BLACK PLAYWRIGHTS, 1823–1977:

AN ANNOTATED BIBLIOGRAPHY OF PLAYS

BLACK PLAYWRIGHTS, 1823–1977:

AN ANNOTATED BIBLIOGRAPHY OF PLAYS

Compiled and Edited by
James V. Hatch
and
OMANii Abdullah

R. R. BOWKER COMPANY
New York & London, 1977

Published by R. R. Bowker Company
1180 Avenue of the Americas, New York, N.Y. 10036

Library of Congress Cataloging in Publication Data

Hatch, James Vernon, 1928–
   Black playwrights, 1823–1977.

   Includes index.
   1. American drama—Afro-American authors—Bibliography. 2. American drama—Afro-American authors—
History and criticism—Bibliography. 3. Drama—Black
authors—Bibliography. I. Abdullah, OMANii, joint
author. II. Title
Z1231.D7H37 [PS338.N4]   016.812'009'352   77-11890
ISBN 0-8352-1032-4

To Owen Dodson, Dean of Black American Theatre.

James V. Hatch

To three "Bubbas"— my stepfather, Caesar Ford; my little
   brother, Jake; and my cousin, Lucious Owens III.

To the memories of my grandfather, Caesar Ford, Sr., and to my
   aunt, Ernestine Durham.

To my road buddies, Kelvin and Kenneth Mercer and Michel Perry.

To Mable J. Henderson, Hilda David, Dr. John Cotlin, Mamie Cash,
   and Warren Burdine II.

OMANii Abdullah

Contents

Foreword

The clues to the architectural and political structure of almost every age of civilization, from the cave to the golden climates of Greece and Rome, or the Middle Ages until our present order—even the sleeping and eating habits—have been uncovered by archaeologists in buried monuments, cathedrals, lost cities, reconstructed skeletons, pottery, manuscripts carved in stone or written on parchment. These are physical evidences of life on this planet. But where do we find clues to the heart and mind of human beings, their gods, their attitudes, their relationships to themselves, their families, their communities? The answer lies mostly in the works of artists, poets, dramatists, and the religious seers. They bring to us the illuminations of the soul of humankind and of existence itself.

The importance of this bibliography to those interested in slavery, freedom, and the truth of the Blacks, is provided in this special, specific account of the black artist's thinking and survival in the Western world, a world almost completely dominated by other races.

James V. Hatch and OMANii Abdullah, with loving scholarship, have found in their research two thousand seven hundred sources of the spiritual rivers of the black mind and soul and existence through his and her written drama. It is now our task to follow them along the rivers into the vast oceans of terror, pleasure, achievement, and exultation. This record will never be complete, for there are generations now growing and those unborn who will keep adding to this already incisive work.

Owen Dodson

Preface

This bibliography, designed for directors and producers in search of plays to meet their specific production requirements and for scholars and researchers who are seeking historical data, lists over 2700 plays by approximately 900 black American playwrights. Included for the first time anywhere are definitive, annotated play lists of many playwrights, such as Ed Bullins, Alice Childress, Owen Dodson, Lorraine Hansberry, Langston Hughes, Willis Richardson, and Theodore Ward. This book is a reference tool which theatre scholars have needed for some time.

As recently as ten years ago, students of black American drama and theatre had to rely upon brief and often inaccurate lists of plays called "Negro Dramas." These bibliographies, compiled by Frederick Bond, Hilda Lawson, Alain Locke, and others, contained plays by black and white playwrights who had written about "Negro characters" and who left the reader to ascertain that Em Jo Basshe was white and that Andrew Burris was black. Even theses and dissertations concerned with "The Negro in American Drama" seldom distinguished playwrights by race (Fannin Belcher, Jr., excepted). The lists of "Negro plays," compiled by the WPA Federal Theatre Project (FTP) for production by their segregated theatre units, included both black and white authors. As recently as 1970, when one of the editors of this work published *Black Image on the American Stage: A Bibliography of Plays and Musicals, 1770-1970*, a book of 2000 entries, he did not identify black and white authors.

This kind of pseudo-integration, perhaps a tacit assertion that the race of an artist was of no consequence in judging a work of art, resulted in an American theatre in which black playwrights had little or no recognition. Not until the 1960s, with the publication of Loften Mitchell's *Black Drama: The Story of the American Negro in the Theatre* and Doris Abramson's *Negro Playwrights in the American Theatre* did white American theatre begin to realize that black American theatre included not only distinguished performers, but talented writers.

The flowering of Black Studies, with its demand for tools and data, brought forth in the 1970s five seminal bibliographies: *The Black Teacher and the Dramatic Arts: A Dialogue, Bibliography and Anthology*, written by William Reardon and Thomas Pawley and published in 1970; *Black Theatre: A Resource Directory*, edited by Marc Primus and published by Joan Sandler of the Black Theatre Alliance in 1973; "A Checklist of Original Plays, Pageants, Rituals, and Musicals by Afro-American Authors Performed in the United States from 1960-1973," edited by Geneviève E. Fabre and published by *Black World* in April 1974; "Checklist of Black Playwrights: 1823-1970," edited by Basil Busacca and published in *The Black Scholar*, September 1973, with its important addendum by Mary V. Jackson of The City College of New York; and "An Annotated Bibliography of Black Drama, 1959-1974," by John Grace (OMANii Abdullah), a Masters thesis at the University of Tennessee, June 1974. As the editors of the present work, we are deeply indebted to these scholars whose pioneering efforts laid the basis for this comprehensive annotated listing of plays by Afro-Americans.

The bibliography focuses on plays written by Afro-Americans from 1823 to 1977. Some plays by Caribbean and other black nationals have been included when their plays have been produced in the United States. For example, one playwright, Victor Séjour, was American born but lived in France and wrote in French; his plays are rarely produced in America, according to the available sources.

The approach we have taken has been inclusive rather than exclusive. Although this work is an annotated list of stage plays, we have included some film, television, and radio plays. This policy of inclusion has perhaps netted a few works which may never have been completed by their authors. Many titles in the border areas of poetry readings and variety shows have also been listed if they contained some dramatic form of dialogue or story.

In an effort to provide a comprehensive and original work, we consulted not only available research sources, but placed notices in journals, magazines, and newspapers and attempted to contact each living playwright and/or his or her agent, if there was one. We are concerned about a number of plays entered that remain without any or with only partial annotation. Readers, scholars, teachers, playwrights, and directors are invited to submit additional data and corrections for future editions to Hatch-Billops Archives, 491 Broadway, New York, N.Y. 10012

Finally, on the basis of the data collected here, we wish to suggest several areas in which research might profitably be conducted: the black minstrel shows of the nineteenth and twentieth centuries; ragtime operas and musicals of the *fin de siècle;* the jazz musicals of the 1920s; vaudeville skits by black artists; productions at small colleges, little theatres, lodges, and churches; and popular entertainments from carnivals, fairs, radio, and Theatre Owners' Booking Association (TOBA) circuit theatres.

James V. Hatch
OMANii Abdullah

Acknowledgments

Because this bibliography is an effort in a large collective process, we wish to give special credit to the following persons, publications, and organizations. We owe a special debt of thanks to Madame Geneviève E. Fabre who, with her husband Michel, so generously shared files and private sources of data. Appreciation also goes to Leslie Sanders of York College, Toronto, who shared her extensive Langston Hughes bibliography, and to Professor Thomas Pawley for annotations of the plays of Paul L. Dunbar.

The following librarians were generous in their efforts of reviewing lists of plays, searching for titles, and answering inquiries: Ernest Kaiser and Ruth Ann Stewart of the Schomburg Center for Research in Black Culture, New York; Rod Bladel and Don Fowle of the Performing Arts Library, New York; Ruth M. Harry of the Louisville Free Public Library, Kentucky; Laura V. Monti, University Libraries, Gainesville, Florida; Ann Allen Shockley of Special Collections, Fisk University, Nashville, Tennessee; and Anne Whelpley of the James Weldon Johnson Collection, Yale University.

Individuals who assisted in locating plays and playwrights were: Oscar Brockett, Lorraine Brown, Dick Campbell, Dominique de Lerma, Brooks Dendy III, Owen Dodson, Winona Fletcher, Errol Hill, Helen A. Johnson, Loften Mitchell, John O'Connor, Yemi Ogunbiyi, Juanita Oubre, Ted Shine, Dorothy and Reuben Silver, Ellen Simon, and Theodore Ward. A special note of thanks is due to the curator of the Negro Ensemble Company library, Steve Carter, and to the director of the New Federal Theatre, Woodie King, Jr.

A number of persons and publications gave space to our appeals to playwrights and others for information. Appreciation goes to Joan Sandler of the Black Theatre Alliance; Garland Lee Thompson and Niamani Mutima of the Frank Silvera Writers' Workshop; Vivian Robinson of AUDELCO; the *Amsterdam News*, the *Black American*; Hannah Hedrick of *Black American Literature Forum*; Hoyt Fuller of *Black World*; Robert Christman of *The Black Scholar*; Virginia Scott of *Educational Theatre Journal*; and Eileen Southern of *The Black Perspective in Music*.

We would also like to acknowledge the assistance of the playwrights and agents who submitted annotated entries:

Robert Abney, Jr.	Norma Blacke-Bragg
Donald Alexander	William Branch
Yvette Allen	Roger L. Brewer
Mrs. Hughes Allison	Townsend Brewster
T. Dianne Anderson	Theodore R. Browne
Regina M. Andrews	Warren Burdine II
Dudley Archer	Steve Carter
Russell Atkins	Alice Childress
Nathan Barrett	China Clark
Damali Bashira	Buriel Clay II
George Houston Bass	Kelsie Collie
Black Spectrum Theatre Co.	Kathleen Collins

J. Douglas Comer
Jimmy Davis Compton, Jr.
Michael Donnell Connor
Mel Conway
Theodore G. Cooper
Scott Cunningham
Lorraine Currelley
Helen Daniel
Dharvi Darrelle
N. R. Davidson
A. I. Davis
Fai Walker Davis
Milburn Davis
Melvin Dixon
Owen Dodson
Shirley Graham Du Bois
Daisy Dumas
Ann Early
Don Evans
J. E. Franklin
Levi Frazier
Charles Fuller
Roger Furman
Clay Goss
Alfred Rudolph Gray, Jr.
Gertrude Greenidge
Bill Gunn
Bill Harris
Paul Carter Harrison
Victoria Hershey
Ralph Hicks
Yusef Iman
International Creative Management
C. Bernard Jackson
Gertrude Jeannette
Helen Marie Jones
Adrienne Kennedy
Scott Kennedy
Bertha Klausner
Erma L. Kyser
Whitney Leblanc
Leslie lee
David Lewis
Frederick Lights
Darryle Lloyd
Melody Maris McDowell
Jerry Eugene McGlown
William Wellington Mackey

Jo-Anne McKnight
Sister Malika
Sharon Stockard Martin
Clifford Mason
John F. Matheus
May Miller (Sullivan)
Loften Mitchell
Barbara Jean Molette
William Morris Agency
Kimya Abudu Mungu
Niamani Mutima
NASABA
Robert Nemiroff
Yemi Ogunbiyi
Regina O'Neal
Thomas Pawley
Eugene Perkins
Andrew Phillips
Charles Pole, Jr.
Jim Potts
Aishah Rahman
Eugene Redmond
Reverse Music Company
Robert E. Richardson Productions
    Ltd.
Willis Richardson
Louis Rivers
Flora Roberts Agency
D. B. Roderick
Fred Rohan
Insan Sauti
John Scott
Saundra Sharpe
Tito Shaw
Ted Shine
Edward Smith
Lois A. Smith
The Society of Creative Concern,
    Inc.
Thomas Stanback
Thelma Jackson Stiles
Harold Stuart
Vincent Terrell
The Theatre of Reality
Valerie Thomas
Chezia B. Thompson
Richard Toussaint
Urban Arts Corp.

WPA Theatre
Evan Walker
Rudy Wallace
Theodore Ward
Charles Brown Washington
Edgar White

James E. White III
Grady D. Whitfield
Curtis L. Williams
Samm Williams
Elton C. Wolfe
George C. Wolfe

To all of them and to Barbara Lekatsas and Ruth Helfrich, who spent so many hours ferreting out the editors' errors, we offer our gratitude.

How to Use This Book

The format of the entries in *Black Playwrights, 1823-1977* and the reasons for it are set forth below. There is a maximum of eleven items that may be annotated for any given play and they include the following:

Authors. Playwrights are listed alphabetically by surname. Whenever possible, pseudonyms have been used as main entries and cross-referenced. There are a few white playwrights in this book who share joint authorship or who collaborated with black playwrights on particular plays; they are so designated by the use of an asterisk.

Titles. Play titles are listed alphabetically in the body of the text and in the index without regard to articles, including those in a language other than English; for example, *L'Ouverture* is listed under the O's. Alternate titles appear after the main title and are preceded by an "or"; for example, *The Black Doctor* or *The Lovers of Bourbon.* Alternate titles are indexed separately; subtitles appear in the descriptions of plays and are not indexed.

Dates. Dates refer to the date(s) of composition or the copyright date.

Genres. All the standard dramatic genres, such as comedy, tragedy, drama, musical, ritual, and pageant appear. Some plays have more than one genre and in that case they are separated by an oblique line (/); for example, "Ritual/Drama." Often the standard genres are accompanied by descriptive words, especially when the playwrights themselves provided genres; for example, "Political Drama." Some entries of plays do not cite genres but rather descriptive words; for example, "Historical" or "Historical Didactic." The use of genres is connotative, rather than denotative. It is intended to suggest a general type, style, subject, or philosophy. For instance, the category "Morality Play" does not denote here the form of medieval drama, but it connotes an attitude in which the forces of virtue and evil are clearly drawn in order to impart a moral lesson to the audience. The genres are not mutually exclusive; some entries have no designations.

Descriptions. The statements about each play are sometimes thematic, sometimes a summary of the plot; at times they are lengthy, at other times, brief. These variations, as well as a diversity of composition styles, stem from three sources: entries written by playwrights and their agents; entries written by the editors; and entries quoted from critics, reviews, and scholars. When a play could not be obtained, the editors relied upon published reports when there were such. In annotating less contemporary plays, the dissertations of Leonard Archer, Fannin Belcher, Jr., Frederick Bond, Sister Francesca Thompson, and Margaret Wilkerson have been frequently cited. (See the Bibliography of Dissertations and Theses on the American Theatre, pp. 259-264, in this volume.) Reviewers often quoted are Eugene Perkins, Peter Bailey, and Jeanne-Marie Miller of *Black World.* Professor Townsend Brewster, writing in the Harlem Cultural Council's *Newsletter*, has made the listing of many recent plays possible, as have the reviewers writing in the *Amsterdam News.*

Cast. The number of characters in plays is listed by race and by sex, with special mention of roles for children, teenagers, dancers, musicians, chorus, and extras, as well as the doubling of roles. Where there was no indication of race, none has been noted. Some playwrights have indicated that white roles should be played by Blacks in whiteface.

Length. The number of acts or scenes is noted; a few authors have designated these as "movements" or "episodes." When a one-act play is deemed long enough to fill a program by itself, it has been noted as "full length." These data, it should be observed, are frequently altered by playwrights in the course of revision and the reader might find revised scripts at variance with the data published here.

Productions. The term "productions" embraces the words "produced" and "performed." Whenever possible, the premiere date and place are listed; in many cases, it was not possible to verify if the performance was the premiere. Where a second production is listed, it is a professional one. The reader who wishes to ascertain a precise production history should investigate each case thoroughly.

Publications. Because scripts by black playwrights have suffered not only the common fate of most plays, that is, no publication, as well as the neglect caused by discrimination, the editors have made a serious attempt to locate every play published by a black American. That was not possible. In some cases, a reference indicated that a play was published, but a copy could not be located; however, these quasi-publications have been included. In other cases, publication was announced, but no copy could be found; these are marked "possibly never published."

Library Sources. Whenever possible, a source for securing a copy of a script has been indicated—either from a library or from an author or his or her agent. Although many scripts are widely available, the editors have restricted their efforts to listing a single source for each play.

Permissions. The rights to produce a play are held by the authors and/or by their agents. Anyone wishing to produce a play should contact the author or agent directly.

On the opposite page is an example of an entry that incorporates all eleven items that may be annotated for plays. The numbers used in the sample entry are identifiers only and do not appear in the entries of the book. The eleven items, which have been described above, are:

1. Author's name
2. Play title
3. Date of composition or copyright
4. Genre
5. Description: theme or story line
6. Cast: number, race, and sex
7. Length: acts or scenes
8. Production (Prod): theatre, city, state, date
9. Publication (Pubn): title, editor, place, publisher, date
10. Library Source (Lib Source): library, author, or agent
11. Permission (Perm): author or agent

The final sections of *Black Playwrights, 1823-1977* include a bibliography of books, sources, and anthologies, as well as a list of dissertations and theses on the black American theatre and the theatre in general; appendixes containing a list of taped interviews in the theatre, awards given to black theatre artists, and addresses of playwrights and agents; there is also a title index.

Sample Entry:

[1]WARD, THEODORE

[2]*Big White Fog.* [3](1938). [4]Domestic Drama. [5]Victor Mason, husband, father, and Garveyite (follower of Marcus Garvey), fights to keep his dream of independence alive while his family and the world fall down around him. [6]*Cast:* 6 BM, 6 BF, 4 BC, 2 WM, extras. [7]*Length:* 3 Acts. [8]*Prod:* FTP, Great Northern Theatre, Chicago, Ill., Apr. 1938. [9]*Pubn: Black Theater USA*, ed. by James V. Hatch and Ted Shine, New York: Free Pr., 1974. [10]*Lib Source:* HBA. [11]*Perm:* Agency, James V. Hatch.

Key to Abbreviations

ANT	American Negro Theatre
APT	American Place Theatre
B	Black
BB	Black Boy
BC	Black Children
BF	Black Female
BG	Black Girl
BM	Black Male
c.	circa
DPS	Dramatists Play Service Inc.
eds.	editors
F	Female
FST	Free Southern Theatre
FTP	Federal Theatre Project (also Research Center for the Federal Theatre Project at George Mason University)
GMU	George Mason University (Research Center for the Federal Theatre Project)
HBA	Hatch-Billops Archives
ICM	International Creative Management
Lib	Library
M	Male
n.d.	no date
NEC	Negro Ensemble Company
NFT	New Federal Theatre
NHT	New Heritage Theatre
NLT	New Lafayette Theatre
n.p.	no place
NYPL	New York Public Library
PAL	Performing Arts Library at Lincoln Center, New York Public Library
Perm	Permission
Prod	Produced
Pubn	Publication
SCHOM	Schomburg Center for Research in Black Culture, New York Public Library
SF	Samuel French Inc.
W	White
WC	White Children
WF	White Female
WM	White Male
YL	Yale Library, Yale University

BLACK PLAYWRIGHTS, 1823–1977

ABBENSETTS, MICHAEL

The Museum Attendant. *Prod:* B.B.C. 2-TV, London, Eng., Aug. 1973.

Sweet Talk. Domestic Drama. The marriage of Rita and Tony, a West Indian couple who have immigrated to London, is faltering from the double pressures of problems within the marriage as well as those caused by an alien and hostile society. *Cast:* 3 BM, 3 BF. *Length:* 2 Acts. *Prod:* Theatre Upstairs, Royal Court Theatre, London, Eng., July 1973; Caribbean American Repertory Theatre, Riverside Church, New York, Mar. 1977 *Pubn:* London: Eyre Methuen Ltd., 1974. *Lib. Source:* HBA. *Perm:* Clive Goodwin.

ABDALLAH, MOHAMMAD IBN

Ananse and the Rain God. Children's Play. Based on an African folktale. *Prod:* Spelman College, Atlanta, Ga., Mar. 1975.

The Trial of Mallam Ilya. *Prod:* University of Georgia, Athens, 1976.

ABDULLAH, AHMED MAARIFA

A Malcom Play. [sic] Children's Play. The children have a lesson on Malcolm X and what is black and beautiful. *Cast:* 5 BB, 5 BG. *Length:* 2 Acts. *Pubn: Connection*, ed. by Curtiss Porter, Pittsburgh, Pa.: Oduduwa Production, 1970. *Lib Source:* HBA.

ABDU-RAHMAN, ANADOULA

Ghetto Sounds. A melange of songs and poems about the black struggle. Presented at a benefit for Eldridge Cleaver and other Black Panthers in jail. *Prod:* Theatre Black, Fillmore East, New York, May 1968.

ABIODUNJI, SYL

For Malcolm X. Didactic. The words of Malcolm X are woven into a skit in which the figure of America is brought to trial, found guilty, and executed. *Cast:* 2 BM, 2 WM, extras. *Length:* 1 Act. *Pubn: Connection*, ed. by Curtiss Porter, Pittsburgh, Pa.: Oduduwa Production, 1970. *Lib Source:* HBA.

ABNEY, ROBERT, JR.

The Interview. (1974). Morality Play. Explores the distortion of the image of women by depicting them as sex objects.   *Cast:* 4 BM, 2 BF. *Length:* 1 Act. *Perm:* Author.

Killing Me Softly. (1974). Ritual/Pantomime. A story about growing old gracefully.   *Cast:* 3 BM, 2 BF, extras. *Length:* 1 Act. *Perm:* Author.

The Liquor Store. (1974). Ritual. The story of four drunks who share their wisdom, knowledge, understanding, and love with various segments of the black community that are groping for direction and clarification of their purpose in life.   *Cast:* 9 BM, 2 BF. *Length:* 6 Movements. *Perm:* Author.

Loving Conversation. (1975). Morality Play. What is said in bed by two people having an affair.   *Cast:* 1 BM, 1 BF. *Length:* 1 Act. *Perm:* Author.

Maybe We Should Call Ourselves I Don't Know. (1975). Ritual/Morality Play. Centers around the collective dreams of four young black men, their singular attempts to reach their dreams, and their brush with the devil.   *Cast:* 6 BM, 2 BF, 2 WM. *Length:* 6 Movements. *Perm:* Author.

On the Verge of the Lying Truth. Ritual/Morality Play. About the roles that society sets up for men and women and the rebellion against and alternatives to those roles.   *Cast:* 3 BM, 3 BF. *Length:* 1 Act. *Perm:* Author.

The Sofa. (1973). Morality Play. The story of the conflict of one black man trying to choose between a black woman and a white "queen."   *Cast:* 1 BM, 1 BF, 1 WF. *Length:* 1 Act. *Perm:* Author.

What Momma Don't See. (1974). Ritual/Children's Play. The story of some very street-wise black youngsters who hook school and spend the day discussing their already grown-up lives.   *Cast:* 1 BM, 1 BF, 10 BC. *Length:* 1 Act. *Perm:* Author.

What We Said We Was. (1974). Morality Ritual. The story of a black community worker, the death of his younger sister from an overdose of drugs, and the search for answers concerning the inability to cope with a death-oriented environment.   *Cast:* 9 BM, 4 BF. *Length:* 3 Acts. *Perm:* Author.

Who's Driving This Bus? (1975). Children's Play. The story of some black school children who act up on the bus and the response they get.   *Cast:* 2 BM, 3 BF, 6 BC. *Length:* 1 Act. *Perm:* Author.

ABRAMSON, DOLORES

The Light. (1971). Ritual. The Devil and God have verbal conflict over the role of a black woman, who the two of them deem is not adhering to what is "proper" behavior for black women.   *Cast:* 2 M, 1 BF. *Length:* 1 Act. *Pubn: Three Hundred Sixty Degrees of Blackness Comin' at You*, ed. by Sonia Sanchez. New York: 5X Pub. Co., 1971. *Lib Source:* HBA.

ABUBAKARI, DAMANI

The Inn Crowd.   *Prod:* Mwanzi Arts, Detroit, Mich., 1973.

Pvt. Huckleberry.   *Prod:* Concept East Theater, Detroit, Mich., 1973.

ACADEMY THEATRE COMPANY

African Collage. *Length:* 1 Act. *Prod:* Group conceived and directed by Ernie McClintock, New York, c. 1965.

Two Rooms. *Length:* 1 Act. *Prod:* Group conceived and directed by Ernie McClintock, New York, c. 1965.

ACAZ, MBA

The Ambassadors. Drama. The plot centers around a teenaged gang who are engaged in a rumble with a rival gang. *Prod:* The Other Stage, New York, 1972.

ACHILLES, MARCEL

Askia the Great. (1970). Historical. Askia, the Songhai warrior, carries the religious war forward amid the tumult of his wives and children. *Cast:* 6 BM, 7 BF, extras. *Length:* 1 Act.

The Black Mexican. Historical. Estevanico, the black adventurer, leads Franciscan friars through Indian territory and is killed by Indians. *Cast:* 1 BM, 4 IM, 2 WM, 3 IF. *Length:* 1 Act.

ACREE, NATE

Black Is 1976. Futuristic Ritual. *Prod:* Humanist Theater, Cleveland, Ohio, 1973.

ADAMS, RAY

A Ritual of the Blacks. (1974). Comedy/Drama. The death of Louise's son prompts a family get-together that reveals the hypocrisy of the well-wishers. *Cast:* 4 BM, 8 BF. *Length:* 3 Acts.

ADDERLEY, JULIAN CANNONBALL, and NAT ADDERLEY

Big Man. (1975). Musical. The story of the black folk hero, John Henry. *Prod.* Concert Version, Carnegie Hall, New York, July 1976.

ADELL, ILUNGA. *See* Stevenson, William Adell, III

AFRO-AMERICAN FOLKLORIC TROUPE

High John de Conqueror. *Prod:* City Center, New York, Apr. 1969.

AFRO-AMERICAN STUDIO

Where It's At. Group conceived and directed by Ernie McClintock. Made up of poetry, modern dance, mime, and improvisation; the play offers a serious look at the black condition in America. *Prod:* Afro-American Studio, New York, 1968.

AHMAD, DOROTHY

Papa's Daughter. Domestic Drama. A girl, thrust into pivotal roles of mother for a younger sister and platonic companion for father, is not allowed to develop

AHMAD, DOROTHY *(Cont.)*

a meaningful relationship for herself. *Cast:* 1 BM, 2 BF. *Length:* 1 Act. *Prod:* Dillard University, New Orleans, La., 1969. *Pubn: Drama Review*, vol. 12, no. 4, Summer 1968. *Lib Source:* PAL.

AIDOO, CHRISTINA AMA ATA

The Dilemma of a Ghost. This play deals with what happens when a Ghanaian takes his black American wife home. *Prod:* Harlem School of the Arts, New York, n.d.

AJAMU. *See* Crawford, Robert

AJAYI, AFOLABI

Akokawe. (1970).

ALAMAJI,   JIWE

The Long-Game Mefy.

The Soul of Willy.

Space Brother. (1974). Futuristic Fantasy. Black man from another planet is befriended and bewildered by a black family that is headed by a strict moralist. *Cast:* 4 BM, 3 BF, 1 BB. *Length:* 2 Acts. *Lib Source:* Typescript, SCHOM.

ALDRIDGE, IRA

The Black Doctor or *The Lovers of Bourbon.* (1847). Melodrama. Adaptation from the French play of Anicet-Bourgeoiš. Fabian, the black doctor, secretly marries the daughter of a French aristocrat, is separated, imprisoned, and goes mad. *Cast:* 2 BM, 1 BF, 5 WM, 5 WF, extras. *Length:* 3 Acts. *Pubn: Black Theater USA*, ed. by James V. Hatch and Ted Shine, New York: Free Pr., 1974. *Lib Source:* HBA.

Titus Andronicus. Tragedy. Adaptation. "The play was adapted from the point of the Negro, the Moor, for Aldridge turned the central villain, Aaron the Moor, into a hero!"—Herbert Marshall and Mildred Stock, *Ira Aldridge, The Negro Tragedian. Prod:* n.p., Nov. 1849.

ALEXANDER, DONALD W.

Ask Your Mama. (1973). Morality Drama. The interaction of a black woman, who may or may not be a woman, with a white male. *Cast:* 1 BF, 1 WM. *Length:* 1 Act. *Pubn: Time to Grease*, ed. by Buriel Clay. *Perm:* Author.

Blind Rats. (1975). Domestic Drama. A black woman, up alone at night while her husband sleeps, brings out all her frustration and fear, eventually finding a solution. *Cast:* 1 BM, 1 BF. *Length:* 1 Act. *Perm:* Author.

Omens. (1974). Drama. A black man and his wife are trapped inside their home by unknown persons and realize their vulnerability. *Cast:* 2 BM, 1 BF, 2 WM, 1 Asian M. *Length:* 1 Act. *Prod:* The American Conservatory Theater, San Francisco, Calif., May 1975. *Perm:* Author.

Tricks. (1974). Musical Comedy/Drama. Old Uncle Sam watches some of his various tricks that he is playing on niggahs, tricks that make some act in the ways that they do. *Cast:* 15 BM, 12 BF, 5 BB. *Length:* 2 Acts. *Perm:* Author.

We Don't Play That in the Projects. (1975). Drama. Conflicts that erupt within a gang of young teens and the violent and sad outcome. *Cast:* 9 BM, 3 BF. *Length:* 1 Act. *Perm:* Author.

ALEXANDER, LEWIS

Pierrot at Sea. Fantasy. *Length:* 1 Act.

ALI, LATEEF

How Long How Long How Long. Ritual. The Devil (white) destroys the minds and bodies of black people by teaching them to be niggers. *Cast:* 5 BM, 2 BF, 1 WM, 1 WF. *Length:* 1 Act. *Pubn: Connection*, ed. by Curtiss Porter, Pittsburgh, Pa.: Oduduwa Production, 1970. *Lib Source:* HBA.

ALLADICE, DARRYL E.

Bobby and Evelyn. (1976). Comedy/Drama. Young man and woman, after making love for the first time, begin to verbally and emotionally spar until each feels secure with the other. *Cast:* 1 BM, 1 BF. *Length:* 1 Act.

Buddies. Comedy/Drama. Two young lovers have a late night/early morning discussion of love, life, and relationships, which establishes that they are buddies as well as lovers. *Cast:* 1 BM, 1 BF. *Length:* 1 Act. *Prod:* Reading, Frank Silvera Writers' Workshop, City College of New York, Mar. 1977.

ALLEN, PAUL

Blues Life of Billie Holiday. *Prod:* Possibly at the New Black American Theatre, Washington, D.C., n.d.

Raise Up. The story of a portable numbers operation. *Prod:* Possibly at the New Black American Theatre, Washington, D.C., n.d.

ALLEN, RICHARD

Take Me to Your Leader. Children's Play/Comedy. Visitors from Mars and their reaction to the American automobile. *Cast:* 9 B, 3 G. *Length:* 1 Act. *Pubn: We Are Black*, Chicago: Science Research Assn., 1969. *Lib Source:* HBA.

ALLEN, THOMASENA

Songs My Father Taught Me. Based on true-to-life experiences of black Americans and relates the truths and values instilled by their forefathers. *Prod:* The New Black American Theatre, Washington, D.C., Mar. 1973.

ALLISON, HUGHES

It's Midnight over Newark. Living Newspaper/Drama. Dramatizes the problems of Negro physicians who, as of 1941, were denied access to practicing medi-

ALLISON, HUGHES (*Cont.*)

cine in city hospitals. *Cast:* 11 BM, 8 BF, 6 WM, 5 WF. *Length:* 2 Acts. *Prod:* Mosque Theater, Newark, N.J., May 1941. *Lib Source:* HBA.

The Trial of Dr. Beck. Courtroom Drama. About the trial of a brilliant Negro physician, Dr. Beck, whose theories on race "improvement" led him to murder his wife. *Cast:* 7 BM, 5 BF, 15 WM, 2 WF. *Length:* 3 Acts. *Prod:* Maxine Elliot Theatre, New York, Aug. 1937; Copley Theatre, Boston, Mass., June 1939. *Lib Source:* HBA.

ALONZO, CECIL

Beaulah Johnson. "Soap Opera written for the stage. It takes the plight of a real sister, a day worker who supports her perennially unemployed aspiring actor-husband."—*Amsterdam News*, June 25, 1977. *Prod:* Alonzo Players, Brooklyn, N.Y., June 1977.

Black Voices. Poetic Revue.

Breakfast Is Served. *Prod:* Alonzo Players, Seafood Playhouse, New York, June 1975.

400 Years Overdue. *Prod:* Alonzo Players, New York, June 1975.

O.T.B.

Somewhere between Us Two. *Prod:* Seafood Playhouse, New York, June 1975.

ALONZO, CECIL, and ROD TAYLOR

Strike One Blow. *Length:* 1 Act.

ALONZO, CECIL, and JOHN AJALA WILLIAMS

1999 or Ghetto 1999. (1974). *Length:* 1 Act. *Prod:* Alonzo Players, Harlem Cultural Council, New York, Jan. 1975.

AMIS, LOLA E.

The Deal. Melodrama. Four characters make a deal from which each hopes to exploit the others; greed brings disaster to them all. *Cast:* 2 M, 2 F. *Length:* 2 Acts. *Pubn: Exploring the Black Experience in America*, Franklin Square, N.Y.: F. Peters, 1976. *Lib Source:* HBA. *Perm:* Author.

Helen. Domestic Drama. Helen treats her teenaged daughter as her sister and loses the girl to their mutual lover. *Cast:* 1 M, 3 F. *Length:* 2 Acts. *Pubn: Three Plays*, New York: Exposition, 1965. *Lib Source:* NYPL. *Perm:* Author.

The New Nigger or *Who's Afraid of William Faulkner?* (1975). A satire on racism in America. A young man (the New Nigger) writes and produces his own play over white boy's objections. *Cast:* 2 BM, 1 BF, 1 WM, 1 WF, extras. *Length:* 2 Acts. *Pubn: Exploring the Black Experience in America.* Franklin Square, N.Y.: F. Peters, 1976. *Lib Source:* HBA. *Perm:* Author.

The Other Side of the Wall. Domestic Drama. A conflict between a sensitive wife and cloddish husband results in tragedy. *Cast:* 1 M, 2 F, 1 B. *Length:*

3 Acts. *Prod:* Morgan State College, Baltimore, Md., 1971. *Pubn: Three Plays,* New York: Exposition, 1965; *Janus,* Spring 1973. *Lib Source:* HBA. *Perm:* Author.

Places of Wrath. Domestic Drama. An unfaithful husband suffers the wrath of his wife and the suicide of his daughter. *Cast:* 4 M, 5 F. *Length:* 3 Acts. *Pubn: Three Plays,* New York: Exposition, 1965. *Lib Source:* NYPL. *Perm:* Author.

ANDERSON, GARLAND

Appearances or **Don't Judge by Appearances.** (1925). Melodrama. First full-length drama by a black American on Broadway. A black bellhop, falsely accused of rape, proves his superiority to those who accused him. *Cast:* 2 BM, 1 BF, 12 WM, 3 WF. *Length:* 3 Acts. *Prod:* Frolic Theater, New York, Oct. 1925. *Pubn: Black Theater USA,* ed. by James V. Hatch and Ted Shine, New York: Free Pr., 1974. *Lib Source:* HBA.

ANDERSON, ODIE

Trial of God. Verse Play. God is charged with the evils of both past and present, indicted as omnipotent conspirator against all mankind, and placed on trial. *Cast:* 25 M, 1 B. *Length:* 5 Movements *Pubn:* New York: Exposition, 1970. *Lib Source:* HBA.

ANDERSON, T. DIANNE

Black Sparrow. (1972). Drama About black Vietnam veteran who comes home with his mind messed up from the war. *Cast:* 2 BM, 1 BF, 1 WM, 2 WF. *Length:* Full Length. *Prod:* University of South Florida, Tampa. *Lib Source:* HBA. *Perm:* Author.

Come Yesterday. Tragedy. About a young man's search for faith and his subsequent disillusionment. *Cast:* 3 M, 2 F. *Length:* 1 Act. *Prod:* West Side YMCA Theater, New York, 1964. *Perm:* Author.

Home to Roost. Domestic Comedy. Middle-aged woman comes home unexpectedly after six years and throws the male household (her husband, son, and his friend) into chaos. *Cast:* 1 BM, 1 BF, 2 WM, 1 WF. *Length:* 3 Acts. *Prod:* West End Repertory Theater, New York, 1966. *Perm:* Author.

Just Friendly. Tragi-Comedy. Lawyer and his client meet a year after the client is acquitted and reenact their own private trial. *Cast:* 2 M, 1 extra. *Length:* 1 Act. *Prod:* West Side YMCA Theater, New York, 1964. *Perm:* Author.

Nightcap. Situation Comedy. Man forces himself into a woman's apartment for a nightcap and the woman's virtue is compromised until the landlady comes down with frying pan and discovers that the gentleman is an old acquaintance. *Cast:* 2 M, 2 F. *Length:* 1 Act. *Prod:* West Side YMCA Theater, New York, 1964. *Perm:* Author.

The Unicorn Died at Dawn. (1971). Domestic Drama. Generation gap between parents and their grown children is heightened by shifting social and moral values, and parents are asked to account for values that seem hypocritical

ANDERSON, T. DIANNE (*Cont.*)

to the young adults. *Cast:* 2 BM, 2 BF. *Length:* 2 Acts. *Prod:* Back Alley Theater, Washington, D.C., 1971. *Perm:* Author.

ANDREWS, REGINA

Climbing Jacob's Ladder. Drama. A story of a lynching that takes place while people are in church praying. *Prod:* Harlem Experimental Theatre, New York, 1931.

Underground. Drama. A story of slaves escaping through the underground railway. *Prod:* Harlem Experimental Theatre and by the Drama Committee of the New York Public Library at the New School, c. 1933.

ANGELOU, MAYA

Adoja Amissah. (1967).

And Still I Rise! A theatrical adaptation of a wide variety of Afro-American poetry, music, and dance. *Prod:* Oakland Ensemble Theatre, Calif., Aug. 1976.

The Best of These. (1966).

The Clawing Within. (1966–1967).

ANONYMOUS

Asheeko. African Pageant. *Prod:* Philadelphia, Pa., 1922.

Bessie, Billie & Bo. Musical. *Prod:* Chicago, Ill., 1975.

The Capricious Crump. An adaptation of *L'Histoire du Soldat*, updated to fit the black-white conflict. *Prod:* Possibly at Detroit Repertory Theatre, Mich., 1968 or 1969.

The Dozens. A drama dealing with the conversion of a "typical castrating black woman" to an African one. *Prod:* TIAFA Builders, Chicago, Ill., 1973.

Earth Has No Sorrow. *Prod:* Weeksville Actors Co., Eubie Blake Theatre, Brooklyn, N.Y., Nov. 1974.

The Ghetto. Children's Play. *Prod:* Buffalo Drama Workshop, State College, New York, n.d.

Give Me Back My Drum. A dramatization of the black man's problem in mass communication. *Prod:* Oakland, Calif., 1969.

Gooped Up. *Length:* 1 Act. *Prod:* National Ethiopian Art Theatre, New York, Oct. 1924.

The Greatest Show on Earth. The scene is a circus; the ringmaster announces to the audience that they are about to see the greatest show on earth. "You will see your uncle, brother, sister, friend, maybe your mama." *Prod:* Third World Revelationist, New York, 1969.

The Lonely Crowd. Musical Revue. *Prod:* PASLA, Los Angeles, Calif., 1969.

Runaround. Short piece on the vicious cycle in which whites have caught Blacks. *Length:* 1 Act. *Prod:* Black Magicians, New York, 1972.

ARCHER, DUDLEY   9

Theme for Aunt Sarah.   *Prod:* Freedom Theatre, Philadelphia, Pa., 1971.

A Train South. "It is a gripping tragic little drama which is sure to make you think."—Sister Francesca Thompson, *Chicago Defender*, Feb. 24, 1923.

The Vicious Pronouns. Musical/Children's Play.   *Prod:* Possibly at Detroit Repertory Theatre, Mich., 1968 or 1969.

Walls of the Ghetto. Surrealistic Drama. Tells of the destructive consequences of drug addiction. *Prod:* Atlantic Avenue Theatre Group, Brooklyn, N.Y., 1972.

ANTHONY, EARL

Charlie Still Can't Win No Wars on the Ground. Comedy. A group of people of different political and social backgrounds and of different ages meet to watch Neil Armstrong land on the moon. *Cast:* 5 BM, 4 BF. *Length:* 1 Act. *Prod:* NFT, New York, 1971.

A Long Way from Here.

The (Mis)Judgment. A black militant organization eliminates an informer only to find the real informer is the "baad" militant. *Cast:* 6 BM, 1 BF, 3 Cops. *Length:* 1 Act. *Prod:* NFT, New York, 1971.

Picking Up the Gun. First production of the group founded by Woodie King, Jr. *Prod:* NFT, New York, 1970.

ARANHA, RAY

The Estate. Drama. Thomas Jefferson's confrontation with a free black scientist, Benjamin Banneker, and with his own anguished love for his slave mistress. *Length:* Full Length. *Prod:* Hartford Stage Company, Conn., Feb. 1976.

My Sister, My Sister. (1973). Drama. Story of a young black schizophrenic woman. *Cast:* 3 BM, 6 BF, 1 WM. *Length:* 2 Acts. *Prod:* Hartford Stage Company, Conn., 1973; U.R.G.E.N.T. Theatre, New York, Apr. 1974. *Lib Source:* HBA. *Perm:* SF

ARCHER, DUDLEY

Anatomy of a Rebel. Drama. Courtroom protestation and justification of a potential martyr. *Cast:* 1 M, Judge, and Jury. *Length:* 1 Act. *Prod:* New York, 1960. *Perm:* Agency, Brown-Tiwoni.

Captive. Traumatic, conscience-stricken brooding of state executioner in preparation for upcoming assignment. *Cast:* 1 M. *Prod:* New York, 1967. *Perm:* Agency, Brown-Tiwoni.

Christmas Carrol. [sic] Satire. Centers around a man, broken by life, whose only crutch at present is excessive drinking. *Cast:* 1 M. *Prod:* New York, Dec. 1965. *Perm:* Agency, Brown-Tiwoni.

The "Crier." Allegory. A man urging men to take control of their own lives. *Cast:* 1 M and throngs of males and females; adults and children. *Prod:* New York, 1964. *Perm:* Agency, Brown-Tiwoni.

ARCHER, DUDLEY (*Cont.*)

The Eavesdropper. An exchange between Merchant Marine officers of different nationalities, races, etc., as observed by writer at the Seaman's Club in Calcutta, India. *Cast:* 3 WM, 1 East Indian. *Length:* 1 Act. *Prod:* Calcutta, India, 1960. *Perm:* Agency, Brown-Tiwoni.

Letter to a Parish Priest. Insight into the problems and dilemma of a Latin-American peasant, husband, and father. *Cast:* 1 M. *Prod:* New York, 1961. *Perm:* Agency, Brown-Tiwoni.

Mushay Man. Tragi-Comedy. A Caribbean folktale based on life in the Islands. *Cast:* 1 BM, 4 BF, 2 BB, 2 BG. *Length:* 4 Acts. *Prod:* Jamaica, W.I., 1958. *Perm:* Agency, Brown-Tiwoni.

On Liberty. Short discourse on political freedom. *Cast:* 1 M. *Prod:* New York, 1964. *Perm:* Agency, Brown-Tiwoni.

Street Scene. Skit. A confrontation that takes place between black ghetto residents and police. *Cast:* 3 BM, 2 BF. *Prod:* New York, 1964. *Perm:* Agency, Brown-Tiwoni.

AREMU, ADUKE

Babylon II. Children's Play/Satire. A look at the parallels of a modern-day society and the Babylon of ancient Biblical times. *Prod:* Harlem Children's Theatre Co., New York, 1974.

Land of the Egyptians. Children's Play. *Prod:* Harlem Children's Theatre Co., New York, Oct. 1974.

The Liberation of Mother Goose. *Prod:* Harlem Children's Theatre Co., New York, Mar. 1973.

ARRINGTON, JOHN N.

Strange Generation. Drama. The story of the young black generation of the 1950s in the South who are determined to change the world. *Cast:* 13 BM, 6 BF. *Length:* 3 Acts. *Pubn:* New York: Vantage, 1976. *Lib Source:* HBA.

ASHBY, WILLIAM MOBILE

The Road to Damascus. *Length:* 7 Scenes. *Pubn:* Boston: Christopher Pub. Co., 1935.

ASHLEY, RICHARD

Nothing for Elizabeth. (1967). Drama. Black playwright forces white friend and his black wife to recognize their racial identities. *Cast:* 2 BM, 1 BF, 2 WM, 1 WF. *Length:* 2 Acts. *Perm:* Author.

ASHLEY, WILLIAM

Booker T. Washington. (1939).

ASTRAL PLAYERS

Soul Journey into Truth. *Prod:* National Black Theatre, New York, May 1975.

ATKINS, RUSSELL

The Abortionist. Drama. Poem in play form to be set to music. Doctor avenges himself by giving a hated colleague's daughter a violent abortion. *Cast:* 1 BF, 1 WM. *Length:* 1 Act. *Pubn: Free Lance,* 1954; Revised title *Two by R. Atkins,* New York: Johnson Reprint Co., 1969. *Perm:* Author.

The Corpse. Drama. Poem in play form. Deranged widow revisits dead husband's tomb each year to watch his body deteriorate and lose identity. *Cast:* 2 BM, 1 WF. *Length:* 1 Act. *Pubn: Western Review,* University of Iowa, Iowa City, 1954. *Perm:* Author.

The Drop of Blood. (1959). Drama. Poem in play form. Older woman married to young man is driven to a state of hallucination by her mistrust of him. *Cast:* 1 M, 1 F. *Length:* 1 Act. *Pubn: Phenomena,* Wilberforce University Press, Ohio, 1961. *Perm:* Author.

The Exoneration. (1959). Poetic Drama. False arrest of a black suspect set against a background of police violence. *Cast:* 1 BM, 3 WM. *Length:* 1 Act. *Pubn: Phenomena,* Wilberforce University, Ohio, 1961. *Perm:* Author.

The Nail. (1957). Poetic Libretto. For an opera suggested, but not written, by composer Hale Smith. Story adapted from the short story of the same name by Pedro Antonio de Alarcon. Woman fugitive, concealing her real name and identity, is hunted down by the man who loves her, surrenders to the police, and her lover collapses. *Cast:* 4 M, 1 F (Spanish), 10 minor parts. *Length:* 3 Acts. *Pubn: Free Lance,* 1971. *Perm:* Author.

The Seventh Circle. (1957). Poem/Psychological Play. A day in the life of a man contemplating involvement and noninvolvement. *Cast:* 4 M voices, 1 F voice. *Pubn: Experiment Magazine,* 1957; *Heretofore,* Heritage Series, London, 1968. *Perm:* Author.

AURANSIA. *See* Williams, Sandra Beth

AURELIUS, NEVILLE

Reflections of a Man. *Cast:* 1 BM, 1 WM, 1 WF. *Length:* 1 Act. *Prod:* Reading, Frank Silvera Writers' Workshop, Martinique Theatre, New York, Nov. 1974.

AWEUSI, ALI

Agent among the Just. Political. About the infiltration of a Black Liberation Front by informers. *Pubn:* New York: Amuru Pr., c. 1974, possibly never published.

The Day Pop Threw Out the Tee Vee. *Pubn:* New York: Amuru Pr., c. 1973, possibly never published.

AYBAR, TRUDY

Morning Train. *Length:* 1 Act. *Prod:* Reading, Frank Silvera Writers' Workshop, Martinique Theatre, New York, Dec. 1974.

AYERS, VIVIAN

Bow Boly. Musical Tragi-Comedy.

BAHATI, AMIRH T.

Castles in the Air.   *Prod:* Reading, Frank Silvera Writers' Workshop, The Teachers Inc., New York, Dec. 1975.

BAILEY, LARRY J.

Timetha and Two Thousand Years from Home. Satire/Fantasy. The Hill family deals with life and death.   *Cast:* 3 BM, 6 BF. *Length:* 1 Act.

BAILEY, ROBERTA

New Life.

BALDWIN, JAMES

The Amen Corner. (1968). Domestic Morality Drama. Black woman becomes engulfed in religious life as she attempts to protect her son from the sin-filled world and forget her problem-ridden marriage.   *Cast:* 5 BM, 9 BF, extras. *Length:* 3 Acts. *Prod:* Howard University, Washington, D.C., 1954; Ethel Barrymore Theatre, New York, Apr. 1965. *Pubn: Black Theatre USA*, ed. by James V. Hatch and Ted Shine, New York: Free Pr., 1974; SF. *Lib Source:* HBA. *Perm:* SF.

Blues for Mister Charlie. (1964). Protest Drama. The struggle of black people in southern town pits father against son as the latter questions the relevance of Christianity in relationship to the survival of Blacks.   *Cast:* 6 BM, 2 BF, 7 WM, 4 WF. *Length:* 3 Acts. *Prod:* ANTA Theatre, New York, Apr. 1964. *Pubn:* New York: Dial, 1964; SF. *Lib Source:* HBA. *Perm:* SF.

One Day, When I Was Lost. Screenplay. A scenario based on *The Autobiography of Malcolm X.* Pubn: London: Michael Joseph, 1972. *Lib Source:* HBA.

Running through Paradise. Drama.

BARAKA, AMIRI

Arm Yrself or Harm Yrself. (1967).   *Prod:* Spirit House, Newark, N.J., 1967. *Pubn:* Newark, N.J.: Jihad Productions, 1967.

The Baptism. (1967). Ritual/Morality Play. The black church is shown as a hypocritical institution, in which a homosexual is the only person capable of acknowledging his perversion.   *Cast:* 3 BM, 2 BF. *Length:* 1 Act. *Prod:* Present Stages, Writer's Stage Theatre, New York, Mar. 1964. *Pubn:* New York: Grove, 1967. *Lib Source:* HBA.

BA-RA-KA. (1972). Ritual/Poem/Play. Celebrates the birth of the black race. *Cast:* 4 BM, 4 BF. *Length:* 1 Act. *Pubn: Spontaneous Combustion (8 New American Plays)*, ed. by Rochelle Owens, New York: Winter House Ltd., 1972. *Lib Source:* HBA.

A Black Mass. (1965). Ritual. Dealing in mysticism and other things; black magician creates new life that he cannot control (the White Beast).   *Cast:* 3 BM, 3 BF, 1 WM. *Length:* 1 Act. *Prod:* Proctor's Theatre, Newark, N.J., May 1966.

Pubn: Four Black Revolutionary Plays, ed. by LeRoi Jones, Indianapolis: Bobbs-Merrill, 1966. *Lib Source:* HBA. *Perm:* Agency, Ronald Hobbs.

Black Power Chant. (1971). *Prod:* Spirit House, Newark, N.J., 1968. *Pubn: Black Theatre*, no. 4, 1971. *Lib Source:* HBA.

Bloodrites. (1971). Ritual. This piece relates the need for Blacks to secure a sense of purpose and awareness about themselves. *Cast:* 10-14 B. *Length:* 1 Act. *Pubn: Black Drama*, ed. by Woodie King, Jr. and Ron Milner, New York: Signet, 1971. *Lib Source:* HBA.

Board of Education.   *Length:* 1 Act. *Prod:* Spirit House, Newark, N.J., 1968.

Chant. Ritual. Directions and words for a chant and ritual.   *Pubn: Black Theatre*, no. 5, 1971. *Lib Source:* HBA.

Columbia, Gem of the Ocean. "Performed against a background of slide projections featuring scenes from the Black man's American experiences, this piece made clear its purpose: to free black minds from the evils of Euro-Americanism and to build Black solidarity."—Jeanne Marie A. Miller, *Black World*, vol. 23, no. 6, Apr. 1974.   *Prod:* Spirit House Movers, Howard University, Washington, D.C., 1973.

The Coronation of the Black Queen. Ritual. A piece modeled after African ceremonies.   *Pubn: Black Scholar*, vol. I, no. 8, June 1970. *Lib Source:* HBA.

The Death of Malcolm X. (1969). Historical Ritual. The murder of Malcolm X, by white conspirators, is explored. *Cast:* 15-20 B, 6 WM. *Length:* 1 Act. *Pubn: New Plays from the Black Theatre*, ed. by Ed Bullins, New York: Bantam, 1969. *Lib Source:* HBA.

Dutchman. Morality Play. Black man is provoked by white woman and forced to remove his facade, thus revealing his true feelings about her and white people. Obie Award for Best Off-Broadway Play. *Cast:* 1 BM, 1 WF. *Length:* 1 Act. *Prod:* Cherry Lane Theatre, New York, Mar. 1964. *Pubn:* New York: Morrow, 1964. *Lib Source:* HBA.

The Eighth Ditch (Dante). Drama. A short play about an interracial homosexual rape in an army camp in 1947.   *Prod:* New Bowery Theatre, New York, 1964. *Pubn: The System of Dante's Hell*, New York: Grove, 1965. *Lib Source:* HBA.

Experimental Death Unit #1. White "dudes" consorting with black prostitutes: the revolution comes and they are decapitated. *Cast:* 3 BM, 1 BF, 2 WM. *Length:* 1 Act. *Prod:* St. Marks Playhouse, New York, Mar. 1965. *Pubn: Four Black Revolutionary Plays*, ed. by LeRoi Jones, Indianapolis: Bobbs-Merrill, 1969. *Lib Source:* HBA.

A Good Girl Is Hard to Find.   *Prod:* Possibly at Sterlington House, Bloomfield, N.J., 1958.

Great Goodness of Life. (1969). Ritual/Drama. A Negro father must redeem himself for an alleged crime, his son's death, so that he can return to his role as a responsible Negro in the post office. Subtitled: *A Coon Show.   Cast:* 3 BM, 1 BF, 5 WM. *Length:* 1 Act. *Prod:* Spirit House, Newark, N.J., Nov. 1967. *Pubn: A Black Quartet*, New York: New Amer. Lib., 1970. *Lib Source:* HBA.

BARAKA, AMIRI (*Cont.*)

Home on the Range. Absurd Comedy. A collage of satire on white America that ends with Blacks surviving the apocalypse. *Cast:* 4 BM, 2 BF, 2 WM, 2 WF, extras. *Length:* 1 Act. *Prod:* Spirit House, Newark, N.J., Spring 1968. *Pubn: Drama Review,* vol. 12, no. 4, Summer 1968. *Lib Source:* HBA.

Insurrection. *Length:* 1 Act. *Prod:* Spirit House, Newark, N.J., 1968.

J-E-L-L-O. (1970). Comedy/Drama. The psychic liberation of Jack Benny's manservant, Rochester. *Cast:* 1 BM, 3 WM, 1 WF. *Length:* 1 Act. *Prod:* Black Arts Repertory Theatre, New York, 1965. *Pubn:* Chicago: Third World Pr., 1970.

Junkies Are Full of (Shhh. . .). (1971). Morality Drama. A black pusher and his counterparts are killed by black men in an effort to demonstrate what will happen to such infiltrators of the black community. *Cast:* 8 BM, 5 WM. *Length:* 1 Act. *Prod:* 1969. *Pubn: Black Drama,* ed. by Woodie King, Jr. and Ron Milner, New York: Signet, 1971. *Lib Source:* HBA.

Madheart. (1966). Morality Drama. An attempt is made to give black life to a mother and sister who possess "white" souls. *Cast:* 1 BM, 4 BF. *Length:* 1 Act. *Prod:* Black Arts Alliance, San Francisco State College, Calif., c. 1967. *Pubn: Black Fire,* ed. by LeRoi Jones and Larry Neal, New York: Morrow, 1968. *Lib Source:* HBA.

Police. Ritual. Black community wants an end to the black-and-white, police-killing-black people cycle. *Cast:* 5 BM, 4 BF, 4 WM. *Length:* 1 Act. *Pubn: Drama Review,* vol. 12, no. 4, Summer 1968.

A Recent Killing. Drama. A play about evolution and the development of airman Pearson from poet to activist. *Cast:* 4 BM, 2 BF, 13 WM, 2 WF. *Length:* 3 Acts. *Prod:* NFT, New York, Jan. 1973. *Lib Source:* Typescript, HBA.

Revolt of the Moonflowers.

S-1. (1976). Didactic Drama. An examination of the repressive dangers in U.S. Senate bill S.1, a piece of legislation that would affect the rights of all Americans and particularly Afro-Americans. *Prod:* Congress of Afrikan People, Newark, N.J., Apr. 1976; Afro-American Studio, New York, Aug. 1976.

The Sidnee Poet Heroical or If in Danger of Suit, The Kid Poet Heroical. Satirical Comedy. Sidnee, the poet/actor, arrives innocent from the West Indies determined to "make it." The play is his odyssey to fame in the white world and his rejection of it for a black culture. *Cast: 14 B & W. Length:* 29 Scenes. *Prod:* NFT, New York, May 1975. *Perm:* Agent, Ronald Hobbs.

The Slave. (1964). Drama. A revolutionary confronts problems inherited from association with white culture and tries to erase evidence of his white past by attempting to destroy his mulatto daughters. *Cast:* 1 BM, 1 WM, 1 WF. *Length:* 2 Acts. *Prod:* St. Marks Playhouse, New York, Dec. 1964. *Pubn:* New York: Morrow, 1964. *Lib Source:* HBA.

Slave Ship. (1967). Historic Ritual. Depicted in this chronicle are the Middle Passage of slavery, early attempts at revolution, Uncle Tomism, and liberation struggle. *Cast:* 5 BM, 3 BF, extras. *Length:* 1 Act. *Prod:* Chelsea Theatre Center, New York, season 1969–1970. *Pubn:* Newark, N.J.: Jihad Productions, 1967. *Lib Source:* HBA.

The Toilet. (1964). Morality Drama. The problems of developing meaningful relationships among some high school black and white males are explored. *Cast:* 9 BM, 2 WM. *Length:* 1 Act. *Prod:* St. Marks Playhouse, New York, Dec. 1964. *Pubn: Black Drama in America*, ed. by Darwin Turner, Greenwich: Fawcett, 1971. *Lib Source:* HBA.

BARBOUR, FLOYD

The Bird Cage. (1971). Contemporary drama set in small southern town. *Pubn:* Scene in *Black Scenes*, ed. by Alice Childress, New York: Doubleday, 1971. *Lib Source:* HBA.

BARNES, AUBREY

The Superheroes. Comedy/Drama. The forces of honkyism. *Cast:* 11 Characters. *Length:* 2 Acts. *Pubn:* Amuru Pr., n.d., possibly never published.

BARNES, HAROLD C.

Quite at Random. Fantasy Drama. Phillip, caught in a maddening conflict over homosexuality and race, rapes a white girl. *Cast:* 2 BM, 2 WM, 1 WF. *Length:* 1 Act.

BARNETT, MARGO, and DOUGLAS JOHNSON

Black Is a Beautiful Woman. This work consists of such black writers as Margaret Walker, Nikki Giovanni, Mari Evans, and Langston Hughes. *Prod:* Black Alley Theatre, Washington, D.C., 1973.

BARRETT, LINDSAY

Sighs of a Slave. Dream. *Length:* 1 Act.

BARRETT, NATHAN

Aunts of Antioch City. (1966). Comedy. About a black grandmother's determination to advance the interests of her mulatto granddaughter by moving in on the white aunts. The focus is on the girl's education as she moves between these two forces. *Cast:* 2 BF, 2 WF, 1 M, 1 F mulatto. *Length:* 4 Scenes. *Prod:* Great Jones Theatre, New York, Feb. 1977. *Perm:* Author.

Baker-Maker. (1971). Farce. The times and loves of a Harlem baker whose bread comes alive; familial and community involvement in creating the lives of its people. *Cast:* 4 BM, 5 BF. *Length:* 2 Acts. *Perm:* Author.

Bird Food. Protest Drama. White cripple has physically enslaved a black man in attempt to take over his mind and the black man revolts. *Cast:* 1 BM, 1 WM. *Length:* 1 Act. *Perm:* Author.

Cut-ups & Cut-outs. (1973). Black Comedy. Sixteen ex-heroes live out their lives and die in a forgotten, deserted home by the sea. *Cast:* 6 BM, 10 WM. *Length:* 2 Acts. *Perm:* Author.

BARRETT, NATHAN (Cont.)

Engagement in San Dominique. (1966). Historical Melodrama. Set in the final days of the French departure from Haiti. Mulatto girl decides to throw her lot with the fleeing whites when love enters and revulsion at the horrors of revolutionary truths lead her to self-betrayal. *Cast:* 1 BM, 3 F (B or W), 1 BB, 4 WM. *Length:* 3 Acts. *Perm:* Author.

For Love of Mike. (1967). *Perm:* Author.

Lead Ball. (1965). *Length:* 1 Act. *Perm:* Author.

Losers: Weepers. (1962). *Length:* 1 Act. *Perm:* Author.

Room of Roses. (1965). Melodrama. A town honors a mother on the return of her son in a pine box, but she is run out of the town because she misbehaves. *Cast:* 5 BF, 1 BB, 1 WM. *Length:* 3 Scenes. *Perm:* Author.

S-C-A-R-E-W-E-D. (1960). *Perm:* Author.

Sitting and Chipping. (1965). *Length:* 1 Act. *Perm:* Author.

Square Root of Mother. (1967). Domestic Farce. About an interracial, liberated couple who receive a visit, simultaneously, from their mothers and a first anniversary surprise. *Cast:* 2 BM, 2 BF, 1 WM, 2 WF. *Length:* 6 Scenes. *Perm:* Author.

While Dames Dine. (1965). *Length:* 1 Act. *Perm:* Author.

Why Lily Won't Spin. Children's Play. Music by Lucas Mason. Lily cannot and will not learn to spin; yet, she finds a way to marry the prince. *Cast:* 1 M, 6 F. *Length:* 5 Scenes. *Prod:* Greenwich Mews Theatre, New York, Oct. 1976. *Perm:* Author.

BASCOMBE, RONALD D.

The Unifier. (1971). Satire. White man's puppet is doing his job of keeping Blacks contented by leading them in a vicious cycle that goes nowhere. *Cast:* 2 BM, 1 WM (voice), extras. *Length:* 1 Act. *Pubn: Three Hundred and Sixty Degrees of Blackness Comin' at You*, ed. by Sonia Sanchez, New York: 5X Pub. Co., 1971. *Lib Source:* HBA.

BASHIRA, DAMALI

Just Like His Mama. (1974). Drama. Set in an inner city laundromat. Street-wise mother shares her life experiences with middle-class black coed. Deals with the questions of black man-woman relationships and the responsibility of raising a child. *Cast:* 1 BB, 2 BF, 10–15 extras. *Length:* 1 Act. *Perm:* Author.

A New Day. (1970). Drama. A series of monologues reveals the events and feelings of Blacks and whites from the sit-ins of the sixties to the development of the Pan-African interest of the seventies. *Cast:* 7 BM, 3 BF, 6 WM, 3 WF. *Length:* 3 Acts. *Perm:* Author.

BASS, GEORGE HOUSTON

African Vibrations. Mythic Ritual. Music by Ndikho Xaba. *Prod:* n.p., July 1973. *Perm:* Author.

Black Blues. A collage of incidents (scenario for improvisations). *Prod:* Black Arts Theatre, New Haven, Conn., June 1968. *Perm:* Author.

Black Masque. Historical Ritual. Music by Clinton Utterbach. *Cast.* 8 M, 10 F. *Prod:* Rites and Reason, Brown University, Providence, R.I., Apr. 1971. *Perm:* Author.

The Booby Prize, The Booby Hatch, The Booby Trap, The Booby. A ritual of schizophrenia. *Cast:* 6 M, 5 F. *Length:* 1 Act. *Prod:* Yale School of Drama, New Haven, Conn., Mar. 1967. *Perm:* Author.

Function at the Junction. Two plays for a barroom, *Lonely Women* and *Buckwheat Revue,* a collective work improvised by the actors. *Prod:* New Junction, Providence, R.I., May 1972. *Perm:* Author.

The Funhouse. Music by Noel Da Costa. *Cast:* 8 M, 5 F. *Length:* 2 Acts. *Prod:* Long Wharf Summer Theatre, New Haven, Conn., Sept. 1968. *Perm:* Author.

Games. Children's Play. White youngsters exclude a peer from their merriment because of color difference. *Cast:* 1 BG, 3 WB, 4 WG. *Length:* 1 Act. *Prod:* Mobilization for Youth Drama Group, New York, May 1966. *Pubn: Introduction to Black Literature in America,* ed. by Lindsay Patterson, Washington, D.C.: Associated Publishers, 1968. *Lib Source:* HBA. *Perm:* Author.

How Long Suite. *Length:* 9 Masks. *Prod:* New Haven Black Arts Theater, for Onyx Conference on the Arts, New York, Nov. 1968. *Perm:* Author.

Knee-High Man and Babu's JuJu. Children's Plays. Music by Noel Da Costa. *Length:* Two 1 Act Plays. *Prod:* Country Day School, New York. *Perm:* Author.

Mama Etta's Chitlin Circuit. Soul Revue. A series of famous black singers, dancers, and musicians perform their specialties. *Length:* 3 Scenes. *Prod:* Brown University, Providence, R.I., Apr. 1973. *Pubn: Rites and Reason,* ed. by Scott Purdin, Hellcoal Playbook Series, vol. 1, no. 6, 1973. *Lib Source:* HBA. *Perm:* Author.

Oh Lord, This World. Musical. Music by Clinton Utterbach. Lyrics by George Houston Bass. Subtitled: *Get It Together.* *Cast:* 11 M, 11 F. *Prod:* Queen of Angels Players, Newark, N.J., Nov. 1970. *Perm:* Author.

Once I Heard Buddy Bolden Play. (1965). Musical. Lyrics and music by Mildred Kayden. *Cast:* 5 M, 3 F, 1 B, extras. *Perm:* Author.

One into Another. Vaudeville Ritual. "Two Moves Plus Tag," "Remnants of a Dream," "Encore," "A New Recipe." *Cast:* 6 M, 4 F. *Length:* 1 Act. *Prod:* Wastepaper Theater, Providence, R.I., Dec. 1974. *Perm:* Author.

The Providence Garden Blues. Two plays with music by Jonas Gwangwa. Based on the results of an oral history research project on racism in Providence, R.I., from 1920 to the present. *Cast:* 9 M, 9 F. *Length:* 1 Act. *Prod:* Brown University, Providence, R.I., Mar. 1975. *Perm:* Author.

The Third Party. (1968). *Perm:* Author.

A Trio for the Living. Music by Noel Da Costa. "Loop-de-Loo," "Catch Us Alone," and "Mourners at the Bier." *Cast:* 5 M, 5 F. *Length:* Three 1 Act Plays. *Prod:* Yale University, New Haven, Conn., Apr. 1968. *Perm:* Author.

BASS, GEORGE HOUSTON, and DOROTHY CLARK

Dreamdust. Music by Kambon. Six African-American folktales adapted by Bass, Clark, and the performers. *Prod:* As Street Theatre throughout Rhode Island, June–Aug. 1974. *Perm:* Author.

BASS, KINGSLEY B., JR.

We Righteous Bombers. (1968). Drama. Confused revolutionaries who have not ascertained what revolution is all about. The play is probably Ed Bullins' adaptation of Camus' *The Just Assassins. Cast:* 5 BM, 2 BF, 3 WM. *Length:* 3 Acts. *Prod:* NLT, New York, Apr. 1969. *Pubn: New Plays from the Black Theatre,* ed. by Ed Bullins, New York: Bantam, 1969. *Lib Source:* HBA. *Perm:* Agency, Don Farber.

BATCHELOR, RONALD

At Home in the Sun. Historical Musical. *Prod:* Ferris-Booth Hall, Wollman Auditorium, New York, Apr. 1975.

BATES, H. JACK

Black Acres.

Cinda. *Prod:* Bijou Theatre, Boston, Mass., 1933. *Lib Source:* FTP, GMU.

Dear Morpheus. (1970). Fantasy. An epic contest between Adam and Eve about love and marriage from the Garden of Eden to the present, when they finally marry. *Cast:* 16 BM, 9 BF (doubling). *Length:* 9 Scenes. *Lib Source:* Typescript, HBA.

The Legend of Jo Emma.

The Lost Disciple.

Streets of Gold. *Lib Source:* FTP, GMU.

Yulee.

BATSON, SUSAN

Hoodoo Talkin. (1971). Poem/Play. Four black women talk of various things that relate to the black experience. *Cast:* 4 BF. *Length:* 1 Act. *Pubn: Three Hundred and Sixty Degrees of Blackness Comin' at You,* ed. by Sonia Sanchez, New York: 5X Pub. Co., 1971. *Lib Source:* HBA.

BEAL, TITA

A Just Piece. *Length:* 1 Act. *Pubn: Liberator,* June 1970.

BECKHAM, BARRY

Garvey Lives. Historical Ritual. Music by Richard Humes. Directed by George Bass. *Prod:* Rites and Reason, Brown University, Providence, R.I., 1972.

BED-STUY STREET ACADEMY

An Experience in Reality. (c. 1971). Group conceived and directed by Tom Turner. *Prod:* The Bed-Stuy Street Academy Drama Workshop, New York.

BED-STUY THEATRE

Black Evolution. An original company concept.   *Prod:* Bed-Stuy Theatre, New York, Summer 1970.

Three Women. An original company concept.   *Prod:* Bed-Stuy Theatre, New York, Summer 1969.

BEIM, NORMAN

The Dark Corner of an Empty Room. Melodrama. The pressures of Frank's life involve him in crime until he is finally shot by a white cop.   *Cast:* 4 BM, 4 BF, 1 WM, extras. *Length:* 2 Acts.

BELL, DENISE

Dialogues of the Shadow Women. Drama. The struggle within the evangelical church for power and control, largely among the women.   *Cast:* 3 BM, 10 BF. *Length:* 2 Acts. *Prod:* Directors' Unit, Frank Silvera Writers' Workshop, Urban Art Corps, New York, Jan. 1977.

Lush Life.   *Prod:* Reading, Frank Silvera Writers' Workshop, City College, New York, Jan. 1977.

BELL, ROBERT, JR.

Catch Me! Catch Me! If You Can! (c. 1974). Domestic Drama. The cycles of a black family.   *Cast:* 7 characters. *Length:* 3 Acts. *Pubn:* New York: Amuru Pr., possibly never published.

The Horns the Angels Blow. (c. 1974). Drama. Contemporary play on the theme of black loyalty within the family.   *Length:* 3 Acts. *Pubn:* New York: Amuru Pr., possibly never published.

I Saw the Mornin' Sparrow among the Ashes. (c. 1974). Domestic Drama. The disillusionment and the death of dreams in a ghetto environment.   *Length:* 3 Acts. *Pubn:* New York: Amuru Pr., possibly never published.

BENJAMIN, PAUL

Memoirs of a Junkie. (1971). Morality Drama. Junkie and pusher realize that they're still trapped by America and make vows to kick the habit.   *Cast:* 2 BM, 1 BF. *Length:* 2 Acts. *Prod:* City College, New York, Mar. 1975.

A Twosome.

BENNETT, HARRIET V.

Grandma's Hands.   *Prod:* Mount Vernon College, N.Y., 1976.

BERNIER, BHUNNIE

Ola and B.   *Cast:* 2 BM, 2 BF. *Length:* Full Length. *Prod:* Reading, Frank Silvera Writers' Workshop, Martinique Theatre, New York, Apr. 1975.

Partake of the Goat Meat.   *Prod:* Reading, Frank Silvera Writers' Workshop, Harlem Performance Center, New York, Dec. 1976.

BERRY, KELLY-MARIE

Baku or *How to Save the Whale's Tale.* (1970).

Black Happenin'. (1967). Poetic Dance Drama. Members of a black family, headed by grandma, struggle with themselves and the "Man" to make it. *Cast:* 2 BM, 3 BF, 1 BB, 1 BG. *Length:* 1 Act.

The Boomp Song. (1973).

BEST, GERMAINE

To the Future. Political Drama. A fantasized projection of guerrilla war between blacks and whites. *Cast:* 6 BM, 3 BF, 2 WM, extras. *Length:* 1 Act.

BETTER, ANTHONY

The Window of Our Dreams. Drama. "Dramatized a fight for love and dignity in the environs of a ghetto."—*Black World*, vol. 25, no. 6, Apr. 1976. *Prod:* Federal City College, Washington, D.C., Winter 1975.

BEY, SALOME

And a Little Child Shall Lead Them. Musical. Focuses on two teachers in public schools in charge of Christmas play. *Cast:* 1 M, 1 F, 10 C (ages 8–12), extras. *Length:* 1 Act.

The Sweet Bitter Life. Dramatic Musical. Deals with the problems of society and attempts to find solutions. *Cast:* 20 characters. *Length:* 2 Acts.

BIBB, ELOISE. *See* Thompson, Eloise A.

BIRCHFIELD, RAYMOND

The Diamond Youth. Social Drama. *Cast:* 12 characters. *Length:* 1 Act. *Pubn:* New York: Amuru Pr., c. 1974, possibly never published.

BISMILLAH-R-RAHMANI-R-RAHIM. *See* X, Marvin

BLACK ARTS TROUPE

Angela. A play depicting the struggle of Angela Davis. *Prod:* Black Drama Workshop, Buffalo, N.Y., Apr. 1972.

Tambourra. Documentary. Uses dance, drama, and music, to depict the metamorphosis of the black man in America. *Prod:* Black Drama Workshop, Buffalo, N.Y., Apr. 1972.

BLACKE-BRAGG, NORMA

Herman Jones. (1975). Domestic Drama. A dramatization of the black male's development into a sexual and social being, within the context of a matriarchal family, and his initiation into the larger society. *Cast:* 5 BM, 4 BF, 6 BB (or tape-recorded voices), 2 WM. *Length:* 2 Acts. *Perm:* Author.

BLACKWELL, JAMES

The Money Game. Subtitled: *The Penny Game.*   *Prod:* Chicago South Side Center of the Performing Arts, Ill., 1969.

BLAINE, LAWRENCE

A Rose for Cousin Henry. (1971). Tragedy. Recollections from the life of Henry, once husband, gardener, man, and how he literally wound up in the sewer. *Cast:* 3 BM, 1 BF, 3 WM, 1 WF. *Length:* 2 Acts.

BLAKE, EUBIE, AUBREY LYLES, FLOURNOY MILLER, and NOBLE SISSLE

Shuffle Along. Musical Comedy. Story possibly based on Miller & Lyles' *Mayor of Dixie*, 1907. Concerns the efforts of three candidates to win the mayoralty campaign and the complications when one wins. Subtitled: *Mayor of Jim Town.*   *Cast:* 15 BM, 4 BF, chorus. *Length:* 2 Acts. *Prod:* Sixty-third Street Music Hall, New York, May 1921. *Pubn: Best Plays of 1920-21*, ed. by Burns Mantle, New York: Dodd, 1921.

BLAKE, EUBIE, CECIL MACK, and MILTON REDDIE

Swing It. Revue. "A potpourri of minstrelsy, singing, dancing, mugging, clowning, spirituals, jazz swing, tapping, and the carrying of Harlem's throaty torch."—*New York Times*, July 23, 1937. *Cast:* 19 BM, 7 BF. *Prod:* Adelphi Theatre, New York, July 1937. *Lib Source:* FTP, GMU.

BLAKE, EUBIE, FLOURNOY MILLER, and NOBLE SISSLE

Shuffle Along of 1933. Musical Comedy. About the financing of a molasses factory. *Cast:* 13 BM, 7 BF, extras. *Length:* 2 Acts. *Prod:* Mansfield Theatre, New York, Dec. 1932. *Pubn: Best Plays of 1932-33*, ed. by Burns Mantle, New York: Dodd, 1933.

BLAKE, EUBIE, FLOURNOY MILLER, NOBLE SISSLE, and PAUL GERARD SMITH

Shuffle Along of 1952. Musical Comedy. "Woven around a group of GIs and WACS who meet in the Army just before the end of World War II and then get together to run a dressmaking establishment in New York."—*New York Times*, May 9, 1952. *Cast:* 15 BM, 7 BF. *Prod:* Broadway Theatre, New York, May 1952.

BLAKE, EUBIE, LEW PAYTON, and NOBLE SISSLE

In Bamville. Musical Revue. Deals with aspects of horse racing. *Prod:* Chicago, Ill., 1923-1924; New York, Mar. 1924. *Pubn: Best Plays of 1923-24*, ed. by Burns Mantle, New York: Dodd, 1924.

BLANK, ROGER

Blink (Your Eyes). A showcase of expressions that seeks out the imaginary gulf span within the blink of your eyes. *Prod:* The Astral Players, New York, June 1975.

BOATNER, EDWARD

The Fruits of the Afro-American Tree. (1974). Documentary Drama with Music. Story of Afro-Americans from their life in Africa to the present time. *Cast:* 16 voice choir, 20 actors (9 W), narrator. *Length:* Full Length. *Perm:* Author.

Heaven's Gate Choir. (1931). Drama/Comedy. Life of a choir director in a black church. Subtitled: *He Will Answer.* *Cast:* 30 characters. *Length:* 3 Acts. *Perm:* Author.

One Drop of Blood. (1950). Drama. Southern white plantation owner has son by a slave. *Cast:* 3 BM, 3 BF, 3 WM, 2 WF, extras. *Length:* 3 Acts. *Perm:* Author.

The Whiggers. (1973). Southern Drama with Music. Role reversal: whites are slaves on black plantation. *Cast:* 35 characters. *Length:* 3 Acts. *Perm:* Author.

BOATNER, EDWARD, CELADY SHAW ERSKINS, and IVAN FIRTH

Julius Caesar in Rome Georgia. (1933). Musical Comedy. Parody of Julius Caesar set in Negro Morning Star Lodge. *Cast:* 10 BM, 10 BF, 38 actors and dancers, extras. *Length:* 3 Acts. *Lib Source:* PAL. *Perm:* Author.

BOLAND, GENE

The Unforgiving Minute. Domestic Drama. Story of family living in a housing project and involves a tragic conflict between a strong father and his son. *Cast:* 7 BM, 4 BF. *Length:* 3 Acts. *Perm:* Agency, Brandt and Brandt.

BOND, FREDERICK W.

Family Affairs. Drama. The story of a family that has been victimized by the depression. *Pubn:* Institute: West Virginia State College, 1939.

BONNER, MARITA

Exit, an Illusion. (1929). Surrealistic Drama. A young black man shoots his light-skinned mistress because of "racial" jealousy. *Cast:* 2 M, 1 F. *Length:* 1 Act. *Pubn: Crisis* magazine, Oct. 1929. *Lib Source:* SCHOM.

The Pot-Maker. Domestic Melodrama. Elias Jackson is "called" to be preacher, but he manages to kill his wife's lover. *Cast:* 3 BM, 2 BF. *Length:* 1 Act. *Pubn: Opportunity* magazine, Feb. 1927. *Lib Source:* SCHOM.

The Purple Flower. (1928). Expressionistic Play. The black folks down in the valley of life discover that only blood will buy them the Flower of Life up on the hill that the white devils hold. *Cast:* 7 BM, 5 BF, sundry white devils. *Length:* 1 Act. *Pubn: Black Theater USA*, ed. by James V. Hatch and Ted Shine, New York: Free Pr., 1974. *Lib Source:* HBA.

BONTEMPS, ARNA

Free and Easy. Adaptation of Countee Cullen's musical comedy, *St. Louis Woman. Prod:* Holland, Belgium, and France, 1959–1960.

BONTEMPS, ARNA, and COUNTEE CULLEN

St. Louis Woman. (1944). Musical Comedy. Based on the novel *God Sends Sun-day*, by Arna Bontemps. Lyrics and music later added by Johnny Mercer and Harold Arlen. Little Augie, the world's greatest jockey, wins the big race, and St. Louis' most beautiful woman, Della Green. *Cast:* 22 BM, 7 BF, extras. *Length:* 3 Acts. *Prod:* Gilpin Players, Karamu Theatre, Cleveland, Ohio, Nov. 1933; Martin Beck Theater, New York, Mar. 1946. *Pubn: Black Theater*, ed. by Lindsay Patterson, New York: Dodd, 1971. *Lib Source:* HBA.

BONTEMPS, ARNA, and LANGSTON HUGHES

Cavalcade of the Negro Theatre. (1940). Historical Pageant. The Negro in the theatre from *The Octoroon*, by Dion Boucicault, to 1940s Chicago jazz and gospel singing. *Length:* 21 Scenes. *Prod:* Written for the Negro Expo-sition, Chicago, Ill., Summer 1940. *Lib Source:* Manuscript, possibly incom-plete, YL.

Jubilee, a Cavalcade of the Negro Theatre. Radio Play. Written for CBS, 1941.

When the Jack Hollers. Folk Comedy. Black and white sharecroppers in Mis-sissippi delta both suffer from a merciless landowner until Aunt Billie's voo-doo, an amazing mule, and a fish fry unite the races against the exploiter. *Cast:* 8 BM, 7 BF, 5 WM. *Length:* 3 Acts. *Prod:* Gilpin Players, Karamu The-atre, Cleveland, Ohio, May 1936. *Lib Source:* Typescript, YL; Harold Ober playscript, SCHOM.

BOOKER, SUE

The Flags. A young white civil rights worker stops a very poor black woman from selling Confederate flags and so deprives her of her only income. *Cast:* 1 BF, 1 WM. *Length:* 1 Act. *Pubn: Cry at Birth*, ed. by Merrel Daniel Booker, Sr., et al., New York: McGraw-Hill, 1971. *Lib Source:* HBA.

BOYD, VINETTA

Campaign. The play concerns itself with a black politician running for mayor of a small town and points out that Blacks may become greedy and avaricious when they become involved in politics. *Prod:* Southern University, Baton Rouge, La., 1976.

BRANCH, WILLIAM

Baccalaureate. (1975). Domestic Drama. Young black woman graduate student, rooming with her married sister's family, is forced to choose between com-fortable middle class ambitions and an exciting, but perilous involvement with a young black activist. *Cast:* 3 BM, 3 BF, 3 BB. *Length:* 3 Acts. *Perm:* Agency, Bridget Aschenberg, ICM.

Experiment in Black.

In Splendid Error. (1953). Historical Drama. Frederick Douglass grapples with the practical, personal, and psychological problems of supporting his friend, John Brown, as both seek an effective way to fight slavery. Subtitled: *Fred-*

BRANCH, WILLIAM *(Cont.)*

erick Douglass. *Cast:* 5 BM, 1 BF, 1 BG, 5 WM. *Length:* 3 Acts. *Prod:* Greenwich Mews Theatre, New York, Oct. 1954. *Pubn: Black Theater USA*, ed. by James V. Hatch and Ted Shine, New York: Free Pr., 1974. *Lib Source:* HBA. *Perm:* Agency, Bridget Aschenberg, ICM.

A Medal for Willie. (1951). Protest Drama. Southern town gathers for official U.S. presentation of a medal to a mother of a dead soldier-hero, but the underlying hypocrisy leads to an event not scheduled on the program. *Cast:* 6 BM, 4 BF, 9 WM (or 8 WM and 1 WF, for ed.). *Length:* 7 Scenes, Prologue, and Epilogue. *Prod:* Club Baron, New York, Oct. 1951. *Pubn: Black Drama Anthology*, ed. by Woodie King, Jr. and Ron Milner, New York: New Amer. Lib., 1972. *Perm:* Agency, Bridget Aschenberg, ICM.

To Follow the Phoenix. (1971). Historical Drama. Black college student finds inspiration and courage to participate in potentially dangerous racial demonstrations by recalling the life and example of the extraordinary Mary Church Terrell, a black elitist who fought against racial and sexual discrimination from post-reconstruction days through the sit-ins of the 1960s. *Cast:* 8 BM, 6 BF, 4 WM (doubling), extras. *Length:* 2 Acts. *Prod:* Chicago, Ill., 1960. *Pubn:* Scene in *Black Scenes*, ed. by Alice Childress, New York: Doubleday, 1971. *Perm:* Agency, Bridget Aschenberg, ICM.

A Wreath for Udomo. Morality Drama. Based upon the novel by Peter Abrahams. African prime minister finds that defeating colonialism is the easiest part of acquiring independence; exercising power calls for a diabolical decision in a far more complicated world than he and his fellow revolutionaries ever dreamed of during their student days abroad. *Cast:* 6 BM, 4 BF, 4 WM, 2 WF, 1 Asian M, extras. *Length:* 3 Acts. *Prod:* Karamu Theatre, Cleveland, Ohio, 1959; London, 1961. *Perm:* Agency, Bridget Aschenberg, ICM.

BRANCHCOMB, SYLVIA WOINGUST

If the Shoe Fits. (1972). Musical. The reflections, the distortions, and the overprotectiveness of black families, caused by environmental and inherited prejudices, is complicated by a lack of communication. *Cast:* 28 BM, 25 BF, 10 WM, 3 WF. *Length:* 2 Acts. *Perm:* Author.

It's Our Time to Speak. (1975). Comedy. Today's youth is both bored and hyperactive, as well as frustrated, and is prepared for less disciplined behavior in the future. *Cast:* 17 BM, 6 BF, 4 WF (doubling). *Length:* 2 Acts. *Prod:* Getty Square Neighborhood Center, Yonkers, N.Y., Nov. 1975. *Lib Source:* Typescript, HBA. *Perm:* Author.

BRANDON, JOHNNY

Sing Me Sunshine. Musical. The story of a prizefighter's daughter set in the period of early swing and boogie-woogie. *Prod:* Off-Broadway, New York, 1974.

BRENNER, ALFRED

Black Jesus (Death of). Black Jesus likens the historical Jesus and his times to that of a contemporary Black and his conditions.

BREWER, ROGER L.

He Who's Ugly. Satire/Children's Play. Involves an imagined society where ugly people are arbitrarily discriminated against by the beautiful people. (Dialogue is in rhyme.) *Cast:* 4 M, 2 F, chorus. *Length:* 1 Act. *Prod:* Hartford, Conn., 1973. *Perm:* Author.

A Little Red Chicken. Protest Drama. Shows the evil of an educational system that has become highly commercialized. *Cast:* 3 M, 4 F. *Length:* 2 Acts. *Prod:* Hartford, Conn., 1973. *Perm:* Author.

No Grace for a God. (1973). Fantasy. Clarence, recently released from prison, conceives the idea that he may be God and should build an ark, but he kills someone before his plan can materialize. *Cast:* 6 BM, 5 BF. *Length:* 1 Act. *Perm:* Author.

What Is a Home without a Mother. Domestic Drama. A comment on motherhood, focusing on the problems involved with raising children and on a mother imposing her desires on her children. *Cast:* 2 M, 4 F. *Length:* 2 Acts. *Prod:* Hartford, Conn., 1973. *Perm:* Author.

BREWSTER, TOWNSEND

The Adventurous Petticoat. (1974). Comic Opera Libretto. Patriotic girl, though she has been told that women can take no active part in the American Revolution, is instrumental in making Paul Revere's ride possible. *Cast:* 1 BM, 1 BF, 5 WM, 2 WF (1 girl disguised as boy). *Length:* 1 Act. *Perm:* Author.

Amator, Amator. (1973). Television Comedy. Modern adaptation of the myth of the judgment of Paris. Strikingly handsome Greek and Latin teacher attributes the effect he has on the ladies to awe of his erudition rather than to his appearance. *Cast:* 5 BM, 7 BF. *Length:* 3 Acts. *Perm:* Author.

Andromeda. (1948). Lyric Comedy. Explores the myth of the rescue of Ethiopian princess, Andromeda, by Perseus. National Theatre Conference Award. *Cast:* 6 BM, 8 BF, 11 WM, 17 WF, B & W chorus. *Length:* Full Length. *Perm:* Author.

The Anonymous Lover. Translation of opéra comique, *L'Amant Anonyme,* the only fully extant opera by Joseph Boulogne (Chevalier de Saint-Georges) the eighteenth-century black composer. Translated under a grant from the Harlem Cultural Council, 1976. *Cast:* 3 WM, 3 WF, chorus, ballet. *Length:* 2 Acts. *Perm:* Author.

Arthur Ashe and I. (1975). Comedietta. A young black teacher is almost browbeaten into letting some of his colleagues take advantage of a black student, but rises to the occasion when Arthur Ashe wins at Wimbledon. *Cast:* 2 BM, 3 WM. *Length:* 1 Act. *Perm:* Author.

Black-Belt Bertram. (1974). Farce. Wealthy Bertram Butterworth tries to avoid paying off a bet he has lost by pretending to be a karate expert, but is exposed by a real black belt who wins Bertram's fiancée. *Cast:* 3 BM, 3 BF. *Length:* 1 Act. *Prod:* Reading, Frank Silvera Writers' Workshop, New York, Sept. 1974.

The Botany Lesson. *Length:* 1 Act. *Prod:* Circle in the Square, New York, Dec. 1972.

BREWSTER, TOWNSEND (Cont.)

The Cable. (1955). Musical. Adaptation of the *Rudens* of Plautus, the only Roman comedy to take place in Africa. A long lost daughter, who has fallen into the clutches of a pimp, finds her parents and marries her lover. *Cast:* 14 BM, 3 BF, 1 BB, BM chorus. *Length:* 5 Acts. *Perm:* Author.

Chocolat Volatil. (1975). Musical. Adapted from three one act musicals, *The Harlequin Twins*, *Hot Love in Harlem*, and *No More Ego Tripping*, all adapted from French comedies of the eighteenth, nineteenth, and twentieth centuries, respectively. *Cast:* 4 BM, 3 BF. *Length:* 3 Acts. *Perm:* Author.

The Cocktail Sip. (1975). Comic Opera. Score by Noel Da Costa. A parody of T. S. Eliot's play *The Cocktail Party* that takes place among some high-toned Blacks in Newark, New Jersey. *Cast:* 3 BM, 3 BF, B chorus. *Length:* 1 Act. *Perm:* Author.

Ebur and Ebony. (1975). Comedy. Aided by Hamlet, Harlequin, and O-Kuni of Izume, and opposed by Beelzebub, St. Genesius, the patron saint of actors, tries to devise a script for the future without racial conflict. *Cast:* 1 BM, 3 WM, 1 Japanese F. *Length:* 1 Act. *Perm:* Author.

The Ecologists. (1973). Radio Play. In the next century, the ecologists deal with the problem of people pollution. *Cast:* 1 BM, 3 WM, 3 WF, 1 Chinese F. *Perm:* Author.

The Finger Hole in the River. (1975). Musical Proverbs. Powerful aide to black cabinet member learns that no one is indispensable. *Cast:* 6 BM, 5 BF. *Length:* 1 Act. *Perm:* Author.

The Harlequin Twins.

Idomeneus. (1976). Verse Comedy. A black writer who has at last made it big, but at the expense of his personal life, experiences regret when he sees a young black father in the subway. *Cast:* 2 BM, 1 WF. *Length:* 1 Act. *Perm:* Author.

The Jade Funerary Suit. (1975). Comedy. Poor black family steals priceless ancient Chinese burial suit for their father's interment. *Cast:* 4 BM, 2 BF, 2 WM, 1 WF. *Length:* 1 Act. *Perm:* Author.

Johnny Renaissance. (1974). Lyric Comedy. The attainments of a twentieth-century Renaissance man. *Cast:* 1 BM, 1 BF, chorus. *Length:* 1 Act. *Perm:* Author.

Little Girl, Big Town. Revue. *Cast:* 1 BM, 1 BF, 2 WM, 1 WF. *Length:* 2 Acts. *Prod:* Queens College, New York, 1953. *Perm:* Author.

The Main-Chance Rag. (1972). Comedy. Adapted from a play by Alexander Dumas, *Fils*. Young businessman from the streets wrests his company from white control and wins the girl he loves despite disapproval of upper-class Blacks. *Cast:* 3 BM, 3 BF, 1 BB. *Length:* 1 Act. *Perm:* Author.

Medora and the Rustics. (1954). Comic Opera Libretto. A fashionable lady loses the man of her choice because, during her stay in Paris, he, along with the rest of her set, has succumbed to the craze for folksy things. *Cast:* 1 BM, 1 BF, chorus. *Length:* 2 Acts.

Mood Indigo. (1976). Verse Play. A black bishop is doomed to disappointment in his hopes that his way of life will bring him the acclaim that, instead, goes to the great black actor Paul Robeson. *Cast:* 2 BM, 1 WM, 2 WF, 2 Indian M. *Length:* 1 Act. *Perm:* Author.

Oh My Pretty Quintroon. Jazz Opera. Music by Sam Rivers. *Prod:* Harlem Cultural Center, New York, May 1975. *Perm:* Author.

Oh, What a Beautiful City! (1954). Verse Comedy. By passing an examination, a committee chosen by the mayor of New York can win Heaven for all humanity. *Cast:* 2 BM, 1 BF, 1 Chinese M, 9 WM, 3 WF. *Length:* 2 Acts. *Perm:* Author.

The Palm-Leaf Boogie. (1975). Comedy. Adapted from a play by Alexander Dumas, *Père.* A widow who has sent a young man away while her husband was still alive, finds him barely recognizable when he returns from fighting in Angola. *Cast:* 4 BM, 3 BF. *Length:* 1 Act. *Perm:* Author.

Please Don't Cry and Say "No." (1972). Comedy. A young woman, basically happily married but dissatisfied with the position of women in society, decides that one thing she may do that her husband may not is have an affair with a teenager. *Cast:* 7 BM (6 teenagers), 3 BF (1 teenager), extras. *Length:* 1 Act. *Prod:* Circle in the Square, New York, Dec. 1972. *Perm:* Author.

The Reversed Deception. (1950). Comic Opera. Through tricks and counter-tricks, Harlequin loses and regains a winning lottery ticket. *Cast:* 2 BM, 2 BF. *Length:* 1 Act. *Perm:* Author.

Thirteen Ways of Looking at Merle. (1976). Verse Play. A beautiful young black woman evokes varying responses from passengers on a subway. *Cast:* 1 BM, 2 BF, 3 WF, 7 WM, 1 Asian M. *Length:* 1 Act. *Perm:* Author.

Though It's Been Said Many Times Many Ways. Comedy. Black Piet, Santa Claus's assistant, effects a jailbreak using Santa Claus's sleigh. *Cast:* 6 BM, 1 WM. *Length:* 1 Act. *Perm:* Author.

To See the World in a Drop of Brine. (1975). Verse Comedy. The kings of the Atlantic and Pacific Oceans threaten to engulf the earth in their territorial disputes. *Cast:* 5 WM, 3 WF, 1 Pacific-Islands M, courtiers. *Length:* 1 Act. *Perm:* Author.

The Tower. Comic Opera. King Solomon attempts to prevent the realization of a prophecy that his daughter will marry the poorest man in the land, but is unsuccessful. *Cast:* 4 BM, 3 BF. *Length:* 1 Act. *Prod:* Santa Fe Opera, N. Mex., 1957. *Perm:* Author.

Waiting for Godzilla. (1973). Comedy. Dracula, the Wolf Man, the Frankenstein monster, and company find themselves outdone as monsters by some solid citizens from whose murderous clutches they rescue a little black boy. *Cast:* 1 BB, 7 WM, 3 WF, 1 Japanese boy (Baby Godzilla). *Length:* 1 Act. *Perm:* Author.

The Washerwomen. Children's Musical. With the help of some washerwomen a poor young girl on the Caribbean island of Desirade marries a young man who returns home after having made a great success in television commercials. *Cast:* 4 BM, 8 BF, chorus. *Length:* 1 Act. *Perm:* Author.

BREWSTER, TOWNSEND (Cont.)

What Are Friends For? (1968). Musical. Through pull, the second most meritorious candidate beats out both a thoroughly incompetent candidate and
the most meritorious one (a Black) to win a federal arts grant. *Cast:* 8 BM,
1 BF, 17 WM, 4 WF, 1 Chinese M, B & W chorus. *Length:* 2 Acts. *Perm:* Author.

BROME, GEORGE

Before Black Was Beautiful. Tragi-Comedy. A group of college students (c.
1964) get into a contest of who's blackest. *Cast:* 6 BM. *Length:* 1 Act.

BROOKS, CHARLOTTE

Firm Foundations. (1954). Radio Skit. A skit prepared for Negro History Week
in which a class of ninth graders show their enthusiasm for the pending celebration. Some of the noted blacks discussed include James Rapier, Henry
Highland Garnett, and Crispus Attucks. *Pubn: Negro History Bulletin*, Mar.
1954. *Lib Source:* SCHOM.

BROOME, BARBARA CUMMINGS

The Fat Sisters. Comedy. About weight watchers. *Prod:* Fourth International
Black Writers Conference, Chicago, Ill., 1975.

BROWN, AARION

*Onica Mitchell Is in Double Jeopardy: She's Black and Female . . . (AND SHE
HATES EVERYBODY?).* This play concerns the inner growth of a black
girl and her determination to keep her individuality despite the negative
implications that being born Black and female can bring. She engages in a
crusade to save herself. *Prod:* Nat Horne Theatre, New York, Jan. 1977.

BROWN, ARROW

All for the Cause. *Length:* 1 Act. *Prod:* Kuumba Workshop, Chicago, Ill., 1971.

BROWN, B. S.

The Snake Chief. *Length:* 1 Act. *Pubn: Negro History Bulletin,* Mar. 1971.

BROWN, CECIL M.

The African Shades. Comedy. Exploitative white film producer gets exploited by a
young black theatre producer. *Cast:* 3 BM, 1 BF, 3 WM, 2 WF, extras. *Length:*
1 Act. *Pubn: Yardbird Reader,* ed. by Ishmael Reed, vol. 1, Berkeley, Calif.:
Yardbird Pub. Co., 1972. *Lib Source:* HBA.

The Gila Monster.

Our Sisters Are Pregnant. *Prod:* Potrero Hill Neighborhood House, San Francisco, Calif., 1973.

The Real Nigger: On the Minstrel Revolution.

BROWN, HENRY

The Drama of King Shotaway. Historical Drama. Based on facts of the Insurrection of the Caravs on the island of St. Vincent; possibly the first play written by a Black and acted by Blacks in America.   *Prod:* African Grove Theater, New York, June 1823.

BROWN, JAMES NELSON

Tomorrow Was Yesterday.   *Pubn:* New York: Exposition, 1966.

BROWN, LENNOX

Ballet behind the Bridge. Drama. Escaped convict in Trinidad returns to "behind the bridge slum," where dreams of past glory are coupled with European exploitation.   *Cast:* 10 BM, 5 BF, 2 WM, 1 Chinese M, extras. *Length:* 2 Acts. *Prod:* NEC, New York, 1969.

The Captive. Subtitled: *Snow Dark Sunday.*   *Cast:* 6 M, 1 F. *Length:* 1 Act. *Prod:* Toronto, Can., 1965. *Pubn: Ottawa Little Theatre,* Ranking Play Series 2, Catalogue No. 43, Ottawa, Can., Sept. 1965.

Devil Mas'. (1974). Mythic Ritual. This play deals with black Caribbean ghetto life and the occult. *Cast:* 3 BM, 2 BF, 2 WM, 1 WG, 1 Chinese M, extras. *Length:* 3 Acts. *Pubn: Kuntu Drama,* ed. by Paul Carter Harrison, New York: Grove, 1974. *Perm:* Agency, William Morris.

Fire for an Ice Age.   *Cast:* 3 M, 1 F. *Length:* 1 Act. *Prod:* University of Toronto, Can., 1968.

Fog Drifts in the Spring. (1970). Part of a cycle of plays entitled *The Crystal Tree.* *Cast:* 2 M. *Length:* 1 Act. *Prod:* Caribbean-American Repertory Theatre Company, Billie Holiday Theatre, New York, Feb. 1976.

I Have to Call My Father. Subtitled: *Jour Ouvert.*   *Cast:* 2 M, 1 F, dancers. *Length:* 1 Act. *Pubn: Drama and Theatre,* vol. 8, no. 2, Winter 1970.

The Meeting.   *Cast:* 3 M, 1 F, extras. *Length:* 1 Act. *Pubn: Performing Arts in Canada,* vol. 8, no. 2, Winter 1970.

The Night Class. (1969). Morality Drama. A storm traps Catholic fathers and students in night class, forcing realization about suicide.   *Cast:* 2 BM, 2 BF, extras. *Length:* 2 Acts.

Night Sun.   *Cast:* 2 M, 1 F. *Length:* 1 Act.

Prodigal in Black Stone.   *Cast:* 9 M, 4 F. *Length:* 2 Acts. *Prod:* Staged reading at the National Playwrights Conference of the Eugene O'Neill Memorial Theatre Center, Waterford, Conn., Summer 1972.

Saturday's Druid.   *Cast:* 2 M, 2 F. *Length:* 1 Act. *Prod:* CBC Radio, Can., 1969.

The Scent of Incense.

The Sisterhood of a Spring Night. Three black women living in Canada search for companionable black males, but find sex and disappointment.   *Cast:* 3 BM, 5 BF, dancer. *Length:* 2 Acts. *Prod:* Queens College, New York, Oct. 1974. *Perm:* Agency, William Morris.

BROWN, LENNOX *(Cont.)*

Snow Dark Sunday. See *The Captive*

Song of the Spear. Radio Drama. *Length:* 1 Hour. *Prod:* CBC Radio, Can., 1970.

Summer Screen. (1970). Part of a cycle of plays entitled *The Crystal Tree.*   *Cast:* 3 M, 1 F. *Length:* 1 Act.

The Throne in the Autumn Room. (1970). Part of a cycle of plays entitled *The Crystal Tree.*   *Cast:* 3 M, 1 F, dancers. *Length:* 2 Acts.

The Trinity of Four.   *Cast:* 3 M, 1 F. *Length:* 1 Act. *Prod:* Caribbean-American Repertory Theatre Company, Billie Holiday Theatre, New York, Feb. 1976. *Pubn: Caribbean Rhythms*, New York: Simon & Schuster, 1974.

The Twilight Dinner. Drama. Two middle-aged black men reminisce about their militant college days and what has happened since.   *Cast:* 2 BM, 1 WF. *Length:* Full Length. *Prod:* IRT Loft Theatre, New York, Feb. 1977.

The Voyage Tonight.   *Cast:* 4 M, 2 F, extras.

Wine in Winter.   *Cast:* 2 M, 1 F. *Length:* 1 Act. *Prod:* Radio 610, Trinidad, W. I., 1971.

Winti Train. Melodrama. "Six people aboard a train bound for Harlem and a Black World Festival when it is learned that the state troopers have been brought in because two Festival members plan to blow up the train."—*Amsterdam News*, Mar. 19, 1977.   *Cast:* 6 M, 1 F, dancers. *Length*: 2 Acts. *Prod*: Billie Holiday Theatre, New York, Mar. 1977.

BROWN, OSCAR, JR.

Joy. (1970). Musical Revue. A cabaret theatre event built around three talents: Oscar Brown, Jr., Jean Pace, and Sivuca.   *Cast:* 1 BM, 1 BF, 1 WM, 3 musicians. *Length:* Full Length. *Prod:* Sunbar Productions, the New Theatre, New York, Jan. 1970.

Kicks & Company. Musical. Directed by Lorraine Hansberry.   *Length:* 2 Acts. *Prod:* Arie Crown Theatre, Chicago, Ill., Oct. 1961. *Pubn: Best Plays of 1961-1962*, ed. by Henry Hewes, New York: Dodd, 1962.

Summer in the City. (1965). Musical.

Sunshine and Shadows. Folk Drama. The poetry of Paul Laurence Dunbar with original music by Phil Cohran.   *Prod:* Black Heritage Theatrical Players, Chicago, Ill., 1974.

BROWN, RHOZIER T. (ROACH)

Xmas in Time. Length: 1 Act. *Prod:* Inner Voices, Washington, D.C., 1969.

BROWN, WESLEY

And Now, Will the Real Bud Jones Stand Up. (1971). Ritual. Black man examines the question of what is the truth.   *Cast:* 2 BM, 1 BF. *Length:* 1 Act. *Pubn: Three Hundred and Sixty Degrees of Blackness Comin' at You*, ed. by Sonia Sanchez, New York: 5X Pub. Co., 1971. *Lib Source:* HBA.

BROWN, WILLIAM WELLS

The Escape or *A Leap for Freedom.* Historical Melodrama. Story of the humiliations of slavery and the escape of a husband and wife to Canada. Oldest extant published drama by a black American. *Cast:* 5 BM, 4 BF, 1 BB, 10 WM, 1 WF, 1 WG, extras. *Length:* 5 Acts. *Prod:* Emerson College, Boston, Mass., Dec. 1971. *Pubn:* Boston: R. F. Wallcut, 1858; *Black Theatre USA*, ed. by James V. Hatch and Ted Shine, New York: Free Pr., 1974. *Lib Source:* HBA.

Experience or *How to Give a Northern Man a Backbone.* Protest Melodrama. The Reverend Dr. Nehemiah Adams, a northern preacher with southern sympathies, is accidentally sold into slavery, which changes his attitude. May have been entitled *Dough Face.* *Prod:* Read aloud in Apr. 1856, according to William Edward Farrison's biography on William Wells Brown, playwright and historian.

BROWNE, ROSCOE LEE

A Hand Is on the Gate. A potpourri of Afro-American poetry, music, and dance. *Prod:* Afro-American Studio, New York, Oct. 1974.

BROWNE, THEODORE R.

A Black Woman Called Moses or *Go Down Moses.* Historical Drama. Harriet Tubman conducts a small band of slaves to freedom via the Underground Railroad at the outbreak of the Civil War, then goes on to serve as nurse, scout, and spy for the Union Army. *Cast:* 14 BM, 6 BF, 12 WM (doubling). *Length:* 2 Acts (9 Scenes). *Lib Source:* GMU. *Perm:* Author.

The Day of the Midnight Ride of Paul Revere. (1975). Historical. *Length:* 2 Acts.

The Gravy Train. (1940). Domestic Drama. An aspiring young Black finds himself in conflict with his young bride over his attending New York's City College. *Length:* Full Length. *Lib Source:* Typescript, SCHOM.

Lysistrata of Aristophanes. An anachronistic adaptation (African version) of the Aristophanes farce about a successful demonstration against war, led by women, on the steps of the Acropolis at Ebonia. *Prod:* FTP, Seattle, Wash., 1937. *Perm:* Author.

Natural Man. Legendary Drama. Hero John Henry, the "steel-drivin' man," pits his raw strength against a machine. *Cast:* 20 BM, 10 BF, 5 WM. *Length:* 8 Episodes. *Prod:* FTP, Seattle, Wash., 1937; ANT, New York, 1940. *Pubn: Black Theatre USA*, ed. by James V. Hatch and Ted Shine, New York: Free Pr., 1974. *Lib Source:* HBA.

Ring the Janitor's Bell. Comedy. Takes place in a Harlem basement apartment during the 1930s; a janitor goes on a short-lived spree with the rent collection. *Cast:* 10 BM, 4 BF. *Length:* 3 Acts. *Perm:* Author.

The Seven Cities of Gold. Legendary Drama. The fantasy-conceived story of Stephen (Esteban) Dorantes, the blackamoor who helped explore the Southwest at the time of the Spanish conquistadores. About his lust for glory and power that led him to betray the two Franciscan friars whom he was leading to the fabled Cibola, and his massacre at the hands of the Zuni Indians. *Cast:* 1 BM, 2 WM, 4 Indian M, 2 Indian F. *Length:* 2 Acts and Epilogue. *Perm:* Author.

BROWNE, THEODORE R. (*Cont.*)

Steppin' High. Minstrel. Book for a musical extravaganza in the genre of *Show Boat;* traces the rise of a Negro performer from the "under-canvas" minstrel shows down South to the Broadway stage of the Bert Williams and George Walker ragtime era. *Cast:* 31 BM, 11 BF, 4 WM (doubling). *Length:* 5 Acts. *Perm:* Author.

BROWNING, ALICE

It's Fun to Be Black. Comedy. *Prod:* Malcolm X College, Chicago, Ill., 1973.

BROWNSVILLE LABORATORY THEATRE

Ghetto Corner—Sounds of Brownsville. A living experience of Brownsville. *Length:* 1 Act. *Prod:* Brownsville Laboratory Theatre, New York, Nov. 1970.

Variations of Freedom. Group Concept. *Prod:* Brownsville Laboratory Theatre, Billie Holiday Theatre, New York, Nov. 1972.

BRUCE, RICHARD

Sadjhi. African Ballet. No dialogue. Ballet score by Grant Still. A chanter relates the story of the Azandé chieftain who goes hunting while his favorite wife has an affair with his heir apparent. The king dies in the hunt, and the wife must kill herself. *Cast:* 6 BM, 8 BF, extras. *Length:* 1 Act. *Prod:* Howard University, Washington, D.C., n.d. *Pubn: Plays of Negro Life,* ed. by Alain Locke and Montgomery Gregory, New York: Harper, 1927. *Lib Source:* HBA.

BRUCE, RICHARD, and ROSE McCLENDON

Taxi Fare. (1931). *Length:* 1 Act.

BRUNO, JOANN

Sister Selena Got the Gift. Comedy. Music by Jackie McLean. Sister Selena leaves her lover to establish her own business in religion, but he follows her and she has to rid herself of him. *Prod:* D.C. Black Repertory Company, Washington, D.C., 1975.

Uncle Bud's No Stranger.

BRUNSON, DORIS, and ROGER FURMAN

Three Shades of Harlem. Life in Harlem shown in three moods: Shade One—the Blues; Shade Two—Joy; Shade Three—Hope for the Future. *Length:* 3 Acts. *Prod:* NHT, New York, June 1965.

BRYANT, FREDERICK JAMES, JR.

Lord of the Mummy Wrappings. (1967).

BRYANT, HAZEL

Attica Trick or Truth. Prod: Afro-American Total Theatre, Riverside Church Tower, New York, Oct. 1971.

Black Circles, Black Spirits.   *Prod:* Afro-American Total Theatre, New York, 1974.

Black Circles round Angela.   *Prod:* Afro-American Total Theatre, International House, New York, Feb. 1970.

Jimmy's Place.   *Prod:* Afro-American Total Theatre, Arts Foundation, New York, June 1973.

Kingmaker. Music by Jimmy Justice.   *Prod:* Afro-American Total Theatre, New York, Nov. 1973.

Mae's Amees.   *Prod:* Afro-American Total Theatre, Riverside Church Theatre, New York, Aug. 1969.

On Being Black in White America.   *Prod:* Afro-American Total Theatre, International House, New York, Jan. 1970.

Sheba.   *Prod:* Riverside Church Theatre, New York, Dec. 1972.

Star. Christmas Play.   *Prod:* Martinique Theatre, New York, Dec. 1973.

BRYANT, HAZEL, GERTRUDE GREENIDGE, and WALTER MILES

Makin' It.   *Prod:* Afro-American Total Theatre, International House, New York, Jan. 1972.

BRYANT, HAZEL, and JIMMY JUSTICE

Jimmy's Carousels.   *Prod:* Afro-American Total Theatre, New York, May 1972.

Soul Politiken.   *Prod:* Afro-American Total Theatre, Street Theatre, Lincoln Center, New York, July 1973.

BRYANT, HAZEL, and B. TODD

Origins.   *Prod:* Afro-American Total Theatre, Riverside Church Theatre, New York, Oct. 1969

BULLINS, ED

The American Flag Ritual. (1969). Protest Ritual. A black man makes a solemn ritual of pissing on the American flag.   *Cast:* 1 BM. *Length:* 1 Act. *Pubn: The Theme Is Blackness*, New York: Morrow, 1973. *Lib Source:* HBA. *Perm:* Agency, Don Farber.

Black Commercial #2. (1972). TV Didactic Sketch. Two fighting black men become black brothers. *Cast:* 2 BM, extras. *Length:* 1 Act. *Pubn: The Theme Is Blackness*, New York: Morrow, 1973. *Lib Source:* HBA. *Perm:* Agency, Don Farber.

The Box Office. (1970). Scenario. This was written for a short film about the rebirth of the New Lafayette Theatre.   *Cast:* 2 BM, B Children. *Pubn: Black Theatre*, no. 3, ed. by Ed Bullins, 1970. *Lib Source:* HBA. *Perm:* Agency, Don Farber.

Clara's Ole Man. (1965). Comedy/Drama. Depicts the life-styles of ghetto dwellers that consist of alcoholics and gang members, as well as a conflict between a lesbian and a middle class college youth.   *Cast:* 5 BM, 4 BF. *Length:* 1 Act. *Prod:* Firehouse Repertory Theatre, San Francisco, Calif., Aug. 1965. *Pubn: Five*

BULLINS, ED *(Cont.)*

   Plays, Indianapolis: Bobbs-Merrill, 1968. *Lib Source:* HBA. *Perm:* Agency, Don Farber.

The Corner. (1968). The activities of a group of drinkers on "Liquor St. and Wine Ave." come into conflict with the protagonist as he tries a new life-style. *Cast:* 5 BM, 1 BF. *Length:* 1 Act. *Prod:* Theatre Company of Boston, Mass., 1968. *Pubn: The Theme Is Blackness*, New York: Morrow, 1973. *Lib Source:* HBA. *Perm:* Agency, Don Farber.

Daddy. Domestic Drama. This is the sixth play in a twenty play cycle about Blacks in contemporary American life. A father returns to the family he had abandoned and attempts to make amends for his neglect. *Cast:* 5 BM, 5 BF. *Length:* Full Length. *Prod:* NFT, New York, June 1977.

Deathlist. (1970). Didactic Drama. A black militant plans to assassinate all the Negro leaders who had signed a newspaper ad supporting Israel against the Arabs. *Cast:* 1 BM, 1 BF. *Length:* 1 Act. *Prod:* Theatre Black, University of the Streets, New York, Oct. 1970. *Pubn: Four Dynamite Plays*, New York: Morrow, 1972. *Lib Source:* HBA. *Perm:* Agency, Don Farber.

Dialect Determinism or The Rally. (1965). Satire. A bizarre meeting of Blacks in which their leader toys with different identities. *Cast:* 7 BM, 4 BF. *Length:* 1 Act. *Prod:* Firehouse Repertory Theatre, San Francisco, Calif., Aug. 1965. *Pubn: The Theme Is Blackness*, New York: Morrow, 1973. *Lib Source:* HBA. *Perm:* Agency, Don Farber.

Do-Wah. Musical. Set in the fifties.

The Duplex: A Black Love Fable (1969). Set during the early sixties in a duplex in southern California, this play tells the story of Velma Best's search for completeness, for a love that transcends sex. *Cast:* 7 BM, 5 BF. *Length:* 4 Movements. *Prod:* NLT, New York, May 1970. *Pubn:* New York: Morrow, 1971. *Lib Source:* HBA. *Perm:* Agency, Don Farber.

The Electronic Nigger. (1966). Satire. The failure of a writer to hold his own against a Negro programmed to defend statistics, law, and order. *Cast:* 2 BM, 1 BF, 1 WM, 2 WF, extras. *Length:* 1 Act. *Prod:* APT, New York, Mar. 1968. *Pubn: Five Plays,* Indianapolis: Bobbs-Merrill, 1968. *Lib Source:* HBA. *Perm:* Agency, Don Farber.

The Fabulous Miss Marie. (1971). Ritual/Drama. The various dilemmas and confusions of the so-called black middle class. *Cast:* 6 BM, 4 BF. *Length:* 1 Act. *Prod:* NLT, New York, Mar. 1971. *Pubn: The New Lafayette Theatre Presents,* ed. by Ed Bullins, New York: Anchor Pr., 1974. *Lib Source:* HBA. *Perm:* Agency, Don Farber.

The Gentleman Caller. (1968). Didactic Melodrama. Black domestic sheds the robes of servitude and dons those of a black princess. *Cast:* 2 BM, 2 BF. *Length:* 1 Act. *Prod:* Chelsea Theatre Center, New York, Apr. 1969. *Pubn: A Black Quartet,* New York: Signet, 1970. *Lib Source:* HBA. *Perm:* Agency, Don Farber.

Goin' a Buffalo. (1966). Drama. A black hustler learns that his good buddy is not his "brother." *Cast:* 4 BM, 1 BF, 1 WF, extras. *Length:* 3 Acts. *Prod:* Staged reading, APT, New York, June 1968. *Pubn: New Black Playwrights*, ed. by William

Couch, Jr., Baton Rouge: Louisiana State Univ. Pr., 1968. *Lib Source:* HBA. Perm: Agency, Don Farber.

The Helper. (1968). Protest Satire. A white family engages the aid of a black man and then demonstrates their ignorance in various ways.   *Cast:* 1 BM, 2 WM, 2 WF. *Length:* 1 Act. *Prod:* New Dramatists Workshop, New York, June 1970. *Pubn: The Theme Is Blackness*, New York: Morrow, 1973. *Lib Source:* HBA. *Perm:* Agency, Don Farber.

Home Boy. (1972). Drama. Music by Aaron Bell. Two southern black men plan to emigrate to the North. One does, but both are victims, survivors, and casualties of the America of the 1950s and 1960s.   *Cast:* 4 BM, 5 BF. *Length:* Full Length. *Prod:* Perry Street Theater, New York, Sept. 1976. *Perm:* Agency, Don Farber.

House Party, a Soul Happening. "Another of Ed Bullins' photo plays which tells it like it is and nothing else (you can see the same thing for one drink at your local bucket-of-blood bar on almost any weekend night . . .)"—Peter Bailey, *Black World*, vol. 23, no. 6, Apr. 1974.   *Prod:* APT, New York, Oct. 1973. *Perm:* Agency, Don Farber.

How Do You Do. (1965). Satire/Nonsense Drama. Two stereotypes needle each other, reflecting the resentments they have inherited from a white society. *Cast:* 2 BM, 1 BF. *Length:* 1 Act. *Prod:* Firehouse Repertory Theatre, San Francisco, Calif., Aug. 1965. *Pubn: Black Fire,* ed. by LeRoi Jones and Larry Neal, New York: Morrow, 1968. *Lib Source:* HBA. *Perm:* Agency, Don Farber.

I Am Lucy Terry. Historical Fantasy. This play for young Americans concerns Lucy Terry, a young slave poet illegally educated by her mistress, who falls in love and marries Abijah Prince, a free black man. Commissioned by the N.Y. State Council on the Arts.   *Cast:* 1 BM, 1 BF, 1 WM, 1 WF, 1 Indian. *Length:* 1 Act. *Prod:* APT, New York, Feb. 1976. *Perm:* Agency, Don Farber.

In New England Winter. (1967). Domestic drama. The problems two brothers face as the elder tries to recapture his wife. A continuation of the life of Cliff Dawson, one of the characters from *In the Wine Time,* by the same playwright.   *Cast:* 6 BM, 2 BF. *Length:* 1 Act. *Prod:* NFT, New York, Feb. 1971. *Pubn: New Plays from the Black Theatre,* ed. by Ed Bullins, New York: Bantam, 1969. *Lib Source:* HBA. *Perm:* Agency, Don Farber.

In the Wine Time. (1967). Drama. The interaction of ghetto dwellers focusing on a black man who wants to leave his present setting for a new world.   *Cast:* 7 BM, 7 BF. *Length:* 3 Acts. *Prod:* NLT, New York, Dec. 1968. *Pubn: Five Plays*, Indianapolis: Bobbs-Merrill, 1968. *Lib Source:* HBA. *Perm:* Agency, Don Farber.

It Bees Dat Way. (1970). Ritual. Street people interacting with liberal-minded whites and the former's realization of what must be done about the genocidal plot of the white establishment.   *Cast:* 4 BM, 2 BF. *Length:* 1 Act. *Prod:* Ambiance Lunch-Hour Theatre Club, London, Eng., Sept. 1970. *Pubn: Four Dynamite Plays*, New York: Morrow, 1972. *Lib Source:* HBA. *Perm:* Agency, Don Farber.

It Has No Choice. (1965). Drama. A white woman tries to sever her relationship with her black lover.   *Cast:* 1 BM, 1 WF. *Length:* 1 Act. *Prod:* Black Arts West

BULLINS, ED *(Cont.)*

Repertory Theatre School, San Francisco, Calif., Spring 1966. *Pubn: The Theme Is Blackness*, New York: Morrow, 1973. *Lib Source:* HBA. *Perm:* Agency, Don Farber.

Jo Anne! (1976). Drama/Satire. An examination of the Jo Anne Little rape/murder case in a North Carolina prison.   *Cast:* 5 BM, 5 BF, 5 WM, 2 WF. *Length:* 2 Acts. *Prod:* Riverside Church Theatre, New York, Oct. 1976. *Perm:* Agency, Don Farber.

Malcolm: '71; or Publishing Blackness. (1971). Mr. Blackman, a black writer and revolutionary, receives an inquiry about publishing from a white girl whose dog is named "Malcolm."   *Cast:* 1 BM, 1 WF. *Length:* 1 Act. *Pubn: The Black Scholar,* vol. 6, no. 9, June 1975. *Lib Source:* HBA. *Perm:* Agency, Don Farber.

The Man Who Dug Fish. (1967). Absurd Comedy. A black man buys a large fish and a shovel and places them in a deposit box at the bank for ten years—an absurd action taken in an absurd white world.   *Cast:* 1 BM, 3 WM. *Length:* 1 Act. *Prod:* The New Dramatists, New York, June 1970. *Pubn: The Theme Is Blackness,* New York: Morrow, 1973. *Lib Source:* HBA. *Perm:* Agency, Don Farber.

A Minor Scene. (1966). Drama. A black man picks up a white woman; their interactions are the focus of this play.   *Cast:* 1 BM, 1 WF. *Length:* 1 Act. *Prod:* Black Arts West Repertory Theatre, San Francisco, Calif., Spring 1966. *Pubn: The Theme Is Blackness,* New York: Morrow, 1973. *Lib Source:* HBA. *Perm:* Agency, Don Farber.

The Mystery of Phillis Wheatley. (1975). Historical Children's Musical. A struggle of black and white forces for the soul of the famous poet as she rises to international fame.   *Cast:* 2 BM, 1 BF, 2 WM, 2 WF. *Prod:* NFT, Feb. 1976.

Next Time. (1972). Protest Drama. The incident is based on the shooting of the black poet, Henry Dumas, by a white policeman.   *Cast:* 1 BM, 1 BB, 1 WM, 1 Narrator. *Length:* 1 Act. *Pubn: Spirit, the Magazine of Black Culture,* vol. I, no. 1, Spring 1975. *Lib Source:* HBA.

Night of the Beast. (1969). Drama. Revolutionary group combats the forces of police brutality as it attempts to govern its own community.   *Cast:* 3 BM, 2 BF, extras. *Length:* 1 Act. *Pubn: Four Dynamite Plays,* New York: Morrow, 1972. *Lib Source:* HBA. *Perm:* Agency, Don Farber.

One Minute Commercial. (1969). For Black Community Broadcasting.   *Pubn: The Theme Is Blackness,* New York: Morrow, 1973. *Lib Source:* HBA. *Perm:* Agency, Don Farber.

The Pig Pen. (1969). Drama. Pot smokers, wine drinkers, and a need for white sex partners make up a group of pseudo Blacks who think they have it all together, but don't.   *Cast:* 7 BM, 1 BF, 2 WM, 1 WF. *Length:* 1 Act. *Prod:* APT, New York, May 1970. *Pubn: Four Dynamite Plays,* New York: Morrow, 1970. *Lib Source:* HBA. *Perm:* Agency, Don Farber.

The Play of the Play. (1970). Media Happening. Invites audience participation. *Pubn: The Theme Is Blackness,* New York: Morrow, 1973. *Lib Source:* HBA. *Perm:* Agency, Don Farber.

A Short Play for a Small Theatre. (1971). Ritual. A black man applies ritual makeup and then shoots each white person in the audience, one by one.   *Cast:* 1 BM. *Length:* 1 Act. *Pubn: Black World,* vol. 2, no. 6, Apr. 1971. *Lib Source:* HBA. *Perm:* Agency, Don Farber

A Son, Come Home. (1967). Domestic Drama. Flashbacks in the lives of a black mother and her son whom she hasn't seen in years.   *Cast:* 2 BM, 2 BF. *Length:* 1 Act. *Prod:* APT, New York, Mar. 1968. *Pubn: Five Plays,* Indianapolis: Bobbs-Merrill, 1968. *Lib Source:* HBA. *Perm:* Agency, Don Farber.

State Office Building Curse. (1969). A "planned" happening of the opening and closing of the State Office Building in Harlem, a building built, despite community objections, in Harlem by then governor of New York, Nelson Rockefeller. *Length:* 1 Act. *Pubn: The Theme Is Blackness,* New York: Morrow, 1973. *Lib Source:* HBA. *Perm:* Agency, Don Farber.

A Street Party. (1970). A suggested dialogue about political-racial events that invites improvisation. *Pubn: The Theme Is Blackness,* New York: Morrow, 1973. *Lib Source:* HBA. *Perm:* Agency, Don Farber.

Street Sounds. (1970). Sundry voices of the black population of inner cities.   *Cast:* 12 BM, 5 BF. *Prod:* La Mama Experimental Theatre Club, New York, Oct. 1970. *Pubn: The Theme Is Blackness,* New York: Morrow, 1973. *Lib Source:* HBA. *Perm:* Agency, Don Farber.

The Taking of Miss Janie. Satirical Drama. This play is the sequel to Bullins' *The Pig Pen.* Set in California in the 1960s, it follows the lives, loves, and political attitudes of nine black and white students.   *Cast:* 3 BM, 2 BF, 2 WM, 2 WF. *Length:* Full Length. *Prod:* NFT, New York, Mar. 1975.

The Theme Is Blackness. (1966). To be performed before predominantly white audiences. The house and stage lights are turned off for twenty minutes.   *Cast:* 1 BM. *Length:* 1 Act. *Prod:* City College, New York, 1973, San Francisco State College, Calif., 1966. *Pubn: The Theme Is Blackness,* New York: Morrow, 1973. *Lib Source:* HBA. *Perm:* Agency, Don Farber.

We Righteous Bombers. See Bass, Kingsley B., Jr.

You Gonna Let Me Take You Out Tonight, Baby? (1969). Comedy. Black man tries to hustle one of his girl friend's friends.   *Cast:* 1 BM. *Pubn: Black Arts,* ed. by Ahmad Alhamisi and Harum Wangara, Detroit: Black Arts Pub. Co., 1969. *Lib Source:* HBA. *Perm:* Agency, Don Farber.

BULLINS, ED, and MILDRED KAYDEN*

Sepia Star. (1977). Musical. Music and lyrics by Mildred Kayden. About a rhythm-and-blues singer. *Prod:* Stage 73, New York, Aug. 1977.

Storyville. Musical Comedy. Music and lyrics by Mildred Kayden. "Set in New Orleans in 1917, a singer gets involved with a musician and they form their own band as they work their way up river."—*The Black American,* vol. 16, no. 21, May 1977.   *Prod:* Mandeville Theatre, University of California, La Jolla, May 1977.

BULLINS, ED, and SHIRLEY TARBELL

The Game of Adam and Eve. (1966). *Length:* 1 Act.

BURDINE, WARREN, II

a.k.a. Deadwood Dick. Ritual. This Afro-Western odyssey with music is a passage-to-manhood rite that several tribes in West Africa practice. It has been Americanized and set in the mythical West. The protagonist, Nat "Deadwood Dick" Love, makes a symbolic journey in search of his manhood. *Cast:* 15-20 M & F, 5 musicians. *Length:* Full Length. *Prod:* Dillard University, New Orleans, La., Dec. 1976. *Perm:* Agency, Ed Lawrence.

Down thru the Chimney. (c. 1970). Fantasy. Farce about what would happen if two black cops arrested Santa Claus for breaking and entering. *Cast:* 3 BM (1 in whiteface). *Length:* 1 Act. *Perm:* Agency, Ed Lawrence.

Jake Jackson's Revolution. (1974). Drama. An adaptation of Richard Wright's novel, *Lawd Today,* set in Chicago in 1937. A day in the life of a young black postal worker and a look at the social and emotional factors that keep him running on a never-ending treadmill of apathy and the possibility of his redemption. *Cast:* 9 BM, 4 BF, 2 WM, 1 WF, extras. *Length:* 3 Acts. *Perm:* Agency, Ed Lawrence.

Jitterbug Champagne. Tragi-Comedy. Set in a small drugstore-restaurant-general store in rural east Tennessee in the summer of 1967. Deals with ignorance and naiveté of people with preconceived notions about others and the games and rituals blacks must act out to survive. A work in progress. *Cast:* 1 BM, 2 WM, 1 WF, 1 Afro-Latin. *Length:* 1 Act. *Perm:* Agency, Ed Lawrence.

A Night Class at Harlem U. (1972). The hopes, frustrations, and fears of sundry characters in inner city communities. *Cast:* 8 BM, 6 BF, 1 BB, 1 WM. *Length:* 2 Acts. *Prod:* Humanist Theatre, Cleveland, Ohio, June 1974. *Perm:* Agency, Ed Lawrence.

Snowbound. Historical Drama. Set in the 1800s. A group of Blacks who have plotted to revolt against their masters are trapped by a blizzard in a plantation house. *Cast:* 4 BM, 2 BF, 1 WM, 1 WF, offstage voice. *Length:* 3 Acts. *Perm:* Agency, Ed Lawrence.

BURGESS, IVAN

Horseshoe House. (1970). Drama. Conflict of black man and white woman living in a boardinghouse in Canada. *Cast:* 1 BM, 1 WM, 2 WF. *Length:* 2 Acts.

BURGHARDT, ARTHUR, and MICHAEL EGAN

Frederick Douglass . . . through His Own Words. *Cast:* 2 BM, 1 BF. *Prod:* NEC, New York, May 1972.

BURKE, INEZ

Two Races. Pageant. This piece (for junior high school) concerns a white boy and a black boy who compare what each race has done throughout history. *Cast:* 2 BB, 2 WB. *Length:* 1 Act. *Pubn: Plays and Pageants from the Life of the Negro,* ed. by Willis Richardson, Washington, D.C.: Associated Publishers, 1930. *Lib Source:* HBA.

BURR, ANNE

Brothers. An assortment of situations representing the life of city streets and their happenings, utilizing props, film, mime, etc.   *Cast:* Assortment of characters of all colors, sexes, and ages; number is flexible. *Length:* Full Length.

BURRILL, MARY

Aftermath. Returning black veteran of World War I learns that his father has been hanged by white neighbors and he seeks revenge.   *Cast:* 1 BM, 3 BF. *Length:* 1 Act. *Prod:* Krigwa Players, Little Negro Theatre, New York, May 1928. *Pubn:* *The Liberator,* Apr. 1919. *Lib Source:* FTP, GMU.

They That Sit in Darkness. (1919). Drama. Malinda Jasper dies from too much hard work and too many children.   *Cast:* 1 BF, 1 WF, 6 children. *Length:* 1 Act. *Pubn: Black Theater USA,* ed. by James V. Hatch and Ted Shine, New York: Free Pr., 1974. *Lib Source:* HBA.

BURRIS, ANDREW

You Mus' Be Born Again. Drama. Blacks, outraged by Clem Coleman's "nationalism" toward their established institutions, contrive to make him accept their standards.   *Cast:* 6 BM, 6 BF. *Length:* 3 Acts. *Prod:* Gilpin Players, Karamu Theatre, Cleveland, Ohio, 1931. *Lib Source:* FTP, GMU.

BURROUGHS, NANNIE

The Slabtown Convention. Rustic Burlesque. This piece was performed by Bert Williams and George Walker, the vaudevillian comedy team.

BURROWS, VINIE

Dark Fire. Program of oral literature of Africa with myths, folktales, legends, and proverbs from throughout Africa.   *Cast:* 1 BF. *Prod:* Pratt University, New York, 1965. *Perm:* Author.

Echoes of Africa. Readings. These are selections in English and French of modern day African poets and writers.   *Cast:* 1 BF. *Perm:* Author.

The Female of the Species. One woman show. Incidental score composed by Ulysses Kay. Vignettes of seven characters from drama and literature with selections from Lewis Carroll, Shakespeare, Oscar Wilde, Edgar Allen Poe, Langston Hughes, and others.   *Cast:* 1 BF. *Perm:* Author.

From Swords to Plowshares. Readings. About the strife of war and the strife of peace.   *Cast:* 1 BF. *Perm:* Author.

Shout Freedom. Dramatic Readings. About struggle: the child breaking away from the parent; the woman from the traditional domination of the male; the maverick chafing against conformity.   *Cast:* 1 BF. *Prod:* Antioch College, Yellow Springs, Ohio, 1963. *Perm:* Author.

BURROWS, VINIE *(Cont.)*

Sister! Sister! Written on commission from the A. M. E. Church. Martha's Vineyard performance subtitled "theatre celebration of International Women's Year"; gala at Ford's Theatre subtitled "all sorts and conditions of women." *Cast:* 1 BF. *Prod:* A. M. E. Conference, Los Angeles, Calif., n.d.; Martha's Vineyard, Mass., July 1975. *Perm:* Author.

Walk Together Children. The black journey from auction block to new nation time [black nationalism]. *Cast:* 1 BF. *Prod:* Greenwich Mews Theatre, New York, 1968. *Perm:* Author.

BUSEY, DE REATH IRENE BYRD

The Yellow Tree. *Length:* 1 Act. *Prod:* Howard Players, Washington, D.C., 1922.

BUSH, OLIVIA WARD

Memories of Calvary. Religious Easter Pageant. *Cast:* 4 M, 2 F, chorus 15-20. *Pubn:* Philadelphia, Pa.: A. M. E. Book Concern, c. 1915.

BUSH, R. W.

Two Daughters. *Prod:* AMAS Repertory Theatre, Inc., New York.

BUTCHER, JAMES W., JR.

Milk and Honey. (Before 1940).

The Seer. (1941). Comedy. The seer forbids the marriage of a young woman because he plans to marry her himself. *Cast:* 4 BM, 1 BF. *Length:* 1 Act. *Pubn:* *The Negro Caravan,* ed. by Sterling Brown, Arthur P. Davies, and Ulysses Lee, New York: Arno, 1969. *Lib Source:* HBA.

BUTLER, GLEN ANTHONY

19th Nervous Breakdown.

Obsolete Bird. (1972). Melodrama. Wolf Moore, king pimp, reaches for a moment of beauty and is killed. *Cast:* 5 BM, 4 BF, 2 WM. *Length:* 1 Act.

Resurrection and Kingly Rights. Morality Play. The personalized story of Dr. Martin Luther King and his struggle. *Cast:* 13 BM, 5 BF, 6 WM, 1 WF.

BUTLER, RUFUS

Pushkin. Adaptation of a series of the Russian poet Alexander Pushkin's letters. *Prod:* Black Theatre, Los Angeles, Calif., 1973.

BUTLER, TOMMY

Selma. Dramatic Musical. *Prod:* Inner City Cultural Center, Los Angeles, Calif., 1975.

BUTTS, HILTON

Zeus on Four Wheels. Tragedy. The American dream and how it ultimately fails, as represented by a mythic fusion of such American heroes of technology as Henry Ford and Thomas Edison. *Cast:* 12 M, 3 F, extras. *Length:* 2 Acts.

CAIN, ORLANDO

Cry of the Still Blacks. "This play deals with a myriad of themes: interracial marriage, homosexuality, alcoholism and family disunity."—Eugene Perkins, *Black World,* vol. 23, no. 6, Apr. 1974. *Prod:* South Side Community Center, Chicago, Ill., Nov. 1973.

CALDWELL, BEN

All White Caste. (1971). Melodrama. The aftermath of the black "revolution" finds a white liberal in a somewhat precarious position. Subtitled: *After the Separation.* Cast: 1 BM, 2 WM. *Length:* 1 Act. *Pubn: Black Drama,* ed. by Woodie King, Jr. and Ron Milner, New York: Signet, 1971. *Lib Source:* PAL. *Perm:* Agency, NASABA.

Family Portrait. (1967). Domestic Drama. The dichotomy that exists between a militant black and his parents. *Cast:* 2 BM, 1 BF. *Length:* 1 Act. *Pubn: New Plays from the Black Theater,* ed. by Ed Bullins, New York: Bantam, 1969. *Lib Source:* PAL. *Perm:* Agency, AFRACA.

The Fanatic or *Testifyin'.* (1968). Morality Play. The "spirit" at a black church causes white man to confess to the evils and wrongdoings he has inflicted upon blacks. *Cast:* 1 BM, 1 WM, 1 WF, extras. *Length:* 1 Act. *Lib Source:* Typescript, HBA. *Perm:* Agency, NASABA

Hypnotism. (1969). Didactic Drama. Magician has enslaved the minds of blacks to be nonviolent. *Cast:* 1 BM, 1 BF, 2 WM. *Length:* 1 Act. *Pubn: Afro-Arts Anthology,* Newark, N.J.: Jihad Productions, 1966. *Lib Source:* HBA. *Perm:* Agency, NASABA.

The Job. (1968). Ritual Drama. The condescending attitude of white man costs him his life. *Cast:* 5 BM, 2 BF, 1 WM. *Length:* 1 Act. *Pubn: Drama Review,* vol. 12, no. 4, Summer 1968. *Lib Source:* PAL. *Perm:* Agency, NASABA.

The King of Soul or *The Devil and Otis Redding.* (1967). Morality Ritual. The manipulation of the career of Otis Redding and the events surrounding his death. *Cast:* 6 BM, 1 WM. *Length:* 1 Act. *Pubn: New Plays from the Black Theatre,* ed. by Ed Bullins, New York: Bantam, 1969. *Lib Source:* HBA. *Perm:* Agency, AFRACA.

Love. *Prod:* Kasisi Yusef Iman Weusi Kuumba Theatre Troupe, New York.

Mission Accomplished. (1967). Historical Satire. Christianity makes its way to an African village. *Cast:* 4 BM, 1 WM, 2 WF. *Length:* 1 Act. *Pubn: Drama Review,* vol. 12, no. 4, Summer 1968. *Lib Source:* PAL. *Perm:* Agency, NASABA.

Prayer Meeting or *The First Militant Minister.* (1966). Comedy. Speaking as the voice of God, a burglar convinces a nonviolent minister to change his attitude about violence. *Cast:* 2 BM. *Length:* 1 Act. *Prod:* Spirit House Movers, Newark, N.J., Apr. 1967. *Pubn: Black Fire,* ed. by LeRoi Jones and Larry Neal, New York: Morrow, 1968. *Lib Source:* HBA. *Perm:* Agency, William Morrow.

Recognition. (1968). Morality Ritual. God assesses the cause of the black man's problems and gives advice as to possible solutions. *Cast:* 3-5 black voices, 2-4 white voices. *Length:* 1 Act. *Lib Source:* Typescript, HBA. *Perm:* Agency, NASABA.

CALDWELL, BEN *(Cont.)*

Riot Sale or ***Dollar Psyche Fake Out.*** (1966). Drama. A parting of the ways between would-be revolutionaries and dedicated ones.   *Cast:* 10-15 B, 5-10 W. *Length:* 1 Act. *Pubn: Drama Review,* vol. 12, no. 4, Summer 1968. *Lib Source:* PAL. *Perm:* Agency, NASABA.

Runaround.   *Length:* 1 Act. *Prod:* Third World House, June 1970.

Top Secret or ***A Few Million after B.C.*** (1967). Drama. A plan is devised to eliminate the black race.   *Cast:* 6 BM. *Length:* 1 Act. *Pubn: Drama Review,* vol. 12, no. 4, Summer 1968. *Lib Source:* PAL. *Perm:* Agency, NASABA.

Un-Presidented or ***What Needs to Be Done.*** (1968). Drama. Spokesman for civil rights group has a bold and surprising confrontation with U. S. president.   *Cast:* 3 BM, 6-8 WM. *Length:* 1 Act. *Lib Source:* Typescript, HBA. *Perm:* Agency, NASABA.

The Wall. (1967). A wall of graffiti is given different strokes by different folks.   *Cast:* 3 BM, 2 BF, 2 WM, 1 WF, teenagers. *Length:* 1 Act. *Pubn: Scripts,* vol. I, no. 7, May 1972. *Lib Source:* HBA. *Perm:* Agency, NASABA.

What Is Going On.   *Prod:* NFT, New York, 1973. *Perm:* Agency, NASABA.

CALDWELL, BEN, and YUSEF IMAN

Yesterday, Today, Tomorrow. Historical Didactic Play. A presentation of the black experience—past, present, and future. Subtitled: **The 7 Principles.**   *Cast:* Large B. *Prod:* Weusi Kuumba Troupe, The East, New York, Aug. 1974. *Perm:* Agency, Sister Malika.

CAMERON, NORMAN E.

Jamaica Joe. Drama. Joe Strong leaves his girl Agnes to come to the U. S. during World War II as laborer; he loses his girl and returns home to help his country toward self-government.   *Cast:* 8 BM, 3 BF, dancers and children. *Length:* 3 Acts. *Pubn:* Georgetown, Guyana: By the author, 1962.

CAMP, HARRY

The Prodigal Son.   *Prod:* Harlem Experimental Theatre, St. Philip's Church Parish House, New York, c. 1932.

CAMPBELL, HERBERT

Goin' Home to Papa.

Middle Class Black. Drama. Depicts the plight of an affluent Negro living in an all-white neighborhood when he comes under attack from some of his militant black relatives.   *Length:* 3 Acts. *Prod:* Bed-Stuy Theatre, New York, June 1970.

Rape.   *Prod:* Bed-Stuy Theatre, New York, Oct. 1971.

CAMPBELL, RALPH

Death of a Crow.

CANNON, STEVE, CORRINE JENNINGS, and JOE OVERSTREET

Snakeshiiit. Pageant Play / Tragic-Comic Farce. Head man at the White House tries to contain the black revolution and is assassinated.   *Cast:* 6 BM, 2 BF, 5 WM, 2 WF, extras. *Length:* 3 Acts. *Prod:* Reading, NFT, New York, 1975. *Lib Source:* Typescript, HBA.

CAPEL, SHARON

Dreams Are for the Dead. A play about the people in a revolutionary black theatre company.   *Length:* 2 Acts. *Prod:* Reading, Frank Silvera Writers' Workshop, Martinique Theatre, New York, Jan. 1975.

CARNIL, PEPE

Shango de Ima. Yoruba Mystery Play. Adapted and translated by Susan Sherman. As performed in Cuba, the play centers on the birth and history of the Orisha figure, Shango.   *Cast:* 5 BM, 5 BF, extras. *Length:* 26 Scenes. *Prod:* JuJu Players, St. Marks-on-the-Bowery, New York, Sept. 1972. *Pubn:* Garden City: Doubleday, 1969. *Lib Source:* HBA.

CARROLL, VINNETTE

But Never Jam Today. Musical Fable. Based on Lewis Carroll's *Adventures of Alice in Wonderland*, interpreted as a black fantasy. Subtitled: *Black Alice.*   *Cast:* Large B. *Length:* 2 Acts. *Prod:* Urban Arts Corps, New York, City Center, Apr. 1969. *Perm:* Author.

Trumpets of the Lord. Contains poems of James Weldon Johnson's in the form of sermons and traditional Negro spirituals and gospel music.   *Cast:* 6 BM, 5 BF. *Prod:* Brooks Atkinson Theatre, New York, Apr. 1969. *Perm:* Author.

Your Arms Too Short to Box with God. Gospel Musical. Music and lyrics by Alex Bradford; additional music by Micki Grant. The story of Christ as conceived from the "Book of Matthew."   *Cast:* 21 singers and dancers. *Prod:* Spoleto Festival, Italy, 1975; Lyceum Theatre, New York, Dec. 1976. *Perm:* Author.

CARROLL, VINNETTE, and MICKI GRANT

Croesus and the Witch. Musical Comedy. While on a hunt in the wilderness, Croesus and his two friends confront the devilish witch I lecuba, managing to outwit her and return home with prized deerskins.   *Cast:* 3 M, 1 F, chorus (variable). *Length:* 1 Act. *Prod:* Urban Arts Corp., New York, Aug. 1971. *Perm:* Authors.

Don't Bother Me, I Can't Cope. Musical Revue. A musical celebration of the present-day black experience.   *Cast:* B M & F. *Length:* 2 Acts. *Prod:* Lincoln Center Auditorium, New York, Oct. 1970; Edison Theatre, New York, Apr. 1971. *Perm:* Authors.

Old Judge Mose Is Dead.   *Prod:* Urban Arts Corps, New York. *Perm:* Authors.

Step Lively, Boy. Dramatic Musical. Based on Irwin Shaw's play *Bury the Dead*. A statement about the horror, futility, and absurdity of war.   *Cast:* Large. *Length:* 1 Act. *Prod:* Urban Arts Corps, New York, Feb. 1973. *Perm:* Authors.

CARROLL, VINNETTE, and MICKI GRANT (*Cont.*)

The Ups and Downs of Theophilus Maitland. Musical Comedy. A rich old man on the island of Jamaica woos and wins a beautiful young girl, and then discovers he may not be up for the ordeal after all.   *Cast:* 5 BM, 5 BF, chorus. *Length:* 1 Act. *Prod:* Urban Arts Corps, New York, Mar. 1975. *Perm:* Authors.

CARSON, GERALD

The Unforgettable Experience of Billy Joe McAlester. Screenplay. Adapted from the ballad of Billy Joe McAlester, the play tells how a black man loved a white woman and was pushed from the bridge by a jealous white rival.   *Cast:* 2 BM, 2 BF, 2 BB, 2 BG, 4 WM, 3 WF, extras. *Length:* Full Length: *Pubn:* New York: Vantage, 1977. *Lib Source:* HBA.

CARTER, BEN, SAUNDRA McCLAIN, and DAVID E. MARTIN

Bitter Trails. Protest Drama with Music. A play depicting the life of migrant workers (the black migrant workers in particular) in the Southwest.   *Cast:* 5 BM, 1 BF, 5 M, 1 F. *Length:* 3 Acts. *Prod:* Reading, Frank Silvera Writers' Workshop, New York, Mar. 1975; Billie Holiday Theatre, New York, Apr. 1975.

CARTER, JAMES

The Masks behind a Clown's Face. (1968). Expressionistic Drama. Black man and white man go off to Vietnam and carry with them American racial backgrounds. *Cast:* 5 BM, 5 WM. *Length:* 2 Acts.

CARTER, JOHN D.

The Assassin. (1971).

CARTER, STEVE

As You Can See. (1968). Comedy. A true blind man can also be a true con man.   *Cast:* 2 M, 2 F, 2—race and sex optional. *Length:* 1 Act. *Perm:* Author.

Eden. (1975). Domestic Drama. The daughter of a West Indian (follower of Marcus Garvey) falls in love with a southern American Black, and both families are thrown into conflict. Set in New York, in 1927.   *Cast:* 2 BM, 4 BF, 2 BM teenagers. *Length:* 3 Acts. *Prod:* NEC, New York, Feb. 1976.

One Last Look. (1967). Comedy/Satire. The mistress, wife, and children of a dead man each speak with him at his funeral, revealing his lusty, sad life.   *Cast:* 5 BM, 7 BF. *Length:* 1 Act. *Prod:* NEC, New York, 1968; ABC/TV, 1970. *Pubn: Black Scenes*, ed. by Alice Childress, New York: Doubleday, 1971. *Lib Source:* HBA. *Perm:* Author.

Rampart Street. (1974). Musical. Story based on the life of jazz musician Buddy Bolden. *Length:* Full Length. *Perm:* Author.

Terraced Apartment. (1968). Comedy/Satire. A couple with middle-class aspirations moves into middle income housing and can't pull it off.   *Cast:* 1 BM, 1 BF. *Length:* 1 Act. *Prod:* Old Reliable Theatre Tavern, New York, 1968. *Perm:* Author.

Terraces. (1974). Comedy/Satire. Simultaneous actions of different couples in a new apartment building when a woman falls from a terrace.   *Cast:* 3 BM, 3 BF (doubling). *Length:* Full Length. *Prod:* NEC, New York, 1974. *Perm:* Author.

CARTER, THOMAS G., JR.

Angel of the Mourning. A black love story involving a young married couple living in a small urban city. They are confronted with the pressures of racism and unpleasant working conditions.   *Cast:* 5 M, 1 F. *Prod:* University of Southern California, Los Angeles, 1976.

CÉSAIRE, AIMÉ

A Season in the Congo. (1968). Historical. Based on the activities of African leader Patrice Lumumba.   *Cast:* Large B cast. *Length:* 3 Acts. *Pubn: Kuntu Drama,* ed. by Paul Carter Harrison, New York: Grove, 1974. *Lib Source:* HBA. *Perm:* Agency, Ninon Karlweis.

CHAKA TA

The Sun Force.   *Prod:* The Black Butterfly, Philadelphia, Pa., 1970.

CHAMBERS, CHARLOTTE

Equation X.   *Prod:* Black Repertory Group, Berkeley, Calif., 1973.

CHAMBERS, E. MORRIS

July Jones. Domestic. A young woman's struggle to leave home.   *Cast:* 2 BM, 3 BF. *Length:* 2 Acts.

CHAMBERS, KENNETH

Miller High Life.   *Prod:* Atlanta University Summer Theatre, Ga., 1974.

CHARLES, MARTIE

African Interlude.

Black Cycle. (1971). Domestic Drama. The conflict of ideals and priorities is questioned by a mother and her daughter.   *Cast:* 3 BM, 5 BF. *Length:* 2 Acts. *Prod:* NLT Workshop, New York, 1971. *Pubn: Black Drama,* ed. by Woodie King, Jr. and Ron Milner, New York: New Amer. Lib., 1971. *Lib Source:* PAL. *Perm:* Agency, NASABA.

An Invocation. Social Drama. A black girl's rebellion against the established order and the older generation.   *Perm:* Agency, NASABA.

Jamimma. (1972). Drama. Jameena, beautiful, sensitive, and in love, is crushed by the death of her lover, Omar.   *Cast:* 5 BM, 3 BF. *Length:* 3 Acts. *Prod:* NFT, New York, Mar. 1972. *Lib Source:* Typescript, HBA. *Perm:* Agency, NASABA.

Job Security. (1972). Drama. The conditions of the ghetto educational system entice a black girl to take drastic action.   *Cast:* 4 BF, 1 BG. *Length:* 1 Act. *Prod:* Black Magicians, Third World House, New York, June 1970. *Pubn: Black Theater USA,* ed. by James V. Hatch and Ted Shine, New York: Free Pr., 1974. *Lib Source:* HBA. *Perm:* Agency, NASABA.

CHARLES, MARTIE *(Cont.)*

Where We At. (1969). Depicts the humiliation and degradation of a black woman who refused to help an unfortunate sister.   *Cast:* 2 BM, 4 BF, whiteface used. *Length:* 1 Act. *Prod:* NEC Workshop, New York, Jan. 1971. *Lib Source:* Typescript, HBA. *Perm:* Agency, NASABA.

CHARLES, NORMAN

Friends.   *Length:* 1 Act. *Prod:* Regal Roots for the Performing Arts, St. Joseph Hospital Auditorium, Paterson, N.J., July 1975.

Infirmity Is Running. Domestic Drama.   *Length:* 2 Acts. *Prod:* The Theatre of Renewal, Stagelights Theatre, New York, Sept. 1976.

Jenny. Comedy/Drama.   *Length:* 1 Act. *Prod:* The Theatre of Renewal, Stagelights Theatre, New York, Sept. 1976.

CHATMAN, XAVIER

And It's Time for a Big Celebration. Musical. Music by Isaiah Jones, Jr.   *Prod:* Performing Arts Society, Los Angeles, Calif., 1973.

CHAUNCEY, HARRELL CORDELL

It's Mary's Boy.   *Prod:* MLK Players, New York University, N.Y., Jan. 1977

CHILDRESS, ALICE

The African Garden. The Afro-American search for deeper African identification. *Pubn:* Excerpt in *Black Scenes,* ed. by Alice Childress, New York: Doubleday, 1971. *Lib Source:* HBA. *Perm:* Agency, Flora Roberts.

Florence. A black mother, en route to New York to retrieve her daughter Florence from a theatre career, converses with a hypocritical white actress and decides to stay home and encourage her daughter to fight on.   *Cast:* 4 B, 1 WF. *Length:* 1 Act. *Prod:* ANT, New York, 1951. *Pubn: Masses and Mainstream,* vol. 3, Oct. 1950. *Lib Source:* HBA. *Perm:* Agency, Flora Roberts.

The Freedom Drum. Historical. Music by Nathan Woodard. Story of the Montgomery bus strike. Subtitled: *Martin Luther King at Montgomery, Alabama.*   *Cast:* 5 B, 4 W (doubling). *Length:* Full Length. *Prod:* Performing Arts Repertory Theatre, on tour, 1970. *Perm:* Agency, Flora Roberts.

Gold thru the Trees. Musical Revue. The parallel of the freedom struggle in South Africa with the fight in the United States. First performed in celebration of South African Blacks' 300-year-old struggle for freedom.   *Length:* Full Length. *Prod:* Club Baron, New York, Apr. 1952. *Perm:* Agency, Flora Roberts.

Hero Ain't Nothin' but a Sandwich. Screenplay. Story of a thirteen–year–drug addict and the adults in his life.   *Prod:* Film produced by Radnitz & Mattel; to be released in 1977.

Just a Little Simple. Musical Revue. Derived from Langston Hughes' book, *Simple Speaks His Mind,* plus original material by Alice Childress.   *Length:* Full Length. *Prod:* Club Baron, New York, Sept. 1950. *Perm:* Agency, Flora Roberts.

A Man Bearing a Pitcher. Drama. A fictional account of the family in whose home Jesus Christ and his disciples held their last supper, and the family's attempt to save Christ from crucifixion.   *Length:* Full Length.

Mojo. (1970). Domestic Drama. Black couple reminisces about the past and how things could have been.   *Cast:* 1 BM, 1 BF. *Length:* 1 Act. *Prod:* NHT, New York, Nov. 1970. *Pubn: Black World,* vol. 21, no. 6, Apr. 1971. *Lib Source:* HBA. *Perm:* Agency, DPS.

String. (1971). Domestic Drama. The credibility of an aging man is questioned when he is accused of stealing.   *Cast:* 2 BM, 3 BF, 1 BG. *Length:* 1 Act. *Prod:* NEC, New York, 1969. *Pubn:* DPS. *Lib Source:* HBA. *Perm:* Agency, DPS.

Trouble in Mind. (1970). During the first rehearsal of a play dealing with a Negro lynching in the South, the leading black actress refuses to play her stereotypic role.   *Cast:* 2 BM, 2 BF, 3 WM, 2 WF. *Length:* 2 Acts. *Prod:* Greenwich Mews Theatre, New York, Nov. 1955. *Pubn: Black Theatre,* ed. by Lindsay Patterson, New York: Dodd, 1971. *Lib Source:* HBA. *Perm:* Agency, Flora Roberts.

Wedding Band. (1973). Drama. An interracial romance set in South Carolina, circa World War I.   *Cast:* 1 BM, 4 BF, 2 WM, 2 WF, 1 BG, 1 WG. *Length:* 3 Acts. *Prod:* University of Michigan, Ann Arbor, 1967; Public Theater, New York Shakespeare Festival, N.Y., Nov. 1972; national television, 1974. *Pubn:* SF. *Lib Source:* HBA. *Perm:* Agency, Flora Roberts.

When the Rattlesnake Sounds. Drama. One summer in New Jersey, Harriet Tubman works as laundress in a hotel to help the abolitionist cause; the play reveals the extent of her courage and commitment.   *Cast:* 3 BF. *Length:* 1 Act. *Pubn:* New York: Coward, 1975. *Lib Source:* HBA. *Perm:* Agency, Flora Roberts.

Wine in the Wilderness. (1969). Comedy/Drama. An artist who had contempt for a black woman of "uncultured" background discovers that she is the true wine in the wilderness for the Revolution.   *Cast:* 3 BM, 3 BF. *Length:* 1 Act. *Prod:* WGHB-IV, Boston, Mass., Mar. 1969. *Pubn:* DPS. *Perm:* Agency, DPS.

The World on a Hill. Drama. An unhappy white woman and her son meet a fourteen-year-old black boy on a picnic in the West Indies and glimpse their lives in the isolation of the setting.   *Cast:* 1 BB, 1 WF, 1 WB. *Length:* 1 Act. *Pubn: Plays to Remember,* New York: Macmillan, 1968. *Perm:* Agency, Flora Roberts.

CHILDRESS, ALVIN, and ALICE HERNDON

Hell's Alley. Drama. "The scene takes place in an alley, in which a gangster carries on his trade of swindling and victimizing unsuspecting persons who pass."—Frederick Bond.   *Prod:* Lafayette Players, New York, 1930.

CHIMBAMUL

How the Spider Becomes the Hero of Folk Tales. (1971). Children's Play.

CHISHOLM, EARLE

Black Manhood.

Two in the Back Room.   *Prod:* Freedom Theatre, Philadelphia, Pa., 1971.

CLARK, CHINA

In Sorrow's Room. Domestic Drama. Focuses on the problem of a young woman named Sorrow who is trying to establish her identity.   *Cast:* 3 BM, 4 BF. *Length:* 3 Acts. *Prod:* African Total Theatre, New York, 1975. *Pubn: Neffie and In Sorrow's Room*, New York: ERA Pub. Co., 1976. *Lib Source:* HBA.

The Madwoman's Room.   *Perm:* Author.

Neffie. (1972). Mythic Fantasy. About a beautiful African woman whose love for one man lasts through eternity.   *Cast:* 6 BM, 6 BF, 1 BB. *Length:* 2 Acts. *Prod:* Reading, Frank Silvera Writers' Workshop, New York, 1975. *Pubn: Neffie and In Sorrow's Room*, New York: ERA Pub. Co., 1976. *Lib Source:* HBA.

Perfection in Black. (1972). Drama. Concerns black woman's conflicts with black man/white woman.   *Cast:* 2 M, 1 F. *Length:* 1 Act. *Prod:* NEC Workshop, New York, Jan. 1971. *Pubn: Scripts*, vol. 1, no. 7, May 1972. *Lib Source:* HBA. *Perm:* Author.

The Sabian.

Why God Hates Rev. Chandler.

The Willow Lottery.

CLARK, DOROTHY, and GEORGE HOUSTON BASS

Dreamdust. Music by Kambon. Six African-American folktales adapted by Bass, Clark, and the performers.

CLARKE, SEBASTIAN

Helliocentric World. (1971). Morality Drama. A series of brief monologues and vignettes showing the decline and fall of city life.   *Cast:* 3 BM, 2 BF, 3 WM, 1 WF. *Length:* 1 Act. *Pubn: Scripts*, vol. 1, no. 7, May 1972. *Lib Source:* HBA. *Perm:* Agency, Hattie Gossett.

Lower Earth.

CLAY, BURIEL, II

Buy a Little Tenderness. (1971). Domestic Drama. A look into some of the socio-psychological pressures on persons living under ghetto conditions and the kinds of response those conditions demand.   *Cast:* 2 BM, 4 BF. *Length:* 1 Act. *Prod:* NEC, New York, Feb. 1975. *Lib Source:* Typescript, HBA. *Perm:* Author.

The Creation of the World. (1952). African Ballet/Ritual. An adaptation of a Ugandan folktale. The creation of the world, of man and woman, and the gift of love as represented through poetry, music, song, and dance.   *Cast:* 5 BM, 3 BF, 6 chorus, 3 musicians. *Length:* 1 Act. *Lib Source:* Typescript, HBA. *Perm:* Author.

A Dance for Demons. (1973). Concerns the damnation of two souls and the attempt to salvage one of them.   *Cast:* 1 BM, 1 BF, 1 WM, 1 WF, 1 bass player. *Perm:* Author.

The Gentle Rose Decays. (1975). Psychodrama. Focuses on the futility of placing too much hope in the trust and love of one person and the problems, the insanity, and the horror of women incarcerated. *Cast:* 3 BF, 2 WM, 1 WF, 1 Latin F. *Length:* 2 Acts. *Perm:* Author.

Greasy Spoon. (1975). Morality Drama. Depicts the struggle of four people waiting for a change to come and what each does or does not do to effect that change. *Cast:* 3 BM, 2 BF. *Length:* 2 Acts. *Perm:* Author.

Jezebelle. (1973). Morality Drama. Focuses on the inadequacies of the present political, economic, social, and psychological state of black people. *Cast:* 5 BM, 2 BF, 1 WF. *Perm:* Author.

Liberty Call. (1974). Morality Drama. Explores life's encounters through grief, conflict, fear, joy, aspirations, etc., of three sailors from different political, educational, and social backgrounds. *Cast:* 4 BM, 1 WM, 1 Asian M, 3 Asian F. *Length:* 2 Acts. *Prod:* Reading, Frank Silvera Writers' Workshop, Martinique Theatre, New York, Jan. 1975. *Perm:* Author.

No Left Turn. (1973). Drama. This play explores the theory that "They's mo to bein' black than meets the eye!" It presents the attitudes, realities, and experiences of seven childhood friends reunited in a rural Texas community. *Cast:* 7 BM, 1 WM. *Length:* 1 Act. *Prod:* Reading, Frank Silvera Writers' Workshop, Harlem Performance Center, New York, Nov. 1976. *Perm:* Author.

Raw Head and Bloody Bones. (1972). Ritual. Hoodoo ritual drama that explores the enlightenment, conflict, and consequences of a young lady who copulates with a forbidden mate. *Cast:* 1 BM, 5 BF, 2 WM, 1 WB. *Length:* 1 Act. *Lib Source:* Typescript, HBA.

X's. (1972). Domestic Drama. Centers on the desires, fears, and strife three people encounter because of confused priorities. *Cast:* 3 BM, 3 BF, 1 WM, 1 WF. *Length:* 2 Acts. *Perm:* Author.

CLAY, CARL

2000 Black. *Prod:* Spectrum Theatre, New York, July 1975.

CLAY, MELVIN, and SAM GREENLEE

The Spook Who Sat by the Door. Melodrama. An adaptation of Sam Greenlee's novel of the same name, about a black revolution that begins on Chicago's South Side. *Length:* Full Length.

CLEVELAND, CARLES, and JAMES DE JONGH

Hail, Hail, the Gang's. (1976). Musical Drama. The tragic and sometimes comic struggle of street gangs to maintain their images and their survival. *Cast:* 12 BM, 1 BF. *Length:* Full Length. *Prod:* New York Theatre Ensemble, May 1976. *Perm:* Author.

CLIMONS, ARTIE

My Troubled Soul. A school and family drama. *Prod:* San Francisco Bay Area, Calif., 1970–1971.

CODLING, BESS
The Assassin.

COFFMAN, STEVEN
Black Sabbath. Drama. When Onus, the poet, finds his best friend, The Kid, shot in a riot, Onus walks into the burning church to die.   *Cast:* 6 BM, 2 BF, 1 WM, 1 WF, extras. *Length:* 1 Act.

COGMAN, GEORGE
Little Stone House.   *Prod:* Harlem Experimental Theatre, St. Philip's Church Parish House, New York, c. 1932.

COLE, BOB
Belle of Bridgeport. Musical Revue. A "white show" (for white performers and a white audience) to which Cole contributed.
Coontown Carnival. (1900).
King of Spades. (1900). Musical Comedy.   *Length:* 2 Acts.

COLE, BOB, and JAMES W. JOHNSON
The Shoo-fly Regiment. Comic Opera.   *Prod:* Possibly Grand Opera House, New York, June 1907 or Bijou Theatre, New York, Aug. 1907.

COLE, BOB, and ROSAMUND JOHNSON
The Red Moon. Comic Opera. "A musical story in which lawyer Slim Brown and Dr. Plunk Green, both quacks, rescue a maiden who has been taken from her mother's home to her father's wigwam on a western reservation."— Fannin Belcher.   *Prod:* Majestic Theatre, New York, May 1909.

COLE, BOB, JAMES W. JOHNSON, and ROSAMUND JOHNSON
Humpty Dumpty. Musical Revue. "A 'white show' [for white performers and a white audience] to which these black artists contributed."—Fannin Belcher.
In Newport. Musical Revue. "A 'white show' [for white performers and a white audience] to which these black artists contributed."—Fannin Belcher. *Prod:* n.p., 1904.

COLE, BOB, and WILLIAM JOHNSON
A Trip to Coontown. Musical. "The story concerned two bunko operators who pursued a naive provincial with money to burn."—Fannin Belcher.   *Prod:* Third Avenue Theatre, New York, Apr. 1898.

COLE, BOB, et al.
Black Patti Troubadours or *A Darktown Frolic on the Rialto.*

COLEMAN, ANNIE R.

Gaslight Square. Drama. Black novelist discovers through interracial love affair that he has to make it on his own.   *Cast:* 3 BM, 2 BF, 2 WF. *Length:* 3 Acts.

COLEMAN, RALF

Swing Song. (1937). Protest Melodrama. Classic story of pregnant white girl, her black lover, and a lynch mob in Deep South.   *Cast:* 5 BM, 3 BF, 1 WF. *Length:* 1 Act. *Prod:* FTP, Boston, Mass., c. 1938. *Lib Source:* Typescript, HBA.

COLEMAN, WARREN

Juba.   *Length:* 1 Act. *Lib Source:* Typescript, FTP, GMU.

COLES, ROBERT

Woke Up This Mornin', Good Thing on My Mind. Drama. The setting is rural Georgia during the sixties. A black couple gropes toward a reconciliation with their activist son who appears on stage as a ghost.   *Cast:* 2 BM, 1 BF. *Length:* Full Length. *Prod:* Arizona State University, Tempe, Sept. 1975. *Pubn:* Arizona State Univ. Pr., 1975. *Perm:* Author.

COLES, ZAIDA

Scenes and Songs on Love and Freedom. One-Woman Show   *Prod:* Urban Arts Corp., New York, Apr. 1975.

COLLIE, KELSEY E.

Ash Wednesday. (1967). Morality Drama. Based on Ash Wednesday scriptures. Several persons at a cocktail party are revealed to be jealous, petty, and lustful, as they share the bread and wine served by the host, who is a priest. *Length:* 1 Act. *Perm:* Author.

Black Images/Black Reflections. (1975). Children's Historical Ritual. A chronicle narrative of Afro-American experiences and contributions to the United States' development depicted through song, movement, and dramatization. *Cast:* Ensemble. *Perm:* Author.

Celebration. (1973). Children's Play with Songs. A selfish, egotistical prime minister who has been voted out of office by the people of a West Indian nation almost gets away with stealing all the money from the treasury and preventing the people from holding an Independence Day celebration.   *Cast:* 6 M, 1 B, 12 F, 1 G. *Prod:* Drama Department, Howard University, Washington, D.C., 1973. *Perm:* Author.

Fiesta! Children's Musical. A young man's search for truth and happiness leads him to a South American village where he saves the fiesta from becoming a fiasco when it is discovered that the ceremonial donkey has been stolen. *Cast:* 8 M, 12 F, 1 G. *Length:* 1 Act. *Pubn:* MFA Thesis, George Washington University, Washington, D.C., 1970. *Perm:* Author.

COLLIE, KELSEY E. *(Cont.)*

The Gift. Sermon in three dramatic sketches, utilizing a litany. Depicts how humans are often mindless of the gift of love that God has given. *Cast:* 3 M, 1 B, 7 F, 2 narrators. *Length:* 1 Act. *Pubn: Youth Ministry Notebook*, 7, New York: Seabury, 1973. *Perm:* Author.

Good Friday, or The End and the Beginning. (1962). Morality Drama. Ten persons seek shelter from an atomic holocaust in a cave; they attempt to come to grips with themselves and each other. *Cast:* 5 M, 5 F. *Length:* 1 Act. *Perm:* Author.

Hell's Belles. (1965). Musical Comedy. An angel is sent from heaven as an emissary and promptly falls in love with an attractive hellion. *Cast:* 8 M, 4 F, extras (children). *Length:* 2 Acts. *Perm:* Author.

How to Succeed with a Little Bit of Luck. (1964). Musical Comedy. A young woman visits her cousin in New York and gets a big theatrical break; but she encounters some minor romantic problems. *Cast:* 8 M, 2 B, 9 F, 2 G. *Length:* 2 Acts. *Perm:* Author.

It Happens Every Summer. (1963). Musical Comedy. Deals with experiences shared by a group of young people who are working as summer camp counselors for a church youth program. *Cast:* 11 M, 6 B, 11 F, 4 G. *Length:* 2 Acts. *Perm:* Author.

It's a Mad, Mad, Mad, Mod World We Live In. (1967). Musical Revue. Topical issues including politics, religion, and minority problems are satirized in song and dance. *Cast:* Ensemble. *Length:* 1 Act. *Perm:* Author.

Kids! (1966). Musical Comedy. The girls want to know what the boys are doing in their clubhouse, so they send in a spy. The parents would like to know what they are all up to. *Length:* 1 Act. *Perm:* Author.

Maybe Some Day. (1968). Domestic Drama with Music. A young woman's conflict with her mother's teachings and the desire to have a good time with her friend and neighbor, who is very hip and popular. *Cast:* 2 WM, 4 F. *Length:* 1 Act. *Perm:* Author.

Randy's Dandy Circus. (1974). Children's Musical. A young boy inherits a circus and his envious aunt and uncle sabotage the opening by stealing all the animals; but the boy triumphs after all with the help of his friends. *Cast:* 4 M, 1 B, 6 F, 1 G, 3 puppets (1 F, 2 M), extras (children). *Perm:* Author.

Where Is Love? (1964). Children's Drama. A little girl runs away from an orphanage in search of love. *Cast:* 9 M, 6 B, 13 F, 8 G. *Length:* 1 Act. *Perm:* Author.

COLLIER, EUGENIA

Ricky. Length: 1 Act. *Prod:* Kuumba Workshop, Eugene Perkins Theatre, Chicago, Ill., Oct. 1976.

COLLIER, SIMONE

In a City.

Straw Baby with Hay Feet.

COLLINS, KATHLEEN

Love Comes But Once. (1972). Poetic Drama. A woman is in love but the man is not in love with her. *Cast:* I BM, 1 BF. *Length.* 1 Act. *Perm:* Author.

Portrait of Kathleen. (1974). Musical Fantasy. A reflection of the marriage of a middle-aged, middle-class black couple going back in the past to the wife's childhood and forward through their courtship, marriage, etc. *Cast:* 3 BM, 8 BF, 1 G. *Length:* 5 Acts. *Perm:* Author.

Where Is the Love. (1972). Television Drama. A middle-aged black man reflects on a love affair that happened a long time ago and that he cannot seem to get over. *Cast:* 1 BM, 2 BF. *Length:* 9 Scenes. *Perm:* Author.

COLLINWOOD ARTS CENTER

Cleveland Speaks. Combines poetry, dance, music, and lights as the media for making strong statements about the effects of urban life on contemporary artists. *Prod:* Collinwood Arts Center, Cleveland, Ohio, 1973.

COMER, J. DOUGLAS, and WILLIAM H. GRAHAM

Beyond the City. Musical Comedy. Community life is the theme, as a semiprofessional basketball player's weak knee forces him to change professions and work in an out-of-the-way community. *Cast:* 6 BM, 1 BB, 1 BF, 1 WM, 1 WF. *Length:* 3 Acts. *Perm:* Author.

The Continuous Struggle, Part II. Domestic Drama. Problem of family where parents are both college graduates. Subtitled: *Stand by East High.* *Cast:* 3 M (2 teenaged twins), 2 F (1 teenager). 6 extras (females). *Length:* Full Length. *Perm:* Author.

Mable Jones and the Devil. Musical Comedy. A domestic situation comedy about poor people. *Cast:* 7 BM (2 teenagers), 6 BF (3 teenagers), 1 WM, 1 WF. *Length:* 3 Acts. *Perm:* Author.

Outta This World. Musical Comedy. A poor black family, headed by a hypochondriac father, inherits money from a rich uncle in Texas and strikes oil. The consequences are that a son in rebellion becomes a hippie and his mother, in order to get rid of him, hires a black ex-astronaut to take her son "outta this world," which, with the help of a janitor at Cape Kennedy, is accomplished and the duo lands on Planet Soul. *Cast:* 7 BM, 1 BB, 3 BF, 2 WM, 9 dancers. *Length:* 3 Acts. *Prod:* East High School, Columbus, Ohio, Mar. 1970. *Perm:* Author.

Six Broken Wires. Drama. Six adults in graduate school at Kent State University are rehabilitation counselors and are going to rehabilitate the world—the result is that two women become pregnant. *Cast:* 2 BM, 1 BF, 2 WM, 1 WF. *Perm:* Author.

COMPTON, JIMMIE DAVIS, JR.

Why Chickens, Turkeys, and Ostriches Don't Fly. Children's Mythic Play. Illustrates how one's greed will lead to one's own destruction. Subtitled: *Why Chickens, Turkeys, and Ostriches Don't Be Around Other Birds.* *Cast:* 8 BM, 19 extras. *Perm:* Author.

CONNOR, MICHAEL DONNEL

Make Mad the Guilty. Satirical Drama. The play depicts and examines two men's view of hypocrisy and hatred in America. Third place in Randolph Edmond's Playwright's Contest. *Cast:* 2 M (B or W). *Length:* 1 Act. *Prod:* Shaw University, Charlotte, N.C., Mar. 1973.

CONWAY, MEL

Best One of 'em All. Domestic Ritual. Deals with a preacher, his daughters, his son from a previous marriage, and how the preacher is pushed by his family to a higher level of consciousness. *Cast:* 14 BM, 12 BF. *Length:* 3 Acts. *Prod:* Parkway Community House, Chicago, Ill., Feb. 1975. *Perm:* Author.

COOK, ERNESTINE

Checkers. *Prod:* Reading, Frank Silvera Writers' Workshop, Harlem Cultural Council, New York, May 1976.

Peanut Butter and Jelly. *Prod:* Reading, Frank Silvera Writers' Workshop, Harlem Performance Center, New York, Jan. 1977.

COOK, WILL MARION

Casino Girl. (1900). Musical.

COOK, WILL MARION, and PAUL L. DUNBAR

Clorindy or *The Origin of the Cakewalk.* Musical. "A story of how the cakewalk came about in Louisiana in the early eighteen eighties."—Will Marion Cook. *Prod:* Casino Roof Garden, New York, Oct. 1898.

Jes Lak White Folks. Musical. *Prod:* Cherry Blossom Theatre Roof Garden, New York, June 1900.

The Lucky Coon. (c. 1898). Musical Revue.

COOK, WILL MARION, and JESSE A. SHIPP

The Policy Players. Musical Revue. Subtitled: *4-11-44.* *Prod:* 1900.

COOPER, ANNA JULIA

Christmas Bells. Children's Play in Verse. *Length:* 1 Act.

COOPER, JOAN

How Now? *Prod:* Black Repertory Group, Berkeley, Calif., 1973.

COOPER, RALPH

Chocolate Blondes. Musical.

COOPER, T. G.

Chickenbone Special. (1972). Mythic Drama. Malcolm X returns to convince the black man of the need to love one another. *Cast:* 6 BM, 1 BF. *Length:* 1 Act. *Perm:* Author.

Chocolate Boy. (1968). Morality Drama. The principles of a righteous white family are challenged when the son brings home a black friend for Christmas. *Cast:* 7 BM, 3 BF, 6 WM, 1 WB, 6 WF, 1 WG. *Length:* 3 Acts. *Perm:* Author.

Goodnight Mary Beck. (1974). Morality Melodrama. A young black woman finds it is more convenient to have a male roommate to the distaste of her boyfriend. *Cast:* 3 BM, 4 BF. *Length:* 3 Acts. *Perm:* Author.

Have You Seen Mommy Lately. (1970). Morality Drama. A black man's attempt at finding reality in insanity. *Cast:* 1 BM. *Length:* 1 Act. *Perm:* Author.

Portrait of a Woman. (1972). Morality Drama. A middle-class black woman's attempt to free herself from the social restrictions placed on her by family ties. *Cast:* 3 BM, 3 BF. *Length:* 3 Acts. *Perm:* Author.

Queen's Chillun. (1970). Domestic Comedy. The potential husband of a black woman with three children by three different men must accept the already formed family. *Cast:* 3 BM, 1 BB, 2 BF, 1 BG. *Length:* 1 Act. *Perm:* Author.

A Town Called Tobyville. (1971). Protest Drama. A brother investigates the unusual death of his sister that occurs while she is on a freedom ride in the South. *Cast:* 7 BM, 1 BB, 3 BF, 4 WM. *Length:* 3 Acts. *Perm:* Author.

CORT, HARRY, and ALEX ROGERS

Charlie. (1923).

COTTER, JOSEPH SEAMON, JR.

On the Fields of France. Drama. White and black officers, both mortally wounded in World War I, face death together. *Cast:* 1 BM, 1 WM. *Length:* 1 Act. *Pubn:* *Crisis* magazine, June 1920. *Lib Source:* SCHOM.

Paradox. *Pubn:* *Saturday Evening Quill*, Boston, Mass., June 1913.

COTTER, JOSEPH S., SR.

Caesar Driftwood. Mythic Drama. Several baffling characters wait and talk of a Caesar Driftwood's arrival, who never arrives because he is dead. *Cast:* 6 M, 4 F. *Length:* 1 Act. *Pubn:* *Negroes and Others at Work and Play*, ed. by Joseph S. Cotter, Sr., New York: Paebar, 1947. *Lib Source:* SCHOM.; Typescript, Louisville Free Public Library, Ky.

Caleb, the Degenerate: A Study in Types, Customs, and Needs of the American Negro. (1901). Morality Drama in Verse. Caleb, a drinking, dishonest, villain competes with an honest, upright bishop and the bishop's daughter to lead Negroes in the "right" direction. *Cast:* 9 BM, 4 BF, extras, children. *Length:* 4 Acts. *Pubn:* *Black Theater USA*, ed. by James V. Hatch and Ted Shine, New York: Free Pr., 1974. *Lib Source:* HBA.

The Chastisement. Father wants to punish his son for bad habits he has picked up—from him. *Cast:* 3 M, 3 F. *Length:* 1 Act. *Pubn:* *Negroes and Others at Work and Play*, ed. by Joseph S. Cotter, Sr., New York: Paebar, 1947. *Lib Source:* SCHOM.; Typescript, Louisville Free Public Library, Ky.

COTTON, WALTER

Candyman's Dance. *Prod:* Masque Theatre, New York, Oct. 1974.

Monday Morning of Homing Brown.

COUSINS, LINDA

Free Groceries Thursday Morning. Domestic Drama. Lillie, thirty-five years old, tries to hold the family together with pride and without welfare. *Cast:* 1 BM, 3 BF. *Length:* 1 Act.

Night before the Buryin'. Poetic Drama. Miz Jen recalls her life with her now deceased husband Frank by means of monologue and flashbacks. *Cast:* 1 BM, 3 BF. *Length:* 1 Act.

Sheer Guts. A "poemsical." A series of poems on black life. *Cast:* 2 BM, 3 BF. *Length:* Full Length.

COX, JOSEPH MASON ANDREW

Ode to Dr. Martin Luther King. *Length:* 3 Acts.

COX, TONY

Man's Best Friend. Situation Comedy. About a widow and son and the son's introduction to women while a shy boy and after. *Cast:* 3 BM, 2 BF. *Length:* 1 Act. *Perm:* Author.

Man's Best Friend. Situation Comedy. Depicts young boy's sexual conflict as he approaches manhood and his struggle and that of his father, a widower, as they rebuild a family with a new woman. *Cast:* 7 BM, 7 BF. *Length:* 3 Acts. *Lib Source:* Typescript, HBA. *Perm:* Author.

Take a Look. (1971). Ritual. Mentally incarcerated Blacks are unaware of what it takes to free themselves from their mental imprisonment. *Cast:* 4 BM, 3 BF. *Length:* 1 Act. *Lib Source:* Typescript, HBA. *Perm:* Author.

CRAWFORD, ROBERT

The Brass Medallion. Drama. "Set in a reformatory, it dealt with the black male's illusions of manhood."—*Black World*, vol. 25, no. 6, Apr. 1976. *Prod:* Howard University, Washington, D.C., 1975.

CRAWLEY, HAZEL L.

The Square Root of Two. *Prod:* Reading, Frank Silvera Writers' Workshop, Martinique Theatre, New York, Jan. 1976.

The Sunset Gun. *Prod:* Reading, Frank Silvera Writers' Workshop, Harlem Cultural Council, New York, June 1976.

Ten Past. *Cast:* 1 BF, 1 WM, 2 WF. *Length:* 1 Act. *Prod:* Reading, Frank Silvera Writers' Workshop, Martinique Theatre, New York, May 1975.

CREAMER, HENRY, and WILLIAM DUNCAN

Three Showers. Musical. *Prod:* 1920. *Pubn: Best Plays of 1920-21*, ed. by Burns Mantle, New York: Dodd, 1921. *Lib Source:* PAL.

CREAMER, HENRY, and TURNER J. LAYTON

Strut Miss Lizzie. Musical Comedy. Prod: Times Square Theatre, New York, June 1922.

CREAMER, HENRY, and ALEX ROGERS

The Old Man's Boy. Musical Farce. *Prod:* n.p., 1914.

The Traitor. (1912). Musical.

CULLEN, COUNTEE

Byword for Evil. Tragedy. An adaptation of *Medea* by Euripides. *Cast:* 8 M, 2 F, 2 children, extras. *Length:* 2 Acts. *Prod:* Fisk University, Nashville, Tenn., 1945. *Lib Source:* Manuscript, YL.

One Way to Heaven. Comedy. Mattie and Sam decide to get married, but many problems, such as Christian salvation, Freudian analysis, etc., intervene. *Cast:* 13 BM, 9 BF, 1 BB. *Length:* 4 Acts. *Prod:* Hedgerow Theatre, Moylan-Rose Valley, Pa., Sept. 1936. *Lib Source.* Typescript, YL.

CULLEN, COUNTEE, and ARNA BONTEMPS

St. Louis Woman. (1944). Musical Comedy. Based on the novel, *God Sends Sunday*, by Arna Bontemps. Lyrics and music later added by Johnny Mercer and Harold Arlen. Little Augie, the world's greatest jockey, wins the big race, and St. Louis' most beautiful woman, Della Green. *Cast:* 22 DM, 7 BF, extras. *Length:* 3 Acts. *Prod:* Gilpin Players, Karamu Theatre, Cleveland, Ohio, Nov. 1933; Martin Beck Theater, New York, Mar 1946 *Pubn: Black Theater*, ed. by Lindsay Patterson, New York: Dodd, 1971. *Lib Source:* HBA.

CULLEN, COUNTEE, and OWEN DODSON

Medea in Africa. Tragedy. Adaptation of the Greek story of Medea to Africa. Subtitled: *The Medea. Cast:* 5 M, 4 F, 2 children, chorus. *Prod:* Howard University, Washington, D.C., Sept. 1959. *Pubn:* New York: Harper, 1935. *Lib Source:* Typescript, HBA.

The Third Fourth of July. Poetic Dance Drama. A black family moves into a white neighborhood on July 4, but battles two years before they are accepted. *Length:* 1 Act. *Prod:* 1945. *Pubn: Theatre Arts*, Aug. 1946.

CUMMINS, CECIL

Young Blood, Young Breed. (1969). Drama. Shows how pushers ply their destructive trade in our communities. *Cast:* 4 BM, 4 BF, 1 BB. *Length:* 1 Act. *Prod:* Brownsville Laboratory Theatre, Junior High School 263, New York, Dec. 1969.

CUNEY-HARE, MAUD

Antar of Araby. (1929). Romantic Drama. Abyssinian Antar wins freedom, the war, and the daughter of the Arab chieftain. *Cast:* 13 BM, 6 BF, extras. *Length:* 1 Act. *Pubn: Plays and Pageants from the Life of the Negro*, ed. by Willis Richardson, Washington, D.C.: Associated Publishers, 1930. *Lib Source:* HBA.

CUNNINGHAM, SCOTT

Beautiful Dreamer. Historical Drama. Tracing the history of the civil rights movement, from Mrs. Rosa Parks to the assassination of Dr. Martin Luther King. *Cast:* 6 BM, 3 BF, 9 WM, 3 WF. *Length:* 34 Scenes. *Prod:* Resurrection City, Washington, D.C., May 1968. *Perm:* Author.

CURRELLEY, LORRAINE

And the Gang Played On. Drama. Concerns itself with a youth street gang and the conflicts of individual members in choosing between good and bad. *Cast:* 7 BM, 3 BF. *Length:* 4 Acts. *Perm:* Author.

Breasts Oppressed. (1974). Drama. Deals with conflicting beliefs between a divorced couple. The woman has a homosexual relationship with a woman she has known and loved since high school. *Cast:* 6 BM, 5 BF. *Length:* 7 Acts. *Perm:* Author.

The Unsuccessful Raping of James's Mother. (1974). Domestic Drama. Concerns itself with conflicts arising between a mother and her son when she remarries. *Cast:* 2 BM, 2 BF. *Length:* 6 Acts. *Perm:* Author.

CURRIE, RANDY, and EDWARD WISE

Zelda and Lucas Plotz. *Length:* 1 Act. *Prod:* Regal Roots for the Performing Arts, St. Joseph Hospital Auditorium, Paterson, N.J., July 1975.

CURTIS, PATRICIA TAYLOR. *See* Taylor, Patricia

D.C. BLACK REPERTORY DANCE CO.

Dance Theatre Concert. Musical. A collage of black music and dance. *Prod:* D.C. Black Repertory Dance Co., Washington, D.C., Apr. 1973.

DAFORA, ASADATA

Kykunkor. Dance/Opera. Based on nature rites of courtship and marriage, including a variety of associated ceremonies. Subtitled: *Witch Woman.* *Cast:* 4 BM, 5 BF, musicians. *Prod:* Little Theatre, New York, May 1934. *Pubn: Best Plays of 1933-34,* ed. by Burns Mantle, New York: Dodd, 1934.

DALLAS, WALTER

Manchild. *Prod:* Black Ensemble Theatre, Afro-American Studies, University of California, Berkeley, 1973.

Willie Lobo. *Prod:* Black Ensemble Theatre, Afro-American Studies, University of California, Berkeley, 1973.

DALZON, WILFRID, and CALVIN KENLY

The Second Visitation. (1972). Historical Mythic. A black community seizes power over its own destiny through violence, and this action is then judged by ten great black leaders of the past. *Cast:* 15 BM, 8 BF (doubling). *Length:* 3 Acts.

DAMU. *See* Stokes, Herbert

DANIEL, GLORIA

The Male Bag.

DANIEL, HELEN

The Hidden Knowledge. (1975). Drama. The question of what to do with the shameful, sinful soul of a man, and at the same time keep a promise to the devil. *Cast:* 7 M. *Length:* 1 Act. *Perm:* Author.

DANIELS, RON

Swing Low Sweet Steamboat. Drama. "Set in a New Orleans waterside environment, the drama centered around the wine-drinking denizens of that community."—*Black World*, vol. 25, no. 6, Apr. 1976. *Prod:* D.C. Black Repertory Company, Washington, D.C., 1975.

DARRELLE, DHARVI

Goodbye to Yesterday. (1972). Domestic Musical Drama. Love story concerning a black couple's conflict between their domestic life and the woman's striving for success in her career as a dancer. The underlying conflict between them is that the man wants contact with only the black world, while the woman's cultural background is interracial. *Cast:* 1 BM, 5 BF, 1 WM, 1 WF. *Length:* 3 Acts. *Perm:* Author.

New Couple. Domestic Dance Drama. Black woman falls in love with black homosexual who is having an affair with white European man and all three struggle to accept a new life-style. Subtitled: *Lovers.* *Cast:* 1 BM, 2 BF, 1 WM, dancers. *Length:* 2 Acts. *Prod:* Reading, Frank Silvera Writers' Workshop, Martinique Theatre, New York, June 1975.

DAVIDSON, N. R.

The Contraband. (1973). Epic Drama. A group of slaves are held in bondage in Texas long after the Emancipation and the end of the Civil War by a cruel slave master. *Cast:* 5 BM, 6 BF, 2 WM, 1 WF. *Perm:* Author.

El Hajj Malik. (1968). Historical Ritual. Key events in the life of Malcolm X. *Cast:* 6 BM, 4 BF, 2 dancers. *Length:* 1 Act. *Prod:* Dillard University, New Orleans, La., Fall 1968; Afro-American Studio, New York, Oct. 1970. *Pubn: New Plays from the Black Theatre*, ed. by Ed. Bullins, New York: Bantam, 1969. *Lib Source:* HBA. *Perm:* Author.

Falling Scarlet. (1972). Musical Comedy. Happy times down South during slavery days. *Cast:* 8 BM, 6 BF, chorus. *Length:* 2 Acts. *Perm:* Author.

DAVIDSON, N. R. (*Cont.*)

The Further Emasculation Of. (1970). Comedy. A mental patient finds his road to recovery blocked by the social and family forces that originally drove him insane. *Cast:* 2 BM, 2 BF, 1 WF. *Length:* 1 Act. *Perm:* Author.

Jammer. (1970). Expressionistic Comedy. The sexual myths surrounding a black stud-hustler and his sportive combat with a white woman are the subject of entertainment and admiration for a neighborhood youth. *Cast:* 1 WF, 4 BM (3 teenagers). *Length:* 1 Act. *Perm:* Author.

Jimy Cry. Musical Comedy. Happy times down South during the Great Depression. Subtitled: ***The Reason Why.*** *Cast:* 8 BM, 6 BF, 2 WM. *Length:* 2 Acts. *Prod:* Dashiki Theatre, New Orleans, La., Apr. 1975. *Perm:* Author.

Nicey. (1975). Verse Drama. A black woman questions her life and her relationship with her present lover. Subtitled: ***Arias for Carol.*** *Cast:* 1 BM, 1 BF. *Length:* 1 Act. *Perm:* Author.

Short Fun. (1970). Comedy. Some neighborhood winos discuss their sexual and drinking habits while sharing a bottle in an alley. *Cast:* 3 BM. *Length:* 1 Act. *Lib Source:* Typescript, HBA. *Perm:* Author.

Window. (1971). Psychological Drama. Two young black college professors attempt to aid a Vietnam veteran (a former student) who is suffering from a nervous breakdown, but find their own homosexuality and the failure of the American educational system muddles their efforts. *Cast:* 4 BM, 1 BF. *Length:* 3 Acts. *Perm:* Author.

DAVIS, A. I.

Better Make Do. Domestic Drama. Confrontation with and realization of the effects of the "hand-me-down" attitudes of unaware adults. *Cast:* 1 BM, 2 BF. *Length:* 1 Act. *Perm:* Author.

Black Sunlight. Drama. African political play. Crisis between a head of state (in a fictitious African country) and a government official. Together, they led the revolution for independence; now, individual concepts of their country's political directions have torn them apart. Assassination, or compromise? *Cast:* 4 BM, 1 BF. *Length:* 2 Acts. *Prod:* NEC, New York, Apr. 1974. *Perm:* Author.

Cirema the Beautiful. Morality Drama. The desires of black folk. A meeting of five stereotyped characters with diverse needs, unknowingly acquired from the same source. *Cast:* 4 BM, 1 BF. *Length:* 3 Acts. *Perm:* Author.

The Cock Crows. Domestic Drama. Confrontation and crisis over the deteriorative effects of welfare and the necessity of a cohesive black family unit. *Cast:* 1 BM, 1 BF. *Length:* 1 Act. *Prod:* Afro-American Total Theatre, Riverside Church Theatre, New York, Feb. 1972. *Perm:* Author.

The Crab Barrel. Screenplay Treatment. The chase-love-death of a disillusioned black revolutionary—his love story—the morality of black and white policemen—the mother-and-son relationship—the inner decay of the black community—with the overall concept of society being a "horde of giant crabs in a barrel." *Cast:* 5 BM, 3 BF, 3 WM. *Perm:* Author.

Episode. Domestic Drama. About the effects of drugs, with the theory that, under their influence, we destroy each other, particularly those who are most sacred to us and for nothing. *Cast:* 2 BM, 1 BF. *Length:* 1 Act. *Perm:* Author

Homeward Bound. Morality Drama. The revelation of the unconscious mind, manifested after death, concerning the moral character of war. *Cast:* 4 BM, 1 WM. *Length:* 1 Act. *Perm:* Author.

Man I Really Am. (1969).

A Man Talking. *Length:* 1 Act. *Prod:* Afro-American Total Theatre, Riverside Church Theatre, New York, 1972.

Short Change. Domestic Drama. Two reactions (and the results thereof) to the cold and loveless relationships between a father and his two sons. *Cast:* 2 BM, 2 BF. *Length:* 1 Act. *Perm:* Author.

Study War No More. Domestic Drama. The alienation of a black father and daughter, the destruction it has caused, and their awkward coming together. *Cast:* 3 BM, 4 BF. *Length:* 3 Acts. *Perm:* Author.

DAVIS, FAI WALKER. *See* Walker, Fai

DAVIS, GERI TURNER

A Cat Called Jesus. *Length:* 1 Act.

DAVIS, LAWRENCE E.

Three Blind Mice. Satire. A black middle class family crouches in the cellar during a racial shoot-out in the suburbs, only to be shot by their white friends and neighbors. *Cast:* 1 BM, 1 BF, 1 BG, voices. *Length:* 1 Act. *Pubn: Connection,* ed. by Curtiss Porter, Pittsburgh, Pa.: Oduduwa Production, 1970. *Lib Source:* HBA.

DAVIS, LLOYD

The Code of Military Justice. Drama. A play about racism in the U.S. Navy. *Cast:* 6 characters. *Length:* 1 Act. *Pubn:* New York: Amuru Pr., 1976, possibly never published.

DAVIS, MILBURN

Black Rage in Suburbia. (1974). Drama. About a young black domestic worker, her white employer in Great Neck, Long Island, and the Blacks in Harlem who intend to rip off the wealthy whites. *Cast:* 3 BM, 3 BF, 1 WM, 1 WF. *Length:* 3 Acts. *Perm:* Author.

Galivanting Husband. Drama. A play about contemporary domestic problems of a young black couple in Harlem. Husband searches for and finds pleasure in another woman's arms, abandoning his wife and infant son. *Cast:* 4 BM, 2 BF. *Length:* 2 Acts. *Prod:* NEC, New York, 1973. *Perm:* Author.

Love Song. Skit for Street Theatre. Singer is interrupted by heckler (actor) who demands the vocalist sing the truth (hate) instead of love, but the singer continues to sing love. *Cast:* 2 BM, 2 BF. *Perm:* Author.

DAVIS, MILBURN *(Cont.)*

More Power to the Grape. (1974). Domestic Comedy. An East Villager (in New York), Kwame Okidi, is a proud and devoted father who has newly discovered his African heritage. There is humorous interaction between Kwame and his wife, who prefers to hold onto her "slave" name, and their best friends—a wife, and a husband, who are opposed to having children.   *Cast:* 2 BM, 2 BF. *Length:* 1 Act. *Perm:* Author.

Nightmare. (1970). Tragi-Fantasy. The courier of truth appears to a black man in his dreams and turns the brother onto Blackness and how he must relate it to his life.   *Cast:* 3 BM, 3 BF, extras. *Length:* 1 Act. *Lib Source:* Typescript, SCHOM. *Perm:* Agency, NASABA.

The $100,000 Nigger or You Can Take the Nigger Out of the Country but . . . Comedy. Situation deals with hustler who hires a phoney medium to help him rip off his cousin, who has inherited $100,000.   *Cast:* 4 BM, 2 BF. *Length:* 1 Act. *Prod:* Reading, NLT, New York, 1970; NEC, New York, 1973. *Perm:* Author.

Precious. (1975). Drama. A black family that endures trials and tribulations as the father, who is raising two teenaged daughters by himself, grapples with denizens of the black street experience.   *Cast:* 3 BM, 5 BF. *Length:* 3 Acts. *Perm:* Author.

Sometimes a Switchblade Helps. (1969). Drama. A play advocating black consciousness with action occurring in the cafeteria of a major corporation in mid-Manhattan. Black man asserts his Blackness when he sees a white manager flirting with a black sister.   *Cast:* 1 BM, 2 BF, 1 WM. *Length:* 1 Act. *Prod:* NLT Workshop, New York, 1970. *Perm:* Author.

Sporting Times. (1973). Comedy. A prostitute induces a young dude from Harlem to become her pimp, after which he goes about composing scatological ghetto rhymes in a search for johns.   *Cast:* 6 BM, 2 BF, 1 WF. *Length:* 1 Act. *Prod:* Reading, NEC Workshop, New York, 1973. *Perm:* Author.

DAVIS, OSSIE

Alexis Is Fallen. (1947).

Alice in Wonder. Historical. This work is highly critical of the federal government for withholding passports from unpopular group members.   *Prod:* Elks Community Theatre, New York, Sept. 1952.

The Big Deal. Possibly a rewrite of *Alice in Wonder*, by the same playwright. *Prod:* New Playwrights Theatre, New York, 1953.

Clay's Rebellion. (1951).

Curtain Call, Mr. Aldridge Sir. Historical. Moments in the life of the black tragedian, Ira Aldridge.   *Cast:* 3 BM, 1 BF, 1 WM, extras. *Length:* 1 Act. *Prod:* University of California, Santa Barbara, Summer 1968. *Pubn: The Black Teacher and the Dramatic Arts*, ed. by William Reardon and Thomas Pawley, Westport: Negro Universities Pr., 1970. *Lib Source:* HBA.

A Last Dance for Sybil. (c. 1950).

The Mayor of Harlem. (1949).

Montgomery Footprints. (1956).   *Length:* 1 Act.

Point Blank. (1949).

Purlie. Musical. Music by Gary Geld, lyrics by Peter Udell, book by Ossie Davis-Rose Udell. Based on the play *Purlie Victorious,* by the same playwright. *Cast:* 2 BM, 4 BF, 2 WM, chorus. *Length:* 2 Acts. *Prod:* Broadway Theatre, New York, Mar. 1970.

Purlie Victorious. (1961). Comedy. Black preacher tries to reacquire the local black church from white plantation head to use as a battleground for freedom fighting. *Purlie,* by the same playwright, was based on this play.   *Cast:* 2 BM, 3 BF, 4 WM, extras. *Length:* 3 Acts. *Prod:* Cort Theatre, New York, Sept. 1961. *Pubn: Black Drama in America: An Anthology,* ed. by Darwin T. Turner, Greenwich: Fawcett, 1971. *Lib Source:* HBA. *Perm:* Agency, SF.

They Seek a City. (1947).

What Can You Say to Mississippi? (1955).   *Length:* 1 Act.

DAVIS, WILLIAM ANGELO

Dalton's Dream. Drama. In poetic prose, the author has written a contemporary allegory of the presidency of the United States and the dream of universal brotherhood.   *Cast:* 4 M, 1 F, chorus. *Length:* 3 Acts. *Pubn:* New York: Vantage, 1975. *Lib Source:* HBA.

DEAN, PHILLIP HAYES

The Dream Time. (1975). A passage through history showing white characters who believe and claim they know more about black people than Blacks know about themselves. Subtitled: *The Rip-Off.*   *Cast:* 1 BM, 1 BF, 1 WM, 1 WF. *Length:* 2 Acts. *Perm:* Author.

Every Night When the Sun Goes Down. Drama. Former racket boss returns home from prison to his old haunts and friends, but he has some new ideas.   *Cast:* 3 BM, 3 BF. *Length:* 2 Acts. *Prod:* APT, New York, 1969 and Feb. 1976.

Freeman. (1973). Domestic Drama. Ambitious black man feels handicapped by his wife, parents, and best friend.   *Cast:* 3 BM, 2 BF. *Length:* 2 Acts. *Prod:* APT, New York, Jan. 1973. *Pubn:* DPS. *Lib Source:* HBA. *Perm:* Agency, DPS.

Johnny Ghost. (1969). Television Script.

The Last American Dixieland Band. The exploitation of a black entertainer as seen through the point of view of the family.   *Cast:* 4 BM, 1 BF, 1 WM, 1 WF. *Length:* 2 Acts. *Prod:* Reading, APT, New York, June 1975. *Perm:* Author.

The Minstrel Boy. (1972). Historical. A study of an aging black vaudevillian whose haunting memories are the best—and the worst—of what life has brought him. Part of Dean's trilogy entitled *American Night Cry.*   *Cast:* 1 BM, 1 BF. *Length:* 1 Act. *Pubn:* DPS. *Lib Source:* HBA. *Perm:* Agency, DPS.

The Owl Killer. (1971). Domestic Drama. Black man not able to cope with the pressures of white society takes out his bitterness on family, thus turning son against him.   *Cast:* 1 BM, 2 BF. *Length:* 1 Act. *Prod:* Afro-American Total Theatre, New York, Dec. 1973. *Pubn: Black Drama Anthology,* ed. by Woodie

DEAN, PHILLIP HAYES (*Cont.*)

King, Jr. and Ron Milner, New York: New Amer. Lib., 1972. *Lib Source:* HBA. *Perm:* Agency, SF.

The Sty of the Blind Pig. (1972). Domestic Drama. A look at four characters displaced by time and how this displacement affects their lives. *Cast:* 2 BM, 2 BF. *Length:* 3 Acts. *Prod:* NEC, New York, Nov. 1971. *Pubn:* Indianapolis: Bobbs-Merrill, 1973. *Lib Source:* HBA. *Perm:* Agency, SF.

This Bird of Dawning Singeth All Night Long. (1971). Drama. Black woman seeking equality with white woman loses her life. Part of Dean's trilogy *American Night Cry.* *Cast:* 1 BF, 1 WM. *Length:* 1 Act. *Prod:* Chelsea Theatre, New York, 1967–1968. *Pubn:* DPS. *Lib Source:* HBA. *Perm:* Agency, DPS.

Thunder in the Index. (1972). An examination of racial antipathy in its confrontation between a Jewish psychiatrist and his young black patient. Part of Dean's trilogy *American Night Cry.* *Cast:* 1 BM, 1 WM, 1 WF, extras. *Length:* 1 Act. *Prod:* Chelsea Theatre Center, New York, 1968–1969. *Pubn:* DPS. *Lib Source:* HBA. *Perm:* Agency, DPS.

DeANDA, PETER

Ladies in Waiting. (1966). Domestic Drama. A liberal-minded white girl gets an inside view of prison conditions while incarcerated with a black lesbian, a prostitute, and a psychotic. *Cast:* 3 BF, 3 WF. *Length:* 2 Acts. *Prod:* n.p., Summer 1968. *Pubn: Black Drama Anthology,* ed. by Woodie King, Jr. and Ron Milner, New York: New Amer. Lib., 1972. *Lib Source:* HBA.

Sweetbread. Drama. Ernest, a young man, finds self pride in the Muslim religion in spite of his brother's opposition; he is finally shot by a white policeman for refusing an order to leave the park. *Cast:* 9 BM, 1 BF. *Length:* 3 Acts.

DECOY, ROBERT H.

The Castration. (1970).

DEDEAUX, RICHARD

And Baby Makes Three. Comedy/Drama. *Prod:* Mafundi Institute, Los Angeles, Calif., 1973.

The Decision.

A Duel with Destiny. Television Play.

The Rip Off. Screenplay.

DEDEAUX, RICHARD, KILLU ANTHONY HAMILTON, and OTIS SMITH

The Rising Sons—Wisdom and Knowledge. *Pubn:* Los Angeles: The Watts Prophets, 1973.

DEE, RUBY

Twin Bit Gardens. Comedy/Drama. The Lord gives mankind thirty days to get things in order. *Prod:* Reading, Frank Silvera Writers' Workshop, Martinique Theatre, New York, Mar. 1976.

DELLIMORE, CRAIG, and KIM DEJAH LYNCH

Black Odyssey: 200 Years in America. Historical Play with Music and Dance. *Length:* 2 Acts. *Prod.* The New World Theatre, Columbia University, New York, Apr. 1976.

DENDY, J. BROOKS, III

Environmental Dramas. A series of sketches exploring one's character response to object, person, etc. *Prod:* CreataDrama Centers in Philadelphia and Pittsburgh, Pa., 1970s. *Lib Source:* HBA. *Perm:* Author.

Julius Caesar's Doomsday. An adaptation of the death of Julius Caesar that focuses on the reaction of the crowd to Caesar's assassination and/or Caesar himself. *Cast:* 6 M, 16 F. *Length:* 1 Act. *Perm:* Author.

DENT, TOM

Feathered Stuff. *Prod:* FST Workshop, New Orleans, La., early 1970.

Inner Blk Blues. Poem/Play. The black dreams that are so often deferred. *Cast:* 4 BM, 3 BF. *Length:* 1 Act. *Pubn:* Nkombo, no. 8, Aug. 1972. *Lib Source:* HBA.

Negro Study Number 34A. Drama. Black couple dupe white businessman into financing bogus project. *Cast:* 1 BM, 2 BF, 1 WM. *Length:* 1 Act *Prod:* FST, BLKARTSOUTH, New Orleans, La., Winter 1969. *Lib Source:* Typescript, HBA.

Riot Duty. Drama. Black plainclothesman is mistaken for rioter and subjected to mistreatment by white policemen. *Cast:* 3 BM, 2 WM. *Length:* 1 Act. *Prod:* FST, BLKARTSOUTH, New Orleans, La., Winter 1969. *Lib Source:* Typescript, HBA.

Ritual Murder. *Length:* 1 Act. *Prod:* FST, New Orleans, La., Fall 1967.

Snapshots. *Length:* 1 Act. *Prod:* FST, BLKARTSOUTH, New Orleans, La., Fall 1969.

DENT, TOM, and KALAMU YA SALAAM

Song of Survival. *Length:* 1 Act. *Prod:* FST, BLKARTSOUTH, New Orleans, La., Dec. 1969.

DE JONGH, JAMES, and CARLES CLEVELAND

Hail, Hail, the Gang's. (1976). Musical Drama. The tragic and sometimes comic struggle of street gangs to maintain their images and their survival. *Cast:* 12 BM, 1 BF. *Length:* Full Length. *Prod:* New York Theatre Ensemble, May 1976. *Perm:* Author.

DE RAMUS, BETTY

That's Just What I Said. (1971).

DEVEAUX, ALEXIS

Circles. Domestic Drama. The dreams of a young dancer are met with ridicule by her fiercely protective grandmother. *Cast:* 1 BM, 2 BF. *Length:* Full Length. *Prod:* Frederick Douglass Creative Arts Center, New York; PBS-TV, Dec. 1976.

DEVEAUX, ALEXIS (*Cont.*)

Tapestry. Drama. Concerns an ambitious twenty-three-year-old black woman who is cramming for the bar exam and is haunted by visions of her own girlhood of southern piety.   *Cast:* 3 BM, 2 BF, extras. *Length:* Full Length. *Prod:* Frank Silvera Writers' Workshop Unit's "Getting off Uptown," May 1976; PBS-TV, Dec. 1976.

DeWINDT, HAL

Us Versus Nobody.   *Length:* 1 Act. *Prod:* NEC Workshop, New York, Feb. 1971.

DICKERSON, GLENDA

Jesus Christ—Lawd Today. Places the story of Jesus in urban black America in 1976. His followers are the poor Blacks.   *Prod:* Black American Theatre Co., Washington, D.C., 1971.

The Torture of Mothers. (1973). An adaptation of Truman Nelson's book of the same title that tells the story of six black mothers whose sons allegedly played key roles in igniting the Harlem riots in 1964.   *Prod:* Back Alley Theatre, Washington, D.C., 1972.

DICKERSON, GLENDA, OWEN DODSON, and MIKE MALONE

Owen's Song. Poetic Musical Tribute. Conceived and directed by Glenda Dickerson and Mike Malone. A collage of Owen Dodson's poetry and plays with music and dance.   *Cast:* 14 BM, 11 BF (doubling). *Length:* 2 Acts. *Prod:* D.C. Black Repertory Theatre, Washington, D.C., Oct. 1974; John F. Kennedy Center for the Performing Arts, Washington, D.C., Dec. 1974. *Lib Source:* HBA. *Perm:* Authors.

DIXON, MELVIN

Confrontation. Drama. A chance encounter between two men on a deserted subway exposes the barriers of social class and political opinions that separate them and the discovery of their common goal.   *Cast:* 2 BM. *Length:* 1 Act. *Prod:* 1969. *Perm:* Author.

Kingdom, or The Last Promise. Ritual. After death, characters attempt to gain the freedom that has been denied them in life while facing the approaching menace of further damnation and betrayal.   *Cast:* 4 BM, 1 BF, 1 WM, chorus. *Length:* 3 Acts. *Prod:* 1972. *Lib Source:* Typescript, HBA. *Perm:* Author.

Ritual: For Malcolm. (1970).

DODSON, OWEN

Amistad. Historical Drama. Story of Cinque's rebellion aboard the Spanish ship and his subsequent landing in America, eventual freedom, and return to Africa.   *Cast:* 33 BM, 4 BF, 31 WM (doubling). *Length:* 5 Scenes. *Prod:* Talledega College, Ala., 1939. *Lib Source:* Typescript, HBA. *Perm:* Author.

The Ballad of Dorrie Miller. Poetic Drama. Music by E. Hathcock. Dorrie Miller, a black messman at Pearl Harbor, takes over a gun and shoots down four planes. *Cast:* 4 M, singers, speakers, extras. *Length:* 1. Act. *Prod:* Great Lakes Naval Training Station, Ill., Feb. 1943. *Pubn: Theatre Arts*, July 1943. *Lib Source:* PAL. *Perm.* Author.

Bayou Legend. (1948). Allegorical Poetic Legend. Reve Grant bedevils his mother and neighbors, falls in love, runs away to travel the world, and returns home to die. *Cast:* 8 BM, 8 BF, 4 WM, 2 WF (doubling). *Length:* 2 Acts. *Prod:* Howard University, Washington, D.C., 1951; AMAS Repertory Theatre, Inc., New York, 1975. *Pubn: Black Drama in America: An Anthology*, ed. by Darwin T. Turner, Greenwich: Fawcett, 1971. *Lib Source:* PAL. *Perm:* Author.

A Christmas Miracle. (1955). Opera. Music by Mark Fax. A black family with a blind daughter is driven from their home because of father's militancy; they find shelter and are visited by three men who return the daughter's sight. *Cast:* 5 BM, 1 BF, 1 G, chorus of males off-stage. *Length:* 1 Act. *Prod:* Howard University, Washington, D.C., 1955. *Lib Source:* Typescript, HBA. *Perm:* Author.

Climbing to the Soil. Historical Drama. The life of the black American botanist, George Washington Carver (1864-1943) and his discoveries. *Cast:* 8 M, 3 F. *Length:* 1 Act. *Prod:* Great Lakes Naval Training Station, Ill., Jan. 1943. *Lib Source:* Typescript, YL. *Perm:* Author.

Climbing to the Soil. Historical Drama. Adapted for radio. The life of the black American botanist, Dr. George Washington Carver, (1864-1943) and his discoveries. *Cast:* 8 M, 2 F, extras. *Lib Source:* Typescript, HBA. *Perm:* Author.

Divine Comedy. Poetic Drama. Music by Morris Mamorsky. A people in economic duress turn to charismatic leader for salvation. *Cast:* 12 BM, 8 BF, chorus (doubling). *Length:* 2 Acts. *Prod:* Yale University, New Haven, Conn., 1938. *Pubn: Black Theater USA*, ed. by James V. Hatch and Ted Shine, New York. Free Pr., 1974. *Lib Source:* Manuscript, HBA. *Perm:* Author.

Don't Give Up the Ship. Historical Drama. Concerns Commodore Matthew Perry's battle in 1812 with the British. *Cast:* 3 M, extras. *Length:* 1 Act. *Prod:* Great Lakes Naval Training Station, Ill., May 1943. *Lib Source:* Typescript, YL. *Perm:* Author.

Doomsday Tale. (1941). Drama. On Good Friday a part of the little village burns down and Sarah emerges from her religious retreat to give hope to the people toward rebuilding. *Cast:* 7 BM, 8 BF, extras. *Length:* Full Length. *Lib Source:* Typescript, HBA. *Perm:* Author.

The Dream Awake. (1969). Radio Drama and Filmstrip. A series of episodes from black history of Africa to the present day, involving Cinque, Attucks, cowboys, Malcolm X, etc. Adaptable to the stage. *Prod:* Spoken Arts Recordings. *Lib Source:* HBA.

Everybody Join Hands. Dance/Drama. The struggle of the Chinese people to free themselves from Western tyranny. *Cast:* 1 M, 1 F, chorus. *Length:* 1 Act. *Prod:* Great Lakes Naval Station, Ill.; Spelman College, Atlanta, Ga. *Pubn: Theatre Arts*, Sept. 1943. *Lib Source:* PAL; Typescript, HBA. *Perm:* Author.

DODSON, OWEN (*Cont.*)

Freedom, the Banner. Dance/Drama. The struggle of the U.S.S.R. against Nazi tyranny. *Length:* 1 Act. *Prod:* Great Lakes Naval Training Station, Ill., 1942. *Lib Source:* Typescript, HBA. *Perm:* Author.

The Garden of Time. Poetic Drama/Mythic. The Medea/Jason tragedy begins in Colchis and transmogrifies to the American southern dilemma. Subtitled: *The Golden Fleece. Cast:* 6 BM, 6 BF, 1 BB. *Length:* 3 Acts. *Prod:* Yale University, New Haven, Conn., 1939; ANT, New York, Mar. 1945. *Lib Source:* Typescript, HBA & YL. *Perm:* Author.

Gargoyles in Florida. Drama. Based on Langston Hughes' story "Red Headed Baby." Red-headed sailor returns to Betsy, whose virginity he took three years earlier, to find a deaf and dumb red-headed child. *Cast:* 1 BM, 2 BF, 1 WM. *Length:* 1 Act. *Prod:* Yale University, New Haven, Conn., 1936. *Lib Source:* Typescript, HBA. *Perm:* Author.

Including Laughter. (1936). Poetic. Incomplete script of black and white college students in New England who are caught in racial dilemmas by their sensitivity. *Cast:* 3 parts. *Lib Source:* Manuscript, HBA. *Perm:* Author.

Including Laughter. Rewrite and completion of a play of the same name begun at Bates College, Lewiston, Maine. First full-length play written by Owen Dodson. Black and white friendships begun at a New England college are tested in later years of violence. *Cast:* 4 BM, 1 BF, 3 WM, 1 WF, chorus. *Length:* 3 Acts. *Lib Source:* Typescript, YL.

Lord Nelson, Naval Hero. Historical Drama. The British admiral Lord Nelson's naval victory over the Spanish Armada. *Cast:* 5 M. *Prod:* Great Lakes Naval Training Station, Ill., Jan. 1943. *Lib Source:* Typescript, YL.

The Midwest Mobilizes. Radio Documentary. Midwestern Negro community participation in World War II. *Prod:* WBBM, Chicago, Ill., May 1943. *Lib Source:* Typescript, HBA.

Migration. (1945). A second version of the screen treatment of the great migration of Blacks from the rural South to the industrial North. Subtitled: *Journey to Paradise. Lib Source:* Typescript, HBA. *Perm:* Author.

The Morning Duke Ellington Praised the Lord and Seven Little Black Davids Tap-Danced Unto. Ceremonial Entertainment. Music by Roscoe Gill. With blues, jazz, and dance. Billie Holiday, Bessie Smith, Charlie Parker, and Dinah Washington come before Jesus to be judged for their lives on earth. *Cast:* 3 BM, 3 BF, 7 dancers, 12 extras, chorus. *Length:* Full Length. *Prod:* Reading, Frank Silvera Writers' Workshop, Martinique Theatre, New York, Jan. 1976. *Lib Source:* Manuscript, HBA. *Perm:* Author.

New World A-Coming. Pageant. Struggle over hope for freedom of black people all over the world. *Prod:* Madison Square Garden, New York, 1943. *Lib Source:* Typescript, HBA, YL. *Perm:* Author.

New World A-Coming. Historical Radio Drama. Adapted from *They Knew Lincoln.* Dramatizes the story of four Blacks who met President Lincoln. *Cast:* 4 BM, 1 BF, 2 WM. *Prod:* WMCA, Feb. 1945. *Lib Source:* Typescript, HBA. *Perm:* Author.

Old Ironsides. Radio Script. The story of the ship U.S.S. *Constitution.* Part of the series of plays, *Heroes on Parade. Length:* 1 Act. *Prod:* Great Lakes Naval Training Station, Ill., 1942. *Perm:* Author.

Potsy Played Poison. Allegory. Children dramatize the function of the United Nations in maintaining peace. Subtitled: **Miss Susie Dumbarton's Proposals.** *Cast:* 2 M, 2 F. *Length:* 1 Act. *Lib Source:* Typescript, HBA. *Perm:* Author.

Robert Smalls. Historical Radio Drama. Story of black naval captain in the Civil War. *Length:* 1 Act. *Prod:* Great Lakes Naval Training Station, Ill., Dec. 1942. *Lib Source:* Typescript, YL.

St. Louis Woman. (1943). Pilot script for a radio series. *Lib Source:* Manuscript, HBA. *Perm:* Author.

The Shining Town. (1937). Drama. White woman comes to subway to bargain with black woman for day-work during the depression. *Cast:* 2 BM, 7 BF, 2 WM, 7 WF, 1 C (doubling). *Length:* 1 Act. *Lib Source:* Manuscript, HBA. *Perm:* Author.

Someday We're Gonna Tear the Pillars Down. Poetic Dialogue. The slaves plan to revolt against the "big house." *Cast:* 4 BM, 3 BF. *Pubn: The Negro Quarterly,* no. 1, Summer 1942; *Powerful Long Ladder,* New York: Farrar, 1946. *Lib Source:* HBA. *Perm:* Author.

The Southern Star. Opera. Original version of *A Christmas Miracle,* by the same playwright. *Length:* 1 Act. *Lib Source:* Typescript, HBA.

They Seek a City. (1945). First version screenplay of the great migration of Blacks from the rural South to the industrial North. Subtitled: **Migration.**

Till Victory Is Won. Opera. Music by Mark Fax. Poetic documentary of Blacks from African diaspora to the present time. Written for the centennial celebration of Howard University, Washington, D.C. *Cast:* 11 BM, 5 BF, 4 WM, 6 C, chorus. *Length:* Full Length. *Prod:* John F. Kennedy Center for the Performing Arts, Washington, D.C., Mar. 1974. *Lib Source:* Typescript, HBA. *Perm:* Author.

Untitled. (1932). An unfinished story of a black playwright caught in a class/racial/artistic struggle. *Cast:* 3 M, 1 F. *Length:* 1 Act. *Lib Source:* Typescript, HBA. *Perm:* Author.

Where You From? (1945). Screenplay. Documentary on migration in America with special emphasis on the Negro. *Lib Source:* Typescript, HBA. *Perm:* Author.

With This Darkness. (1939). Drama. Original version of *The Garden of Time,* by the same playwright. *Length:* 3 Acts. *Lib Source:* Typescript, HBA. *Perm:* Author.

DODSON, OWEN, and COUNTEE CULLEN

Medea in Africa. Tragedy. An adaptation of the Greek story to Africa. Based on the *Medea* by Countee Cullen. Subtitled: **The Medea.** *Cast:* 5 M, 4 F, 2 C, chorus. *Prod:* Howard University, Washington, D.C., Sept. 1959. *Pubn:* Harper, 1935. *Lib Source:* Typescript, HBA.

DODSON, OWEN, and COUNTEE CULLEN (*Cont.*)

The Third Fourth of July. Poetic Dance Drama. A black family moves into a white neighborhood on July 4, but battles two years before they are accepted.   *Length:* 1 Act. *Prod:* n.p., 1945. *Pubn: Theatre Arts*, Aug. 1946.

DODSON, OWEN, GLENDA DICKERSON, and MIKE MALONE

Owen's Song. Poetic Musical Tribute. Conceived and directed by Glenda Dickerson and Mike Malone. A collage of Owen Dodson's poetry and plays with music and dance.   *Cast:* 14 BM, 11 BF (doubling). *Length:* 2 Acts. *Prod:* D.C. Black Repertory Theatre, Washington, D.C., Oct. 1974; John Kennedy Center for the Performing Arts, Washington, D.C., Dec. 1974. *Lib Source:* HBA. *Perm:* Author.

DODSON, OWEN, and WILLIAM SWALLOW

Jane. (1933). An incomplete script based on a story by Somerset Maugham.   *Cast:* 2 M, 2 F. *Length:* 2 Scenes. *Lib Source:* Typescript, HBA. *Perm:* Author.

DOLAN, HARRY

The Iron Hand of Nat Turner. Drama. A play of yesterday's events repeated today. "It establishes a clear connection between the abortive Nat Turner insurrection and the Watts revolt."—Margaret Wilkerson.   *Length:* 3 Acts. *Prod:* Watts Writers' Workshop, Los Angeles, Calif., 1970.

Losers Weepers. Domestic Drama. In an attempt to secure his manhood, man loses his wife to death and his children to estrangement.   *Cast:* 6 BM, 1 BB, 3 BF, 1 BG, 3 WM, 1 WF. *Length:* 2 Acts. *Prod:* NBC-TV, Feb. 1967, under title *Love Song for a Delinquent. Pubn: From the Ashes: Voices of Watts*, ed. by Budd Schulberg, New York: New Amer. Lib., 1967. *Lib Source:* SCHOM.

DONOGHUE, DENNIS

Legal Murder. Drama. Adaptation of the Scottsboro case.   *Cast:* 10 BM, 2 BF, 2 WF. *Length:* 3 Acts. *Prod:* President Theatre, New York, Feb. 1934. *Pubn: Best Plays of 1933-34*, ed. by Burns Mantle, New York: Dodd, 1934.

DONOGHUE, DENNIS, and JAMES H. DUNMORE

The Black Messiah. Comedy. About the life of Father Divine. Subtitled: *The Demi-God.   Prod:* Cooperative Players, Transport Playhouse, New York, June 1939. *Pubn: Best Plays of 1938-39*, ed. by Burns Mantle, New York: Dodd, 1939.

DORR, DONALD, and MARGARET WALKER

Jubilee. Opera. Music by Ulysses Kay. Libretto by Donald Dorr. Adapted from Margaret Walker's novel *Jubilee*. The story of Vyry, a plantation slave, who survives to make a place for herself as a free woman, mother, and wife. *Length:* Full Length. *Prod:* Opera/South, Jackson State University, Miss., Nov. 1976.

DORSEY, ROBERT

Get Thee behind Me, Satan. *Prod:* Harlem Experimental Theatre, St. Philip's Church, New York, c. 1932.

DOUGLAS, RODNEY K.

The Marijuana Trip.

Voice of the Ghetto. (1968). Drama. After addressing a street crowd concerning the racial and economic injustices imposed upon them, a ghetto politician appears, unannounced, at a suspension hearing to protest the suspending of his goddaughter from school. *Length:* 1 Act. *Prod:* Town House, New York, Jan. 1968. *Pubn:* SF. *Lib Source:* HBA. *Perm:* Agency, SF.

DOWNING, HENRY FRANCIS

The Arabian Lovers, or *The Sacred Jar.* *Pubn:* London: Francis Griffiths, 1913. *Lib Source:* NYPL.

Human Nature or *The Traduced Wife.* Melodrama. Wife forgives her husband after scandal, intrigue, and attempted murder. *Cast:* 8 M, 4 F. *Length.* 4 Acts. *Pubn:* London: Francis Griffiths, 1913. *Lib Source:* NYPL.

Incentives. (c. 1914). Melodrama. A secret that is about to be revealed could cause pain and anguish to the innocent. *Cast:* 6 M, 4 F. *Length:* 4 Acts. *Lib Source:* SCHOM.

Lord Eldred's Other Daughter. *Pubn:* London: Francis Griffiths, 1913. *Lib Source:* NYPL.

Melic Ric.

The Pulcherian War Loan.

The Shuttlecock or *Israel in Russia.* Melodrama. Love and intrigue between Jews and Christians in Czarist Russia. *Cast:* 20 M, 8 F, extras. *Length:* 4 Acts. *Pubn:* London: Francis Griffiths, 1913. *Lib Source:* NYPL.

The Sinews of War.

The Statue and the Wasp.

Voodoo. Melodrama. Disappointed suitor pursues heroine from England to Barbados amid intrigue and voodoo magic. *Cast:* 4 BM, 1 BF, 36 WM, 10 WF, extras. *Length:* 4 Acts. *Pubn:* London: Francis Griffiths, 1914. *Lib Source:* NYPL.

DOWNING, HENRY FRANCIS, and MRS. DOWNING

Placing Paul's Play. *Pubn:* London: Francis Griffiths, 1913. *Lib Source:* NYPL.

Which She Should Have Saved.

DRAYTON, RONALD

Black Chaos. (c. 1960).

The Conquest of Africa. (1968).

DRAYTON, RONALD (*Cont.*)

Nocturne on the Rhine. Domestic Ritual. Priest tries to save the soul of black man convicted of stealing money to build hospital. *Cast:* 2 BM. *Length:* 1 Act. *Pubn: Black Fire*, ed. by LeRoi Jones and Larry Neal, New York: Morrow, 1968. *Lib Source:* HBA. *Perm:* Agency, William Morrow.

Notes from a Savage God. Domestic Ritual. A black boy in dire need of love and companionship feels hopeless in his plight. *Cast:* 4 BM. *Length:* 1 Act. *Prod:* Back Alley Theatre, Washington, D.C., 1975. *Pubn: Black Fire*, ed. by LeRoi Jones and Larry Neal, New York: Morrow, 1968. *Lib Source:* HBA. *Perm:* Agency, William Morrow.

DU BOIS, SHIRLEY GRAHAM

Coal Dust. *Length:* 1 Act. *Prod:* Morgan State College, Baltimore, Md., 1930; Gilpin Players, Karamu Theatre, Cleveland, Ohio, Apr. 1938.

Dust to Earth. Drama. Father, owner of a coal mine, attempts to rescue his own son in a coal mine disaster and dies with him. *Length:* 3 Acts. *Prod:* Possibly at Oberlin College, Ohio, c. 1940; possibly at Yale University, New Haven, Conn., 1941.

Elijah's Ravens. Comedy. A preacher believes the ravens will feed him by means of an inheritance from a sister in Hollywood. *Length:* 3 Acts. *Prod:* Gilpin Players, Cleveland, Ohio, c. 1930; Atlanta University Summer Theatre, Ga., 1941.

I Gotta Home. Comedy. Possibly the alternate title for *Elijah's Ravens*, by the same playwright. *Length:* 3 Acts. *Prod:* Gilpin Players, Karamu Theatre, Cleveland, Ohio, Nov. 1939.

It's Morning. Tragedy. A mother kills her own daughter rather than permit her to be sold away in slavery. *Length:* 3 Acts. *Prod:* Yale University, New Haven, Conn., 1940.

The Swing Mikado. Adaptation to swing music of the Gilbert & Sullivan opera, *The Mikado*. *Prod:* FTP, Chicago, Ill., 1938.

Tom-Tom. Opera. Libretto and music by Shirley Graham Du Bois. Based on African rhythms and situations. Original production starred Jules Bledsoe, Charlotte Murry, and Luther King. *Prod:* Morgan State College, Baltimore, Md.; Cleveland Opera series, Summer 1932.

Track Thirteen. Radio Comedy. About life in a pullman car. *Length:* 3 Acts. *Prod:* Mutual Network Radio, 1942. *Pubn:* Boston: Expression Co., c. 1940.

DU BOIS, SHIRLEY GRAHAM, and CHARLOTTE CHORPENNING*

Little Black Sambo. Children's Musical. Music by Shirley Graham Du Bois. Adaptation of the children's tale about an African boy who must outwit the tigers to get home. *Prod:* FTP, Chicago, Ill., 1938.

DU BOIS, W. E. B.

George Washington and Black Folk. Historical. A pageant for the bicentenary, 1732–1932. Characters include Phillis Wheatley, Benjamin Banneker,

Thomas Jefferson, Paul Cuffee, and Prince Hall. All quotations are in the approximate original words of the speakers. *Length:* 5 Scenes. *Pubn: Crisis* magazine, Apr. 1932. *Lib Source:* SCHOM.

The Star of Ethiopia. Pageant. "Listen to the tale of the eldest and strongest of the races of mankind, whose faces be Black. Hear ye, hear ye of the gifts of Black men in this world."—Leonard Archer, *Crisis* magazine, Nov. 1913. *Cast:* 350. *Length:* Prelude, 6 Episodes, Epilogue. *Prod:* The Emancipation Exposition, New York Armory, Oct. 1913; Washington, D.C., 1914.

DUDLEY, S. H.

The Smart Set. (1896).

DUDLEY, S. H., and HENRY TROY

Dr. Beans from Boston. (1911).

DUKE, BILL

An Adaptation: Dream. Subtitled: *Dreams. Length:* 1 Act. *Prod:* NEC Workshop, New York, Jan. 1971.

Sonata. Prod: Theatre Genesis, St. Marks-on-the-Bowery, New York, June 1975.

DUMAS, AARON

Encounter: Three Acts in a Restaurant. Prod: Black Arts West, Seattle, Wash., 1970.

Poor Willie. Prod: Black Arts West, Seattle, Wash., 1970.

DUMAS, DAISY

Jumeau's Mama. Subtitled: *La Maman de Jumeau. Prod:* Reading, Frank Silvera Writers' Workshop, The Teachers, Inc., New York, Jan. 1977.

Wamba's Mother. Domestic Drama. Problem of an unmarried, professional, black female dealing with conflicting cultural and moral values among the black elite, with the need of the black professional to be better than his white counterpart, and with the often destructive results that occur as Blacks struggle to be accepted. *Cast:* 7 BM, 1 BB, 11 BF. *Length:* 3 Acts. *Perm:* Author.

DUNBAR, PAUL L.

Dream Lovers. Operatic Romance. Music by Samuel Coleridge Taylor. "Two friends woo and win two sisters."—Thomas Pawley. *Cast:* 2 M, 2 F. *Pubn:* London and New York: Bosby, 1898.

Herrick. (c. 1901). Comedy. "An attempt to thwart a romance between the poet and Lady Cynthia ends disastrously for his rivals."—Thomas Pawley. *Cast:* 8 WM, 2 WF. *Length:* 3 Acts. *Lib Source:* Dunbar Collection, Ohio Historical Society, Columbus.

DUNBAR, PAUL L. (*Cont.*)

The Quibbler's Wife. Melodrama. "A neglected wife seeks to escape a tedious marriage by eloping with her lover."—Thomas Pawley. *Cast:* 1 BM, 1 BF, 1 WF. *Lib Source:* Manuscript (fragment), Dunbar Collection, Ohio Historical Society, Columbus.

The Stolen Calf. (1892).

Uncle Eph's Christmas. Vaudeville Sketch. "Uncle Eph, Aunt Chloe and their neighbors celebrate Christmas morning with song, dance and end with the cakewalk."—Thomas Pawley. *Length:* 1 Act. *Prod:* Boston Music Hall, Mass., 1899.

Untitled Play probably *On the Island of Tanawana.* Musical fragment. "A millionaire American soap manufacturer is crowned king of a mythical island only to discover his daughter has eloped with a native prince."—Thomas Pawley. *Cast:* Numerous speaking and supernumerary roles that are not racially identified. *Lib Source:* Dunbar Collection, Ohio Historical Society, Columbus.

Winter Roses. "Two former lovers rediscover one another in old age. Referred to in Brawley's *Paul Lawrence Dunbar, Poet of His People.*"—Thomas Pawley.

DUNBAR, PAUL L., and WILL MARION COOK

Clorindy or *The Origin of the Cakewalk.* Musical. "A story of how the cakewalk came about in Louisiana in the early eighteen eighties."—Will Marion Cook. *Prod:* Casino Roof Garden, New York, Oct. 1898.

Jes Lak White Folks. Musical Revue. *Prod:* Cherry Blossom Theatre Roof Garden, New York, June 1900.

The Lucky Coon. (c. 1898). Musical Revue.

DUNBAR, PAUL L., ALEX ROGERS, and JESSE A. SHIPP

In Dahomey. Musical Comedy. The president of the Dahomey Colonization Society hires two detectives (Bert Williams and George Walker) to find a missing treasure. They all end up in Dahomey, where they are nearly executed. They decide there's no place like home. *Cast:* 15 BM, 3 BF. *Length:* Prologue, 2 Acts. *Prod:* Boston Music Hall, Mass., Sept. 1902.

DUNBAR-NELSON, ALICE

The Author's Evening at Home. *Length:* 1 Act. *Pubn: The Smart Set*, Sept. 1900.

Mine Eyes Have Seen. (1918). Drama. A young black man refuses induction into the army in World War I but ultimately submits to family pressure and goes. *Cast:* 3 BM, 2 BF, 1 WM, 2 WF. *Length:* 1 Act. *Pubn: Black Theater USA*, ed. by James V. Hatch and Ted Shine, New York: Free Pr., 1974. *Lib Source:* HBA.

DUNCAN, THELMA MYRTLE

Black Magic. Folk Comedy. Israel Jenkins thinks that his wife has left him and invokes the art of the voodoo fakir. *Cast:* 3 BM, 2 BF. *Length:* 1 Act. *Pubn: The Yearbook of Short Plays*, 1st series, ed. by Wise and Snook, Evanston, Ill.: Row Peterson, 1931. *Lib Source:* NYPL.

The Death Dance. (1923). African Play. Kumo is to stand trial by drinking the Red Water, but his girl friend has bribed the medicine man. *Cast:* 3 BM, 1 BF, extras. *Length:* 1 Act. *Prod:* Howard University, Washington, D.C., Apr. 1923. *Pubn: Plays of Negro Life*, ed. by Alain Locke and Montgomery Gregory, New York: Harper, 1927. *Lib Source:* NYPL.

Sacrifice. (1930). Domestic Drama. Son steals chemistry exam, which nearly kills his mother. *Cast:* 2 M, 2 F. *Length:* 1 Act. *Pubn: Plays and Pageants from the Life of the Negro*, ed. by Willis Richardson, Washington, D.C.: Associated Publishers, 1930. *Lib Source:* HBA.

DUNCAN, WILLIAM, and HENRY CREAMER

Three Showers. Musical. *Prod:* 1920. *Pubn: Best Plays of 1920-21*, ed. by Burns Mantle, New York: Dodd, 1921. *Lib Source:* PAL.

DUNDEE, KULUA

Rainlight. *Prod:* Reading, Frank Silvera Writers' Workshop, Harlem Performance Center, New York, Jan. 1977.

Running Fast through Paradise. *Prod:* 1975.

DUNDY, CALUA. See Dundee, Kulua

DUNHAM, KATHERINE, and EUGENE B. REDMOND

Ode to Taylor Jones. (1967-1968).

DUNMORE, JAMES H., and DENNIS DONOGHUE

The Black Messiah. Comedy. Concerns the life of Father Divine. Subtitled: *The Demi-God.* *Prod:* Cooperative Players. Transport Playhouse, New York, June 1939. *Pubn: Best Plays of 1938-39*, ed. by Burns Mantle, New York: Dodd, 1939.

DUNN, ALLAN, and ERNEST HOGAN

A Country Coon. (1900). Musical Farce. *Length:* 3 Acts.

DURRAH, JAMES

Available in Winter. Play deals with the memories of an old man. *Prod:* New York, Dec. 1973.

The Ho-Hum Revolution.

How Do You Spell Watergait? Musical Satire. Music by Victor Willis and Donna Brown. Lyrics by James Durrah. The subject is Watergate and politics. *Prod:* Sutton East Theatre, New York, Jan. 1977.

DURRAH, JAMES (*Cont.*)

Miss DoFunny Speaking. A takeoff on two homosexuals as mental hospital intake workers. *Prod:* New York, Dec. 1973.

One of Them Lonely Families Trying to Dance Out of It but Too Many People Are Looking.

The Saturday Militant. Futuristic Play. Forecasts a time when the earth will be ruled by the "Perfect White" and robots. *Prod:* New York, Dec. 1973.

The Wonder Stuff.

EARLY, ANN

Do You Take This Woman. Domestic Drama. Slice-of-life play about a religious mother who is forced to accept her son's common-law wife in the house, while her other son deteriorates with drugs. *Cast:* 3 BM, 2 BF. *Length:* 1 Act. *Prod:* Writers in Residence, Great Neck, N.Y., n.d. *Perm:* Author.

Is George Responsible. Comedy. Courtroom play that tries George Washington for the failure of the American system. *Cast:* 10 M, 7 F. *Prod:* Writers in Residence, Great Neck, N.Y., n.d. *Perm:* Author.

Mishap. Drama. Black slice-of-life play dealing with incest—about an unmarried woman who raised her son to believe he was her brother until he falls in love with a neighbor's daughter, his sister. *Cast:* 3 BM, 2 BF, 1 WM. *Length:* 2 Acts. *Prod:* Writers in Residence, Great Neck, N.Y., n.d. *Perm:* Author.

EARLY, ANN, and RIKER'S ISLAND INMATES

I Am. Blues Musical.

EARLY, JACQUELINE

Sheba. Improvisational Sing Play. *Prod:* Tompkins Square Park, New York, Aug. 1971.

EAST CLEVELAND COMMUNITY THEATRE

Our Way. Musical Revue. "The depiction of the real world and a man's place within it; begins with man and his creator and ends with man's compassion for his fellowman."—*Black World*, vol. 25, no. 6, Apr. 1976. *Prod:* Cleveland Ensemble, Ohio, Feb. 1975.

EASTON, SIDNEY

Miss Trudie Fair. (1953).

EASTON, WILLIAM EDGAR

Christophe. Tragedy. Dessalines, former emperor of Haiti, is assassinated and Christophe is declared emperor. This is the story of how the revolution leads to the despoilment and overthrow of Christophe. *Cast:* 9 BM, 4 BF, extras. *Length:* 4 Acts. *Pubn:* Los Angeles: Grafton, 1911. *Lib Source:* SCHOM.

Dessalines, a Dramatic Tale; a Single Chapter from Haiti's History. Historical Drama. Dessalines, emperor of Haiti, rallies the black men of Haiti against the French and their mulatto allies. *Cast:* 5 BM, 1 BF, extras. *Length:* 4 Acts. *Prod:* Haitian Pavilion, World's Fair, Chicago, Ill., Jan. 1893. *Pubn:* Galveston: J. W. Burson, 1893. *Lib Source:* HBA.

EBONY TALENT

Second Coming Last Chance (SCLC). Expressions and impressions of the life of Dr. Martin Luther King and what might happen if he should have a second coming. *Prod:* Ebony Talent School of Total Theatre, Chicago, Ill., 1974.

ECHOL, ANN J.

Black Hands Play Noisy Music.   *Prod:* Kuesma, Chicago, Ill., 1974.

EDMONDS, HENRIETTE

Mushy Mouth. Children's Play. *Prod:* Howard University, Washington, D.C., 1975.

EDMONDS, RANDOLPH

Bad Man. (1934). Folk Drama. A rough, tough, gambling man becomes defender and hero of black people. *Cast:* 7 BM, 1 BF. *Length:* 1 Act. *Pubn: Black Theater USA,* ed. by James V. Hatch and Ted Shine, New York: Free Pr., 1974. *Lib Source:* HBA.

The Black Highwayman. (1925). Tragedy. Plot suggested by Alfred Noyes' poem "The Highwayman." Sheriff of a small southern town arrests the sweetheart of a young, romantic bootlegger who is supposed to come and see her one night; although she tries to warn him, he walks into the trap set by the sheriff. *Cast:* 1 BM, 1 BF, 3 WM. *Length:* 1 Act. *Perm:* Author.

Bleeding Hearts. Protest Drama. Wife of sharecropper dies of pneumonia; the husband vows to kill "Marse Tom" for starving them. *Cast:* 4 BM, 3 BF, 1 WM. *Length:* 1 Act. *Pubn: Six Plays for a Negro Theater,* Boston: Baker, 1934. *Lib Source:* HBA. *Perm:* Author.

The Breeders. Protest Drama. The slaves on the plantation resist forced breeding. *Cast:* 2 BM, 2 BF, 1 WM. *Length:* 1 Act. *Pubn: Six Plays for a Negro Theater,* Boston: Baker, 1934. *Lib Source:* HBA. *Perm:* Author.

The Call of Jubeh. (1935). Folk Tragedy. Aunt Sarah, raising her nephew as her own son, is devastated when he is lynched by a mob incited by a formerly friendly farmer. Her grief and despair lead her to an hallucination that her nephew is calling her from the swamps, and one night she finally gives in and follows the lights and her nephew's voice into the swamp. *Cast:* 3 BM, 3 BF. *Length:* 1 Act. *Perm:* Author.

Career or College. (1956). Purpose Play. Four high school students, two of whom want to go to college and two of whom want to go directly into a career, debate the justification of their choices under the questioning of their lawyers. *Cast:* 5 M, 3 F. *Length:* 1 Act. *Perm:* Author.

EDMONDS, RANDOLPH (*Cont.*)

Christmas Gift. (1923). Drama. Two con men, hearing that an old lady has a considerable sum of money hidden in her house, visit her on the pretext of soliciting a donation for a Christmas gift for a returning town hero. When the old lady reveals the hiding place, the con men attempt to rob her; the result is that she outsmarts them.   *Cast:* 2 BM, 1 BF, 3 WM. *Length:* 1 Act. *Perm:* Author.

Denmark Vesey. (1929). Historical Drama. Story of the betrayal and last days of the leader of a slave insurrection in Charleston, South Carolina, in 1822. *Cast:* 10 BM, 8 WM, 6 WF. *Length:* 1 Act. *Perm:* Author.

The Devil's Place. Fantasy. Set in the nowhere kingdom of Blufuster. John's been falsely accused and robbed by the king. He has a dream—in which good and bad angels come to him. He accepts the bad angel. Through a battle, John becomes king and is worse than the old king. The devil comes to claim John. *Cast:* 9 M, 2 F, extras. *Length:* 4 Acts. *Pubn: Shades and Shadows*, Boston: Meador Pub. Co., 1930. *Perm:* Author.

Doom. (1924). Tragedy. Despite the fact that Old Aunt Sallie White tries to rear her son to follow in the footsteps of Booker T. Washington and to make a man of himself, Eddie turns out to be a bootlegger and a ne'er-do-well, with the result that he is brought home one night after being shot at the "still" by the sheriff. Sallie becomes hysterical but soon reconciles herself to the doom she has prophesied for her son.   *Cast:* 4 BM, 3 BF. *Length:* 1 Act. *Perm:* Author.

Drama Enters the Curriculum. (1930). Purpose Play. A (symbolic) curriculum committee of a college holds a meeting to review its departmental courses, with the result that after much argument, the subject of drama is admitted as part of the curriculum.   *Cast:* 3 M, 2 F, extras. *Length:* 1 Act. *Perm:* Author.

EAMU's Objective IV. Purpose Play. Depicts Florida A&M University's emphasis upon fine arts as a feature of its curriculum. Professor Claude debates the importance of the arts with his students.   *Cast:* 2 M, extras. *Length:* 1 Act. *Perm:* Author.

Earth and Stars. (1946). Historical Drama. In the 1946 version, the problems of southern leadership following World War II are explored. The revised version emphasizes the civil rights struggle of the 1960s.   *Cast:* 4 BM, 3 BF, 5 WM. *Length:* 3 Acts. *Pubn: Black Drama in America: An Anthology*, ed. by Darwin T. Turner, Greenwich: Fawcett, 1971. *Lib Source:* Typescript, HBA. *Perm:* Author.

Everyman's Land. Fantasy. Two soldiers are killed in France. Their souls search the void together; then the one from Georgia learns the other was "colored." Mars comes in his chariot and says in death they are equal.   *Cast:* 1 BM, 1 WM, extras. *Length:* 1 Act. *Pubn: Shades and Shadows*, Boston: Meador Pub. Co., 1930. *Perm:* Author.

For Fatherland. Melodrama. In the days of Nazi Germany, Fritz, a member of Hitler's guards, returns home to hide in order to escape the purge of the organization; his destination is Switzerland. After avoiding the searchers for a while, he is caught and sentenced to Nazi justice.   *Cast:* 5 M, 2 F, extras. *Length:* 1 Act. *Prod:* The School of Drama, Yale University, New Haven, Conn., 1934. *Perm:* Author.

Gangsters over Harlem. Melodrama. Double crossing and double dealing over control of the numbers rackets in the 1930s. *Cast:* 4 BM, 1 BF. *Length:* 1 Act. *Prod:* Dillard University, New Orleans, La., 1939. *Pubn: The Land of Cotton and Other Plays,* Washington, D.C.: Associated Publishers, 1942. *Lib Source:* HBA. *Perm:* Author.

Hewers of Wood. Mythic Drama. The Blacks are hewing wood and drawing water to build a church for the white man. They pray for release. The devil appears as God and tells them to get to work. One refuses to accept and prays to an idol—God of Ethiopia. He disappears in fire. An angel appears and says they've been tested, and they all get their reward. *Cast:* 4 BM, extras. *Length:* 1 Act. *Pubn: Shades and Shadows,* Boston: Meador Pub. Co., 1930. *Lib Source:* NYPL. *Perm:* Author.

The High Court of Historia. Pageant. The historians of many races arrive at the High Court to tell how they distort history to the benefit of their own people— all except the African, who is reproached for not teaching Black History. *Cast:* 12 M, 7 F, extras (doubling). *Length:* 1 Act. *Prod:* Dillard University, New Orleans, La., 1939. *Pubn: The Land of Cotton and Other Plays,* Washington, D.C.: Associated Publishers, 1942. *Lib Source:* HBA.

Illicit Love. (1927). Tragedy. Interracial Romeo and Juliet story set in the 1920s. The girl is the white daughter of a southern planter. The boy is the son of a black farmer. Caught at their rendezvous near a spring between the two farms, their romance ends tragically with the boy receiving southern justice. *Cast:* 2 BM, 1 BF, 5 WM, 2 WF. *Length:* 1 Act. *Perm:* Author.

In Florida's Everglades. Farce/Comedy/Skit. Two black soldiers, members of the troops President Kennedy had stationed in Florida during the Cuban Missile Crisis, go fishing in the Everglades without a fishing license and flee when they spy a game warden. They find themselves in a Seminole Indian camp and encounter unexpected adventures, including marriage. *Cast:* 2 BM, 2 Indian M, 4 Indian F. *Length:* 1 Act. *Perm:* Author.

Job Hunting. (1922). Blackfaced Skit. Two men sit in the park on a bench—but would rather complain about the hot weather and how difficult it is to find a job. Won honorable mention in the *Opportunity* magazine literary contest, 1922. *Cast:* 4 BM, 1 BF. *Length:* 1 Act. *Perm:* Author.

The Land of Cotton. Protest Drama. Black and white sharecropper unite against wealthy landowners. *Cast:* 18 M, 8 F (doubling). *Length:* 3 Acts. *Prod:* People's Community Theatre, New Orleans, La., 1941. *Pubn: The Land of Cotton and Other Plays,* Washington, D.C.: Associated Publishers, 1942. *Lib Source:* HBA. *Perm:* Author.

The Man of God. (1931). Domestic Drama. Reverend Diggs, a prosperous minister, gets assistance from his Sunday school teacher with his sermons and church work. As a result, the affair nearly wrecks the church when the wife finds out that more than religion is involved. *Cast:* 5 BM, 5 BF, extras. *Length:* 3 Acts. *Perm:* Author.

A Merchant in Dixie. (1923). Drama. Black boy and white boy grow up together in a southern town and fight in France together during World War I. Upon return-

EDMONDS, RANDOLPH (*Cont.*)

ing from war, each leads his own life—the black man becoming a member of the NAACP and a teacher, the white man, a merchant—yet they continue their friendship, and the merchant gets his friend out of a jam when he can't get mortgage money to build a house because of his NAACP activities.   *Cast:* 3 BM, 2 BF, 3 WM. *Length:* 1 Act. *Perm:* Author.

Nat Turner. Historical Drama. The black insurrectionist Nat Turner (1800–1831) is shown before and after his rebellion.   *Cast:* 10 BM, 1 BF. *Length:* 1 Act. *Pubn:* *Six Plays for a Negro Theater,* Boston: Baker, 1934. *Lib Source:* HBA. *Perm:* Author.

The New Window. Melodrama. A mean bootlegger, Bulloch Williams, is finally killed by a young country boy.   *Cast:* 5 BM, 2 BF. *Length:* 1 Act. *Pubn: Six Plays for a Negro Theater,* Boston: Baker, 1934. *Lib Source:* HBA. *Perm:* Author.

Old Man Pete. Domestic Drama. Middle class Harlemites ask "down home" parents to live with them, but conflicts draw parents from the apartment to their death.   *Cast:* 4 BM, 3 BF, extras. *Length:* 1 Act. *Pubn: Six Plays for a Negro Theater,* Boston: Baker, 1934. *Lib Source:* HBA. *Perm:* Author.

One Side of Harlem. (1928). Domestic Drama. Set in the early 1920s, the play involves a family from the rural South who insist on keeping their country ways, to the shame and dismay of other migrant families who adopt more sophisticated, New York ways.   *Cast:* 10 BM, 12 BF. *Length:* Full Length. *Perm:* Author.

The Other Room. Mystery Melodrama. The chief of a numbers gang in Harlem comes early to a pre-arranged meeting at the headquarters and happens to overhear a plot by the other members in the next room to kill him.   *Cast:* 6 M. *Length:* 1 Act. *Perm:* Author.

Peter Stith. (1933). Domestic Drama. Version of *Old Man Pete,* by the same playwright. Middle class Harlemites invite their parents to leave the South and come and live with them in New York. The children soon tire of their country ways and the conflicts that arise drive the old folks from their children's home to a tragic death in New York's Central Park.   *Cast:* 5 BM, 4 BF, extras. *Length:* Full Length. *Perm:* Author.

The Phantom Treasure. Jerry tells of dreams that his father had and that he also has of a treasure buried by his slave grandfather when General William Tecumseh Sherman marched through Georgia during the Civil War. The boys dig, find it, and lose it.   *Cast:* 2 BM. *Length:* 1 Act. *Pubn: Shades and Shadows,* Boston: Meador Pub. Co., 1930. *Lib Source:* NYPL. *Perm:* Author.

Prometheus and the Atom. Historical Fantasy. The theme of the play is that man has never possessed great power without misusing it. The first act dramatizes the Prometheus story and the second act, the development of the atom bomb. Each act has a spectacular ending.   *Prod:* The Florida A&M University Players, Tallahassee, 1955. *Perm:* Author.

Rocky Roads. (1936).   *Perm:* Author.

Shades and Shadows. Mystery Melodrama. Young author, Reggie, is to be declared insane by stepfather and crooked psychiatrist. Plot is foiled by

Reggie's girl friend and detective. Only character mentioned as Black is the chauffer. *Cast:* 1 BM, 5 WM, 1 WF. *Length:* 1 Act. *Pubn: Shades and Shadows,* Boston: Meador Pub. Co., 1930. *Lib Source:* NYPL. *Perm:* Author.

The Shadow across the Path. (1943). Symbolic Fantasy. When an unexplainable shadow falls across a man who is cruel, unjust, and unmerciful, tragedy results. *Cast:* 3 M, 3 F. *Length:* 1 Act. *Perm:* Author.

The Shape of Wars to Come. (1943). Farce/Comedy. Depicts life in 2500 A.D., when women will go out to fight the wars and men will stay home to rear the babies. *Cast:* 2 M, 2 F. *Length:* 1 Act. *Prod:* The Fort Huachuca Soldier Show Players, University of Arizona, Tucson, 1944. *Perm:* Author.

Silas Brown. Folk Drama. A stingy, cruel father drives his son from home and lives to regret it. *Cast:* 3 BM, 3 BF. *Length:* 1 Act. *Prod:* Oberlin High School, Ohio, Mar. 1927. *Pubn: The Land of Cotton and Other Plays,* Washington, D.C.: Associated Publishers, 1942. *Lib Source:* HBA. *Perm:* Author.

Simon in Cyrene. Historical. *Length:* 1 Act. *Prod:* 1939. *Perm:* Author.

Simon in Cyrene. Biblical Drama. Simon, the man from Cyrene who helped the Savior bear his cross up Golgotha, inspired by the experience, returns to his native country to become the first apostle and instead becomes the first martyr. *Cast:* 15 BM, 9 BF, extras. *Length:* 4 Acts. *Prod:* The Dillard Players, New Orleans, La., 1943. *Perm:* Author.

Sirlock Bones. Mystery Comedy. Instead of using the intellectual brilliance of Sherlock Holmes, Sirlock Bones, Holmes' counterpart, uses a method all his own to solve a crime. *Cast:* 3 M, 2 F, extras. *Length:* 1 Act. *Prod:* Morgan Players, Apollo Theatre, New York, 1928. *Perm:* Author.

Stock Exchange. (1927). Blackfaced Negro Musical. A black group decides to organize their own stock exchange and sell stocks and bonds and engage in high finance in general. The scheme fails when a rival group corners the market. *Cast:* 9 BM, 6 BF, extras. *Length:* Full Length. *Perm:* Author.

Takazee, "A Pageant of Ethiopia." (1928). Historical Pageant. With dialogue, music, pantomime, dance, and song. The significant incidents of the history of Ethiopia are told. Special emphasis is placed upon the rule of King Menelik. Over 1,000 people were in the cast when the play was presented in 1934. *Cast:* 10 M, 6 F, extras. *Length:* Full Length. *Prod:* Division of Recreation, Baltimore, Md., 1934. *Perm:* Author.

The Trial and Banishment of Uncle Tom. Purpose Play. Uncle Tom, one of the most hated of black stereotypes, is summoned by the High Court of Justice to answer for the crime of creating a false image of black people in drama and literature. His sentence is banishment forever from the stage and literature. *Cast:* 10 BM, 6 BF, extras. *Length:* 1 Act. *Prod:* The Dillard Players, New Orleans, La., 1945. *Perm:* Author.

The Tribal Chief. Melodrama. Set in a mosque in Tibet. Tribal chief buries man and woman alive for fornicating. Priest objects, chief kills him too and buries all three. Then Death comes for the chief. *Cast:* 4 BM, 2 BF, extras. *Length:* 1 Act. *Pubn: Shades and Shadows,* Boston: Meador Pub. Co., 1930. *Lib Source:* NYPL. *Perm:* Author.

EDMONDS, RANDOLPH *(Cont.)*

The Virginia Politician. (1927). Tragedy. Hattie Jones, a good-looking maid and cook, is forced to yield to James Barrows, a Virginia politician and rabble-rouser who goes about the state preaching against race-mixing. Out of this union are born two children and tragic results.   *Cast:* 1 BM, 1 BF, 2 WM, 2 WF. *Length:* 1 Act. *Perm:* Author.

Whatever the Battle Be. Pageant. A narration of the history of A&M University in Tallahassee, Florida, from its beginning in 1887 to the days of the presidency of Dr. George W. Gore, Jr. in 1947.   *Cast:* 16 BM, 8 BF, extras. *Length:* Full Length. *Prod:* Florida A&M University Playmakers and Music Department, Tallahassee, 1947. *Perm:* Author.

Wives and Blues. (1938). Romantic Melodrama. Dramatization of Ralph Matthews' Afro-American Newspaper serial story. Three wives shape the life of Leslie Kayne, lawyer and songwriter; one of them gets him convicted for murder. *Cast:* 9 BM, 9 BF, 1 BB, 1 BG, extras. *Length:* Full Length. *Perm:* Author.

Yellow Death. (1935). Historical Melodrama. A black regiment in the Spanish-American War volunteers for dangerous fever hospital duty.   *Cast:* 10 BM. *Length:* 1 Act. *Pubn: The Land of Cotton and Other Plays*, Washington, D.C.: Associated Publishers, 1942. *Lib Source:* HBA. *Perm:* Author.

EDMONDS, RANDOLPH, and WILBUR STRICKLAND

G. I. Rhapsody. G. I. Musical Revue. Features skits, solos, music, and dance numbers.   *Cast:* 18 M, 5 F, extras. *Prod:* The Special Service Division, Fort Huachuca, Ariz., 1943.

EDWARD, H. F. V.

Job Hunters. (1931). Documentary Drama. The story shows the hope and despair of the Great Depression in a Harlem employment agency.   *Cast:* 14 BM, 1 BF. *Length:* 1 Act. *Pubn: Black Theater USA,* ed. by James V. Hatch and Ted Shine, New York: Free Pr., 1974. *Lib Source:* HBA.

EDWARDS, LAURA L.

Heaven Bound. Ritual/Drama. Incorporates the elements of ceremonial worship, which include heaven, earth, and hell. *Prod:* FTP, 1936.

EDWARDS, S. W.   *See* Sublette, Walter

EGAN, MICHAEL, and ARTHUR BURGHARDT

Frederick Douglass . . . through His Own Words.   *Cast:* 2 BM, 1 BF. *Prod:* NEC, New York, May 1972.

EKULONA, ADEMOLA

Last Hot Summer.

Mother of the House.

Three Black Comedies.

EL, LEATRICE

Black Magic Anyone? (1971). Pageant. The black people's search for God in his many manifestations. *Cast:* 3 BM, 3 BF, extras. *Length:* 2 Acts. *Prod:* NEC Workshop, New York, Jan. 1971. *Perm:* Author.

EL MUHAJIR. *See* X, Marvin

ELDER, LONNE, III

Ceremonies in Dark Old Men. (1965). Domestic Drama. A black family begins to fall apart under the pressures of its hopes and desires in a world limited by racism. *Cast:* 5 BM, 2 BF. *Length:* 3 Acts. *Prod:* NEC, New York, Feb. 1969. *Pubn: Black Theater,* ed. by Lindsay Patterson, New York: Dodd, 1971. *Lib Source:* HBA.

Charade on East 4th Street. (1971). Drama. A kidnapped white policeman is harassed by black gang for crimes he allegedly committed against the black community. *Cast.* 6 BM, 1 BF, 1 WM. *Length:* 1 Act. *Pubn: Black Drama Anthology,* ed. by Woodie King, Jr. and Ron Milner, New York: New Amer. Lib., 1972. *Lib Source:* HBA.

A Hysterical Turtle in a Rabbit Race. (1961). Domestic Drama. Domineering mother struggles with her children and her husband in their attempts to break away from her. *Cast:* 5 BM, 4 BF, 2 WM. *Length:* 3 Acts. *Lib Source:* Typescript, HBA.

Kissin' Rattlesnakes Can Be Fun. (1966). *Length:* 1 Act.

Seven Comes Up, Seven Comes Down. (1966). *Length:* 1 Act.

Sounder. Screenplay. A poor, southern, black family fights for father when he steals a ham to feed them. *Prod:* Twentieth Century Fox Film Corp., 1972.

The Terrible Veil. (1963).

ELLINGTON, DUKE

Skrontch!! Songs composed by Ellington come "from three produced shows plus revues for the Cotton Club. There are six from *Pousse-Cafe* and two each from *Beggar's Holiday* and *Jump for Joy."*—Townsend Brewster, *Newsletter* of the Harlem Cultural Council, vol. 2, no. 6. *Prod:* Theatre at Noon, St. Peter's Church, New York, 1975.

ELLINGTON, DUKE, et al.

Jump for Joy. Sun-Tanned Revu-sical. A series of comedy sketches and songs built around the idea that Uncle Tom dies and is replaced by new images. *Length:* 2 Acts, 31 Scenes. *Prod:* Mayan Theatre, by American Revue Theatre, Los Angeles, Calif., Summer 1941.

EMERUWA, LEATRICE W. *See* El, Leatrice

ERSKINS, CELADY SHAW, EDWARD BOATNER, and IVAN FIRTH

Julius Caesar in Rome Georgia. (1933). Musical Comedy. Parody of Julius Caesar set in Negro Morning Star Lodge. *Cast:* 10 BM, 10 BF, 38 actors and dancers, extras. *Length:* 3 Acts. *Lib Source:* PAL. *Perm:* Author.

ETIENNE

The Jazzman and His Lady Fare. Poetic. Young black man laments his white woman's passion for jazz and dope. *Cast:* 5 M, 4 F. *Length:* 1 Act. *Pubn:* Paris: Privately published, 1965.

EUBA, FEMI

Crocodiles. *Prod:* NEC, New York, Feb. 1973.

The Riddle of the Palm Leaf. *Prod:* NEC, New York, Feb. 1973.

EULO, KEN

Black Jesus. (1972). Drama. A blind black American helps steal a Guatemalan Black Jesus and regains his sight just before dying. *Cast:* 3 BM, 1 Indian. *Length:* 3 Scenes. *Perm:* Agency, William Morris.

EVANS-CHARLES, MARTIE. *See* Charles, Martie

EVANS, DON

Change of Mind. Domestic Comedy. Adam, a young man from the South, comes up North to start his revolution by turning some of the ugly things said about black men into "love-talk." *Length:* 2 Acts. *Perm:* Agency, Karen Baxter, NASABA.

Matters of Choice. Domestic Comedy. Focuses on the problem of ownership and privacy in a society where people are programmed to take what they can't buy. *Cast:* 5 BM, 4 BF, 1 WM. *Length:* 2 Acts. *Prod:* Karamu Theatre, Cleveland, Ohio, Feb. 1975. *Perm:* Agency, Karen Baxter, NASABA.

Orrin. Domestic Drama. Orrin, a young man with a history of drug abuse and thievery, returns home and causes his father and mother to reaffirm their trust in the "family." *Cast:* 2 BM, 2 BF. *Length:* 1 Act. *Perm:* Agency, Karen Baxter, NASABA.

Showdown. Comedy. A black version of Shakespeare's *The Taming of the Shrew,* set in Philadelphia. *Cast:* 9 BM, 4 BF. *Length:* Full Length. *Prod:* NFT, New York, Feb. 1976.

Sugar-Mouth Sam Don't Dance No More. Domestic Drama. Centers on the conflicts of a middle-aged pair of lovers. Verda Mae & Sammy have been lovers for ten years, in spite of marriage (to others), jail, and the rigors of day-to-day poverty. *Cast:* 1 BM, 1 BF. *Length:* 1 Act. *Prod:* NEC, New York, May 1975. *Pubn: Black World,* vol. 23, no. 6, Apr. 1973. *Lib Source:* HBA. *Perm:* Agency, Karen Baxter, NASABA.

EVANS, ZISHAW

Zetta. *Prod:* Chicago, Ill., 1975.

EVERETT, RON

The Babbler. *Prod:* Neo-Otundila Theatre Company, Philadelphia, Pa., 1971.

A Cup of Time. *Prod:* Neo-Otundila Theatre Company, Philadelphia, Pa., 1971.

Wash Your Back. *Prod:* Neo-Otundila Theatre Company, Philadelphia, Pa., 1971.

EZILE

Have You Seen Sunshine?

FABIO, SARAH WEBSTER

M. L. King Pageant. (1967).

FAIR, RONALD L.

Sails and Sinkers. (1969).

FANN, AL

King Heroin. About the destructiveness of the new slavery—drug addiction—and how the community has aided its spread. *Prod:* Al Fann's Theatrical Ensemble, New York, 1970.

Masks in Black (Brown). A celebration of the black experience in America through poetry, music, dance, and scenes from Broadway dramas and comedies. *Prod:* Hofstra University Playhouse, Hempstead, N.Y., Jan. 1974.

Masks in Black '75. Musical Revue. Salutes contributions of black Americans in building the country from the Revolution to the present. *Prod:* Al Fann Theatrical Ensemble, St. Philips Church, New York, June 1975.

FANN, AL, and MARGARET F. TAYLOR SNIPES

The Hymie Finkelstein Used Lumber Company. Musical. *Prod:* Karamu Theatre, Cleveland, Ohio, 1973-74 season.

FANN, ERNIE

Blue, Green, Yellow, Orange, Red and Brown. This play is about racial confrontations.

A Fair and Impartial Verdict. *Prod:* Rome, Ohio, 1976.

The First Tuesday in November. *Prod:* Horse Show Lodge Country Club, Rome, Ohio, Sept. 1975.

FARLEY, RICHARD

The Great American Race War. Drama. White liberal believes he's not a racist until the race war begins. *Length:* 3 Acts. *Perm:* Author.

FEDERAL THEATRE PROJECT (SEATTLE)

An Evening with Dunbar. Operetta. The life of Paul Lawrence Dunbar told through his poetry and stories. *Length:* 3 Acts. *Prod:* Possibly FTP, Seattle, Wash., n.d. *Lib Source:* Typescript, FTP, GMU.

FERDINAND, VAL. *See* Salaam, Kalamu Ya

FERGUSON, LOU

Elton. *Prod:* Greenwich Village-base Players Workshop, New York, 1973.

FIELDS, MAURICE

The Dead Are Never Forgotten Easy. (1974). Domestic Drama. Concerns black man running for public office and his son, whom he thought dead, who returns to taste the good life his father is about to come into.   *Cast:* 3 BM, 1 BF, 2 WM, 1 WF. *Length:* 1 Act. *Perm:* Author.

Nowhere to Go, Nowhere to Get Over. (1974). Domestic Drama. A play about a Black Muslim who comes home from jail and the conflict his religion causes within his mother's household.   *Cast:* 11 BM, 5 BF, 1 WM. *Length:* 3 Acts. *Perm:* Author.

FIGGS, CARRIE LAW MORGAN

Bachelor's Convention.   *Pubn:* Chicago: Privately published by author, 1923.

Jepthah's Daughter.   *Pubn:* Chicago: Privately published by author, 1923.

The Prince of Peace.   *Pubn:* Chicago: Privately published by author, 1923.

Santa Claus Land.   *Pubn:* Chicago: Privately published by author, 1923.

FIRTH, IVAN, EDWARD BOATNER, and CELADY SHAW ERSKINS

Julius Caesar in Rome Georgia. (1933). Musical Comedy. Parody of Julius Caesar set in Negro Morning Star Lodge.   *Cast:* 10 BM, 10 BF, 38 actors and dancers, extras. *Length:* 3 Acts. *Lib Source:* PAL. *Perm:* Author.

FISHER, RUDOLPH

The Conjure Man Dies. Comedy/Mystery. The Conjure Man is apparently murdered, but during a seance he reappears and is shot again.   *Cast:* 16 M, 6 F, extras. *Length:* 3 Acts. *Prod:* Lafayette Theatre, New York, Mar. 1936. *Lib Source:* Typescript, SCHOM.

FLAGG, ANN

Great Gettin' Up Mornin'. (1964). Domestic Drama. This is the day the family's six-year-old daughter is to attend a previously all-white school. First Prize Winner in National Collegiate Playwriting Contest.   *Cast:* 4 BM, 2 BF, 1 BG, 1 BB. *Length:* 1 Act. *Prod:* APT, New York. *Pubn:* SF. *Lib Source:* HBA. *Perm:* Agency, SF.

FLETCHER, B. B.

Do Unto Others. (1973). Parable. White desk clerk tries "to make it" with black Saundra, but she is too clever and takes him instead.   *Cast:* 1 BF, 1 WM. *Length:* 3 Scenes.

The Letter of the White Law. (1973). Protest Drama. Mr. Henderson refuses to pay rent until the landlord makes his building safe.   *Cast:* 2 BM, 2 BG, 4 WM, 1 WF, 2 Puerto Rican M, 2 Puerto Rican F (doubling). *Length:* 4 Scenes.

FLOYD, RONALD. *See* Ekulona, Ademola

FOARD, SYLVIA-ELAINE

A Fictional Account of the Lives of Richard and Sarah Allen. Drama. "An account of the eighteenth-century black minister who founded the AME Church, his wife, his activist brother, and a Philadelphia conjur woman."—Townsend Brewster, *Newsletter* of the Harlem Cultural Council, vol. 2, no. 10. *Length:* 16 Scenes. *Prod:* NEC Season-within-a-Season, New York, Spring, 1976.

FOLANI, FEMI

A Play for Zubena. (1972).

FOLAYAN, OMODELE

Ju Ju Man. Children's Play.   *Prod:* Harlem Children's Theatre, New York, Dec. 1974.

FORDE, B. BIL

African Song, Daddy Beethoven. Melodrama. Eddie and B. G. rob and kill all the rich white folks, then flee with the black maid.   *Cast:* 3 DM, 1 BF, 2 WM, 1 WC, *Length:* 1 Act. *Perm:* Author.

FOSTER, ALEX

Community Kitchen. Comedy/Drama. A group of black working-class people, faced with automation, lose their jobs and consider suicide.   *Cast:* 2 BM, 2 BF. *Length:* 3 Acts. *Prod:* Harlem YMCA, New York, 1974.

FOSTER, GREGORY

The Life in Lady Day.   *Prod:* Ebony Talent Associates, Chicago, Ill., 1973.

FOWLER, JERI. *See* Chimbamul

FRANKLIN, CLARENCE

Copper Pig.

FRANKLIN, HAROLD

Guilty or Not Guilty.   *Length:* 1 Act. *Prod:* Tanzia-Mystique Productions, Brooklyn Academy of Music, N.Y., June 1974.

FRANKLIN, J. E.

Black Girl. (1969). Domestic Drama. A young black woman struggles with the jealousy of her half sisters and with her own inner fears of separating herself from her family in order to study dancing.   *Cast:* 1 BM, 5 BF, 1 BB, 1 BG. *Length:* 2 Acts. *Prod:* NFT, New York, June 1971. *Pubn:* DPS. *Lib Source:* HBA. *Perm:* Agency, DPS.

Cut Out the Lights and Call the Law. Drama. A group of black students in a white college prepare to fight when attacked by whites.   *Cast:* 4 BM, 5 BF. *Length:* 2 Acts. *Prod:* NFT, New York, Apr. 1972. *Perm:* Agency, Bohan-Neuwald.

FRANKLIN, J. E. *(Cont.)*

First Step to Freedom. (1964). Was part of a Mississippi CORE-SNCC program designed to interest students in reading. *Perm:* Author.

Four Women.

The In-Crowd. (1965). Play for young bloods. A gang of young kids decides to judge the cruelty of their parents toward them, but when they kill the parents in effigy, they realize that parents are family after all. *Cast:* 8 M, 2 F. *Length:* 1 Act.

Mau-Mau Room.   *Prod:* NEC Workshop, New York, c. 1972.

Two Flowers.   *Prod:* New Feminist Theatre.

FRANKLIN, J. E., and MICKI GRANT

The Prodigal Sister. (1974). Musical. Music and lyrics by Micki Grant. Book and lyrics by J. E. Franklin. Jackie, a young black woman in conflict with parents, becomes pregnant and leaves home for the freedom of the big city, only to return home to find love and acceptance. *Cast:* 7 BM, 7 BF. *Length:* 8 Scenes. *Prod:* NFT, New York, July 1974. *Pubn:* SF; Music by Fiddleback Music Co., New York. *Lib Source:* HBA. *Perm:* Agency, SF.

FRANKLIN, SANDRA

The Magic Yam. Dance/Drama. Choreography by Stanley Dalton. *Prod:* Rites and Reason, Brown University, Providence, R. I., July-Aug. 1972.

FRANKLIN, SANDRA, and CLEVELAND KURTZ

A Voice in the Wilderness. Gospel Song/Historical Play. *Length:* 1 Act. *Prod:* Congdon Street Baptist Church, Providence, R. I., Nov. 1973.

FRAZIER, HANK

A Black Market. (1976). Mystery/Comedy. A twin seeks the murderer of his twin brother. *Cast:* 5 BM, 2 BF, 2 WM. *Length:* 2 Acts. *Prod:* Reading, Frank Silvera Writers' Workshop, Studio Museum, New York, Mar. 1977. *Lib Source:* HBA. *Perm:* Author.

The Businessman. (1972). Confused black man cannot find what he is looking for in terms of fulfillment because he has not ascertained exactly what it is he desires. This is due in part to his prejudice against knowledge. *Cast:* 4 BM, 1 BF, 3 WM, 1 WF. *Length:* 1 Act. *Lib Source:* Typescript, SCHOM. *Perm:* Author.

Nothing but the Truth. Drama. An aggregation of death row: Blacks who have sundry views about God and the white man's morality. *Cast:* 4 BM, 1 BF, 1 WM. *Length:* 1 Act. *Lib Source:* Typescript, SCHOM. *Perm:* Author.

FRAZIER, LEVI, JR.

Down on Beale. Historical Drama. Deals with the life of W. C. Handy from his boyhood days in Florence, Alabama, through his days on the notorious Beale Street, and ends with Handy relinquishing his job as a musician in order to devote more time to record publishing.   *Cast:* 19 BM, 4 WM (doubling). *Length:* 3 Acts. *Prod:* Lemoyne-Owen College, Memphis, Tenn., 1973.

'Sis' Moses. Historical Fantasy. Focuses on one of Harriet Tubman's journeys on the Underground Railroad, during which she relates her life story as she and others prepare for their hour of freedom.   *Cast:* 1 BF, 1 WM, 1 WF. *Length:* 1 Act. *Prod:* Memphis Public Library, Tenn., 1975. *Perm:* Author.

A Tribute to Richard Wright. Historical Protest. Compilation of some of Wright's works, conversations, letters, and other memorabilia from the time he spent in Mississippi up until his final departure for France; focuses on both the writer and the man.   *Cast:* 2 BM, 1 BF. *Length:* 1 Act. *Prod:* Southwestern (college), Memphis, Tenn., Mar. 1972. *Perm:* Author.

The Way We Was; or The Wrong Place at the Right Time. Morality Drama. Death-seeking revolutionary writer during 1960s who has relinquished self-love for self-hate and sees his own characters on stage turn against him.   *Cast:* 3 BM, 2 WM, 1 WF. *Length:* 1 Act. *Prod:* Southwestern (college), Memphis, Tenn., May 1973. *Perm:* Author.

FREE SOUTHERN THEATRE

The Bogalusa Story.   *Prod:* FST, Bogalusa, La., c. 1966.

The Jonesboro Story.   *Prod:* FST, Jonesboro, Ark., c. 1966.

They Came This Morning. Fantasy. Blacks are enslaved and plans are made to have them shipped to the moon.   *Cast:* 3 BM, 2 BF, 3 WM. *Length:* 1 Act.

FREEMAN, CAROL

The Suicide. Drama/Satire. The wake of a suicide victim is mixed with confusion and awe that is precipitated by the victim's wife.   *Cast:* 1 BM, 3 BF, 2 WM. *Length:* 1 Act. *Prod:* Black Folks Theater, Northwestern University, Evanston, Ill., 1971 *Pubn: Black Fire,* ed. by LeRoi Jones and Larry Neal, New York: Morrow, 1968. *Lib Source:* HBA.

FREEMAN, HARRY LAWRENCE

An African Kraal. (1902–1903). Opera. Set in Zululand.   *Length:* 1 Act.

An American Romance. (1927). Opera.

Athalia. (1915–1916). Opera. Set in America.   *Length:* 3 Acts, Prologue.

The Flapper. (1929). Opera.

Leah Kleschna. (1931). Opera.

The Martyr. (1893). Dramatic Opera. About the imprisonment and death, by fire, of an Egyptian nobleman who has fallen from the faith of his father and accepted that of Jehovah.   *Cast:* 3 M, 2 F. *Length:* 2 Acts. *Prod:* Freeman Grand Opera Co., Deutches Theatre, Denver, Colo., Sept. 1893.

The Octoroon. (1902–1904). Opera. This adaptation of the play, *The Octoroon* by Dion Boucicault, is by M. E. Braddon.

The Plantation. (1906-1915). Opera. Set in America.   *Length:* 3 Acts.

FREEMAN, HARRY LAWRENCE (*Cont.*)

The Prophecy. (1911). Opera. Set in America. *Length:* 1 Act.

The Tryst. (1909). Dramatic Opera. A pioneer drama, set in Michigan, about a joust in which a young Indian chieftain, believing he has hurled his knife at some brush and slain his "paleface" pursuers, finds instead the lifeless body of his sweetheart. *Cast:* 1 M, 1 F. *Length:* 1 Act. *Prod:* Freeman Operatic Duo, Crescent Theatre, New York, May 1911.

Uzziah. (1934). Opera.

Valdo. (1905). Dramatic Opera. Set in Mexico, about mistaken identity in which the hero is challenged to a fatal duel by his sister's jealous fiancé. *Cast:* 2 M, 2 F. *Length:* 1 Act. *Prod:* Freeman Grand Opera Co., Weisgerber's Hall, Cleveland, Ohio, May 1906.

Vendetta. (1911–1923). Dramatic Opera. Set in Mexico, it concerns the jealous and fatal rivalry between a toreador and an overlord for the hand of a lady of rank. *Cast:* 5 M, 3 F, dancers, extras. *Length:* 3 Acts. *Prod:* Negro Grand Opera Co., Lafayette Theatre, New York, Nov. 1923.

Voodoo. (1912–1914). Opera. Set in Louisiana. *Length:* 3 Acts. *Prod:* Fifty-second Street Theatre, New York, 1928; WCBS Radio, 1928.

Zuliki. (1897–1898). Opera. Set in Africa. *Length:* 3 Acts. *Prod:* In parts, Cleveland, Ohio, 1900.

Zululand. (1932-1947). A tetralogy that includes ballet and symphonic poem: *Nada, Allah, The Zulu King, The Slave.*

FRIEDMAN, KARL

No Balm in Gilead. Drama. About the lives and crumbling dreams of five black people living in a New York City ghetto and particularly a love story about a young man who, in searching for dignity and self-realization in a life on the streets, finds tragedy and degradation for himself, his woman, and his family. *Prod:* Manhattan Cable Television, New York, Mar. 1975.

FUDGE, ANTHONY

Migration. Futuristic. Play depicting one man's spiritual development. *Prod:* Humanist Theatre, Cleveland, Ohio, 1973.

FULLER, CHARLES H.

Ain't Nobody Sarah but Me.

All's Fair. (1972). Domestic Drama. Concerns a young man's coming marriage and the dispute among the three women who love him. *Cast:* 3 BF. *Length:* 1 Act. *Perm:* Agency, Karen Hitzig, William Morris.

Brother Marcus.

The Brownsville Raid. Historical Drama. Concerns the events of August 13, 1906, in Brownsville, Tex., when it was reported that a troop of black soldiers raided the town.   *Cast:* 9 BM, 1 BF, 2 WM. *Length:* 3 Acts. *Prod:* NEC, New York, Nov. 1976. *Perm:* Agency, Karen Hitzig, William Morris.

Cain.

Candidate. (1973). Political Drama. Concerns a black candidate's attempt to win a mayoral primary election.   *Cast:* 8 BM, 3 BF, 4 WM, 1 WF. *Length:* 3 Acts. *Prod:* NFT, New York, Mar. 1974. *Perm:* Agency, Karen Hitzig, William Morris.

Charles Fuller Presents, the Dynamic Jerry Bland and Blandelles, with the Fabulous Miss Marva James. (1974). Domestic Drama. Sequel to *In My Many Names and Days,* a composite of several works by the same playwright. Concerns an old blues singer trying to make a comeback.   *Cast:* 5 BM, 4 BF. *Length:* 3 Acts. *Perm:* Agency, Karen Hitzig, William Morris.

The Conductor. (1969).

Emma. Domestic Drama. Concerns a southern family whose son is killed in a railroad strike.   *Cast:* 2 BM, 2 BF. *Length:* 1 Act. *Prod:* Afro-American Arts Theatre, Philadelphia, Pa., 1970. *Perm:* Agency, Karen Hitzig, William Morris.

First Love. (1970). Drama. Concerns the problems of boys in the eighth grade during the fifties and their girls.   *Cast:* 6 BB, 1 BG. *Length:* 1 Act. *Prod:* Afro-American Arts Theatre, Philadelphia, Pa., 1971. *Perm:* Agency, Karen Hitzig, William Morris.

The Game. (1972). Historical Domestic Drama. Set in 1947, this play concerns the return of a child to his mother after he has lived with his aunt for six years, and the entrance of Jackie Robinson into the national baseball scene.   *Cast:* 2 BM, 2 BF, 1 BB. *Length:* 1 Act. *Perm:* Agency, Karen Hitzig, William Morris.

In the Deepest Part of Sleep. (1974). Domestic Tragedy. Sequel to *In My Many Names and Days,* a composite of several works by the same playwright. Set in 1956, it continues the life of a black family and deals with a young man's development from adolescence to manhood.   *Cast:* 2 BM, 2 BF. *Length:* 2 Acts. *Prod:* NEC, New York, June 1974. *Perm:* Agency, Karen Hitzig, William Morris.

Indian Giver.

JJ's Game.

"Jerry Bland and the Blandettes Featuring Miss Marva James." Musical.   *Prod:* NFT, New York, Spring 1977.

The Layout Letter. (1968). Domestic Drama. Problem centers around family in which the mother has just died and a letter she wrote to them that is delivered after her death.   *Cast:* 3 BM, 4 BF, 1 BB. *Length:* 1 Act. *Prod:* Freedom Theatre, Philadelphia, Pa., 1974. *Perm:* Agency, Karen Hitzig, William Morris.

Love Song for Robert Lee. (1968).   *Length:* 1 Act.

Perfect Party. (1968). Domestic Drama. Problem centers around a group of integrated couples in mixed-marriages; when the black head of the group wants to leave to find his roots, difficulties and murder occur.   *Cast:* 3 BM, 3 BF, 3 WM, 3 WF. *Length:* 2 Acts. *Prod:* Tambellini's Gate Theatre, New York, Mar. 1969. *Perm:* Agency, Karen Hitzig, William Morris.

FULLER, CHARLES H. (*Cont.*)

The Rise. (1968). Historical Drama. Some of the activities of Marcus Garvey as he combatted Negro politicians and agitated whites in Harlem.   *Cast:* 8 BM, 3 BF, 3 WM. *Length:* 3 Acts. *Prod:* Harlem School of the Arts, New York, 1974. *Pubn: New Plays from the Black Theater,* ed. by Ed Bullins, New York: Bantam, 1969. *Perm:* Agency, Karen Hitzig, William Morris.

Sarah Love Sweet Sarah Love. (1971). Domestic Comedy. Concerns the love affair of a woman who has left the South and tries to make it in Philadelphia in 1936. *Cast:* 1 BM, 1 BF. *Length:* 1 Act. *Perm:* Agency, Karen Hitzig, William Morris.

Sunflower Majorette. Concerns a woman who is in love with a married man who has just left her apartment.   *Cast:* 1 BF. *Length:* 1 Act. *Perm:* Agency, Karen Hitzig, William Morris.

The Sunflowers. (1969). General title for a series of plays.

Untitled Play. (1971). Domestic Drama. Concerns a woman whose long lost lover comes to claim her after many years.   *Cast:* 2 BM, 1 BF. *Length:* 1 Act. *Prod:* Afro-American Arts Theatre, Philadelphia, Pa., 1971. *Perm:* Agency, Karen Hitzig, William Morris.

FULLER, DAVID, and LINDA PARIS-BAILEY

Circus Maxim. Circus/Ritual. "Using the form of a circus freak show . . . the freaks are presented as symbols of black American reality. The play ends with 'We must be freaks no longer.' "—Tom Dent, *First World,* vol. 1, no. 2, Mar.-Apr. 1977. *Prod:* Carpetbag Theater, Festival of the Southern Black Cultural Alliance, New Orleans, La., Nov. 1976.

FURMAN, ROGER

Another Shade of Harlem.   *Prod:* Public School I. S. 201, New York, May 1970. *Perm:* Author.

Fool's Paradise. (1952).   *Length:* 1 Act. *Perm:* Author.

The Gimmick. Fantasy. This play should unfold as a dream, possibly a nightmare. The people in this play are all fugitives of a kind and outcasts from so-called "proper" society.   *Cast:* 1 BM, 1 BF, 3 WF. *Length:* 1 Act. *Prod:* Columbia University School of the Arts, New York, Apr. 1970. *Lib Source:* Typescript, HBA. *Perm:* Author.

The Long Black Block. (1971). Drama. A black woman superintendent of a ghetto apartment house survives junkies and crime and still finds beauty.   *Cast:* 7 BM, 8 BF. *Length:* 2 Acts. *Prod:* NHT, New York, Jan. 1972. *Perm:* Author.

The Quiet Laughter. (1952).   *Length:* 1 Act. *Perm:* Author.

Renegade Theatre.   *Prod:* Purple Manor, New York, Mar. 1968. *Perm:* Author.

To Kill a Devil. (1971). Drama. An Oedipal relationship is explored in which an unmarried mother searches for a man and confronts her son with being in her way. *Cast:* 1 BM, 1 BF. *Length:* 1 Act. *Prod:* Columbia University School of the Arts, New York, Apr. 1970. *Pubn: Black Scenes,* ed. by Alice Childress, New York: Doubleday, 1971. *Lib Source:* Typescript, HBA. *Perm:* Author.

FURMAN, ROGER, and DORIS BRUNSON

Three Shades of Harlem. Life in Harlem shown in three moods: Shade One—the Blues; Shade Two—Joy; Shade Three—Hope for the Future. *Length:* 3 Acts. Prod: NHT, New York, June 1965. *Perm:* Author.

FURMAN, ROGER, and DEE ROBINSON

Fat Tuesday or *Drawers Down, Bottoms Up.* Musical Comedy. The action takes place in New Orleans in the "dirty" 1930s, in a run-down brothel, where the girls are a bit too brassy and the house madam on the wrong side of forty has a much too young "loverboy." *Length:* Full Length. *Prod:* NHT, New York, Oct. 1975. *Perm:* Author.

FURMAN, ROGER, et al.

Hip, Black, and Angry. Variety Program. Directed and conceived by Mr. Furman, written by Jim Williams, Nathaniel Juni, Warren Cuney, Tad Joans, Carl Boissiere, Frances E. K. Parks et al. *Prod:* Public School I. S. 201, New York, Apr. 1967. *Perm:* Author.

GAINES, J. E.

Don't Let It Go to Your Head. (1970). Drama. A prisoner returns home only to recognize, painfully, that there was no love there either. *Cast:* 5 BM, 4 BF. *Length:* 3 Acts. *Prod:* NFT, New York, Jan. 1972. *Perm:* Agency, NASABA.

Heaven and Hell's Agreement. Drama. Vietnam veteran returns home to his wife after having been reported as dead and discovers that she has a serious lover. *Cast:* 2 BM, 1 BF. *Prod:* NEC Season-within-a-Season, New York, Apr. 1974. *Perm:* Agency, NASABA.

It's Cullid, It's Negro, It's Black Man! (1970). *Prod:* Kasisi Yusef Iman Weusi Kuumba Theatre Troupe, New York, n.d. *Perm.* Agency, NASABA.

Sometimes a Hard Head Makes a Soft Behind. (1970). Drama. A young black man on dope steals from his own family and is put out. *Prod:* NLT, New York, July 1972. *Perm:* Agency, NASABA

What If It Had Turned Up Heads. (1970). Drama. An aspect of life at the grass roots in which the characters are winos who live a shabby existence. *Cast:* 4 BM, 1 BF. *Length:* 2 Acts. *Prod:* APT, New York, Mar. 1972. *Pubn:* The New Lafayette Theatre Presents, ed. by Ed Bullins, New York: Anchor Books, 1974. *Lib Source:* HBA. *Perm:* Agency, NASABA.

GAINES-SHELTON, RUTH

The Church Fight. (1925). Comedy. Church members conspire to remove the pastor but are afraid to confront him. *Cast:* 4 BM, 6 BF. *Length:* 1 Act. *Pubn:* Black Theater USA, ed. by James V. Hatch and Ted Shine, New York: Free Pr., 1974. *Lib Source:* HBA.

GAINES, SONNY JIM. *See* Gaines, J. E.

GALE, BERESFORD

The Hand of Fate; or, *Fifty Years After.* Historical. On coming of age, Richard Walker, a Negro, finds conditions in the South unbearable and flees. Ten years later he is reunited with his sweetheart and becomes heir to a plantation.   *Cast:* 4 BM, 2 BF, 5 WM, 1 WF. *Length:* 4 Acts. *Prod:* AME Sunday School Union, Nashville, Tenn. n.d.

GALE, WESLEY

A House in Jamaica. Drama. A woman who is a faith healer practices voodoo and is a victim of discrimination by Jamaican islanders.   *Cast:* 7 BM, 7 BF, 1 WF. *Length:* 3 Acts.

GARRETT, JIMMY

And We Own the Night. Drama. A revolutionary feels compelled to kill his mother, who feels he is wrong for fighting the white man.   *Cast:* 6 BM, 1 BF, 1 WM. *Length:* 1 Act. *Prod:* Spirit House Movers, Newark, N. J., 1967. *Pubn: Black Fire,* ed. by LeRoi Jones and Larry Neal, New York: Morrow, 1968. *Lib Source:* HBA.

GATEWOOD, L. A.

Ghetto a Place. (1970).

A Place Jones. About ghetto life and drug addiction.   *Length:* 1 Act. *Prod:* Humanist Theatre, Cleveland, Ohio, 1973.

GAYE, IRVIN

The Spirit of Christmas. Musical. Concerns a wealthy black entrepreneur and his daughter, who is kidnapped. The play deals with the change of heart the father undergoes during his tribulation.   *Length:* 2 Acts. *Prod:* New Concept Theatre, Chicago, Ill., 1974.

GEARY, BRUCE C.

Cadillac Alley. (1972). Ritual. This play deals with the plagues that confront some blacks, namely, dope, pimps, whores, etc.   *Cast:* 10 BM, 1 BF (voice), extras. *Length:* 1 Act. *Pubn: Who Took the Weight (Black Voices from Norfolk Prison),* Boston: Little, 1972. *Lib Source:* HBA.

GENTRY, MINNIE

My House Is Falling Down.   *Prod:* Reading, Frank Silvera Writers' Workshop, Martinique Theatre, New York, May 1975.

GIBSON, P. J.

Miss Ann Don't Cry No More.   *Prod:* Reading, Frank Silvera Writers' Workshop, City College of New York, Mar. 1977.

GIBSON, POWELL WILLARD

Jake among the Indians. Comedy/Drama. Depicts the trials of an Indian maid with her father.   *Pubn:* Winchester, Va.: W. P. Gibson, 1931.

GILBERT, MERCEDES

Environment. Domestic Drama. Mother tries to keep her head above water amidst a
fugitive husband and son who has gotten in with the wrong crowd. *Cast:* 6 M, 6
F, extras. *Length:* 3 Acts. *Pubn: Selected Gems of Poetry, Comedy and Drama,*
ed. by Mercedes Gilbert, Boston: Christopher Pub. Co., 1931. *Lib Source:*
SCHOM.

In Greener Pastures.

Ma Johnson's Harlem Rooming House. Serial. *Prod:* YMCA, Harlem, New York,
1938.

GILL, BILLY

Time Is for White Folks. Black Comedy. *Prod:* Martinique Theatre, New York,
Apr. 1974.

GILLIAM, TED

What You Say? Or How Christopher Columbus Discovered Ray Charles.
(c. 1969). Satire. Based on comedian Flip Wilson's "Columbus" story. Calls for
large groups of children—all black to play roles of Africans, Indians, and
Europeans. *Prod:* Possibly Dashiki Project, New Orleans, La., Summer 1970.

GLADDEN, FRANK A.

The Distant Brother. (1972).

GLANVILLE, MAXWELL

Cindy. Children's Play. An adaptation of the Cinderella fairy tale. *Length:* 1 Act.
Prod: Adam Clayton Powell, Jr. Theatre, New York, Spring 1976.

GLANVILLE, MAXWELL, and ALFRED RUDOLPH GRAY, JR.

Dance to a Nosepicker's Drum. (1970). Domestic Drama. Play explores relationships of three generations of an urban black middle class family and the
effect of a perceptive young boy on his separated parents. *Cast:* 5BM, 4 BF.
Length: 2 Acts. *Prod:* American Community Theatre, New York, 1970. *Perm:*
Author.

GORDON, CHARLES. *See* Oyamo

GORDON, RICHARD

You Can't Kill, J. R. Sociological Drama. A young black man defines his own logic.
Pubn: New York: Amuru Pr., 1974, possibly never published.

GORDONE, CHARLES

Gordone Is a Muthah. (1970). A series of sketches and poems related to the black
experience. *Length:* 1 Act. *Prod:* Carnegie Hall, New York, 1970. *Pubn: Best
Short Plays, 1973,* ed. by Stanley Richards, Philadelphia: Chilton, 1973. *Lib
Source:* HBA.

GORDONE, CHARLES *(Cont.)*

The Last Chord. Melodrama. Bishop Gregory runs afoul of the Mafia in a very complex plot. *Length:* Full Length. *Prod:* Billie Holiday Theatre, New York, Mar. 1976. *Perm:* Agency, William Morris.

No Place to Be Somebody. (1969). Drama. Black man, no longer able to cope with invisibility within white society and incapable of feeling at home with black impulses around him, is slowly coming apart. *Cast:* 5 BM, 3 BF, 5 WM, 3 WF. *Length:* 3 Acts. *Prod:* Public Theatre, New York Shakespeare Festival, N.Y., May 1969. *Pubn: No Place to Be Somebody,* Indianapolis: Bobbs-Merrill, 1969; SF. *Lib Source:* HBA. *Perm:* Agency, SF.

Under the Boardwalk. Screenplay. *Prod:* Reading, Frank Silvera Writers' Workshop, Teachers, Inc., New York, Dec. 1976. *Perm:* Agency, William Morris.

Worl's Champeen Lip Dansuh an' Wahtah Mellon Jooglah. (1969).

GOSS, CLAY

Andrew. Drama. The story of three friends, who were former gang members, and the tragic circumstances surrounding the death of one of them. *Cast:* 3 BM. *Length:* 2 Acts. *Prod:* NFT, New York, Apr. 1972. *Pubn: Homecookin',* Washington, D.C.: Howard Univ. Pr., 1974. *Lib Source:* HBA. *Perm:* Agency, Dorothea Oppenheimer.

Billy McGhee. Domestic Comedy. Young boy has a chance of becoming a professional actor but must give up school friends and normal home life. *Cast:* 2 BM, 2 BF, 2 WM, 1 WF. *Length:* 1 Act. *Prod:* "The Place," WRC-Channel 4 TV, Washington, D.C., Sept. 1974. *Perm:* Agency, Dewey Hughes, Executive Producer.

Hip Rumpelstiltzken. Fantasy. Rock-soul version of the fairy tale. *Cast:* 5 BM, 5 BF. *Length:* 1 Act. *Prod:* Theatre Black, Brooklyn Academy of Music, New York, Nov. 1973. *Perm:* Agency, Dorothea Oppenheimer.

Homecookin'. Drama. Two childhood friends, now adults, have a chance meeting in the subway. One is a college student and aspiring writer, the other a sergeant in the Marines home from Vietnam. *Cast:* 3 BM. extras. *Length:* 1 Act. *Prod:* NFT, New York, Apr. 1972. *Pubn: Homecookin',* Washington, D.C.: Howard Univ. Pr., 1974. *Lib Source:* HBA. *Perm:* Agency, Dorothea Oppenheimer.

Keys to the Kingdom. Domestic Drama. Conflict arises when it is discovered that young member of the family has inherited property left by grandmother. *Cast:* 6 BM, 6 BF. *Length:* 3 Acts. *Perm:* Agency, Dorothea Oppenheimer.

Mars: Monument to the Last Black Eunuch. (1973). Mythic Ritual. Concerns creativity and regeneration of the spirit. A middle-aged man, tired of his dull routine, finds solace in a Muslim newspaper article about black life on Mars. *Cast:* 5 BM, 5 BF. *Length:* 2 Acts. *Pubn: Homecookin',* Washington, D.C.: Howard Univ. Pr., 1974. *Lib Source:* HBA. *Perm:* Agency, Dorothea Oppenheimer.

Of Being Hit. Protest Drama. Portrait of a former boxing great who is now a janitor and dying of a kidney ailment. *Cast:* 3 BM. *Length:* 1 Act. *Pubn: Homecookin',*

Washington, D.C.: Howard Univ. Pr., 1974 *Lib Source:* HBA. *Perm:* Agency, Dorothea Oppenheimer.

Ornette. Mythic Ritual/Drama. Loosely based on the life/death of Charlie Parker (and jazz innovators of the 1940s in general) and the birth/awakening of avant-garde and spiritual jazz. *Cast:* 4 BM, 3 BF, 1 WM, 1 WF. *Length:* 3 Acts. *Prod:* Ira Aldridge Theatre, Howard University, Washington, D.C., 1972. *Perm:* Agency, Dorothea Oppenheimer.

Oursides. Drama. Black man and black woman reach a common bond of mutual understanding and love. *Cast:* 1 BM, 1 BF, 5-7 M & F. *Length:* 1 Act. *Prod:* NFT, New York, Apr. 1972. *Pubn: Homecookin',* Washington, D.C.: Howard Univ. Pr., 1974. *Lib Source:* HBA. *Perm:* Agency, Dorothea Oppenheimer.

GOSS, LINDA

Lil' Man. (1973). Children's Comedy. Little Man struggles with his street friends and his parents to gain independence and self-sufficiency. *Cast:* 15 M, 8 F. *Length:* 1 Act.

GOUGIS, R. A.

The Tenement. *Prod:* Experimental Black Actors Guild, Chicago, Ill., 1974.

GRAHAM, ARTHUR J.

The Last Shine. (1969). Drama. Caught between the humiliation of an impersonal technology and the necessity of survival, an old "shine boy" learns some startling truths about his black identity, which truths are in opposition to his sycophantic and altruistic existence in a white world of make-believe intimacy, of nonreciprocal respect and admiration, and of ostensible financial security. *Cast:* 2 BM, 6 WM. *Length:* 1 Act. *Pubn: The Last Shine,* San Diego: Black Book Production, 1969 *Lib Source:* HBA. *Perm:* Author.

The Nationals. (1968). Mythic Drama. In counterpoint to the arrogance of the white man's "errand into the wilderness"—pimps, prostitutes, and winos turn revolutionaries within the historical and psychological setting of the Watts rebellion and establish a new order based upon cultural awareness and positive self-esteem. *Cast:* 6 BM, 3 BF, 6 WM, 2 WF. *Length:* 3 Acts. *Pubn: The Nationals,* San Diego: Black Book Production, 1968. *Lib Source:* HBA. *Perm:* Author.

GRAHAM, BILLY

The Rape of the South African Man. Straight from the bloodshed and executions of the gestapo-like police and the apartheid regime in South Africa today comes Morris Abbaduumbee, a pleasant man and a pacifist, only to meet five angry women from Harlem. *Prod:* Reading, Frank Silvera Writers' Workshop, Studio Museum, New York, Jan. 1977.

Waiting for Joyce Miller. *Prod:* Reading, Frank Silvera Writers' Workshop, Harlem Performance Center, New York, May 1976.

GRAHAM, OTTIE

Holiday. Drama. Mulatto passes for white actress and gives up colored daughter, daughter learns truth and drowns herself in ocean—mother does likewise, taking the much needed "holiday." *Cast:* 2 BF, 1 mulatto F, extras. *Length:* 1 Act. *Pubn: Crisis* magazine, May 1923. *Lib Source:* SCHOM.

GRAHAM, SHIRLEY. *See* Du Bois, Shirley Graham

GRAHAM SOUTHERN SPECIALTY COMPANY

Sarah Jackson's Reception. Variety Musical. *Prod:* Metropolis Theatre, New York, Apr. 1899.

GRAHAM, WILLIAM H., and J. DOUGLAS COMER

Beyond the City. Musical Comedy. Community life is the theme as a semiprofessional basketball player's weak knee forces him to change professions and work in an out-of-the-way community. *Cast:* 6 BM, 1 BB, 1 BF, 1 WM, 1 WF. *Length:* 3 Acts. *Perm:* Author.

The Continuous Struggle, Part II. Domestic Drama. Problem of a family in which parents are both college graduates. Subtitled: *Stand by East High.* *Cast:* 3 M (2 teenaged twins), 2 F (1 teenager), extras. *Length:* Full Length. *Perm:* Author.

Mable Jones and the Devil. Musical Comedy. A domestic situation comedy about poor people. *Cast:* 7 BM (2 teenagers), 6 BF (3 teenagers), 1 WM, 1 WF. *Length:* 3 Acts. *Perm:* Author.

Outta This World. Musical Comedy. A poor black family, headed by a hypochondriac father, inherits money from a rich uncle in Texas and strikes oil. The consequences are that a son in rebellion becomes a hippie and the mother, in order to get rid of him, hires a black ex-astronaut to take her son "outta this world," which, with the help of a janitor at Cape Kennedy, is accomplished and the duo lands on Planet Soul. *Cast:* 6 BM, 1 BB, 3 BF, 2 WM, 9 dancers. *Length:* 3 Acts. *Prod:* East High School, Columbus, Ohio, Mar. 1970. *Perm:* Author.

Six Broken Wires. Drama. Six adults in graduate school at Kent State University are rehabilitation counselors and are going to rehabilitate the world—in the process of which two women become pregnant. *Cast:* 2 BM, 1 BF, 2 WM, 1 WF. *Perm:* Author.

GRAINGER, PORTER, and FREDDIE JOHNSON

Lucky Sambo. (1925). Musical Comedy. An oil stock swindle in which the tricksters are tricked. *Cast:* 9 BM, 8 BF, chorus. *Length:* 2 Acts. *Pubn: Best Plays of 1924-25*, ed. by Burns Mantle, New York: Dodd, 1925.

GRAINGER, PORTER, and LEIGH WHIPPER

De Board Meetin'. (1925). Comedy. Black pastor is removed from office for flirting with women, bootlegging, and misappropriating church funds. *Cast:* 6 BM, 1 BF, extras. *Length:* 1 Act. *Lib Source:* Typescript, SCHOM.

We's Risin'. (1927). Musical Comedy. The story of the rivalry of two "colored" fraternal organizations in a small town in Mississippi. *Cast:* 15-20 B M & F. *Length:* 2 Acts. *Lib Source:* Typescript, SCHOM.

GRANT, CLAUDE D.
Where Is the Sky. (1972).

GRANT, MICKI

I'm Laughin' but I Ain't Tickled. Musical Revue. Contains a number of poems from *A Rock against the Wind*, an anthology edited by Lindsay Patterson. *Length:* Full Length. *Prod:* Urban Arts Corps, New York, Spring 1976.

GRANT, MICKI, and VINNETTE CARROLL

Croesus and the Witch. Musical Comedy. While on a hunt in the wilderness, Croesus and his two friends confront the devilish witch Hecuba, managing to outwit her and return home with prized deerskins. *Cast:* 3 M, 1 F, chorus. *Length:* 1 Act. *Prod:* Urban Arts Corps, New York, Aug. 1971. *Perm:* Authors.

Don't Bother Me, I Can't Cope. Musical Revue. A celebration of the present-day black experience. *Cast:* B M & F. *Length:* 2 Acts. *Prod:* Lincoln Center Auditorium, New York, Oct. 1970; Edison Theatre, New York, Apr. 1971. *Perm:* Authors.

Old Judge Mose Is Dead. *Prod:* Urban Arts Corps, New York. *Perm:* Authors.

Step Lively, Boy. Dramatic Musical. Based on Irwin Shaw's *Bury the Dead.* A statement about the horror, futility, and absurdity of war. *Cast:* Large. *Length:* 1 Act. *Prod:* Urban Arts Corps, New York, Feb. 1973. *Perm:* Authors.

The Ups and Downs of Theophilus Maitland. Musical Comedy. A rich old man on the island of Jamaica woos and wins a beautiful young girl, and then discovers he may not be up for the ordeal after all. *Cast:* 5 BM, 5 BF, chorus. *Length:* 1 Act. *Prod:* Urban Arts Corps, New York, Mar. 1975. *Perm:* Authors.

GRANT, MICKI, and J. E. FRANKLIN

The Prodigal Sister. (1974). Musical Comedy. Music and lyrics by Micki Grant. Book and lyrics by J. E. Franklin. Jackie, a young black woman in conflict with parents, becomes pregnant and leaves home for the freedom of the big city, only to return home to find love and acceptance. *Cast:* 6 BM, 7 BF. *Length:* 8 Scenes. *Prod:* NFT, New York, July 1974. *Pubn:* SF; Music by Fiddleback Music Co., New York. *Lib Source:* HBA. *Perm:* Agency, SF.

GRANT, RICHARD, and WILL MERCER
The Southerners. (1904).

GRAY, ALFRED RUDOLPH, JR.

The Dean. (1974). Domestic Drama. Personal and professional crisis in the life of the black dean of discipline in an interracial high school. *Cast:* 2 BM, 3 BF, 4 BB, 1 BG, 7 WM, 2 WF. *Length:* 2 Acts. *Prod:* Hunter College Playwrights,

GRAY, ALFRED RUDOLPH, JR. *(Cont.)*

West Side YMCA, New York, n.d. *Lib Source:* Typescript, Hunter College Library. *Perm:* Author.

Eye for an Eye. Drama. Members of a street clique kidnap a white schoolteacher. *Cast:* 6 BM, 1 WM. *Length:* 1 Act. *Prod:* Hunter College, New York, 1972. *Lib Source:* Typescript, Hunter College Library. *Perm:* Author.

Lucy, My Rose Petal. Absurd Comedy. About a married couple, tied together after a robbery. *Cast:* 1 BM, 1 BF. *Length:* 1 Act. *Prod:* NLT, New York, n.d. *Perm:* Author.

Open School Night. Comedy. An absurdist interpretation of a mother and son meeting the teacher on open school night. *Cast:* 1 WM, 1 WF, 1 WM teenager. *Length:* 1 Act. *Prod:* Hunter College Playwrights Unit, New York, 1973. *Lib Source:* Typescript, Hunter College Library. *Perm:* Author.

A Package of Ball Point Pens. Domestic Drama. The marital problems between a bitter civil rights leader and his wife, daughter of a minister, are used to bring out the conflicting values of two generations of Blacks. *Cast:* 4 BM, 4 BF, 1 BB, 1 WM. *Length:* 3 Acts. *Perm:* Author.

Peeling to the Pain. Domestic Drama. An angry black father teaches his son at home in defiance of the public school system and social service hierarchy. *Cast:* 1 BM, 2 BF, 1 BB. *Length:* 1 Act. *Prod:* Company In Black, Clark Center for the Performing Arts, New York, 1971. *Perm:* Author.

The Revenge.

Tryout. Domestic Drama. Frustrated black ex-baseball pitcher tries to relive former glory through his sixteen-year-old son. *Cast:* 1 BM, 1 BF, 1 BB, 1 BG. *Length:* 1 Act. *Prod:* American Community Theatre, New York, 1959. *Perm:* Author.

The Visit. Domestic Drama. Contrast between the real relationship of a black middle class couple and the wife's fantasy life. *Cast:* 1 BM, 1 BF. *Length:* 1 Act. *Prod:* Hunter College Playwrights Unit, New York, 1972. *Lib Source:* Typescript, Hunter College Library. *Perm:* Author.

Young Faustus. Domestic Philosophic Drama. Interpretation of the Faust theme as it relates to the life of a young modern black playwright and his family. *Cast:* 4 BM, 3 BF, 1 WM. *Length:* 3 Acts. *Perm:* Author.

GRAY, ALFRED RUDOLPH, JR., and MAXWELL GLANVILLE

Dance to a Nosepicker's Drum. (1970). Domestic Drama. Play explores relationships of three generations of an urban black middle class family and the effect of a perceptive young boy on his separated parents. *Cast:* 5 BM, 4 BF. *Length:* 2 Acts. *Prod:* American Community Theatre, New York, 1970. *Perm:* Author.

GRAY, COBB

Seventh Heaven. Drama. Based upon the tensions and turmoils of the civil rights movement. *Length:* 3 Acts. *Prod:* D.C. Teacher's College, Washington, D.C., 1973.

GRAY, RUDY. See Gray, Alfred Rudolph, Jr.

GREAVES, DONALD

Kitsu Mensin. (1972). Verse Drama.

The Marriage. (1971). Domestic Drama. A husband who refuses to grow up fails to give his wife the companionship she needs and is also instrumental in his mother's marital problems. *Cast:* 4 BM, 2 BF. *Length:* 2 Acts. *Pubn: Black Drama*, ed. by Woodie King, Jr. and Ron Milner, New York: New Amer. Lib., 1972.

GREEN, DOROTHY TRAVIS

A Black Man's Plea. Didactic Drama. A middle class Black, caught in a riot in the ghetto, learns that he cannot count on his white friends. *Cast:* 5 BM, 3 BF, 1 WM. *Length:* 1 Act. *Pubn: The Light Book of Soul Scripts*, New York. Exposition, 1976. *Lib Source:* HBA.

It's a Crying Shame. Domestic Drama. Sonny gets in trouble with the law, leaves home, his mother dies, and he returns to repent. *Cast:* 5 BM, 5 BF, 1 WM, 3 BM teenagers, 2 BF teenagers. *Length:* 3 Acts. *Prod:* Del Paso Summer Theatre, n.p., July 1975. *Pubn: The Light Book of Soul Scripts*, New York: Exposition, 1976. *Lib Source:* HBA.

We're Gonna Make It. Domestic Comedy. Lou, after a very hard day fighting off bill collectors, realizes when her husband comes home that they're gonna make it. *Cast:* 1 BM, 1 BF. *Length:* 1 Act. *Pubn: The Light Book of Soul Scripts*, New York: Exposition, 1976. *Lib Source:* HBA.

GREEN, EDDIE, and DONALD HEYWOOD

Blackberries of 1932. Musical Revue. Cast included Jackie "Moms" Mabley, Dewey "Pigmeat" Markham, Tim Moore, and Mantan Moreland. *Length:* 2 Acts. *Prod:* Liberty Theatre, New York, Apr. 1932. *Pubn: Best Plays of 1931 - 32*, ed. by Burns Mantle, New York: Dodd, 1932.

GREEN, JOHNNY L.

Black on Black. Mystery. About the uncovering of a black traitor. *Cast:* 5 M & F. *Length:* 1 Act. *Pubn:* New York: Amuru Pr., 1976, possibly never published.

Night of Judgment. Drama. Four black men are judged by a hooded figure. *Cast:* 7 M & F. *Length:* 1 Act. *Pubn:* New York: Amuru Pr., 1976, possibly never published.

The Sign.

The Trials and Tribulations of Ma and Pa Williams. Domestic Drama. About a wife who places social status above the lives of her family. *Cast:* 8 M & F. *Length:* 3 Acts. *Pubn:* New York: Amuru Pr., 1976, possibly never published.

GREEN, MILTON

Mama. Drama. A tightly knit family, held together by love and respect, is shattered by an attractive, illegitimate half sister, who seduces the youngest son and blackmails him into helping her sell drugs.   *Cast:* 10 M, 5 F. *Prod:* Occidental College, Los Angeles, Calif., 1976.

GREENIDGE, GERTRUDE

Bricks. (1971). Protest Drama. A white couple and their teenaged daughter are forced from their car and sealed in the apartment of an inner city building for no apparent reason.   *Cast:* 1 BG, 1 WM, 2 WF, 3 BM (nonspeaking), 2 BF (nonspeaking). *Length:* 1 Act. *Perm:* Author.

Daughters. Play/Ballet. Two generations of daughters struggling to survive and love in a world of decreasing warmth. Subtitled: *Ma Lou's Daughters.*   *Prod:* Afro-American Total Theatre, Martinique Theatre, New York, Mar. 1975; Reading, Frank Silvera Writers' Workshop, New York, Oct. 1975.

The Game. Protest Drama. Deals with a racist white couple living in an isolated diner in the desert and their attempt to play a cruel hoax on a humble black couple who happen to seek shelter from a sandstorm. The racists get more than they bargained for.   *Cast:* 1 BM, 1 BF, 2 WM, 1 WF. *Length:* 1 Act. *Perm:* Author.

Laundry. (1972). Drama. A laundry room holds a terrifying moment of truth for a very self-sufficient young woman.   *Cast:* 1 BM, 2 BF. *Length:* 1 Act. *Perm:* Author.

Ma Lou's Daughters. (1974). Domestic Drama. A woman who has returned South for her mother's funeral finds she must deal with the daughter she has left in her mother's care.   *Cast:* 4 BF. *Length:* 1 Act. *Perm:* Author.

Red Rain. (1965). Protest Drama. The intense struggle for civil rights in a small southern town erupts in violence and results in many casualties, including a prominent white racist who is critically injured. His only hope is the one person with his rare blood type, who happens to be a black man.   *Cast:* 2 BM, 1 BF, 1 WM. *Length:* 1 Act. *Perm:* Author.

Snowman. (1972). Domestic Drama. The devotion of two brothers is put to the test when one is forced to make an unpleasant choice.   *Cast:* 2 BM, 2 BF. *Length:* 1 Act. *Prod:* Reading, Frank Silvera Writers' Workshop, Harlem Performance Center, New York, May 1976. *Perm:* Author.

GREENIDGE, GERTRUDE, HAZEL BRYANT, and WALTER MILES

Makin' It.   *Prod:* Afro-American Total Theatre, International House, New York, Jan. 1972.

GREENIDGE, GERTRUDE, and HOLLY HAMILTON

Something for Jamie. Musical. Jamie, a storefront preacher with a proclivity toward women, winds up in prison after one testifies falsely against him.   *Prod:* Franklin Thomas Little Theatre, New York, 1975.

GREENLEE, SAM

Blues for Little Prez. Musical Drama. The life and junkie-death of Little Prez, a Chicago jazz musician. *Cast:* 4 BM, 3 BF. *Length:* 3 Acts. *Prod:* Reading, Frank Silvera Writers' Workshop, Martinique Theatre, New York, Jan. 1976.

GREENLEE, SAM, and MELVIN CLAY

The Spook Who Sat by the Door. Melodrama. An adaptation of Sam Greenlee's novel of the same name about a black revolution that begins on Chicago's South Side. *Length:* Full Length.

GREENWOOD, FRANK

Burn, Baby, Burn.

Cry in the Night. *Pubn: Liberator*, Sept. 1963.

GREGGS, HERBERT D.

The Ballad of a Riverboat Town. (1968).

GRIMKE, ANGELINA

Rachel. (1916). Protest Drama. Rachel, a young woman, loves children more than herself, but when she realizes the painful future for black children in America, she refuses to marry. *Cast:* 2 BM, 3 BF, 7 BC. *Length:* 3 Acts. *Prod:* Myrtill Miner Normal School, Washington, D.C., Mar. 1916. *Pubn: Black Theater USA*, ed. by James V. Hatch and Ted Shine, New York: Free Pr., 1974. *Lib Source:* HBA.

GRIST, GARY

Grab a Painted Pony. *Length:* 2 Acts. *Prod:* Reading, Frank Silvera Writers' Workshop, Martinique Theatre, New York, Mar. 1975.

GUILLAUME, ROBERT

Montezuma's Revenge and Everybody Else's. *Prod:* Afro-American Total Theatre, International House, New York, Feb. 1970.

GUINN, DOROTHY C.

Out of the Dark. (1924). Pageant. History of Blacks from Africa to the present. *Cast:* 5 BM, 5 BF, extras (doubling). *Length:* 1 Act. *Pubn: Plays and Pageants from the Life of the Negro*, ed. by Willis Richardson, Washington, D.C.: Associated Publishers, 1930. *Lib Source:* HBA.

GUINTA, ALDO

In the Belly of the Beast. (1967). Tragedy. Retelling of the Greek story of Medea in a contemporary setting. *Cast:* 1 BF, 2 BC, 3 WM, 3 musicians. *Length:* 2 Acts.

GUNN, BILL

Black Picture Show. (1975). Drama. The destruction of a black artist who realizes too late that art in white America is just another form of politics. *Cast:* 3 BM, 2 BF, 3 WM, 1 WF. *Length:* 2 Acts. *Prod:* Vivian Beaumont Theatre, Lincoln Center, New York, Jan. 1975. *Pubn:* Berkeley: Reed, Cannon, Johnson Co., 1975. *Perm:* Agency, Ishmael Reed.

Johannas. Tragedy. Deals with the problems of a talented young black boy who attempts to come of age in racist America and finally must commit suicide as the ultimate form of protest. *Cast:* 1 BM, 1 BF, 1 BB, 2 BG, 2 WM. *Length:* 1 Act. *Prod:* Chelsea Theatre Center, New York, 1965–1966. *Pubn:* Drama Review, vol. 12, no. 4, Summer 1968.

Marcus in the High Grass. Melodrama. A youngster, born out of wedlock, searches for his father, not knowing that his "uncle" is really his father. *Cast:* 6 M, 4 F, 2 children. *Length:* Full Length. *Prod:* Greenwich Mews Theatre, New York, Nov. 1960. *Lib Source:* Typescript, PAL.

GUNNER, FRANCES

The Light of Women. (1930). Pageant. A history of black heroines of the past and present. *Cast:* 19 BF, extras (doubling). *Length:* 1 Act. *Pubn: Plays and Pageants from the Life of the Negro,* ed. by Willis Richardson, Washington, D.C.: Associated Publishers, 1930. *Lib Source:* HBA.

GUY, ROSA

Venetian Blinds. (1954). *Length:* 1 Act.

HAKEIN, ABDUL

The Occult Christmas. The play reveals the hidden mysteries of the Christ-mass. *Prod:* University of the Streets, New York, Dec. 1974.

HALL, PHYLLIS, DELORES McKNIGHT, and ELMO MORGAN

Two Wings. Performed as a continuing series for Brown University's Afro-American Studies Program and as a complement to a course, "Images and Myths of African People in New World Consciousness." *Length:* 6 Episodes. *Prod:* Brown University, Providence, R.I., Feb.–May 1975.

HALSEY, WILLIAM

Judgment. Satire. A black artist tried before a white court for advocating "violence," rises up to lead a massacre of the court. *Cast:* 1 BM, 4 WM, extras. *Length:* 1 Act. *Pubn: Black Dialogue,* vol. 4, no. 1, Spring 1969, New York: Black Dialogue Publications. *Lib Source:* HBA.

HAMILTON, HOLLY, and GERTRUDE GREENIDGE

Something for Jamie. Musical. Jamie, a storefront preacher with a proclivity toward women, winds up in prison after one testifies falsely against him. *Prod:* Franklin Thomas Little Theatre, New York, 1975.

HAMILTON, KILLU ANTHONY, RICHARD DEDEAUX, and OTIS SMITH

The Rising Sons—Wisdom and Knowledge. *Pubn:* Los Angeles: The Watts Prophets, 1973.

HAMILTON, ROLAND

Crack of the Whip. (c. 1930). A group of black vacuum cleaner salesmen are fired and are to be replaced by whites, but the black head salesman steals all the clients for his new company. *Cast:* 3 BM, 1 BF, 1 WM. *Length:* 1 Act. *Lib Source:* Typescript, SCHOM.

HANSBERRY, LORRAINE

The Drinking Gourd. (1969). Television Drama. Probes the nature of American slavery through the intensely personal drama of a black woman, a slavemaster, and their two families in the 1850s, culminating in the inevitability of increasing brutalization and black resistance on the plantation, and the Civil War in the nation. Its theme is the absolute contradiction between the human needs of all vis-á-vis the dictates of a dehumanizing society. *Cast:* 3 BM, 1 BB, 2 BF, 8 WM, 2 WB, 3 WF, 1 WG, extras. *Length:* 90 minutes. *Pubn: Les Blancs: The Collected Last Plays of Lorraine Hansberry,* ed. by Robert Nemiroff, New York: Random, 1972. *Lib Source:* HBA. *Perm:* Agency, William Morris.

Les Blancs. (1972). Drama. Set at a Christian mission in Africa on the verge of revolution, *Les Blancs* ("the whites") is an account of the making of a black revolutionary in the inevitable hour of reckoning—when oppressed and oppressor, observer and participant, guilty and innocent alike, can no longer escape the historical imperatives of black liberation and willingly, or otherwise, must choose. *Cast:* 12 BM, 1 BB, 1 BF, 5 WM, 2 WF. *Length:* 3 Acts. *Prod:* Longacre Theatre, New York, Oct. 1970. *Pubn: Les Blancs: The Collected Last Plays of Lorraine Hansberry,* ed. by Robert Nemiroff, New York: Random, 1972. *Lib Source:* HBA. *Perm:* Agency, SF.

Raisin. See Nemiroff, Robert* and Charlotte Zaltzberg*

A Raisin in the Sun. (1958). Domestic Drama. Black identity, pride, and the quest for liberation; assimilation or resistance to the values of the dominant white society; strength and closeness of the black family; the links between black America and black Africa—these are the major themes in this story of a working-class ghetto family that deals with the conflicting dreams and methods of generations, the identity crisis of the son, the daughter's assertion of liberated womanhood, the mother's heroic attempt to hold all together, and, finally, the family's joint refusal to sacrifice human dignity to the demands of a money-driven racist society. *Cast:* 7 BM, 1 BB, 3 BF, 1 WM. *Length:* 3 Acts. *Prod:* Ethel Barrymore Theatre, New York, Mar. 1959. *Pubn:* New York: Random, 1959; Recording, original cast, Caedmon Records. *Lib Source:* HBA. *Perm:* Agency, SF.

The Sign in Sidney Brustein's Window. (1965). Drama. Set against the artistic and intellectual shenanigans of a stormy political campaign in New York's Greenwich Village, the story of a disenchanted egghead and his actress wife and of their unorthodox quest for meaningful lives in an age of corruption,

HANSBERRY, LORRAINE *(Cont.)*

alienation, and cynicism; the resolution turns on recognition of the necessity for individual commitment and activism, no matter what the odds; an important sub-theme is the poisonous effect of racism upon personal and social relationships. *Cast:* 1 (or 2) BM, 4 (or 5) WM, 3 WF. *Length:* 3 Acts. *Prod:* Longacre Theatre, New York, Oct. 1965. *Pubn:* New York: Random, 1965. *Lib Source:* HBA. *Perm:* Agency, SF.

To Be Young, Gifted and Black. (1969). Drama. Woven together from the diaries, journals, letters, speeches, and scenes from Lorraine Hansberry's own works. The life story of the playwright is both the chronicle of a woman and an artist in interaction with the demands of art, of inner need, and of the times that shaped her, and the portrait of a rebel who celebrated, inseparably, the black experience and the human spirit; all the members of the cast portray not only the people in the playwright's life and the characters she created, but Ms. Hansberry herself. Subtitled: *A Portrait of Lorraine Hansberry in Her Own Words.* *Cast:* 3 BF, 1 WM, 2 WF, extras. *Length:* 2 Acts. *Prod:* Cherry Lane Theatre, New York, Jan. 1969. *Pubn:* SF; Recording, original cast, Caedmon Records. *Lib Source:* HBA. *Perm:* Agency, SF.

What Use Are Flowers. (1969). Fantasy. The fable of an embittered hermit who returns to civilization to find only a group of wild children, the sole survivors of atomic holocaust; as the one remaining link between the stored knowledge of mankind and the future, if there is to be one, he finds himself, against his will, in a race against time to impart whatever he can of everything, from Shakespeare and Einstein to music, sex, the concept of the wheel, and what flowers are used for. *Cast:* 1 M, 7 or 8 children (perhaps experimentally, modern dancers). *Length:* 1 Act. *Pubn: Les Blancs: The Collected Last Plays of Lorraine Hansberry,* ed. by Robert Nemiroff, New York: Random, 1972. *Lib Source:* HBA. *Perm:* Agency, William Morris.

HANSFORD, EDWIN

His Honor, the Barber. Musical Comedy. "Comic S. H. Dudley as Raspberry Snow, fell asleep on the White House grounds and dreamed of being appointed barber to the President."—Fannin Belcher. *Prod:* May 1911.

HARRIS, BILL

No Use Cryin'. Domestic Drama. Family is able to come together after an internal crisis threatens to destroy it. *Cast:* 4 BM, 1 BB, 2 BF. *Length:* 3 Acts. *Prod:* 1969. *Perm:* Author.

The Pimp's Pimp. (1974). Comedy. A militant turns the table on a pimp. *Cast:* 3 BM, 2 BF. *Length:* 1 Act. *Perm:* Author.

Warn the Wicked. Domestic Drama. Black family, divided by political and ideological beliefs, tries to determine the true role of an assassinated militant family member. *Cast:* 3 BM, 2 BF. *Length:* Full Length. *Prod:* Experimental Black Actor's Guild, Chicago, Ill., 1974. *Perm:* Author.

What Goes Around. (1975). Domestic Drama. Couple try to find themselves and each other, despite alien forces (societal and psychological) that try to separate them. *Cast:* 12 BM, 4 BF, extras. *Length:* Full Length. *Perm:* Author.

HARRIS, CLARENCE

The Trip. Ritual. Black man uses jungle tactics to kill a white policeman. *Cast:* 3 BM, 1 BF, 5 WM. *Length:* 1 Act. *Pubn: Black Voices from Prison*, ed. by Ethridge Knight, New York: Pathfinder Pr., 1970. *Lib Source:* SCHOM.

HARRIS, HELEN WEBB

Genefred—The Daughter of L'Ouverture. (1935). Historical Children's Play. General L'Ouverture must choose between saving his daughter's fiancé or having him shot for disobeying orders. *Cast:* 6 BM, 1 BF, extras. *Length:* 1 Act. *Pubn: Negro History in Thirteen Plays*, ed. by Willis Richardson and May Miller, Washington, D.C.: Associated Publishers, 1935. *Lib Source:* NYPL.

HARRIS, NEIL

Blues Changes.

Cop and Blow. Melodrama. White detectives try to hustle black bartender to the chagrin of fellow black detectives. *Cast:* 8 BM, 2 BF, 4 WM. *Length:* 1 Act. *Prod:* Public Theatre, New York Shakespeare Festival, N.Y., Feb. 1972. *Pubn: Scripts*, vol. 1, no. 7, May 1972. *Lib Source:* HBA. *Perm:* Agency, NASABA.

Player's Inn. *Cast:* 10 BM, 1 BF. *Length:* 1 Act. *Prod:* Public Theatre, New York Shakespeare Festival, N.Y., Feb. 1972.

The Portrait. *Prod:* New Lafayette Workshop, New York, 1971.

So Nice They Named It Twice. *Prod:* Reading, Frank Silvera Writers' Workshop, Martinique Theatre, New York, Mar. 1975.

The Vampire. (1971). Drama. Billie, the vampire junkie, emerges from his coffin, hooks and kills a young boy, and climbs back into his box. *Cast:* 5 BM, 5 BF, extras. *Length:* 3 Acts. *Perm:* Agency, NASABA.

Yernom.

HARRIS, NEIL, and MIGUEL PIÑERO

Straight from the Ghetto. Musical Revue. Songs, sketches, poems, and mimes about Harlem street life. *Cast:* 5 BM, 2 BF, musicians. *Length:* Full Length. *Prod:* The Family, a Street Theatre, New York, Summer 1976; Theater for the New City, New York, Jan. 1977.

HARRIS, NORMAN

None of Us Are Brave. *Prod:* Franklin Thomas Repertory Theatre, New York, Feb. 1975.

HARRIS, PAUL E.

The Legend of Stacker Lee. Musical Comedy. Traditional character, Stacker Lee, a rambling, gambling man, reforms to become a good husband. *Cast:* 6 BM, 5 BF, 2 WM. *Length:* 2 Acts.

HARRIS, ROSSIE LEE

The Experiment. Historical Drama. *Prod:* Rites and Reasons, Brown University, Providence, R.I., 1974.

HARRIS, TED

Playstreet. Drama. A couple remaining in an abandoned building experience the dissolution of reality and the horrifying repetition of their unfulfilled marriage. *Cast:* 1 BM, 1 BF. *Length:* 1 Act.

Sandcastles and Dreams. Drama. Two middle-aged women on vacation sit in their beach cottages and confront the problems of loneliness, loss of youth, and unfulfilled sexual fantasies. *Cast:* 1 M, 2 F. *Length:* 1 Act.

HARRIS, TOM

Always with Love or *Mother's Little Helper.* Comedy. Faithful servant, Annie manages the deaths of her employer's family to enable her husband and son to realize their dreams of a career. *Cast:* 1 BM, 1 BB, 1 BF, 4 WM, 2 WF. *Length:* 2 Acts. *Pubn: New American Plays*, ed. by William Hoffman, vol. 3, New York: Hill & Wang, 1969. *Lib Source:* HBA.

The A Number One Family. (1958). *Length:* 1 Act.

Beverly Hills Olympics. (1964).

City beneath the Skin. (1961).

Cleaning Day. (1969). *Length:* 1 Act.

Daddy Hugs and Kisses. (1963). *Length:* 1 Act.

The Dark Years. (1968). *Length:* 1 Act.

The Death of Daddy Hugs and Kisses. (1963).

Divorce Negro Style. (1968).

Fall of Iron Horse. (1959).

The Golden Spear. (1969). *Length:* 1 Act.

Moving Day. (1969). *Length:* 1 Act.

Pray for Daniel Adams. (1958). *Length:* 1 Act.

The Relic. (1967).

Shopping Day. (1969). *Length:* 1 Act.

Who Killed Sweetie. (1967).

Woman in the House. (1958). *Length:* 1 Act.

HARRISON, PAUL CARTER

Brer Soul. (1970).

The Experimental Leader. Expressionistic Drama. An impotent black leader confronts an integrationist couple, a black man and white woman, who have come to him with an experiment designed to ease racial tensions. *Cast:* 2 BM, 1 WF. *Length:* 1 Act. *Pubn: Podium Magazine*, Amsterdam, Holland, 1965. *Perm:* Agency, Ronald Hobbs.

Folly 4 Two. Expressionistic Drama. An African meets a colonial Englishman on the desert of Time and liberates himself in a game of folly. *Cast:* 1 BM, 1 WM.

Length: 1 Act. *Pubn: Podium Magazine*, Amsterdam, Holland, 1967. *Perm:* Agency, Ronald Hobbs.

The Great MacDaddy. (1973). Mythic Drama. Drama about the world odyssey of an indolent young black man of means and the forces he encounters that focus his life toward responsibility. *Cast:* 8-10 BM, 5-7 BF, musicians.*Length:* Full Length. *Prod:* Sacramento State College, Calif., May 1972; NEC, New York, Feb. 1974. *Pubn: Kuntu Drama*, ed. by Paul Carter Harrison, New York: Grove, 1974. *Lib Source:* HBA. *Perm:* Agency, Ronald Hobbs.

Pavane for a Dead-Pan Minstrel. Expressionistic Drama with Music. A black man in white mask and a white man in black mask set out to seduce a white girl in a cafe; the play ends in a deadly *pas du trois*. *Cast:* 1 BM, 1 WM, 1 WF.*Length:* 1 Act. *Pubn: Podium Magazine*, Amsterdam, Holland, 1966. *Perm:* Agency, Ronald Hobbs.

Pawns. (1966). Expressionistic Drama. An old Jew in Germany manipulates two puppets—a black enlisted soldier and a white general serving in Vietnam—who engage in a game of chess that determines the fate of the Jew, who awaits the arrival of the Gestapo. *Cast:* 1 BM, 2 WM.*Length:* 1 Act.*Perm:* Agency, Ronald Hobbs.

The Postclerks. (1961). Existential Drama. Three postal clerks bound to the rhythms of sorting out mail while hoping to be relieved by the mythic, god-like force of Time. *Cast:* 1 young M, 1 middle-aged BM, 1 old M. *Length:* 1 Act. *Perm:* Agency, Ronald Hobbs.

Tabernacle. Ritualistic Spectacle. Questioned here is whether one is guilty of a crime because of the crime or because of the color of skin; a spectacle illuminating the forces that create the demise of two black youths in Harlem. *Cast:* 15-18 BM, 5 musicians. *Length:* 2 Acts. *Prod:* Sacramento State College, Calif., 1972. *Pubn: New Black Playwrights*, ed. by William Couch, Jr., New York: Avon, 1970. *Lib Source:* HBA. *Perm:* Agency, Ronald Hobbs.

Top Hat. Expressionistic Drama with Music. A musician plays in his room while the image of a speechless junkie encounters an elegant black/white woman in a park, who takes him on a sexual odyssey (in fantasy) around the world. *Cast:* 1 BM, 1 B or WF, 1 BM musician. *Length:* 1 Act. *Prod:* Buffalo University, N.Y., Summer 1965. *Perm:* Agency, Ronald Hobbs.

HARVEY, SHIRLEY

Where Is the Pride, Where Is the Joy. *Prod:* Experimental Black Actor's Guild, Chicago, Ill., 1974.

HAWKINS, THEODORE W.

Chicago, Chicago. Domestic Drama. A black family is destroyed by dope; only the blind son survives. *Cast:* 8 BM, 5 BF. *Length:* 4 Acts.

HAYDEN, ROBERT E.

Go Down Moses.

HAZZARD, ALVIRA

Little Heads.   *Length:* 1 Act. *Pubn: Saturday Evening Quill,* Apr. 1929.

Mother Liked It.   *Length:* 1 Act. *Pubn: Saturday Evening Quill,* Apr. 1928.

HEMSLEY, JEROLINE

Wade in de Water.   *Length:* 3 Acts. *Prod:* New Negro Theatre, Saunders Trade School, Yonkers, N.Y., Mar. 1931.

HERNANDEZ, JUANO, and TED KOEHLER*

Minnie the Moocher.   *Length:* Full Length. *Lib Source:* FTP, GMU.

HERNDON, ALICE, and ALVIN CHILDRESS

Hell's Alley. Drama. "The scene takes place in an alley, in which a gangster carries on his trade of swindling and victimizing unsuspecting persons who pass."—Frederick Bond.   *Prod:* Lafayette Players, New York, 1930.

HERSHEY, VICTORIA

Heritage House. Drama. A black slice-of-life drama about Christmas Eve in a welfare hotel.   *Cast:* 1 BM, 1 BF, 1 WF, 2 children. *Prod:* Writers in Residence, Great Neck, N.Y., n.d. *Perm:* Author.

HEYWOOD, DONALD

Black Rhythm. Musical Comedy. "An amateur night in Harlem detached and moved onto Broadway with some sort of loose-joined plot to hold the various acts together."—*Best Plays of 1936-37.*   *Cast:* 14 BM, 7 BF. *Length:* 2 Acts. *Prod:* Comedy Theatre, New York, Dec. 1936. *Pubn: Best Plays of 1936-37,* ed. by Burns Mantle, New York: Dodd, 1937.

How Come Lawd? Folk Drama. Big Boy, an Alabama cotton picker, confuses the union organizer's work with that of the Lord, which leads to tragedy. *Cast:* 10 BM, 3 BF. *Length:* 3 Acts. *Prod:* Forty-ninth Street Theatre, New York, Sept. 1937. *Pubn: Best Plays of 1937-38,* ed. by Burns Mantle, New York: Dodd, 1938.

HEYWOOD, DONALD, and EDDIE GREEN

Blackberries of 1932. Musical Revue. Cast included Jackie "Moms" Mabley, Dewey "Pigmeat" Markham, Tim Moore, and Mantan Moreland.   *Length:* 2 Acts. *Prod:* Liberty Theatre, New York, Apr. 1932. *Pubn: Best Plays of 1931-32,* ed. by Burns Mantle, New York: Dodd, 1932.

HEYWOOD, DONALD, J. HOMER TUTT, and SALEM WHITNEY

Jim Crow. Musical Drama.

HEZEKIAH, LLOYD

The Breast of Heaven. (1967). Historical Drama. Mt. Pelee volcano erupts on Martinique, killing nearly everyone but René, who survives to tell in flashback the story of his life and consequent imprisonment. *Cast:* 4 BM, 2 RF. *Length:* 1 Act.

HICKS, RALPH

From Where Confusion Comes. Domestic Drama. A black militant battles with his cousin in his attempts to conceal his actions and beliefs from his drunken father, a dying old man who has colored his life with delusions of wealth and public standing in the white world. *Cast:* 3 BM, 3 BF, 1 WM. *Length:* 3 Acts. *Prod:* Black Workshop Theatre Group, University of Missouri, Columbia, 1969. *Perm:* Author.

The Last Act of a Revolutionary Play. Drama. The principle leaders of a mythical black revolution struggle with decisions they must make regarding the future of their fallen people and their defeated cause. *Cast:* 3 BM, 2 BF. *Length:* 1 Act. *Prod:* Black Workshop Theatre Group, University of Missouri, Columbia, 1970. *Perm:* Author.

The Revolution?—Is It Time? (1972). Drama. Abstract drama of blood black family consisting of Mama, Pimp, Whore, Junkie, Poet, and two opposing revolutionaries struggling to free themselves from a literal "cage," where they are tormented by "colored" trainers, who in turn are controlled by "Great White Mama-Daddy." *Cast:* 6 BM, 4 BF. *Perm:* Author.

Whatever Happens to All Those Motherless Children? (1971). Domestic Drama. Urban black family of brothers and sisters of widely varying ages copes with the problem of battling against both an antagonistic world and the generation differences. *Cast:* 6 BM, 6 BF. *Length:* 3 Acts. *Perm:* Author.

When Am I Gonna Know My Name. (1969). Domestic Drama. Upper middle class black father tyrannically attempts to control the destinies of his three diverse sons. *Cast:* 10 BM, 6 BF, 2 WM. *Length:* 3 Acts. *Perm:* Author.

HIGHTOWER, ROBERT

The Wait. *Prod:* Reading, Frank Silvera Writers' Workshop, Martinique Theatre, New York, Apr. 1975.

HILL, ABRAM

Hell's Half Acre. (c. 1938). Historical Drama. The South some time after the Civil War, amidst lynchings and general mistreatment by whites. Blacks try to combat the injustices perpetrated by the whites. *Cast:* 5 BM, 6 BF, 9 WM, 3 WF, extras. *Length:* 3 Acts. *Lib Source:* Typescript, SCHOM.

So Shall You Reap. (c. 1931). Trench diggers of Suffolk County, Long Island, and their problems, ranging from the nonsupport of a bastard son to the paying of "protection" money. *Cast:* 13 M, 2 F, extras. *Length:* 3 Acts. *Lib Source:* Typescript, SCHOM.

Striver's Row. (1938). Domestic Comedy. Satire on bourgeoisie. The Van Strivers attempt to live beyond their means and to place an unwilling daughter in high society. *Cast:* 7 BM, 10 BF. *Length:* 3 Acts. *Prod:* ANT, New York, 1940; NHT, New York, Oct. 1974.

HILL, ABRAM (*Cont.*)

Walk Hard. (1944). Drama. Young black fighter won't compromise with racism for the corrupt fight game. *Cast:* 5 BM, 2 BF, 9 WM, 3 WF. *Length:* 3 Acts. *Prod:* ANT, New York, Dec. 1944. *Pubn: Black Theater USA*, ed. by James V. Hatch and Ted Shine, New York: Free Pr., 1974. *Lib Source:* HBA.

HILL, ABRAM, and JOHN D. SILVERA

Liberty Deferred. (1936). Drama. Chronicle of the Negro, Federal Theatre epic style. *Cast:* Large B & W M. *Length:* Full Length. *Lib Source:* Typescript, PAL; GMU and FTP.

HILL, ALBERTA

Sunshine, Moonbeam. Fantasy. An adaptation of the folktale about the frog who became a prince. *Prod:* NEC Season-within-a-Season, New York, Spring 1976.

HILL, ERROL

Man Better Man. (1960). Folk Play. This play was inspired by the legends and traditions that have grown around the Island of Trinidad's stick-playing game, the calinda. *Cast:* 12 M, 5 W. *Length:* 3 Acts. *Prod:* Yale University, New Haven, Conn., 1960. *Pubn: The Yale School of Drama Presents*, ed. by John Gassner, New York: Dutton, 1964. *Lib Source:* PAL. *Perm:* Author.

The Ping-Pong. Comedy/Drama. A play about a steel band and a theft just before a big contest. *Cast:* 7 M. *Length:* 1 Act. *Prod:* BBC, London, Eng., Oct. 1950. *Pubn: The Ping-Pong: A Backyard Comedy-Drama in One Act*, Jamaica: UCWI Extra-mural Dept., 1958. *Lib Source:* HBA.

Strictly Matrimony. (1971). Domestic Play. Things go awry when common-law couple are duped into marriage. *Cast:* 3 BM, 2 BF. *Length:* 1 Act. *Prod:* Yale University, New Haven, Conn., 1960. *Pubn: Black Drama Anthology*, ed. by Woodie King, Jr. and Ron Milner, New York: New Amer. Lib., 1972. *Lib Source:* HBA. *Perm:* Agency, Lucy Kroll.

Wey-Wey. Comedy. A Caribbean play about a quaint form of illegal lottery involving dreams and superstitions. *Cast:* 8 M, 2 F. *Length:* 1 Act. *Prod:* Trinidad, 1957. *Pubn: Wey-Wey: A Play in One Act*, Jamaica: UCWI Extra-mural Dept., 1958. *Lib Source:* HBA.

HILL, J. LEUBRIE, and WILLIAM LeBARON

Hello Paris. Musical. *Prod:* 1911. *Pubn: Best Plays of 1909-1912*, ed. by Burns Mantle and Garrison Sherwood, reprint of 1933 ed., Books for Libraries, Inc.

HILL, J. LEUBRIE, and ALEX ROGERS

Darktown Follies. Musical Revue. According to Fannin Belcher the 1916 show, *My Friend from Kentucky (Dixie)*, was a reworking of this piece. *Prod:* Lafayette Theatre, New York, 1913.

My Friend from Kentucky (Dixie). See Darktown Follies.

HILL, LESLIE P.

Jethro. Pageant.

Toussaint L'Ouverture. Historical Drama. About the black revolution of Haiti led by Toussaint L'Ouverture. *Cast:* Many B & W and mulatto M & F. *Prod:* Boston, Mass., 1928. *Lib Source:* Typescript, SCHOM.

HILL, MARS

The Buzzards.

The Cage.

Eclipse. *Cast:* 5 BM, 3 BF. *Length:* 3 Acts. *Prod:* Staged reading, Frank Silvera Writers' Workshop, New York, Sept. 1974; Arbor Hill Community Center, Albany, N.Y., Dec. 1974.

First in War.

First Movement. Didactic Ritual. Articulated here is the fact that liberation is the natural state of man. Various city dwellers relate their predicaments in America and the denouement finds the *Nguzo Saba* (7 principles) as being one possible panacea. *Cast:* 10-15 B. *Length:* 16 Movements. *Lib Source:* Typescript, SCHOM. *Perm:* Author.

House and Field. Drama. "Field Hand" confronts "House Nigger" and wins an ideological struggle. *Cast:* 2 BM, chorus. *Length:* 1 Act. *Perm:* Author.

The Huzzy. Drama. Two older sisters gossip and disapprove as man and girl meet and neck on the bus from Chicago. *Cast:* 1 BM, 3 BF. *Length:* 1 Act. *Prod:* Reading, Frank Silvera Writers' Workshop, Harlem Performance Center, New York, Jan. 1977. *Perm:* Author.

Malice in Wonderland. Domestic Drama. Melisa, an alcoholic sister, goes crazy and lets family secrets out of the closet, causing a family crisis. *Cast:* 5 BM, 5 BF, 2 WM. *Length:* 2 Acts. *Perm:* Author.

The Man in the Family. Domestic Comedy. Cleophis returns home with his wife, who is mistaken for his girl friend by Lulu, Cleophis' ersatz mother, the "man" of the family. *Cast:* 2 BM, 2 BF. *Length:* 1 Act. *Perm:* Author.

Occupation.

Peck.

The Street Walkers. In this play, the hustler is hustled and has a serious confrontation with his conscience. Subtitled: *From the Black Experience.* *Cast:* 4 BM, 1 BF, extras. *Length:* 1 Act. *Lib Source:* Typescript, SCHOM. *Perm:* Author.

To Have and to Have Not.

Two Ten.

A Very Special Occasion.

The Visitors.

You Ain't Got No Place to Put Yo Snow.

HILL, PHILLIP

The Fruits of Poverty. (1973). Drama. Young, pregnant black girl is duped into believing that her black, hustler, "mainliner" man is different, but he isn't. *Cast:* 3 BM, 4 BF, extras. *Length:* 2 Acts. *Lib Source:* Typescript, SCHOM.

HILL, ROBERT KYA

The Trial of Secundus Generation Blackman versus Hannah and William A. Blackman. Drama. A trial that brings to bear several levels of injustice, ranging from racism to parental cowardice. *Cast:* 5 BM, 4 BF, 5 WM, 4 extras. *Length:* 3 Acts.

HIRSCH, CHARLOTTE TELLER

Hagar & Ishmael. A vignette about the biblical characters Hagar and Ishmael. *Cast:* 1 BM, 1 BF. *Length:* 1 Act. *Pubn: Crisis* magazine, May 1913.

HOGAN, ERNEST, and ALLAN DUNN

A Country Coon. (1900). Musical Farce. *Length:* 3 Acts.

HOGAN, ERNEST, and JOE JORDAN

Rufus Rastus. Musical Revue. *Prod:* n.p., 1905.

HOLDER, LAURENCE

The Journey. (1972). A revolution planned and staged by elite, black, middle class America. *Cast:* 9 BM, 3 BF, 4 WM, 1 WF. *Length:* 3 Acts. *Lib Source:* Typescript, SCHOM. *Perm:* Author.

Open. A bizarre meeting of bizarre people at the Agatha Johnson Memorial Sanatorium. The group includes a playwright, a teacher, and a minister. *Cast:* 7 BM, 3 BF. *Length:* 2 Acts. *Lib Source:* Typescript, SCHOM. *Perm:* Author.

Street Corners. (1972). A corner inhabited by "dead" characters that include transvestites, an interracial "holdup" team, and an ego-tripping, black photographer. *Cast:* 8 BM, 2 BF, 2 WM, 1 WF. *Length:* 3 Acts. *Lib Source:* Typescript, SCHOM. *Perm:* Author.

HOLIFIELD, HAROLD

Cow in the Apartment. (c. 1940).

J. Toth. (1951).

HOLMAN, M. CARL

The Baptizing.

HOOKS, BARNETT ULYSES, II

Judgment Day. Drama. About a white male who kills three black children and their mother, father, and himself, after which he is judged in heaven by an all-black jury of angels and a black God, and is sentenced to be reincarnated as a black man in America during the period of slavery. *Cast:* 9 BM, 7 BF, 2 WM, 1 WF. *Length:* 1 Act. *Prod:* Black Liberated Art Center, Oklahoma City, Aug. 1975. *Perm:* Agency, Tyrone E. Wilkerson.

Who Are You? Drama. An elderly shoeshine-parlor owner arrives at work where a black pharoah appears who forces him to review his past and the past of the black nation from slavery on, to instill in him, before his death, the true knowledge of black people. *Cast:* Large. *Length:* 1 Act. *Perm:* Agency, Tyrone E. Wilkerson.

Why Black Men Die Younger. Black men, using heroin, are shot and killed in a drug robbery. *Cast:* 6 BM. *Length:* 1 Act. *Prod:* Oklahoma University, Oklahoma City, Mar. 1975. *Perm:* Agency, Tyrone E. Wilkerson.

HOPKINS, PAULINE ELIZABETH

One Scene from the Drama of Early Days. "A dramatization of the biblical story of Daniel in the Lion's Den."—Ann Allen Shockley, *Phylon*, vol. 33, no. 1, Spring 1972.

Peculiar Sam or *The Underground Railroad. See Slaves' Escape* or *The Underground Railroad.*

Slaves' Escape or *The Underground Railroad.* Historical Musical Drama. "The drama relates the story of how the underground railroad assisted slaves in their flight to freedom."—Ann Allen Shockley, *Phylon*, vol. 33, no. 1, Spring 1972. The play was later revised and entitled *Peculiar Sam* or *The Underground Railroad. Length:* 4 Acts. *Prod:* Hopkins Colored Troubadours, Oakland Garden, Boston, Mass.. July 1880.

HOUGHLY, YOUNG

Place for the Manchild. (1972).

HOWARD, GARLAND

Change Your Luck. Musical Comedy. Music by J. C. Jackson. An undertaker fills his formaldehyde cans with liquor and does a very good bootleg business. *Cast:* 21 BM, 14 BF. *Length:* 2 Acts. *Prod:* George M. Cohan Theatre, New York, June 1930. *Pubn: Best Plays of 1929-30*, ed. by Burns Mantle, New York: Dodd, 1930.

HOWARD, ROBERT

The Death of Semele. (1966). Tragedy. Adaptation and amalgamation of several of Euripides' plays; questions the relationship between gods and men, or those in power and those who are powerless. *Cast:* 4 BM, 5 BF, 2 WM, 2 WF. *Length:* 2 Acts.

HOWARD, SALLIE

The Jackal. (c. 1950).

HUDSON, EARNEST L.

Rebellion.   *Prod:* Festival Black Company, Wayne State University, Detroit, Mich., July 1971.

HUDSON, FRED

If We Must Die.   *Prod:* B & B Experimental Theatre, Inc., San Francisco, Calif., 1975.

HUDSON, WADE

Sam Carter Belongs Here. Drama.

HUFFMAN, EUGENE HENRY

Hoo-dooed. Subtitled: *The Victory.*   *Prod:* Los Angeles Philharmonic Auditorium, Calif., Apr. 1932.

The Imposter in the Red Mausoleum.

The Last Chord.

St. Peter Is Out.

Unto Us a Child Is Born.

HUGHES, LANGSTON

Adam and Eve and the Apple. Opera.   *Length:* 1 Act. *Lib Source:* Typescript, YL.

The American Negro Speaks. Opera. Contributions possibly made by Clarence Muse and Joe Trent.   *Cast:* 1 BM.

Angelo Herndon Jones. (1936). Political Play. Concerns the plight of the poor and their need for a leader who will lead them in their fight against oppression in which black and white will unite.   *Cast:* 4 BM, 4 BF, 2 WM, extras. *Length:* 1 Act. *Lib Source:* Typescript, YL.

At the Jazz Ball. A collaboration with Abby Mann and Robert Fabian. Lyrics by Langston Hughes.   *Lib Source:* YL.

The Ballad of the Brown King. (1961). Christmas Song Play. Music by Margaret Bonds.   *Length:* 2 Acts. *Prod:* East Side Development, New York.

The Ballot and Me. (1956). Historical Pageant. The Negro's past in suffrage, with historical vignettes about the black vote and the call for black participation in the election process. The play ends with the introduction of current election candidates.   *Cast:* 26 BM, 1 BF. *Length:* 1 Act. *Lib Source:* Typescript, YL.

The Barrier. Historical Opera. Music by Jan Meyerowitz. Version of *Mulatto*, by the same playwright.   *Length:* 3 Acts. *Prod:* Columbia University Opera Workshop, New York, Jan. 1950. *Lib Source:* Typescript, YL; Harold Ober playscript, SCHOM.

Black Nativity. Gospel Pageant. A sermon on the Christmas story, narrated with words, song, mime, and dance.   *Length:* 2 Acts. *Prod:* Forty-first Street Theatre, New York, 1961. *Lib Source:* Harold Ober playscript, SCHOM.

Booker T. Washington in Atlanta. Radio Play.   *Prod:* 1945. *Pubn: Radio Drama in Action*, ed. by Erik Barnouw, New York: Farrar, 1945.

Carmelita and the Cockatoo. (1966). Children's Play. Carmelita admires the cockatoo, begs him for his feathers, then spurns him when she gets them. *Cast:* 1 BM, 1 BF. *Length:* 1 Act. *Lib Source:* Typescript, YL.

Christmas with Christ. (1962).   *Lib Source:* YL.

Cocko' de World. (1931). Musical Comedy. Adapted from a play by Kaj Gynt, with lyrics by Duke Ellington. The play concerns the wanderings of a black sailor from New Orleans who travels through the Caribbean to Paris, where his encounters with white culture, racism, and the bizarre force him to return home again. *Cast:* Large. *Length:* 3 Acts. *Lib Source:* Manuscript, possibly incomplete, YL.

De Organizer. (1939–1941). Blues Opera. Music by James P. Johnson. Play deals with an evening among poor black farmers who are waiting for the organizer to come and finalize their union. *Length:* 1 Act. *Prod:* Possibly Harlem Suitcase Theatre, New York, 1939. *Lib Source:* Harold Ober playscript, SCHOM.

Don't You Want to Be Free? (1938). Historical Pageant. The history of Afro-Americans in dialogue, poetry, and song. Each version brings the story up-to-date; revised 1944, 1946, 1949, 1952, 1960, 1963.   *Cast:* 9 BM, 6 BF, 2 WM, voices, chorus, walk-ons, extras (1938 version). *Prod:* Harlem Suitcase Theatre, New York, 1937. *Pubn: One Act Play Magazine* II, Oct. 1938; *Black Theater USA*, ed. by James V. Hatch and Ted Shine, New York: Free Pr., 1974. *Lib Source:* Harold Ober playscript, SCHOM.; HBA.

Em-Fuehrer Jones. (1938). Parody. A parody of Eugene O'Neill's *Emperor Jones.* Jones is a white resembling Hitler.   *Cast:* 1 BM, 1 WM. *Length:* 1 Act. *Prod:* New Negro Theatre, Los Angeles, Calif., 1939. *Lib Source:* Harold Ober playscript, SCHOM.

Emperor of Haiti. Historical Drama. The play describes the successful revolt led by Jean Jacques Dessalines for the liberation of Haitian slaves, his subsequent rule, betrayal, and death. *Cast:* 20 BM, 13 BF, extras (walk-ons, dancers). *Length:* 3 Acts. *Prod:* Gilpin Players, Karamu Theatre, Cleveland, Ohio, 1938. *Pubn: Black Drama in America: An Anthology*, ed. by Darwin T. Turner, Greenwich: Fawcett, 1971. *Lib Source:* HBA.

Esther. Opera. Music by Jan Meyerowitz.   *Length:* 1 Act. (Also in 3 Act version.) *Prod:* Adelphi Theatre, New York, Jan. 1946; University of Illinois, Urbana, Ill., Mar. 1957.

Five Foolish Virgins. Opera. Music by Jan Meyerowitz. *Length:* 2 Acts. *Lib Source:* Typescript, YL.

For This We Fight. (1943). Historical War Propaganda. History of the Afro-Americans reenacted within the frame of a black soldier speaking to his son. *Length:* 1 Act. *Lib Source:* Manuscript, YL.

Front Porch. Domestic Play. Play concerns the daughter in a black middle class family, her love affair with a working class strike leader, and her family's resistance to her affair, as they prefer the college man who is courting her. Has

HUGHES, LANGSTON *(Cont.)*

alternate endings, one tragic and one happy; one version by Rowena Jellife of Karamu Theatre, Cleveland, Ohio.   *Cast:* 4 BM, 1 BB, 3 BF, 1 WF. *Length:* 3 Acts. *Prod:* Gilpin Players, Karamu Theatre, Cleveland, Ohio, 1938. *Lib Source:* Harold Ober playscript, SCHOM.; Typescript, YL.

The Get-Away. Skit.   *Lib Source:* Unsigned script, YL.

The Gold Piece. (1921). Children's Play. Couple with their first large amount of money give it to a poor woman who appears at their cottage.   *Cast:* 1 BM, 2 BF. *Length:* 1 Act. *Pubn: The Brownie Book*, vol. 2, no. 7, July 1921.

Gospel Glory. The play depicts the life of Christ in song, dance, and mime. Subtitled: *Gospel Glow.   Cast:* Large, with choir. *Length:* 20 Scenes. *Prod:* Brooklyn, N.Y., 1962. *Lib Source:* Harold Ober playscript (*Gospel Glow*), SCHOM.; Typescript (*Gospel Glory*), YL.

Hamlet Jones. Musical. Based on Hughes' *Little Ham.* Adapted by Dorothy Silver. Music by Peyton Dean.   *Prod:* Karamu Theatre, Cleveland, Ohio, Summer 1975.

Hotel Black Majesty. (c. 1943). The play deals with a hotel lobby situation.

Jericho—Jim Crow. Historical Pageant. The history of Afro-Americans is presented in historical vignettes.   *Cast:* 2 BM, 3 BF, 1 WM. *Length:* 1 Act. *Prod:* The Sanctuary, New York, Dec. 1963. *Lib Source:* Typescript, YL; Harold Ober playscript, SCHOM.

Joy to My Soul. Comedy. Depicts the adventures of a good-natured country boy who has come to the city to meet a pen pal and is duped, but goes off with his true love in the end.   *Cast:* 2 BM, 4 BF, 20 extras. *Length:* 3 Acts. *Prod:* Gilpin Players, Karamu Theatre, Cleveland, Ohio, Apr. 1937. FTP. *Lib Source:* Harold Ober playscript, SCHOM.; Typescript, YL.

Just around the Corner. (1951). Lyrics for a two act musical by Abby Mann, Bernard Drew, and Joe Sherman.

Killed but Not Dead. Unfinished.   *Lib Source:* Unsigned manuscript, YL.

Limitations of Life. (1938). Comedy. Parody of film, *Imitation of Life.* White maid serves black family.   *Cast:* 1 BM, 1 BF, 1 WF. *Length:* 1 Act. *Prod:* New Negro Theatre, Los Angeles, Calif., 1939. *Pubn: Black Theater USA*, ed. by James V. Hatch and Ted Shine, New York: Free Pr., 1974. *Lib Source:* HBA.

Little Eva's End. (1938). Satire. Sketch on *Uncle Tom's Cabin.   Length:* 1 Act.

Little Ham. (1935). Comedy. A play about Harlem life in the 1920s: the adventures of Little Ham with women and the numbers and the lives of those who enter the shoeshine parlor in which he works.   *Cast:* 19 BM, 12 BF, 3 WM, 1 BB, 2 BG, extras. *Length:* 3 Acts. *Prod:* Gilpin Players, Karamu Theatre, Cleveland, Ohio, Mar. 1936. *Pubn: Five Plays by Langston Hughes*, ed. by Webster Smalley, Bloomington: Indiana Univ. Pr., 1963. *Lib Source:* HBA.

Love from a Tall Building. (c. 1954). Opera. Story of a woman who threatens suicide before a large crowd because she believes her man no longer loves her.   *Length:* 1 Act, possibly not completed.

The Man Next Door. Unfinished. *Lib Source:* Unsigned manuscript, YL.

Mister Jazz. (1960). Historical Pageant. A panorama in music and motion of the history of Negro dancing. *Cast:* narration, dancers, musicians. *Length:* 1 Act. *Lib Source:* Harold Ober playscript with *Shakespeare in Harlem*, SCHOM.

Mother and Child. (1950). Drama. Women at a meeting gossip about a white woman who has a child by a black man and discuss their admiration for the man, who refuses to leave town. From a short story in *The Ways of White Folk*, by Hughes. *Cast:* 5 BF. *Length:* 1 Act. *Pubn: Sadsa Encore*, 1950; *Black Drama Anthology*, ed. by Woodie King, Jr. and Ron Milner, New York: New Amer. Lib., 1972. *Lib Source:* HBA.

Mulatto. (1931). Historical Tragedy. The tragedy of a southern mulatto who asserts his manhood before his white father, kills him, and is himself hounded to his death. *Cast:* 5 BM, 1 BB, 5 WM, 2 BF, W mob. *Length:* 3 Acts. *Prod:* Vanderbilt Theatre, New York, 1935. *Pubn: Five Plays by Langston Hughes*, ed. by Webster Smalley, Bloomington: Indiana Univ. Pr., 1963. *Lib Source:* HBA.

Pennsylvania Spring. (1953).

Popo and Fifina. (1943). Children's Play. A story of Haiti, from a book of the same name by Arna Bontemps.

Port Town. Opera. Music by Jan Meyerowitz. The adventures and love affairs of Maggie, a woman of the port. *Length:* 3 Acts. *Prod:* Tanglewood, Lenox, Mass., Aug. 1960. *Lib Source:* Harold Ober playscript, SCHOM.

Prodigal Son. Gospel Play. The story of the prodigal son in song, dance, and mime. *Cast:* 9 BM, 6 BF. *Length:* 1 Act. *Prod:* Greenwich Mews Theatre, New York, May 1965. *Pubn: Players Magazine*, vol. 43, no. 1, Oct./Nov. 1967.

St. James: Sixty Years Young. (1955). Historical. The history of St. James portrayed in flashbacks. *Length:* 1 Act.

St. Louis Woman. (1936). Comedy. Possibly a revision of the play of the same name by Countee Cullen and Arna Bontemps. About the high life and love affairs of a jockey, Augie Rivers. *Cast:* 17 BM, 7 BF. *Length:* 3 Acts. *Lib Source:* Typescript, YL.

Scottsboro Limited. Historical. Play presents the history of the Scottsboro case and demands that the audience unite to liberate the Scottsboro boys. *Cast:* 8 BB, 9 WM, 2 WF, voices. *Length:* 1 Act. *Pubn: Scottsboro Ltd./Four Poems and a Play in Verse*, ed. by Langston Hughes, New York: Golden Stair Pr., 1932.

Shakespeare in Harlem. Theatrical Montage. Primarily a stage adaptation of a Hughes' poem, "Montage of a Dream Deferred," describing the daily existence of the people of Harlem. Adapted by Robert Glenn. *Length:* 1 Act. *Lib Source:* Typescript, YL; Harold Ober playscript with *Mister Jazz*, SCHOM.

Simple Takes a Wife. (1957). Comedy. A "Negro Folk Comedy" about Jesse B. Simple's courtship and marriage to Joyce. The play is an adaptation from Hughes' "Simple" newspaper columns. *Length:* 3 Acts. (2 Act version, 1952.) *Lib Source:* Typescript, YL.

Simply Heavenly. (1956). Musical Comedy. Simple's courtship and marriage to Joyce; a musical version of Hughes' *Simple Takes a Wife. Cast:* 12 BM, 6 BF.

HUGHES, LANGSTON (*Cont.*)

Length: 2 Acts. *Prod:* Eighty-fifth Street Playhouse, New York, Aug. 1957. *Pubn:* *Five Plays by Langston Hughes*, ed. by Webster Smalley, Bloomington: Indiana Univ. Pr., 1963. *Lib Source:* HBA.

Soul Gone Home. (1949). Domestic Drama. Mother argues with her son, who has just died, about their lives together.   *Cast:* 1 BM, 1 BF, 2 WM. *Length:* 1 Act. *Prod:* The Little Theatre, New York, Nov. 1963. *Pubn: Five Plays by Langston Hughes*, ed. by Webster Smalley, Bloomington: Indiana Univ. Pr., 1963. *Lib Source:* HBA.

Soul Gone Home. (1954). Opera. Operatic version of the play of the same name. Adapted by Ulysses Kay, who also composed the music. *Length:* 1 Act. *Lib Source:* Typescript, YL.

Street Scene. Opera. Music by Kurt Weill. An adaptation of Elmer Rice's play of the same name. *Length:* 3 Acts. *Prod:* Adelphi Theatre, N.Y., Jan. 1947. *Lib Source:* Harold Ober playscript, SCHOM.

The Sun Do Move. Historical Drama. The play concerns slavery and focuses on a split family, the father's repeated escapes, his return to his wife, and their eventual escape to the North. *Cast:* 16 BM, 4 BB, 14 BF, 6 WM, 2 WF, chorus. *Length:* 3 Acts, Prologue. *Prod:* As *Sold Away*, Skyloft Players, Chicago, Ill., 1942. *Pubn: The Sun Do Move*, ed. by Langston Hughes, New York: International Workers Order, 1942. *Lib Source:* Harold Ober playscript, SCHOM.

Tambourines to Glory. (1949). Musical Comedy. A play about the struggles of a female preacher who has an affair with the devil in disguise. *Cast:* 8 BM, 7 BF, extras, choir. *Length:* 3 Acts. *Prod:* The Little Theatre, New York, Nov. 1963. *Pubn: Five Plays by Langston Hughes*, ed. by Webster Smalley, Bloomington: Indiana Univ. Pr., 1963. *Lib Source:* HBA.

Tell It to Telstar. Historical Poetic Play. Deals with the freedom struggle that connects slavery of Jews, Blacks, and prerevolutionary French poor to Buchenwald, Birmingham, Selma, and Little Rock. Subtitled: **Ready to Live.** *Cast:* 1 BM, 1 BB, 1 BG, 4 soloists, male dancers, chorus. *Length:* 1 Act. *Lib Source:* Typescript, YL.

That Eagle. (1942).

Tropics after Dark. Opera. Music by Margaret Bonds. *Length:* 2 Acts. *Prod:* American Negro Exposition, Chicago, Ill., 1940. *Lib Source:* Typescript, YL.

Troubled Island. Historical Opera. Music by William Grant Still. The musical version of *Emperor of Haiti*, by the same playwright. *Length:* 3 Acts. *Prod:* Gilpin Players, Karamu Theatre, Cleveland, Ohio, Nov. 1936; City Center, New York Opera Company, Mar. 1949. *Lib Source:* Harold Ober playscript, 1949, SCHOM.

Uncle Tommy's Cabin. Mentioned as part of a program including *Em-Fuehrer Jones* and *Limitations of Life*, by the same playwright.

Wide Wide River. Folk Opera. Music by Granville English. Adapted from the play *The Shuffle Town Outlaws*, by William Norman Cox. Possibly not completed. *Lib Source:* Typescript, YL.

The Wizard of Altoona. (1951). Musical. Music by Elie Seigmeister. The story concerns the loves and business affairs of people in a carnival. *Length:* 3 Acts. *Lib Source:* Manuscript, possibly incomplete, YL.

HUGHES, LANGSTON, and ARNA BONTEMPS

Cavalcade of the Negro Theatre. (1940). Historical Pageant. The Negro in the theatre from *The Octoroon*, by Dion Boucicault, to 1940s Chicago jazz and gospel singing. *Length:* 21 Scenes. *Prod:* Written for the Negro Exposition, Chicago, Ill., Summer 1940. *Lib Source:* Manuscript, possibly incomplete, YL.

Jubilee, a Cavalcade of the Negro Theatre. Radio Play. Written for CBS, 1941.

When the Jack Hollers. Folk Comedy. Black and white sharecroppers in Mississippi delta both suffer from a merciless landowner until Aunt Billie's voodoo, an amazing mule, and a fish fry unite the races against the exploiter. *Cast:* 8 BM, 7 BF, 5 WM. *Length:* 3 Acts. *Prod:* Gilpin Players, Karamu Theatre, Cleveland, Ohio, May 1936. *Lib Source:* Typescript, YL; Harold Ober playscript, SCHOM.

HUGHES, LANGSTON, and ZORA NEALE HURSTON

Mule Bone. (1930). Comedy. Jim and Dave, best buddies, quarrel over Daisy; the result is that the entire town divides between the Baptists and the Methodists. *Cast:* 10 BM, 9 BF. *Length:* 3 Acts. *Lib Source:* Typescript, HBA.

HUGHES, LANGSTON, and WOODIE KING, JR.

The Weary Blues. (1966). Adapted from Langston Hughes' book of poetry of the same name. *Prod:* The Adventure Corps, New York, Feb. 1968.

HUGHES, LANGSTON, and BOB TEAGUE

Soul Yesterday and Today. (1969).

HUGHES, LANGSTON, and ELLA WINTER

Blood on the Fields. (1935). Proletarian Drama. Play deals with conditions among migrant cotton workers and their attempts to organize a union. *Length:* 3 Acts. *Lib Source:* Manuscript, possibly incomplete, YL.

HUNKINS, LEE

The Dolls. Ritual. *Prod:* Afro-American Total Theatre, New York, 1969.

Maggie. Drama. Maggie, a prostitute, attempts to change her "habit" by joining a convent. *Cast:* 1 M, 4 BF. *Length:* 1 Act.

26501. Sketch. A metaphysical exercise on existence and death. *Cast:* 2 M, extra. *Length:* 1 Act.

HUNKINS, LEECYNTH. *See* Hunkins, Lee

HUNT, WILLIAM

The Sunshine Train. Gospel Musical.   *Cast:* 5 BM, 5 BF. *Prod:* Abby Theatre, New York, June 1972.

HUNTER, EDDIE

The Battle of Who Run. Vaudeville Sketch.

The Gentleman Burglar. Vaudeville Sketch/Comedy. A burglar attempts to pass himself off as a detective.   *Cast:* 3 M, 1 F.

Going to the Races.

How Come? Musical Revue.   *Cast:* 13 BM, 11 BF. *Prod:* Apollo Theatre, New York, Apr. 1923. *Pubn: Best Plays of 1922-23,* ed. by Burns Mantle, New York: Dodd, 1923.

The Railroad Porter. Vaudeville Sketch.

Subway Sal. Vaudeville Sketch.

What Happens When the Husband Leaves Home. Vaudeville Sketch/Comedy.

HUNTER, EDDIE, and LEE RANDALL

On the Border of Mexico. (1920). Vaudeville Sketch/Comedy.

HUNTER, EDDIE, and ALEX ROGERS

My Magnolia. (1926). Revue.   *Cast:* 9 BM, 5 BF. *Length:* 2 Acts. *Pubn: Best Plays of 1926-27,* ed. by Burns Mantle, New York: Dodd, 1927.

HUNTER, EDDIE, and EARLE SWEETING

The Lady. (1944). Comedy. About a black maid and her boss, Lady Chesterfield. *Cast:* 1 BF, 1 WF. *Length:* 1 Act. *Lib Source:* Typescript, SCHOM.

HUNTLEY, ELIZABETH MADDOX

What Ye Sow. Drama. Illustrates the friction and tension that can result when the Caucasian and Black mingle in the House of God.   *Cast:* 4 BM, 2 BF, 1 WM, 3 WF. *Length:* 4 Acts. *Pubn:* New York: Comet Press Books, 1955. *Lib Source:* HBA.

⋅ HUNTLEY, MADELINE

A Piece of the Action. (1969). Drama. Jasper, an ex-junkie, faced with the opportunity to go back on dope with his girl friend, decides it's better to do manual labor.   *Cast:* 3 BM, 2 BF. *Length:* 1 Act. *Perm:* Author.

The Sheltered. (1968). Drama. A couple who never married, but loved each other for forty years, finally come together to go their separate ways.   *Cast:* 1 BM, 1 BF. *Length:* 1 Act. *Perm:* Author.

HURSTON, ZORA NEALE

Color Struck. Folk Drama. John jilts dark-skinned Emmaline for a light woman at the cakewalk and returns twenty years later to find that Emmaline still hates light-skinned Negroes, even her own illegitimate daughter.   *Cast:* 2 BM, 3 BF, 2 WM, dancers, extras. *Length:* 1 Act. *Pubn: Fire*, vol. 1, no. 1, Nov. 1926. *Lib Source:* YL.

The First One. (1927). Mythic Drama. Noah, drunk one night, curses his own life-loving son, Ham, to be forever black. Ham and his family leave for the land of the sun.   *Cast:* 4 M, 4 F, 2 C. *Length:* 1 Act. *Pubn: Ebony and Topaz*, New York: *Opportunity* magazine (National Urban League), 1927; *Books for Libraries*, Freeport, N.Y., 1971. *Lib Source:* HBA.

From Sun to Sun.

Great Day. (1927).

HURSTON, ZORA NEALE, and LANGSTON HUGHES

Mule Bone. (1930). Comedy. Jim and Dave, best buddies, quarrel over Daisy; the result is that the entire town divides between the Baptists and the Methodists.   *Cast:* 10 BM, 9 BF. *Length:* 3 Acts. *Lib Source:* Typescript, HBA.

HURSTON, ZORA NEALE, and FORBES RANDOLPH, et al.

Fast and Furious. Musical Revue. Cast Included Jackie "Moms" Mabley, Juano Hernandez, Dusty Fletcher, Etta Moten, and Tim Moore.   *Prod:* New York Theatre, Sept. 1931. *Pubn: Best Plays of 1931–32*, ed. by Burns Mantle, New York: Dodd, 1932.

HURSTON, ZORA NEALE, and DOROTHY WARING

Polk County. (1944). Comedy. Based partially on Ms. Hurston's experiences collecting folk materials in Florida. A play of black life in a sawmill camp, with authentic music.   *Cast:* 10 BM, 6 BF, 1 WM, musicians, extras. *Length:* 3 Acts. *Lib Source:* Typescript, PAL.

HYER SISTERS, ANNA and EMMA

Princess Orelia of Madagascar. (c. 1877). Musical. Starring roles shared by Sam Lucas and Tom Fletcher.

HYER SISTERS, ANNA and EMMA, and JOSEPH BRADFORD*

Out of Bondage. Musical. The Hyer sisters acted and sang in this three act musical play that "opens during the time of slavery and traces the Negro through emancipation, ending with his adjustment as a free man."—Mary Frances Cowan. *Length:* 3 Acts. *Lib Source:* Handwritten manuscript, Rare Book Collection, Library of Congress (this version may have been considerably changed by the Hyer sisters into a four act musical comedy).

IHUNANYA, GRACE COOPER

Behold: A Unicorn! (1973). Morality Drama. A conflict in the cultural identity of a "near-white-black" woman.   *Cast:* 4 M, 3 F. *Length:* 1 Act. *Perm:* Author.

A Dress for Annalee. (1972). Domestic Drama. Young unwed mother comes home to find her baby bitten to death by rats.   *Cast:* 1 BM, 2 BF, 1 BB. *Length:* 1 Act. *Perm:* Author.

IHUNANYA, GRACE COOPER *(Cont.)*

Exit: Stage Night. (1974). Domestic Play. Play about black women's liberation. *Cast:* 3 M, 4 F. *Length:* 1 Act. *Perm:* Author.

Finding Easter. (1972). Children's Play. Children find out that the real meaning of Easter is not in material possessions. *Cast:* 5 M, 3 F, 2 B. *Length:* 1 Act. *Perm:* Author.

Kojo and the Leopard. (1973). Children's Musical. A young African boy completes his trial initiation into manhood by conquering the leopard. *Cast:* 7 M, 6 F, 1 B. *Length:* Long 1 Act. *Prod:* Howard University, Washington, D.C., 1973. *Perm:* Author.

The Rain Is Cold in December. (1973). Morality Drama. A black woman's career conflicts with the men she loves. *Cast:* 2 M, 2 F. *Length:* 3 Acts. *Perm:* Author.

IMAN, YUSEF

Blowing Temptation Away. (1972). *Perm:* Agency, Sister Malika.

Book Worm. (1973). Shows how a righteous black man can go about transforming the lives of black women, particularly prostitutes. *Cast:* 1 BM, 2 BF. *Length:* 1 Act. *Prod:* Weusi Kuumba Troupe, New York, 1975.

Confusion. (1970). Mythic Play. Depicts how all the organizations, religions, and sects are against each other and the power struggle that occurs as each attempts to push the other down. *Cast:* 5 BM, 5 BF. *Length:* 1 Act. *Perm:* Agency, Sister Malika.

Dope Pusher. *Perm:* Agency, Sister Malika.

Dope, the Cause, Cure. (1967). Exposes the real dope pushers and tells where dope comes from, how it gets here, and what should be done to stop its importation within black communities. *Cast:* 8 BM, 1 BF, 2 WF, 5 musicians. *Length:* 1 Act. *Perm:* Agency, Sister Malika.

Jihad. (1968). Didactic Drama. Tells why black people in America are in the situation they are in and what can be done about it. *Cast:* 3 BM, 2 BF. *Length:* 1 Act. *Perm:* Agency, Sister Malika.

Joke Is on You. (1970). Protest Play. The president of the U.S. admits his intentions to commit genocide on all the races of color—Black, Chinese, Indian, and Puerto Rican. *Cast:* 3 BM, 1 BF, 1 WM. *Length:* 1 Act. *Perm:* Agency, Sister Malika.

The Junkie. A junkie talks about people always "on his case" and sees the hang-ups they have (cigarettes, homosexuality, prostitution). *Cast:* 1 BM. *Length:* 1 Act. *Prod:* The East, New York, Aug. 1974. *Perm:* Agency, Sister Malika.

Libra. (1972). Morality Play. Depicts the changes people undergo in life, stressing the meaning of death, right and wrong, and giving a new insight on love. *Cast:* 3 BM, 2 BF, 3 WM. *Length:* 2 Acts. *Perm:* Agency, Sister Malika.

Mr. Bad. (1972). A brother who, as he talks to the audience, learns that the practice of martial arts is an ego trip. *Cast:* 2 BM. *Length:* 1 Act. *Prod:* Billie Holiday Theatre, New York, June 1975. *Perm:* Agency, Sister Malika.

A Nigger's House. (1965). Domestic Drama. Reveals the problems and chaotic relationships the average black family has and what can be done about it. *Cast:* 1 BM, 1 BF, 1 BB. *Length:* 1 Act. *Perm:* Agency, Sister Malika.

Praise the Lord, but Pass the Ammunition. Drama. A confrontation between the forces of nonviolence and those of self-defense.   *Cast:* 5 BM, 3 BF, 2 WM. *Length:* 1 Act. *Prod:* Spirit House, Newark, N.J., 1967. *Pubn:* Mimeographed booklet, Newark, N.J.: Jihad Productions, 1967. *Lib Source:* HBA. *Perm:* Agency, Sister Malika.

The Price of Revolution. (1971). Drama. A brother, "into" the revolution, is receiving flack from his woman and is forced to kill her.   *Cast:* 1 BM, 1 BF. *Length:* 1 Act. *Perm:* Agency, Sister Malika.

Respect. (1973). Drama. Displays the negative attitude black men have toward black women and what the consequences will be.   *Cast:* 3 BM, 3 BF. *Length:* 1 Act. *Perm:* Agency, Sister Malika.

Resurrection. (1969). Protest Play. Depicts what is happening and what will happen within the schoolroom.   *Cast:* 3 BB, 3 BF, 1 WF. *Length:* 1 Act. *Perm:* Agency, Sister Malika.

Santa's Last Ride. (1967). Didactic Play. Displays the fallacy of Christmas.   *Cast:* 3 BM, 1 WM, 1 WF. *Length:* 1 Act. *Perm:* Agency, Sister Malika.

Sociology. (1970). Didactic Play. The various life-styles of black prostitutes, homosexuals, and those who are aware of their Blackness. Subtitled: *700 Clean Up Time.*   *Cast:* Large B. *Length:* 1 Act. *Prod:* Sethlow Community Center, New York, July 1970. *Perm:* Agency, Sister Malika.

Verdict Is Yours. (1971). Historical Protest. Puts America on trial as to whether or not she is guilty of the position in which she has put black people. Explores to what extent black people are guilty of their own predicament, due to abuse of power imposed upon their own people centuries ago.   *Cast:* 2 BM, 1 WM. *Length:* 1 Act. *Perm:* Agency, Sister Malika.

We Wear the Mask. (1973). Morality Play. Reveals the problems that black men and women have as they try to win each other's love and respect by making false impressions.   *Cast:* 1 BM, 1 BF. *Length:* 1 Act. *Perm:* Agency, Sister Malika.

IMAN, YUSEF, and BEN CALDWELL

Yesterday, Today, Tomorrow. Historical Didactic Play. A presentation of the black experience—past, present, and future. Subtitled: *The 7 Principles.* *Cast:* Large B. *Prod:* Weusi Kuumba Troupe, The East, New York, Aug. 1974. *Perm:* Agency, Sister Malika.

IRVINE, WELDON

The Priest and the Prostitute.   *Prod:* Reading, Frank Silvera Writers' Workshop, Studio Museum of Harlem, New York, Mar. 1977.

Young, Gifted and Broke. Musical. "Play about two self-proclaimed entertainment managers seeking fame and fortune through the promotion and exploita-

IRVINE, WELDON *(Cont.)*

tion of aspiring community talent."—*The Black American*, vol. 16, no. 21, 1977. *Length:* 3 Acts. *Prod:* Billie Holiday Theatre, New York, May 1977.

ISHAM, JOHN W.

The Octoroons. "A Musical Farce. The first part consisted of an opening chorus and a medley of songs. The middle part was a burlesque sketch in which a number of specialties were strung on a very thin thread of story. The show closed with a cakewalk jubilee, a military drill and a chorus-march-finale."— James W. Johnson, *Black Manhattan. Prod:* New York, 1895.

Oriental America. Musical Revue. "Although it was built on the minstrel model, the afterpiece, instead of being made up of burlesque and specialties, cakewalk, 'hoe-down,' and walk-around finale, was a medley of operatic selections. *Oriental America* broke all precedents by being the first coloured show to play Broadway proper; it opened at Wallack's Theatre at that time called Palmers."—James W. Johnson, *Black Manhattan. Prod:* New York, 1896.

IYAUN, IFA

Drinkwater. Children's Play. A black musical odyssey about a young girl in search of her identity. *Prod:* Henry Street Settlement, New York, Mar. 1975.

JACKMON, MARVIN E. *See* X, Marvin

JACKSON, C. BERNARD

Aftermath. Musical Revue. A selection of highlights from *Earthquake I* and *II. Prod:* Inner City Performing Arts Center, Los Angeles, Calif., Spring 1977. *Perm:* Agency, Reverse Music.

B.C. (Before Completion). (1976). Set in various Moorish households in Spain in the Middle Ages, it explores the interrelationships between African and Spanish music and women. *Cast:* 2 BF. *Length:* Full Length. *Prod:* San Antonio, Tex., Winter 1976. *Perm:* Agency, Reverse Music.

Departure. (1965). Musical Drama. A staged mass for the dead; a musical work that deals with a young black man who refuses to die. *Cast:* 9, chorus, dancers optional. *Length:* Full Length. *Prod:* Inner City Cultural Center, Los Angeles, Calif., 1966. *Perm:* Agency, Reverse Music.

Earthquake I. Musical Revue. Utilizes modified music revue format to explore aspects of life in southern California that tourists seldom see; subjects dealt with include birth control, the construction of the Watts Towers, the increase in Los Angeles' non-white population, the election of Los Angeles' first black mayor, the institution of marriage, aging, theatre criticism, and violence in the schools. *Cast:* 8-11 M & F. *Length:* Full Length. *Prod:* Inner City Cultural Center, Los Angeles, Calif., Dec. 1973. *Perm:* Agency, Reverse Music.

Earthquake II. (1974). Musical Revue. A sequel to *Earthquake I*, which includes such subjects as the demise of a famous southern California amusement park (P.O.P.), theatre reviews and reviewers, aspiring Hollywood actors, institutional religion, street construction, adult nursery rhymes, the "dozens," American violence, and art as entertainment. *Cast:* 6–9 M & F. *Length:* Full Length. *Prod:* Inner City Cultural Center, Los Angeles, Calif., Oct. 1974. *Perm:* Agency, Reverse Music.

Earthquake III. (1975). Musical Revue. Sequel to *Earthquake I* and *II*, this version covers such subjects as Los Angeles trying to cope with the nation's 200th birthday party, mating, piano bars, UFOs, and unemployment. *Cast:* 6–10 M & F. *Length:* Full Length. *Prod:* Inner City Cultural Center, Los Angeles, Calif., 1974. *Perm:* Agency, Reverse Music.

Langston Hughes Said. (1974). A musical evening dedicated to the life of the famous black American writer, Langston Hughes—his poetry, song lyrics, short stories, as well as his one act play *Soul Gone Home.* *Cast:* 4–6 M & F. *Length:* Full Length. *Prod:* Inner City Cultural Center, Los Angeles, Calif., Mar. 1974. *Perm:* Agency, Reverse Music.

Looking Backward. (1974). Adaptation. Derived from the famous Edward Bellamy classic novel dealing with life in America in the year 2000. *Cast:* 3 M, 3 F. *Perm:* Agency, Reverse Music.

Piano Bar and Other California Stories. Musical. The script revolves around the customers, staff, and characters who visit a club. There is a strong message for women's lib and such problems as prostitution, etc. *Cast:* 5 M, 5 F. *Length:* Full Length. *Prod:* Inner City Cultural Center, Los Angeles, Calif., Spring 1976. *Perm:* Agency, Reverse Music.

Sweete Nutcracker. (1974). Christmas Musical. Adapted for the stage from Alexander Dumas' version of the Hoffman story, *The Nutcracker of Nuremburg* (the famous Tchaikovsky ballet, *The Nutcracker*, is based on the Dumas story); this adaptation is sort of an inner city "Nutcracker Suite" dealing with life in the barrios and ghettos of Los Angeles, California. *Cast:* 4 M, 4 F. *Perm:* Agency, Reverse Music.

JACKSON, C. BERNARD, and JAMES V. HATCH*

Fly Blackbird. (1960). Protest Musical. A group of black and white college students picket and go to jail rather than compromise with racist segregation. *Cast:* 6 BM, 6 WM, 4 WF, 1 Japanese M. *Length:* 2 Acts. *Prod:* Shoebox Theatre, Los Angeles, Calif. Aug. 1960; Billy Rose Theatre, New York, Feb. 1962. *Pubn:* Black Theater USA, ed. by James V. Hatch and Ted Shine, New York: Free Pr., 1974; *The Black Teacher and the Dramatic Arts,* ed. by William Reardon and Thomas Pawley, Westport: Negro Universities Pr., 1970. *Lib Source:* HBA. *Perm:* HBA.

JACKSON, DONALD, and SHAUNEILLE PERRY

Last Night, Night Before. (1971). Morality Melodrama. Good people on the block have a party while "The Cat Man" hooks a sixteen-year-old boy on dope that kills him. *Cast:* 11 BM, 10 BF, children. *Length:* 3 Acts. *Prod:* Empoet Productions, New York, n.d.

JACKSON, ELAINE

Toe Jam. (1971). Domestic Drama. Overprotective mother is the cause of rebel-
lious behavior of her daughters. *Cast:* 1 BM, 4 BF. *Length:* 3 Acts. *Pubn:
Black Drama Anthology*, ed. by Woodie King, Jr. and Ron Milner, New York:
New Amer. Lib., 1972. *Lib Source:* HBA.

JACKSON, EUGENIA LUTHER

Everything Is Everything.

Life.

JACKSON, JO

Martin and Malcolm.

JACKSON, JOSEPHINE, and JOSEPH A. WALKER

The Believers. Musical. Action takes place in the "Gone Years" and the "Then and
Now Years." Subtitled: *The Black Experience in Song.*   *Cast:* 7 BM, 6 BF.
Length: 2 Acts. *Prod:* Garrick Theatre, New York, May 1968. *Pubn: Best Plays
of 1967-68*, ed. by Otis L. Guernsey, Jr., New York: Dodd, 1968. *Perm:* Author.

JACKSON, SPENCER

Chi-Star. "The play is an amusing story of a country boy who comes to the city,
where he becomes exposed to the tribulations of urban living."—Eugene
Perkins, *Black World*, vol. 23, no. 6, Apr. 1974.   *Prod:* Black Heritage Theatrical
Players, Chicago, Ill., Dec. 1973.

Come Home.

A New Day.   *Prod:* Black Heritage Theatrical Players, Chicago, Ill., 1973.

Slyster.   *Prod:* Black Heritage Theatrical Players, Chicago, Ill., 1975.

Soul Alley. Drama. Deals with black soldiers in Vietnam.   *Prod:* Hollywood Center
Theatre, Calif., Summer 1976.

JAMES, WILLIAM

Hampton. Domestic Play. A "bicentennial" family love story.   *Prod:* The New
Life Theatre, Metropolitan Community United Methodist Church, New York,
Feb. 1976.

JAMISON, BILL

Soul Bus to Brotherhood. Drama. Bus with Blacks of diverse political and non-
political views picks up a white passenger, who is finally killed at the instigation
of the most middle class black woman.   *Cast:* 8 BM, 1 BF, 1 WM. *Length:* 1 Act.
Perm: Author.

JEANNETTE, GERTRUDE

A Bolt from the Blue. (1946). Drama. Black veteran of World War II returns angry
and alienated, enters rackets, and discovers his own daughter there.   *Cast:*

3 BM, 3 BF. *Length:* Full Length. *Prod:* Elks Community Theatre, New York, 1952. *Perm:* Author.

Light in the Cellar. Domestic Drama/Comedy. Sequel to *This Way Forward.* A father (he is the son of the pioneering woman in *This Way Forward,* by the same playwright) who has uprooted his family from a comfortable middle class existence in the Southwest and come to New York to insure his militant son a better education, finds the same problems in New York. *Cast:* 5 BM, 5 BF (2 teenagers), 1 BB, 1 WM (teenager). *Length:* 3 Acts. *Prod:* Our Theatre, Inc., New York, 1965; Adam Clayton Powell Theatre, New York, May 1975. *Perm:* Author.

This Way Forward. Drama. The struggle of one woman against overwhelming odds to correct the quality, as well as the quantity, of education available to the children in a southwestern farming district from 1924–1930. *Cast:* 6 BM (2 teenagers), 8 F (1 girl, 2 teenagers), 2 WM. *Length:* 3 Acts. *Prod:* ANT, New York, 1950. *Perm:* Author.

JEFFERSON, ANNETTE G.

Drown the Wind. Musical. *Length:* 2 Acts. *Prod:* Freelander Theater, Wooster College, Ohio, May 1975.

In Both Hands. Morality Drama. Portrays the ideological and generational conflict between a black revolutionary and his old-fashioned, preacher father. *Length:* 3 Acts. *Prod:* Humanist Theatre, Cleveland, Ohio, 1973.

JENKINS, FRANK

Last Man Out. (1969). Domestic Drama. A middle class family becomes militant after the father is arrested for no reason. *Cast:* 3 BM, 2 BF. *Length:* 2 Acts. *Perm:* Agency, Alexis Brewer.

JENNINGS, CORRINE, STEVE CANNON, and JOE OVERSTREET

Snakeshiiit. Pageant Play/Tragic-Comic Farce. Headman at the White House tries to contain the black revolution and is assassinated. *Cast:* 6 BM, 2 BF, 5 WM, 2 WF, extras. *Length:* 3 Acts. *Prod:* Reading, NFT, New York, 1975. *Lib Source:* Typescript, HBA.

JOHN, ERROL

Moon on a Rainbow Shawl. Folk Drama. Depicts life in the Port-au-Spain court-yard of a poor tenement teeming with people and problems. *Cast:* 9 BM, 5 BF, 1 BB. *Length:* 3 Acts. *Prod:* Off-Broadway, 1962. *Pubn:* London: Faber & Faber, 1958. *Lib Source:* PAL.

JOHNSON, BRADLON

All behind the Line Is Mine. Satire. Young man, Juan Cancer, who is a hustler, punk, and thug, is treated by his family and society as a nice, misunderstood lad who is not responsible for his crimes. *Cast:* 2 BM, 1 BF, 2 WM, extras. *Length:* 1 Act. *Pubn: Cry at Birth,* ed. by Merrel Booker, New York: McGraw-Hill, 1971. *Lib Source:* HBA.

JOHNSON, CHRISTINE

Zwadi Ya Afrika Kwa Dunwa (Africa's Gift to the World). Historical Children's Play. *Pubn:* Chicago: Free Black Pr., c. 1970.

JOHNSON, DOUGLAS, and MARGO BARNETT

Black Is a Beautiful Woman. This work consists of the works of such black writers as Margaret Walker, Nikki Giovanni, Mari Evans, and Langston Hughes. *Prod:* Black Alley Theatre, Washington, D.C., 1973.

JOHNSON, EUGENE

Spaces in Between.

JOHNSON, FENTON

The Cabaret Girl. *Prod:* The "Shadows" Theatre, Chicago, Ill., 1925.

JOHNSON, FREDDIE, and PORTER GRAINGER

Lucky Sambo. (1925). Musical Comedy. An oil stock swindle where the tricksters are tricked. *Cast:* 9 BM, 8 BF, chorus. *Length:* 2 Acts. *Pubn: Best Plays of 1924-25,* ed. by Burns Mantle, New York: Dodd, 1925.

JOHNSON, GEORGIA DOUGLAS

A Bill to Be Passed. A play concerning the Anti-Lynching Bill before Congress. *Length:* 1 Act.

Blue Blood. (1926). Comedy. A light-skinned young couple, about to be married, discover they have the same father. *Cast:* 2 BM, 3 BF. *Length:* 1 Act. *Pubn: Fifty More Contemporary One-Act Plays,* ed. by Frank Shay, New York: Appleton, 1928. *Lib Source:* HBA.

Blue Eyed Black Boy. A play about a lynching that is avoided. *Length:* 1 Act.

Frederick Douglass. (1935). Historical Children's Play. The story of young Frederick Douglass' escape from slavery. *Cast:* 3 BM, 1 BF. *Length:* 1 Act. *Pubn: Negro History in Thirteen Plays,* ed. by Willis Richardson and May Miller, Washington, D.C.: Associated Publishers, 1935.

Plumes. Folk Drama. The poor mother of a very sick child must decide whether to spend fifty dollars on a doubtful operation or on a beautiful funeral. *Cast:* 1 BM, 3 BF. *Length:* 1 Act. *Pubn: Plays of Negro Life,* ed. by Alain Locke and Montgomery Gregory, New York: Harper, 1927. *Lib Source:* NYPL.

Safe. A play about the effect of lynching. *Length:* 1 Act. *Lib Source:* FTP, GMU.

The Starting Point. Domestic Play. Son, thought to be in medical school, comes home and announces he's in the rackets; his father then gives him his own job as a porter in a bank. *Cast:* 2 BM, 2 BF. *Length:* 1 Act. *Lib Source:* Typescript, YL.

A Sunday Morning in the South: With Negro Church Background. (1925). Protest Drama. A young black man is mistaken for a rapist and lynched. *Cast:* 1 BM, 3 BF, 1 BB, 2 WM, 1 WF. *Length:* 1 Act. *Pubn: Black Theater USA,* ed.

by James V. Hatch and Ted Shine, New York: Free Pr., 1974. *Lib Source:* HBA.

A Sunday Morning in the South: With White Church Background. Drama. An anti-lynching play and companion piece to *A Sunday Morning in the South: With Negro Church Background,* by the same playwright. *Length:* 1 Act.

William and Ellen Craft. (1935). Historical Children's Play. Ellen, a light-skinned slave, disguises herself as a white man and takes her husband William north in an escape plot. *Cast:* 2 BM, 2 BF. *Length:* 1 Act. *Pubn: Negro History in Thirteen Plays,* ed. by Willis Richardson and May Miller, Washington, D.C.: Associated Publishers, 1935. *Lib Source:* NYPL.

JOHNSON, HALL

Run, Little Chillun. Religious Drama with Music. In a southern town, Christians and pagans struggle for the soul of Rev. Jones. Subtitled: *Across the River.* *Cast:* 11 BM, 14 BF, children, extras. *Prod:* Lyric Theatre, New York, Mar. 1933. *Lib Source:* Typescript, SCHOM, GMU.

JOHNSON, HERMAN

The Death of Little Marcus. Domestic Drama. A long gone father-lover returns home to create crisis over his daughter. *Cast:* 2 BM, 2 BF, 1 BG. *Length:* 1 Act.

Nowhere to Run, Nowhere to Hide. (1974). Drama. Two dope peddling icemen directly affect the lives of seven other characters in the ghetto. *Cast:* 5 BM, 3 BF, 2 WM. *Length:* 2 Acts. *Prod:* NEC Season-within-a-Season, New York, Apr. 1974.

17 Sycamore Court. Drama. The play is based on the emotional complexities of people trying to change their bleak past by attempting to accept who they are through the redemptive channels of love and understanding. *Cast:* 5 BM, 3 BF, 1 BG. *Length:* 3 Acts.

JOHNSON, HUGH M.

Justice or Just Us (Part I). (1972). Protest. A look at the judicial system and how it doesn't work for the black man. *Cast:* 4 BM, 5 WM. *Length:* 1 Act. *Pubn: Who Took the Weight (Black Voices from Norfolk Prison),* Boston: Little, 1972. *Lib Source:* HBA.

JOHNSON, J. C.

The Year Around. Musical Revue. *Prod:* Harlem Musical Theatre, New York, Apr. 1953.

JOHNSON, J. C., and LEIGH WHIPPER

Runnin' de Town. (1930). The story is based on the rivalry of two fraternal organizations in a small town in Mississippi.

JOHNSON, JAMES P.

Plantation Days. *Prod:* London, Eng., 1923.

JOHNSON, JAMES W.

God's Trombones. Verse Play. A religious text of Negro sermons often performed as drama. *Pubn:* New York: Viking, 1927.

JOHNSON, JAMES W., and BOB COLE

The Shoo-fly Regiment. Comic Opera. *Prod:* Possibly Grand Opera House, New York, June 1907 or Bijou Theatre, New York, Aug. 1907.

JOHNSON, JAMES W., BOB COLE, and ROSAMUND JOHNSON

Humpty Dumpty. Musical Revue. "A 'white show' [for white performers and a white audience] to which these black artists contributed."—Fannin Belcher.

In Newport. Musical Revue. "A 'white show' [for white performers and a white audience] to which these black artists contributed."—Fannin Belcher. *Prod:* n.p., 1904.

JOHNSON, JAMES W., and ROSAMUND JOHNSON

Toloso. (1898). Comic Opera/Satire. "The setting was an island kingdom in the Pacific. Toloso, the beautiful princess; her prime minister, a crafty old politician; the entrance of an American man-of-war; the handsome heroic American lieutenant; and finally annexation of the island by America."—James W. Johnson, *Along This Way. Length:* Full Length.

JOHNSON, JEAN

The Temple of Holy Love. (1974). Musical. A spell casting, spiritual, gospel singing, musical opera. An ensemble ritual to exorcise Lady Heroin. *Cast:* 17 M & F. *Length:* Full Length. *Prod:* Reading, Frank Silvera Writers' Workshop, Martinique Theatre, New York, Jan. 1975.

JOHNSON, LOUIS, and RON STEWARD

Sambo or *A Black Opera with White Spots.* Jazz Musical. Based on nursery rhymes. Sambo grows up in a white world that evidences its sickness. *Cast:* 2 BM, 2 BF, 3 WM, 2 WF. *Length:* 2 Acts. *Prod:* Public Theatre, New York Shakespeare Festival, N.Y., Dec. 1969.

JOHNSON, REGINALD VEL

Section D. (1974). Drama. A group of young men in a reformatory cottage wrestle with the issues of homosexuality and manhood; the result is violence. *Cast:* 9 M. *Length:* 4 Acts. *Prod:* Seton Hall University, Newark, N.J., July 1975. *Perm:* Author.

The Trap Play. Drama. A plot of cheating and conspiracy to pass an English examination in college in order to play football. *Length:* Full Length. *Prod:* NEC Season-within-a-Season, New York, Spring 1976.

JOHNSON, ROSAMUND, and BOB COLE

The Red Moon. Comic Opera. "A musical story in which lawyer Slim Brown and Dr. Plunk Green, both quacks, rescue a maiden who has been taken from her mother's home to her father's wigwam on a western reservation."—Fannin Belcher. *Prod:* Majestic Theatre, New York, May 1909.

JOHNSON, ROSAMUND, BOB COLE, and JAMES W. JOHNSON

Humpty Dumpty. Musical Revue. "A 'white show' [for white performers and a white audience] to which these black artists contributed."—Fannin Belcher.

In Newport. Musical Revue. "A 'white show' [for white performers and a white audience] to which these black artists contributed."—Fannin Belcher. *Prod:* n.p., 1904.

JOHNSON, ROSAMUND, and JAMES W. JOHNSON

Toloso. (1898). Comic Opera/Satire. "The setting was an island kingdom in the Pacific. Toloso, the beautiful princess; her prime minister, a crafty old politician; the entrance of an American man-of-war; the handsome heroic American lieutenant; and finally annexation of the island by America."—James W. Johnson, *Along This Way. Length:* Full Length.

JOHNSON, WILLIAM, and BOB COLE

A Trip to Coontown. Musical. "The story concerns two bunko operators who pursued a naive provincial with money to burn."—Fannin Belcher. *Prod:* Third Avenue Theatre, New York, Apr. 1898.

JOHNSTON, PERCY

Dawitt. Pubn: New York: Rinjohn Productions, 1973.

Emperor Dessalines. Pubn: New York: Rinjohn Productions, 1973.

John Adams. Historical Drama. *Pubn:* New York: Rinjohn Productions, 1973.

JONES, E. H.

Our Very Best Christmas.

JONES, F. BERESFORD

Ralph and Emma. (1972). Domestic Play. A jealous, out-of-work husband gets a job and is welcomed back home. *Cast:* 1 BM, 2 BF, 1 WM, 2 B. *Length:* 1 Act.

JONES, GAYL

Beyond Yourself (The Midnight Confessions) for Brother Ahh. Ritual/Drama. Letha and Clell, woman and man, strive to become whole and to love themselves and one another, as they are witnessed by two old root folks who have passed through it all before. *Cast:* 2 M, 2 F. *Length:* 1 Act. *Pubn:* BOP (Blacks On Paper), Providence: Brown Univ., 1975. *Lib Source:* HBA.

Chile Woman. (1974). Historical. A "show off" with music by Brother Ahh Folayemi. Contemporary black folk in a bar relate to the near and ancient past. New Play Award, New England Region, 1974. *Cast:* 5 BM, 8 BF, musicians. *Length:* 1 Act. *Prod:* Brown University, Providence, R.I., 1973. *Pubn:* Shubert Playbook Series, ed. by John Emigh, vol. II, no. 5, 1974. *Lib Source:* HBA.

Mama Easter. Prod: Possibly at Brown University, Providence, R.I., 1974.

JONES, GENE-OLIVAR

Based on Cinderella. Two buddies, hooked on drugs in Vietnam, take different routes when they return home; one attempts to join society, and the other gets trapped in the world of crime and drugs. *Cast:* 2 BM, 1 F. *Length:* 1 Act.

No Church Next Sunday. Comedy/Drama. Black woman aspiring for the good life (with a white man) cautions her activist brother about his civil rights endeavors. *Cast:* 3 BM, 4 BF, extras. *Length:* 2 Acts. *Lib Source:* Typescript, SCHOM. *Perm:* Author.

JONES, GWEN. *See* Aremu, Aduke

JONES, HERMAN

Death of a Nationalist.

JONES, JAMES ARLINGTON

Anthology: Attending Skeletons. Domestic Drama. The play concerns Tom Smith's sentence to be hanged and his family's attitudes about it. *Cast:* 5 BM, 1 BF, 1 BB, 2 WM. *Length:* 2 Acts. *Prod:* Bank Street College, New York, Mar. 1974. *Perm:* Author.

JONES, J. J.

Minstrel Quintet. Satire. The theme is the United Nations. *Prod:* FST, New Orleans, La., Dec. 1971.

JONES, LOLA AMIS. *See* Amis, Lola E.

JONES, LeROI. *See* Baraka, Amiri

JONES, ROBERT

Through Black and Back.

JONES, SILAS

Waiting for Mongo. Drama. A nightmare becomes a reality and the black revolution may or may not happen. *Cast:* 5 BM, 4 BF. *Prod:* NEC, New York, May 1975.

JONES, SYL

Dig a Ditch, Dig a Tunnel. "A dream of ethics" about problems of young black girls in search of their expression and their identity. *Length:* 2 Acts. *Pubn:* New York: Amuru Pr., 1974, possibly never published.

JONES, T. MARSHALL, and CURTIS L. WILLIAMS

Ghetto Vampire. (1973). Comedy. A Black tries to gain an apprenticeship in the Vampire Union to escape the ghetto. *Cast:* 6 BM, 3 BF. *Length:* 2 Acts. *Perm:* Authors.

Swap Face. (1974). Children's Musical. Black youth trying to obtain a face, for which he has swapped his own oft-criticized face: a problem of identity. *Cast:* 7 BM, 6 BF. *Perm:* Authors.

JONES, WALTER

The Boston Party at Annie Mae's House.   Prod: Ellen Stewart Theatre, New York, Feb. 1972.

Dudder Lover. (1972).

Fish n' Chips.   Prod: Cornbread Players, New York, 1974.

Jazznite. One member of a ghetto family has completed work on a scholarship (Yale) with the explicit purpose of learning how "the man plays his games." *Cast:* 5 BM, 2 BF. *Length:* 1 Act. *Pubn: Scripts,* vol. 1, no. 6, May 1972. *Lib Source:* HBA.

Nigger Nightmare. Ritual. It seeks to recount four hundred years of black oppression in the West.   *Cast:* 3 BM, 5 BF. *Prod:* Public Theatre's Other Stage, New York Shakespeare Festival, N.Y., June 1971; Langston Hughes' House of KUUMBA, New York, Feb. 1972.

Reverend Brown's Daughter.   Prod: Cornbread Players, New York, 1974.

JONES, WILLA SAUNDERS

The Birth of Christ.

The Call to Arms.

Just One Hour to Live—for the Dope Addict.

The Life Boat.

The Passion Play. (1973).

Up from Slavery.

JOPLIN, SCOTT

A Guest of Honor. (1903). Ragtime Opera.

The Rag-Time Dance. (1903). Folk Ballet.

Treemonisha. (c. 1911). Ragtime Opera. Set in 1884 in Arkansas, this is the story of Monisha, a young woman innocent of her true parentage.   *Cast:* 8 BM, 3 BF. *Length:* 3 Acts. *Prod:* Memorial Arts Center, Atlanta, Ga., Jan. 1972; Palace Theater, New York, Dec. 1975.

JORDAN, JOE, and ERNEST HOGAN

Rufus Rastus. Musical Revue.   *Prod:* n.p., 1905.

JORDAN, NORMAN

Cadillac Dreams. Comedy. Smokey, a domestic worker, concocts a get-rich scheme that would have his girl friend's niece marry a famous and rich professional basketball player.   *Length:* 2 Acts. *Prod:* Theatre Black at Judson Hall, New York, Oct. 1968.

Corrupted American Dollar.   *Length:* 1 Act. *Prod:* Le Theatre Noir, Cleveland, Ohio, Aug. 1967.

In the Last Days. Ritual.   *Prod:* Karamu House Arena Theatre, Cleveland, Ohio, May 1971; Bed-Stuy Theatre, New York, May 1973.

JORDAN, NORMAN *(Cont.)*

We Free Kings. (1967). Two brothers get very high while they wait for the confirmation of their father's death. *Cast:* 2 BM, 1 BF. *Length:* 1 Act. *Prod:* Le Theatre Noir, Cleveland, Ohio, Aug. 1967.

JOSHUA, GEORGE

The Plantation. Prod: Reading, Frank Silvera Writers' Workshop, The Teachers, Inc., New York, Jan. 1977.

JUSTICE, JIMMY, and HAZEL BRYANT

Jimmy's Carousels. Prod: Afro-American Total Theatre, New York, May 1972.

Soul Politiken. Prod: Afro-American Total Theatre, Street Theatre, Lincoln Center, New York, July 1973.

KABAKA, LAWRENCE

Home Grown War. Story of a young revolutionary who was murdered by the police. *Prod:* New Concept Theatre, Chicago, Ill., 1974.

KAIN, GYLAN

Epitaph to a Coagulated Trinity. Length: 1 Act. *Prod:* Group conceived and directed by Ernie McClintock, New York, c. 1965.

KALAMU YA SALAAM. *See* Salaam, Kalamu Ya

KALEEM, BARRY AMYER

Birdland. Historical Drama. Jazz in the fifties and the struggle of jazz greats like James Moody, Art Blakely, Charlie Parker, and others who were ultimately ripped off by the system and the rackets. *Cast:* 5 BM, 4 BF. *Length:* 2 Acts. *Perm:* Author.

One Mint Julep. Tragedy. Homecoming of a cousin leads to family quarrel, resulting in the rape of an in-law; provides a character study of two women. *Cast:* 4 BM, 5 BF. *Length:* 2 Acts. *Perm:* Author.

The System of Green Lantern Solo. Drama. About the year 2000 and the status of black survival in the U.S. *Cast:* 9 M, 4 F. *Length:* 3 Acts. *Perm:* Author.

You Don't Get Off Here to Catch the Express. Musical Comedy. Lyrics by Ifa Iyuan and Amyer Kaleem. Musical arrangements by Palmer Lampkin and Andre Ingram. About the Lower East Side (of New York) melting pot mentality and the caste system that exists within it. *Cast:* 3 BM, 1 BF, 2 WM, 1 WF, 1 Puerto Rican M, 1 Puerto Rican F. *Length:* 1 Act. *Prod:* NFT, New York, July 1975.

KAMBON, OBAYANI

The Pendulum. Surrealistic Drama. Two young men in a shoeshine parlor, who may be brothers or even the same man, feel their "jones" coming down and try to "take off" an old man who may be their father, or even themselves. *Cast:* 3 BM. *Length:* 1 Act. *Pubn: Obsidian,* vol. 1, no. 3, Dec. 1975. *Lib Source:* HBA.

KELLY, JO-ANN

A Gift for Aunt Sarah. *Pubn: Freedom Theatre,* Dec.-Jan. 1970–1971.

Where the Sun Don't Shine.

KEMP, ARNOLD

White Wound, Black Scar.

KENLY, CALVIN, and WILFRID DALZON

The Second Visitation. (1972). Historical Mythic Drama. A black community seizes
power over its own destiny through violence, and this action is then judged by
ten great black leaders of the past. *Cast:* 15 BM, 9 BF (doubling). *Length:*
3 Acts.

KENNEDY, ADRIENNE

A Beast Story. (1969). Poetic Drama. Portrait of inner turmoil of black midwestern
family. *Cast:* 2 BM, 2 BF. *Length:* 1 Act. *Prod:* Public Theatre, New York
Shakespeare Festival, N.Y., Jan. 1969. *Pubn: Cities in Bezique,* SF. *Lib Source:*
HBA. *Perm:* Agency, SF.

Evening with Dead Essex. (1973). A semidocumentary on Mark Essex, shot by
New Orleans police. *Cast:* 3 BM, 1 BF, 1 WM. *Length:* 1 Act. *Perm:* Agency,
Ronald Hobbs.

Funnyhouse of a Negro. (1969). Poetic Drama. A young girl's inability to deal with
an inner conflict and her ultimate suicide. Obie Award for Best Off-Broadway
Play. *Cast:* 1 BM, 7 F. *Length:* 1 Act. *Prod:* Cricket Theatre, New York, Jan.
1964. *Pubn:* SF. *Lib Source:* HBA. *Perm:* Agency, SF.

In His Own Write. See The Lennon Play: In His Own Write, by Adrienne Kennedy,
John Lennon, and Victor Spinetti.

Lesson in a Dead Language. (1967). Poetic Drama. The state of an adolescent girl
and her feelings about family, menstruation, and death. *Cast:* 5 BF. *Length:* 1
Act. *Pubn: Collision Course,* ed. by Edward Parone, New York: Vintage, 1968.
Perm: Agency, Ronald Hobbs.

The Owl Answers. (1969). Poetic Drama. Young woman's inability to accept her
ancestry and how it places her in society. *Cast:* 6 M, 2 F. *Length:* 1 Act. *Prod:*
Public Theatre, New York Shakespeare Festival, N.Y., Jan. 1969. *Pubn: Black
Theater USA,* ed. by James V. Hatch and Ted Shine, New York: Free Pr., 1974;
Cities in Bezique, SF. *Lib Source:* HBA. *Perm:* Agency, SF.

The Pale Blue Flower. (1955). *Length:* 1 Act. *Perm:* Not available.

A Rat's Mass. (1967). Poetic Drama. Inner state of a brother and sister and their
conflicts over religion, family, and sex. *Cast:* 1 BM, 1 BF, 1 WF, extras. *Length:*
1 Act. *Prod:* La Mama E.T.C., New York, Sept. 1971. *Pubn: New Black Playwrights,* ed. by William Couch, Jr., Baton Rouge: Louisiana State Univ., 1968. *Lib
Source:* HBA. *Perm:* Agency, Ronald Hobbs.

Sun. (1969). Monologue. A tribute to Malcolm X. *Cast:* 1 BM. *Length:* 1 Act. *Prod:*
Theatre Upstairs, Royal Court, London, Eng., Aug. 1969. *Pubn: Spontaneous*

KENNEDY, ADRIENNE (Cont.)

Combustion, ed. by Rochelle Owens, The Winter Repertory #6, New York: Winter House, 1972. *Lib Source:* HBA. *Perm:* Agency, Ronald Hobbs.

KENNEDY, ADRIENNE, JOHN LENNON,* and VICTOR SPINETTI*

The Lennon Play: In His Own Write. "This play is about the growing up of any of us; the things that helped us to be more aware. We used John's poems and stories."—Victor Spinetti.   *Cast:* 26 M & F, extras. *Length:* 1 Act. *Prod:* National Theatre Company, London, Eng., 1967. *Pubn:* New York: Simon & Schuster, 1968. *Lib Source:* HBA.

KENNEDY, ADRIENNE, and CECIL TAYLOR

A Rat's Mass/Procession in Shout. Improvizational Jazz Opera. Staged and adapted by Cecil Taylor from Ms. Kennedy's play *A Rat's Mass.*   *Cast:* 17 M & F, 5 musicians. *Length:* 1 Act (2 hours). *Prod:* La Mama E.T.C., New York, Mar. 1976.

KENNEDY, JANIE, and SCOTT KENNEDY

The Poetic Life of Langston Hughes. Protest Morality Drama with Music. Uses poetry, music, and dance. Dramatic sketches as seen through the eyes of Langston Hughes.   *Cast:* 1 BM, 1 BF, dancers. *Length:* 2 Acts. *Prod:* ATRA (African Theatre and the Related Arts), Freetown, Sierra Leone, W. Africa, 1967. *Lib Source:* Kennedy Collection. *Perm:* Author.

The Rivers of the Black Man. Historical Drama with Music. Uses poetry, African drumming, music (gospel, blues, jazz). Depicts the many rivers of the black man, including his indestructible spirit, his connection with endless time, his tears and laughter, his survival, his mask of freedom, his pride, and the African experience.   *Cast:* 1 BM, 1 BF, 2 drummers, 3 dancers, 4 musicians. *Length:* 3 Acts. *Prod:* ATRA (African Theatre and the Related Arts), Accra, Ghana, W. Africa, 1969. *Lib Source:* Kennedy Collection. *Perm:* Author.

KENNEDY, MATTIE

A Love Supreme. MFA Thesis.   *Length:* Full Length. *Prod:* U.C.L.A., Los Angeles, Calif., Spring 1974.

KENNEDY, SCOTT

Behind the Mask. Historical Morality Drama with Music. Conscience of America and dramatic figures of the past come alive to challenge bigotry and call for freedom now.   *Cast:* 3 BM, 1 BF, 2 B, singers, musicians. *Length:* 2 Acts. *Prod:* ATRA (African Theatre and Related Arts), New York, 1965. *Lib Source:* Kennedy Collection. *Perm:* Author.

Beyond the Veil. Historical Mythic Drama with Music. A punchy prize fighter becomes articulate when speaking of black pride and culture. Set in a gym. *Cast:* 2 BM, 1 BF, singers, musicians. *Length:* 2 Acts. *Prod:* ATRA (African Theatre and Related Arts), New York, 1965. *Lib Source:* Kennedy Collection. *Perm:* Author.

Commitment to a Dream. Historical Mythic Ritual/Drama with Music and Dance. A group of players is rehearsing a play that addresses itself to the best way to achieve freedom. The services of a High Priestess from Africa (Ghana) are employed to "infuse the Spirits" in the players and let them "go back in time." Through Ju Ju and a "Trance Dance," some of the players are able to resurrect historical characters such as Joseph Cinque, Fred Douglass, and Nat Turner. *Cast:* 6 BM, 2 BF, 1 WF, dancers, drummers. *Prod:* ATRA (African Theatre and the Related Arts), New York, 1965. *Lib Source:* Kennedy Collection. *Perm:* Author.

Cries from the Ghetto. Protest Morality Drama with Music. Uses poetry and dance. Points a finger at the cancerous color sickness that permeates American society and the world and concerns the struggle for dignity and respect and the clash between morality and values.   *Cast:* 4 BM, 2 BF, musicians, singers. *Length:* 1 Act. *Prod:* ATRA (African Theatre and the Related Arts), New York, 1966. *Lib Source:* Kennedy Collection. *Perm:* Author.

Cries! How African! Drama with Mime. Stresses a need for positive images, racial pride, and group consciousness among Blacks.   *Cast:* 4 BM, 4 BF. *Length:* 1 Act. *Prod:* ATRA (African Theatre and the Related Arts), Adelaide, Australia, 1973. *Lib Source:* Kennedy Collection. *Perm:* Author.

Dramatic Voices of Protest. Historical Drama with Music. Through drama, music, poetry, and improvised black tales, dramatic figures of the past come alive to present the voices of freedom.   *Cast:* 2 BM, 2 BF, singers. *Length:* 2 Acts. *Prod:* ATRA (African Theatre and the Related Arts), New York, 1964. *Lib Source:* Kennedy Collection. *Perm:* Author.

Harn's Children. Morality Drama with Music. Depicts a struggle for dignity and respect in a civil rights conflict as well as a clash of morality and values. Set in a church and a jail in the South.   *Cast:* 5 BM, 3 BF, 2 WM, 12 Mixed M & F. *Length:* 3 Acts. *Prod:* ATRA (African Theatre and the Related Arts), New York, 1962. *Lib Source:* Kennedy Collection. *Perm:* Author.

The King Is Dead. Mythic Ritual/Drama with Music and Dance. Uses Dr. Martin Luther King as a symbolic figure in the struggle for dignity and respect and a clash of morality and values in America.   *Cast:* 3 BM, 2 BF, choir, dancers, extras. *Length:* 2 Acts. *Prod:* ATRA (African Theatre and the Related Arts), New York, 1971. *Perm:* Author.

Negritude: A Speak Out on Color. Protest Morality Drama with Music. Uses poetry and dance. Points a finger at cancerous color sickness that permeates American society and the world and concerns the struggle for dignity and respect and the clash between morality and values.   *Cast:* 4 BM, 4 BF, dancers, singers, musicians. *Length:* 1 Act. *Prod:* ATRA (African Theatre and the Related Arts), New York, 1965. *Lib Source:* Kennedy Collection. *Perm:* Author.

The Spirit that Creates. Mythic Morality Drama with Music and Dance. Depicts the conflict of a human being in a society consumed with greed. The theme is that the spirit that creates must be free.   *Cast:* 10 BC, musicians. *Prod:* ATRA (African Theatre and the Related Arts), Washington, D.C., 1970. *Lib Source:* Kennedy Collection. *Perm:* Author.

KENNEDY, SCOTT (*Cont.*)

They Sang of a Nation. Protest Morality Drama with Poetry, Music, and Dance. Dramatic sketches using the works of Robert Frost, Langston Hughes, and Carl Sandburg. *Cast:* 1 BM, 4 dancers, 4 musicians. *Length:* 2 Acts. *Prod:* ATRA (African Theatre and the Related Arts). Accra, Ghana, W. Africa, 1968. *Lib. Source:* Kennedy Collection. *Perm:* Author.

Threshold of a Dawn. Historical Mythic Ritual/Drama with Music and Dance. Sequel to *Commitment to a Dream.* A group of players is rehearsing a play that addresses itself to the best way to achieve freedom. The services of a high priestess from Africa (Ghana) are employed to "infuse the Spirits" in the players and let them "go back in Time." Through JuJu and a "Trance Dance," some of the players are able to resurrect historical characters such as John Copeland, Frances E. W. Harper, Sojourner Truth, Harriet Tubman, and Dr. William DuBois. *Cast:* 3 BM, 3 BF, 1 WF, chorus, dancers, drummers. *Length:* 2 Acts. *Prod:* ATRA (African Theatre and the Related Arts), New York, 1965. *Lib Source:* Kennedy Collection. *Perm:* Author.

KENNEDY, SCOTT, and JANIE KENNEDY

The Poetic Life of Langston Hughes. Protest Morality Drama with Poetry, Music, and Dance. Dramatic sketches as seen through the eyes of Langston Hughes. *Cast:* 1 BM, 1 BF, dancers. *Length:* 2 Acts. *Prod:* ATRA (African Theatre and the Related Arts), Freetown, Sierra Leone, W. Africa, 1967. *Lib Source:* Kennedy Collection. *Perm:* Author.

The Rivers of the Black Man. Historical Drama with Music. Uses poetry, African drumming, music (gospel, blues, jazz). Depicts the many rivers of the black man, including his indestructible spirit, his connection with endless time, his tears and laughter, his survival, his mask of freedom, his pride, and the African experience. *Cast:* 1 BM, 1 BF, 2 drummers, 3 dancers, 4 musicians. *Length:* 3 Acts. *Prod:* ATRA (African Theatre and the Related Arts), Accra, Ghana, W. Africa, 1969. *Lib Source:* Kennedy Collection. *Perm:* Author.

KENYATTA, DAMON

The Black Experience. (1971).

KENYON, GREGORY

The Piranha Are Waiting. (1972). Morality. The play takes place in Willie Taylor's San Francisco flat, which contains the living room of Sam and Martha. The televised funeral of Jennifer Christe, a "pseudo-black" actress, is the catalyst for flashbacks of time and memory depicting the events leading to her death. *Cast:* 4 BM, 2 BF. *Length:* 3 Acts. *Lib Source:* Typescript, SCHOM.

KILLENS, JOHN O.

Cotillion. Dramatic Comedy. Adapted from Killens' novel, *The Cotillion.* A satire on the black middle class and their imitation of white upper classes. *Cast:* 14. *Prod:* NFT, New York, July 1975. *Perm:* Agency, Phyllis Jackson.

Lower than the Angels. Drama. Adapted from a chapter in Killens' novel *Youngblood.* Set on a Georgia plantation in the late 1950s. Struggle between black and white family exacerbated by the friendship between black boy and white boy.   *Cast:* 15. *Length:* 3 Acts. *Prod:* APT, New York, Jan. 1965. *Perm:* Agency, Phyllis Jackson.

KILLENS, JOHN O., and LOFTEN MITCHELL

Ballad of the Winter Soldiers. Historical Drama. Depicts freedom fighters through-out history.   *Cast:* 4 BM, 2 BF, 1 BG, 3 WM, 4 WF, dancers, singers. *Length:* 2 Acts. *Prod:* Benefit for CORE, Philharmonic Hall, Lincoln Center, New York, Sept. 28, 1964. *Perm:* Agency, Phyllis Jackson.

KILONFE, OBA

Sugar and Thomas. (1970). Melodrama. Sugar loses her man to a white woman because she let her hair go natural. She gets her revenge.   *Cast:* 2 DM, 1 BF, 1 WM, 1 WF, extras. *Length:* 1 Act. *Pubn: Connection,* ed. by Curtiss Porter, Pittsburgh: Oduduwa Productions, 1970. *Lib Source:* HBA.

KIMBLE, KATHLEEN

Jimtown.   Prod: Theatre Genesis, New York, Apr. 1972.

Meat Rack. (1972). Morality Comedy. A play about a street lady who wants to get off the "meat rack."   *Cast:* 11 BM, 6 BF (doubling). *Length:* 1 Act. *Prod:* Afro-American Studio Theatre, New York, Jan. 1975. *Pubn: Scripts,* vol. I, no. 7, May 1972. *Lib Source:* HBA.

KING, CURTIS LAMAR

Development of the Black Man.

Sharecroppers.

A Tribute to the Oppressed.

KING, WOODIE, JR.

Black Dreams. Screenplay. Based on the short story "Beautiful Light and Black Our Dreams."   *Perm:* Author, c/o NFT.

Jet. Screenplay.   *Perm:* Author c/o NFT.

Simple Blues. (1967). Adapted from the poetry and stories of Langston Hughes.

KING, WOODIE, JR., and LANGSTON HUGHES

The Weary Blues. (1966). Adapted from Langston Hughes's book of poetry of the same name.   *Prod:* The Adventure Corps, New York, Feb. 1968.

KIRKSEY, VAN

The Hassle.

KNOWLES, GABRIELLA

What Do We Tell Our Children.   Prod: Reading, Frank Silvera Writers' Workshop, Martinique Theatre, New York, June 1974.

KNUSDEN, K.

There Were Two Tramps, Now There Are None.

KURTZ, CLEVELAND

Sarge. (1974). Two Green Berets visit their former sergeant from Vietnam to recall buddy days and the war, but they discover the war's not yet over. *Cast:* 1 BM, 2 WM. *Length:* 1 Act. *Prod:* Brown University, Providence, R.I., May 1974. *Pubn: Shubert Playbook Series*, vol. 2, no. 1, ed. by John Emigh, 1974. *Lib Source:* HBA.

KURTZ, CLEVELAND, and SANDRA FRANKLIN

A Voice in the Wilderness. Gospel Song Play. *Length:* 1 Act. *Prod:* Congdon Street Baptist Church, Providence, R.I., Nov. 1973.

KYSER, ERMA L.

The Day That Was. Comedy/Drama. Deals with the black-white societal situation in reverse. *Length:* 1 Act. *Perm:* Author.

Pseudo Drama of the Life and Times of Mammy Pleasant. Play about the life of Mary Ellen Pleasant. *Length:* 3 Acts. *Perm:* Author.

She Was a Woman. Domestic Drama. Story about a struggling black family headed by a mother with failing health who tries to hold her family together—each one is fighting to make it in a world of oppression. *Cast:* 3 BM, 5 BF. *Length:* 3 Acts. *Perm:* Author.

LADIPO, DURO

Oba Koso. Yoruba Folk Musical. Based on Nigeria's most famous and revered legend. *Prod:* Felt Forum, New York, Apr. 1975.

LAMB, A. CLIFTON

Black Woman in White. Drama. A courageous black girl, contrary to her mother's desire that she prepare for the concert stage, elects to become a medical doctor and, as a woman in white, fights to establish a hospital for her denied people in a hostile southern community. *Cast:* 7 BM, 8 BF, 3 WM, 1 child, chorus. *Length:* 3 Acts. *Prod:* State University of Iowa, Iowa City, 1940; Rose McClendon Players, Harlem Library, New York, Aug. 1941. *Perm:* Author.

The Breeders.

A Christmas Message for a Little Soul. The story concerns the attempt of a little black boy to reconcile the teaching he has received in Sunday school with what he is being taught in a militant soul school. He is a symbol of those blacks who are groping in the no-man's-land between two camps, the "kneeling Toms" and the "fighting souls." *Cast:* 3 BM, 1 B, 1 BF, extras, children. *Perm:* Author.

Christy Citadel. *Pubn: Intercollegian,* Apr. 1956.

God's Great Acres. Folk Drama. The story concerns the efforts of a black school principal to help tenant farmers who are about to be displaced by machines. Awarded Sergel Prize in Regional Playwriting, State University of Iowa, 1939.

Cast: 4 BM, 3 BF, 1 BB, 3 WM, extras. *Prod:* Prairie View A.&M. U., Tex., 1939. *Perm:* Author.

Mistake into Miracle. Historical Drama. A dramatization of the critical years in the life of black scientist, Dr. George Washington Carver. When he advised farmers, threatened by the devastating boll weevil, to "plow under your cotton and put the land to peanuts," the advice backfired when the bottom dropped out of the peanut market. Ranked among the top ten of the 1600 scripts entered in the Hallmark Hall of Fame Contest in Teleplaywriting. Adapted for stage at Morgan State College. *Cast:* 5 BM, 4 BF, 3 WM, 3 WF, 1 child, extras. *Prod:* Morgan State College, Baltimore, Md., 1957. *Perm:* Author.

The New Window.

Portrait of a Pioneer. Radio Play. The story of the Negro actor, Ira Aldridge, from his apprenticeship as a ship's carpenter in Baltimore, Maryland, to his triumphs on the continental stage. *Cast:* 1 BM, 1 WM, 1 WF, narrator, 3 voices. *Length:* 15 Minutes. *Prod:* WFBR, Baltimore, Md. *Pubn: Negro History Bulletin,* vol. 12, Apr. 1949. *Perm:* Author.

Roughshod up the Mountain. Folk Drama. The story concerns a black storefront preacher who acquires an impressive church in a once white, upper-middle class community. He begins to worship the church building instead of God and attempts to tailor the upper-class Negroes who have settled in the community; he loses the church, but regains his soul. *Cast:* 5 BM, 3 BF. *Length:* Full Length. *Prod:* State University of Iowa, Iowa City, 1953. *Perm:* Author.

Shades of Cottonlips. Expressionistic Drama. A young black playwright fights to break away from the stereotype perpetuated by the old minstrel shows. Winner of the Henry York Steiner Memorial Prize in playwriting, Grinnell College, Iowa, 1932. *Cast:* 1 BM, 1 BF (doubling). *Perm:* Author.

The Two Gifts. (1934). Christmas Play for Negroes. Granny tells her poor and doubting grandchildren the story of Melchior, the black magus, which restores their faith. *Cast:* 2 BM, 2 BF, 1 WM. *Length:* 1 Act. *Prod:* AME, Church, Muscatine, Iowa, Dec. 24, 1932. *Pubn:* Grinnell Plays, Chicago: Dramatic Pub. Co., 1935. *Lib Source:* NYPL. *Perm:* Author.

LANDAU, EL

E' Lollipop. A play that deals with the adventures and friendship of a black child and a white child in the African hinterlands.

LANG, JAMES A.

The Plague. (1972). Drama. Brother is torn between getting himself together for his wife and children or hanging onto his "jones" with the fellows on the block. Sub-titled: *Please Don't Let the Joneses Get You Down.*   *Cast:* 11 BM, 1 BB, 1 BF, 1 BG, 2 WM, extras. *Length:* 1 Act. *Pubn: Who Took the Weight (Black Voices from Norfolk Prison),* Boston: Little, 1972. *Lib Source:* HBA.

LANGE, TED

Day Zsa Voo.

LANGE, TED (Cont.)

A Foul Movement. A play with revolutionary, moral, social, and political imagery. *Prod:* Theatre Black, New York University, May 1972.

Pig, Male and Young.

Sounds from a Flute.

LARK, MORRIS

My Brother's Keeper. *Prod:* Reading, Frank Silvera Writers' Workshop, City College of New York, Mar. 1977.

LAYTON, TURNER J., and HENRY CREAMER

Strut Miss Lizzie. Musical Comedy. *Prod:* Times Square Theatre, New York, June 1922.

LEA

Old MacDonald Had a Camp. Children's Play. The street is the farm and MacDonald is the man, the devil . . . and members of the farm are the people on the street. *Prod:* Theatre Black, House of Kuumba, New York, n.d.

LEAGUE, RAYMOND

Mrs. Carrie B. Phillips. *Prod:* Lambs Club, New York, 1970.

LEAKS, SYLVESTER

My God, My God Is Dead. Screenplay.

Trouble, Blues 'n' Trouble.

LeBLANC, WHITNEY

Dreams Deferred. Ritualistic Historical Fantasy. Set in the Martin Luther King, Jr. civil rights struggle of the 1960s, this play deals with the individual struggles of a Black, a Cuban mulatto, and a white to maintain a life together. *Cast:* 2 BM, 1 Cuban M, 1 WM, 2 WF. *Length:* 2 Acts. *Prod:* Reading, Frank Silvera Writers' Workshop, Martinique Theatre, New York, Feb. 1975. *Perm:* Agency, Lerb Enterprises.

It's a Small World. (1972). Television Script. The coincidental reacquaintance of a black man with a white stripper triggers jealousy in a black woman. *Cast:* 2 BM, 1 BB, 1 BF, 1 WF. *Length:* 1 Act. *Prod:* Tape, Maryland Center for Public Broadcasting, Owings Mills, Md., n.d. *Perm:* Agency, Lerb Enterprises.

The Killing of an Eagle. Expressionist Surrealistic Drama. Explores the difficulty two men—one black, one white—have maintaining a friendship because of what their religions have taught them about "staying with their own kind." *Cast:* 7 BM, 2 BF, 6 WM, 5 WF. *Length:* 3 Acts. *Perm:* Agency, Lerb Enterprises.

LEE, BILLY

A Bench in Central Park.

LEE, HARRY

A Nickel Whistle. Chicago in the early twentieth century. A nickel whistle stolen by a black youngster is the spark that ignites the flame for prejudiced whites and turmoil results. *Cast:* 6 BM, 1 BB, 2 BF, 1 BG, 12 WM, 3 WF, 1 Indian M, 1 Chinese M, extras. *Length:* Full Length. *Lib Source:* 1946 Typescript, SCHOM.

LEE, JAMES

The Rag Pickers. *Cast:* 6 BM, 1 BF. *Length:* 1 Act. *Prod:* Reading, Frank Silvera Writers' Workshop, Martinique Theatre, New York, June 1975.

The Shoeshine Parlor. Melodrama. About men and women in a black ghetto, a dope pusher who eventually has lye thrown in his face by an avenging minister, and a young girl who dies of an overdose. *Length:* Full Length. *Prod:* The Family, Mobile Theatre, New York, Aug. 1975.

LEE, LESLIE

Between Now and Then. Drama. Story of a white middle class family's inability to adjust to social change, as seen from a black point of view. *Cast:* 1 BM, 5 WM, 2 WF. *Length:* 2 Acts. *Prod:* New Dramatists, New York, 1974. *Perm:* Agency, Ellen Neuwald.

Cops and Robbers. Absurd Tragi-Comedy. A play about clinging to tradition and custom and a failure to respond to change. *Cast:* 1 BM, 1 BF, 1 WM. *Length:* 1 Act. *Prod:* Café La Mama, New York, Apr. 1970. *Perm:* Agency, Ellen Neuwald.

Elegy to a Down Queen. Tragi-Comedy. Play concerns revolution within a family as the family accommodates to changing times. *Cast:* 13 B, 6 W. *Length:* 2 Acts. *Prod:* Café La Mama, New York, Feb. 1969. *Perm:* Agency, Ellen Neuwald.

The First Breeze of Summer. Domestic Drama. The life and loves of three generations of a middle class family, with emphasis on Grammer and her grandson. *Cast:* 6 BM, 6 BF, 1 BB, 1 WM. *Length:* 2 Acts. *Prod:* NEC, New York, Feb. 1975. *Perm:* Agency, Ellen Neuwald.

The War Party. Tragedy. Two opposing forces within the black revolutionary movement battle over whether the ends justify the means. *Cast:* 5 BM, 2 BF, 4 WM, 2 WF. *Length:* 2 Acts. *Prod:* New Dramatists, New York, 1973. *Perm:* Agency, Ellen Neuwald.

LERNER, H. ERWIN

Tea. *Prod:* NFT, New York, Jan. 1975.

LEROY, LESLIE HURLEY

Festivities for a New World.

LESLIE, LEW*

From Dixie to Broadway. Musical Revue. Constructed around the life of black actress Florence Mills. This work was created by black and white artists. Book credited to Walter DeLeon, Tom Howard, Sidney Lazarus, and Lew Leslie. Music credited to George Myer, Arthur Johnson, and William Vodrey.

LESLIE, LEW* *(Cont.)*

Lyrics credited to Grant Clark and Roy Turk. Subtitled: *Plantation Revue* and *From Dover to Dixie.*   *Prod:* Broadhurst Theatre, New York, Oct. 1924.

LEWIS, DAVID

Bubba, Connie, and Hindy. Satire. The situation of a job interview is used as a symbol of a black perspective on the afterlife.   *Cast:* 2 BM. *Length:* 1 Act. *Perm:* Author.

Do Your Thing. (1970). Comedy. Oliver comes to visit his friend Andrew in Harlem, but Andrew won't let him in because of paranoia.   *Cast:* 3 BM, 1 BF. *Length:* 1 Act. *Perm:* Author.

Georgia Man and Jamaican Man. (1970). Comedy. A satire about how Afro-Americans and Caribbean West Indians view each other.   *Cast:* 4 BM, 1 B, 5 BF. *Length:* 1 Act. *Perm:* Author.

Gonna Make That Scene. (1967). Morality Play. Two black men get on an elevator to "rise" to upper floors (middle class), but are discouraged by what they see in the middle class elevator operator. They go back down.   *Cast:* 3 BM. *Length:* 1 Act. *Perm:* Author.

Heaven—I've Been There; Hell—I've Been There Too. (1972).   *Perm:* Author.

A Knight in Shining Black Armour. (1971). Domestic Drama. Love story between two members of the middle class—an assistant principal in a junior high school and his former girl friend, with whom he has a moving dialogue minutes before he is to marry a much younger woman.   *Cast:* 1 BM, 3 BF, 1 girl's voice. *Length:* 1 Act. *Perm:* Author.

Miss America of 1910. (1971). Morality Drama. Takes place in a bar and explores the struggle between a barmaid who wants to play an Aretha Franklin record and a drunk who wants to recite Lincoln's Gettysburg Address.   *Cast:* 3 BM, 1 BF, 2 WM. *Length:* 1 Act. *Perm:* Author.

Mr. B. (1971). Domestic Drama. Play takes place in a poolroom in the mid-fifties and describes a poignant love story against a background of two brothers playing pool, with the winner receiving a chicken dinner. The main characters are named after two seldom-remembered presidents.   *Cast:* 6 BM, 1 BF. *Length:* 1 Act. *Perm:* Author.

My Cherie Amour. (1970). Comedy. Lovers, Ronald and Cherie, love, quarrel, and make up at a discotheque.   *Cast:* 1 BM, 1 BF, extras. *Length:* 1 Act. *Perm:* Author.

One Hundred Is a Long Number. (1972). Children's Comedy. Mother and father find themselves confronted with an old antagonism between their two sons; the older boy wants to have his way over the younger son.   *Cast:* 1 BM, 2 BB, 1 BF. *Length:* 1 Act. *Perm:* Author.

Sonny Boy. (1970). Comedy. Curtis stands on the corner trying to hustle a morning paper from various passersby, but finally has to buy his own.   *Cast:* 3 BM, 3 BF, 1 BB. *Length:* 1 Act. *Perm:* Author.

Sporty.   *Perm:* Author.

Those Wonderful Folks (of the First Baptist Church of New Jerusalem in Harlem). (1972). Children's Comedy. Fourteen-year-old girl tries to get the upper hand on her mother before going to church on Sunday morning. A celebration of black cultural values—love of good cooking and the church.   *Cast:* 1 BF, 1 BG. *Length:* 1 Act. *Perm:* Author.

Wally Dear.   *Perm:* Author.

LEWIS, ED "BIM"

The Gun Court Affair. Comedy/Melodrama with Music. "The protagonist, George Bucket, divides his time off from his illegal operations between a long suffering wife and a new mistress."—Townsend Brewster, *Newsletter* of the Harlem Cultural Council, vol. 2, no. 7.   *Length:* Full Length. *Prod:* Jamaica Progressive League and Carib Films, Inc., New York, Spring 1975.

LEWIS, ERMA D.

Our Heritage. Historical Drama. With poetry, song, and dance the play represents a history of the black man from the African era to the present.   *Length:* Full Length. *Prod:* Sojourner Truth Community Theatre, Fort Worth, Tex., n.d. *Perm:* Author.

The Sharecroppers. Melodrama. A black family struggling for survival and dignity by sharecropping on a white plantation manage to assert their independence. *Cast:* 3 BM, 2 BF, 2 WM, 1 WF. *Length:* 1 Act. *Prod:* Jackson State University, Miss., n.d. *Perm:* Author.

LEWIS, RON

Langston, Living. Ritual. Based on the works of Langston Hughes. *Prod:* KUUMBA, Chicago, Ill., 1974.

LIFE, REGGIE

The Natural.   *Prod:* Reading, Frank Silvera Writers' Workshop, Martinique Theatre, New York, Dec. 1975.

LIGHTS, FREDERICK L.

All over Nothin'. Children's Play. This play concerns children at play and the parents who get involved in the children's spats.   *Length:* 1 Act. *Prod:* AMAS Repertory Theatre, Inc., New York, 1975. *Perm:* Author.

Barbershop Boogie. Drama. A Negro student attempts to aid a young white soldier in a dangerous segregated situation in the South.   *Length:* 1 Act. *Perm:* Author.

Boys Like Us. A play about an Ivy League fraternity confronted with its first black pledge.   *Length:* 1 Act. *Perm:* Author.

Mood Indigo. A play that utilizes the music of Duke Ellington.   *Perm:* Author.

Peripity. This play concerns the sudden reversal of fortune in the life of a Negro preacher.   *Length:* Full Length. *Perm:* Author.

LIGHTS, FREDERICK L. *(Cont.)*

Pigeons en Casserole. An adaptation of Bessie Brewer's short story of the same title. The play is about an exiled aristocratic family trying to adjust to America. *Perm:* Author.

Samson and Lilah Dee. A fairy tale for adults. Tells the biblical story of Samson and Delilah through the life of a boxer in Chicago in the 1930s.   *Perm:* Author.

The Underlings. This adaptation of Langston Hughes' poem "Father and Son" is a play about miscegenation.   *Length:* 1 Act. *Perm:* Author.

LINCOLN, ABBEY

A Pig in a Poke.   *Prod:* Mafundi Institute, Los Angeles, Calif., 1975.

A Streak o' Lean. (1967). A scene about the power of money, which a poor black man keeps when he finds it, in spite of conventional morality.   *Pubn: Black Scenes,* ed. by Alice Childress, New York: Doubleday, 1971. *Lib Source:* HBA.

LINDSAY, POWELL

Flight from Fear.

Young Man from Harlem. (1938).

LIPSCOMB, G. D.

Compromise. (1925).

Frances. Melodrama. Black farmer is duped into giving his niece as a concubine to a white landowner, thinking he will be given land.   *Cast:* 2 BM, 1 BF, 1 WM. *Length:* 1 Act. *Pubn: Opportunity* magazine, May 1925. *Lib Source:* SCHOM.

LIVINGSTONE, MYRTLE SMITH

For Unborn Children. (1926). Folk Drama. Son in a southern black family plans to marry a white girl. His grandmother objects because the boy's mother was white and hated her own son.   *Cast:* 2 BF, 1 BM, 1 WF, extras. *Length:* 1 Act. *Pubn: Black Theater USA,* ed. by James V. Hatch and Ted Shine, New York: Free Pr., 1974; *Crisis* magazine, July 1926. *Lib Source:* HBA.

LLOYD, DARRYLE

P. J. Jones. Drama. This play deals with the rise and fall of a ruthless black narcotics dealer in Harlem.   *Cast:* 10 BM, 6 BF, 6 WM. *Length:* 2 Acts. *Prod:* Royal Tyler Theatre, University of Vermont, Burlington, Apr. 1974. *Perm:* Author.

You're Welcome, but You Can't Stay. (1975). Drama. Play deals with a well-to-do black middle class family that is held captive and terrorized in their own home by a gang of white murderers.   *Cast:* 5 BM, 1 BB, 3 BF, 4 WM, 1 WF. *Length:* 2 Acts. *Perm:* Author.

LOMAX, PEARL CLEAGE

Duet for Three Voices. (1969).   *Length:* 1 Act.

Hymn for the Rebels. (1968).   *Length:* 1 Act.

The Sale. (1972).   *Length:* 1 Act.

LONG, BARBARA A.

Midnight Brown. (1968). Mythic. The "Subterranean-Black-Subconscious" is symbolized by seventeen various "black" characters.   *Cast:* 17 B M & F. *Length:* 1 Act. *Lib Source:* Typescript, SCHOM.

LONG, RICHARD A.

Black Is Many Hues. (1969).

Joan of Arc. (1964). Folk Opera.

Pilgrim's Price. (1963). Sketches.

Reasons of State. (1966).

Stairway to Heaven. (1964). Gospel Opera.

LUCAS, W. F.

Africa Foo Young. (1970). Comedy. Black comedy in a Chinese restaurant.   *Cast:* 2 BM, 2 BF, 1 B Chinese. *Length:* 1 Act. *Prod:* Carpetbag Theatre, Knoxville, Tenn., 1971. *Perm:* Author.

Aunt Lottie's Wake. (1970). Mythic Comedy. The funeral and wake of an aged and allegedly well-off black lady.   *Cast:* 6–10 B M & F. *Length:* 1 Act. *Prod:* Carpetbag Theatre, Knoxville, Tenn., 1971; University of Tennessee, Knoxville, 1974. *Perm:* Author.

Bosun's Blues. (1971). Mythic Comedy. A monologue by a black seaman after a long journey at sea.   *Cast:* 1 BM, voices. *Length:* 1 Act. *Prod:* Carpetbag Theatre, Knoxville, Tenn., 1972. *Perm:* Author.

Elevator Stomp. (1970). Mythic Comedy. Blacks and whites are stranded together in a stalled apartment elevator.   *Cast:* 4 B, 4 W. *Length:* 1 Act. *Prod:* Carpetbag Theatre, Knoxville, Tenn., 1971. *Perm:* Author.

Fandango's for Miss X. (1968). Mythic Comedy. A monologue by a housewife declaring her identity.   *Cast:* 1 BF, music and voices. *Length:* 1 Act. *Prod:* Black Arts Spectrum Theatre, Philadelphia, Pa., 1969. *Perm:* Author.

The Mint. (1971). Comedy. Blacks attempting to gain entry into the U.S. Mint.   *Cast:* 10 B M & F. *Length:* 1 Act. *Prod:* Carpetbag Theatre, Workshop performance, Knoxville, Tenn., 1972. *Perm:* Author.

Patent Leather Sunday. (1967). Domestic Comedy. The relationship between two black women, one southern and the other West Indian.   *Cast:* 2 BF. *Length:* 1 Act. *Prod:* Lincoln University, Pa., 1967; University of Tennessee, Knoxville, 1974. *Perm:* Author.

Rudyard's Confections. (1972). Mythic Comedy. The adventures of a West Indian candy store owner and his conflict with a Hassidic rabbi who is almost converted to Christianity.   *Cast:* 2 BM, 1 BF, 1 BC, 1 WM, 1 WF, 1 WC, extras. *Length:* 2 Acts. *Perm:* Author.

LUCAS, W. F. *(Cont.)*

The Triflers, Red, Black, and Green. (1971). Tragi-Comedy. Black academicians in search of their identities. *Cast:* 4 BM, 2 BF, 2 WM, 2 WF. *Length:* 2 Acts. *Perm:* Author.

Wisemen in Stocking Caps or *The First Supper.* (1973). Mythic Comedy. An updated version of the Last Supper; for contemporary audiences. *Cast:* 14 BM, 2 BF, 2 WF. *Length:* 2 Acts. *Perm:* Author.

LUCE, PATRICK

Echoes of Thunder. Morality Drama. Nonviolent Raymond, urged by his white liberal girl friend, kills black militant friend. *Cast:* 2 BM, 1 BF, 1 WF. *Length:* 1 Act.

LUKAS, SONNY THE LION 186. *See* Scott, Joseph

LUTHER, KATIE

He Will Hallow Thee. (1969). Protest Drama. Wealthy southern white woman is lynched for educating black male in the ministry. *Length:* 3 Acts.

LYLE, K. CURTIS

Days of Thunder, Nights of Violence. (1970).

Guerilla Warfare. (1970).

Minstrel Show. (1970).

The Processes of Allusion.

Wichita.

LYLES, AUBREY

Runnin' de Town. Musical Comedy. *Cast:* 15 B M & F. *Length:* 2 Acts. *Prod:* Shubert Theatre, New York, Nov. 1930.

LYLES, AUBREY, EUBIE BLAKE, FLOURNOY MILLER, and NOBLE SISSLE

Shuffle Along. Musical Comedy. Story possibly based on Miller and Lyles' play *Mayor of Dixie,* 1907. Concerns the efforts of three candidates to win a mayoralty campaign and the complications when one wins. Subtitled: *Mayor of Jim Town.* *Cast:* 15 BM, 4 BF, chorus. *Length:* 2 Acts. *Prod:* Sixty-third Street Music Hall, New York, May 1921. *Pubn: Best Plays of 1920–21,* ed. by Burns Mantle, New York: Dodd, 1921.

LYLES, AUBREY, and FLOURNOY MILLER

Keep Shufflin'. (1928). Musical Comedy. Steve and Sam plan to blow up a bank, "thereby releasing a lot of lazy capital loafing in the vaults." *Cast:* 10 BM, 1 BF. *Length:* 2 Acts. *Prod:* Daly's Theatre, New York, Feb. 1928. *Pubn: Best Plays of 1927–28,* ed. by Burns Mantle, New York: Dodd, 1928.

Lazy Rhythm. (c. 1931). Musical.

Rang Tang. Musical Revue.   *Cast:* 10 BM, 10 BF. *Length:* 2 Acts. *Prod:* Royale Theatre, New York, July 1927. *Pubn: Best Plays of 1927-28*, ed. by Burns Mantle, New York: Dodd, 1928.

Runnin' Wild. Musical Comedy. The adventures of Sam Peck (Sharpster) and Steve Jenkins (Boob).   *Cast:* 15 BM, 7 BF. *Length:* 2 Acts. *Prod:* Colonial Theatre, New York, Oct. 1923. *Pubn: Best Plays of 1923-24*, ed. by Burns Mantle, New York: Dodd, 1924.

LYLES, AUBREY, FLOURNOY MILLER, and HAL REID

The Oyster Man. Musical Revue. Music by Henry Creamer, Ernest Hogan, and William Vodrey.   *Prod:* Yorkville Theatre, New York, Dec. 1907.

LYLES, AUBREY, FLOURNEY MILLER, and CHARLES TAZEWELL

Sugar Hill. "A story of the Negro colony in Harlem, having to do with the recent activities of colored racketeers involving Steve Jenkins and Sam Peck, played by Miller and Lyles."—Miller and Lyles.   *Cast:* 8 BM, 6 BF, extras. *Length:* 2 Acts. *Prod:* Forrest Theatre, New York, Dec. 1931 *Pubn: Best Plays of 1931 32*, ed. by Burns Mantle, New York: Dodd, 1932.

LYNCH, KIM DEJAH, and CRAIG DELLIMORE

Black Odyssey: 200 Years in America. Historical Play with Music and Dance. *Length:* 2 Acts. *Prod:* New World Theatre, Columbia University, New York, Apr. 1976.

LYONS, SHEDRICK

A Bird of Passage out of Night. (1970). Domestic Drama. A young poetic son, Kelly, wants to leave his father and the Georgia farm but his father dies before he can leave.   *Cast:* 5 BM, 2 BF. *Length:* Full Length. *Perm:* Author.

MACBETH, ROBERT

A Black Ritual. Ritual. A ritual of Blackness.   *Cast:* B M & F. *Length:* 1 Act. *Pubn: Black Theatre,* no. 2, ed. by Ed Bullins, 1969. *Lib Source:* HBA.

McBROWN, GERTRUDE PARTHENIA

Birthday Surprise. Sketch. About the career of the author, Paul Lawrence Dunbar. *Pubn: Negro History Bulletin,* 16, Feb. 1953. *Lib Source:* NYPL.

Bought with Cookies. Historical Children's Play. The early days in the life of abolitionist Frederick Douglass.   *Cast:* 6 M, 5 F, chorus. *Length:* 1 Act. *Pubn: Negro History Bulletin,* Apr. 1949. *Lib Source:* SCHOM.

McCARLEY, ROBBIE

Wild Flower.   *Prod:* NEC, New York, Jan. 1973.

McCAUGHAN, PAT

A Soft Lullaby. (1974). Domestic Drama. Deals with the problems of five black
women: a mother, granny, and three young daughters in their late teens and
early twenties.   *Cast:* 1 BM, 5 BF. *Length:* 1 Act. *Perm:* Author.

McCLAIN, SAUNDRA, BEN CARTER, and DAVID E. MARTIN

Bitter Trails. Protest Drama with Music. A play depicting the life of migrant workers,
black migrant workers in particular, in the Southwest.   *Cast:* 5 BM, 1 BF, 5 WM,
1 WF. *Length:* 3 Acts. *Prod:* Reading, Frank Silvera Writers' Workshop, New
York, Mar. 1975; Billie Holiday Theatre, New York, Apr. 1975.

McCLENDON, ROSE, and RICHARD BRUCE

Taxi Fare. (1931).   *Length:* 1 Act.

McCOO, EDWARD J.

Ethiopia at the Bar of Justice. (1924). Children's Pageant. A history of black people
from the days of the pharaohs to the present.   *Cast:* 10 BM, 10 BF, extras
(doubling). *Length:* 1 Act. *Prod:* A.M.E. Church Quadrennial Conference, Louisville, Ky., 1924. *Pubn: Plays and Pageants from the Life of the Negro,* ed. by Willis
Richardson, Washington, D.C., Associated Publishers, 1930. *Lib Source:* HBA.

McCRAY, IVY

But There's Gotta Be Music.   *Cast:* 1 BM, 4 BF. *Length:* 1 Act. *Prod:* Reading,
Frank Silvera Writers' Workshop, Martinique Theatre, New York, Nov. 1974.

Run'ers.   *Prod:* Reading, Frank Silvera Writers' Workshop, Teachers, Inc., New
York, Nov. 1976.

Stepping Stones.   *Prod:* Reading, Frank Silvera Writers' Workshop, Martinique
Theatre, New York, Nov. 1975.

McCRAY, NETTIE. *See* Salimu

McDOWELL, MELODIE M.

The Car Pool. Morality Play.   *Cast:* 14 BM, 4 BF. *Perm:* Author.

The Conscience. Morality Drama. The wife of a black mayor is kidnapped by a
group of militants. The drama is viewed from three separate characters' points
of view, and what is most evident is that in spite of all the events that lead up to
the kidnapping, business goes on as usual.   *Cast:* 5 BM, 6 BF, extras. *Length:*
3 Acts. *Prod:* X-Bag, Chicago, Ill., 1975–76 season. *Perm:* Author.

March 22. (1975). Morality Play. On March 22, the lives of three women come together in a dynamic manner—with the backgrounds of each girl depicted.
Cast: 4 BM, 3 BF, extras. *Length:* 3 Acts. *Perm:* Author.

Nigger Knacks. (1974). Satire/Comedy. A series of seventeen vignettes depict
some of the hang-ups that hold Blacks back.   *Cast:* 4 BM, 3 BF. *Length:* 17
Scenes. *Perm:* Author.

McFARLAND, H. S.

Majority, Minority, Etcetera. Poetic. A philosophical discussion of racial America. *Cast:* 1 BM, 1 WM, 1 Indian M, extras. *Length:* 3 Acts. *Pubn: Crest,* New York: Vantage, 1975.

MACGEE, RUCHELL CINQUE

Miscarriage of Justice. Length: 1 Act. *Prod:* Tanzia-Mystique Productions, Brooklyn Academy of Music, N.Y., June 1974.

McGLOWN, JERRY EUGENE

King Uzziah. (1974). Morality Play. A middle-aged white English teacher tries to take a son away from one of his former black students, and the student attempts to force the teacher to confront the absurdity of their previous relationship. *Cast:* 1 BM, 1 WM. *Length:* 1 Act. *Prod:* Memphis State University, Tenn., Mar. 1975. *Perm:* Author.

To Mansions in the Sky. (1974). Domestic Play. Middle class black accountant tries to escape the realities of his Blackness. *Cast:* 3 BM, 4 BF, 2 WM, 3 WF. *Length:* 2 Acts. *Prod:* Memphis State University, Tenn., 1975-1976 season. *Perm:* Author.

McGRIFF, MILTON

And Then We Heard Thunder. Based on a novel of the same name by John O. Killens.

Nigger Killers. Prod: Possibly by Freedom Theatre, Philadelphia, Pa., 1971.

McGUIRE, LOIS

The Lion Writes. (1970).

McIVER, RAY

The Fly in the Coffin. Comedy. Based on an Erskine Caldwell story. Doze Muffin, thought to be dead, rises from his coffin at his funeral. *Cast:* 4 BM, 3 BF, extras. *Length:* 1 Act.

"God Is a (Guess What?)." Satire/Morality Play with Music. God appears as a *deus ex machina* to rescue Jim from a lynch mob. *Cast:* 15 M, 2 F, chorus (doubling). *Length:* 1 Act. *Prod:* NEC, New York, Dec. 1969.

MACK, CECIL, EUBIE BLAKE, and MILTON REDDIE

Swing It. Revue. "A potpourri of minstrelsy, singing, dancing, mugging, clowning, spirituals, jazz swing, tapping, and the carrying of Harlem's throaty torch."—*New York Times,* July 23, 1937. *Cast:* 19 BM, 7 BF. *Prod:* Adelphi Theatre, New York, July 1937. *Lib Source:* FTP, GMU.

MACKEY, WILLIAM WELLINGTON

Behold! Cometh the Vanderkellans. Domestic Play. Focuses on black university president and family of fourth generation "upper class status," who have

MACKEY, WILLIAM WELLINGTON *(Cont.)*

deluded themselves into thinking they were "society," accepted by their peers, and social equals in the white world.   *Cast:* 3 BM, 3 BF. *Length:* 3 Acts. *Prod:* Eden Workshop, Denver, Colo., 1965; Theatre DeLys, New York, Mar. 1971. *Perm:* Agency, Jack Rich.

Billy Noname. Dramatic Musical. A black musical play, with emphasis on song and dance, set against events in American history from the day Joe Louis became heavyweight champ in 1937 up to 1970.   *Cast:* 8 BM, 7 BF. *Length:* 2 Acts. *Prod:* Truck and Warehouse Theatre, New York, Mar. 1970. *Perm:* Agency, Robert E. Richardson.

Death of Charlie Blackman.

Family Meeting. (1968). Surrealistic Psychodrama. Examines the schizoid self-destructive and sadomasochistic tendencies of Blacks unable to accept and cope with their Blackness.   *Cast:* 2 BM, 8 BF, 1 BB, 2 WM, 4–8 WF. *Length:* 1 Act. *Prod:* La Mama, New York, Mar. 1972. *Pubn: New Black Playwrights,* ed. by William Couch, New York: Avon, 1970. *Lib Source:* HBA. *Perm:* DPS.

Homeboys.

Love Me, Love Me, Daddy—or I Swear I'm Gonna Kill You! Domestic Drama. On the eve of the death of one of the richest and most politically powerful black men in America, his seven sons vie for control of the family empire.   *Cast:* 7 BM, 4 BF, 7 BB (ages 3-13). *Length:* 3 Acts. *Perm:* Agency, Jack Rich.

Requiem for Brother X. (1964). Domestic Drama. Play focuses on problems, conflicts, and family disunity that occur on the eve of the assassination of Malcolm X in 1965.   *Cast:* 3 BM, 2 BF. *Length:* 1 Act. *Prod:* Chicago Hull House Parkway Theatre, Ill., 1968; Players Workshop, New York, 1973. *Pubn: Black Drama Anthology,* ed. by Woodie King, Jr. and Ron Milner, New York: New Amer. Lib., 1972. *Lib Source:* HBA.

McKIE, JOHN

Living Is a Hard Way to Die.   *Prod:* Reading, Frank Silvera Writers' Workshop, Harlem Cultural Council, New York, Mar. 1976.

Untitled. (1974). Tragi-Comedy. Two events are interwoven simultaneously: the last days of Poppa, a drunken but lovable man, and the preparation of his son for the funeral at a very strange funeral parlour.   *Cast:* 7 BM, 2 BF, chorus, extras. *Length:* 2 Acts.

McKNIGHT, DELORES, PHYLLIS HALL, and ELMO MORGAN

Two Wings. Performed as a continuing series for Brown University's Afro-American Studies Program and as a complement to a course, "Images and Myths of African People in New World Consciousness." *Length:* 6 Episodes. *Prod:* Brown University, Providence, R.I., Feb.-May 1975.

McKNIGHT, JO-ANNE

Clara. (1971). Domestic Drama. A black woman marries a white man at a time (futuristic) in which America is torn by civil war. Both families are actively engaged in the planning and execution of combat, and they therefore renounce the couple for marrying "the enemy."   *Cast:* 10 BM, 6 BF, 8 WM, 3 WF. *Length:* 2 Acts. *Perm:* Author.

Dialogue between Strangers. (1969). A white man tries to rape a Negro woman; both carry out their individual fantasy influenced by their own cultural background, personal mix-ups, and understandings.   *Cast:* 1 BF, 1 WM. *Length:* 1 Act. *Perm:* Author.

Incense Burners. (1975). Historical Morality Play with Music. A "survivalistic" trip through the stages of spiritual development experienced by black people, starting in Dahomey, Africa, through the plantation, "steal away," Catholicism, the Baptist tradition, and a projection into a future in which black people spiritually return to their traditional African roots.   *Cast:* 9 BM, 4 BF, 2 WM, chorus. *Length:* Full Length. *Perm:* Author.

The Last Day. (1968). A brilliant black man turns into a wino after serving in a war; he stands on a corner and tells imaginary people what he feels about life, death, war, and love.   *Cast:* 1 BM. *Perm:* Author.

Tones of the Lady. (1974). A tribute to Nina Simone and all the other black queens who dare to recognize themselves. Major events of the life of a young southern girl who comes to New York to "make it" as a dancer.   *Cast:* 2 BM, 7 BF. *Length:* Full Length. *Perm:* Author.

Train through Hell. (1970). A white capitalist and his wife each act out the images that they wish the other to see and that are different from their true selves. Their views on the race problem destroy their marriage.   *Cast:* 1 WM, 1 WF. *Length:* 1 Act. *Perm:* Author.

MADDEN, WILL ANTHONY

The Killer and the Girl. Melodrama. Based on the poem "Killer," by Paris Flammonde. A girl delivers a package and a note to a hired killer, not knowing she is to be his next victim.   *Cast:* 1 M, 1 F. *Length:* 1 Act. *Pubn:* Two and One, New York: Exposition, 1961. *Lib Source:* SCHOM.

MAJOR, FRANCIS

Evolution of a Sister.   *Prod:* Afro-American Theatre, New York, May 1975.

MALIK

Get the One with the Star on the Side. The play shows how severe the punishment can be for casting off that precious article called "soul."   *Length:* 1 Act. *Prod:* Afro-American Repertory Co., Masque Theatre, New York, 1974.

MALONE, MIKE, GLENDA DICKERSON, and OWEN DODSON

Owen's Song. Poetic Musical Tribute. Conceived and directed by Glenda Dickerson and Mike Malone. A collage of Owen Dodson's poetry and plays with music and dance.   *Cast:* 14 BM, 11 BF (doubling). *Length:* 2 Acts. *Prod:* D.C. Black Repertory Theatre, Washington, D.C., Oct. 1974; John F. Kennedy Center for the Performing Arts, Washington, D.C., Dec. 1974. *Lib Source:* HBA. *Perm:* Authors.

MALONEY, CLARENCE. *See* Chaka Ta

MANN, CHARLES, BARBARA MOLETTE, and CARLTON MOLETTE

Dr. B. S. Black. Musical. Adaptation of Moliere's *Doctor Inspite of Himself.* *Prod:* Atlanta University, Ga., July 1972; Morehouse-Spelman Players, Atlanta, Ga., Apr. 1973.

MARRYSHOW, HANS

Weekend. *Prod:* Reading, Frank Silvera Writers' Workshop, Teachers, Inc., New York, Dec. 1976.

MARTIN, DAVID E., BEN CARTER, and SAUNDRA McCLAIN

Bitter Trails. Protest Drama with Music. A play depicting the life of migrant workers, black migrant workers in particular, in the Southwest. *Cast:* 5 BM, 1 BF, 5 M, 1 F. *Length:* 3 Acts. *Prod:* Reading, Frank Silvera Writers' Workshop, Martinique Theatre, New York, Mar. 1975; Billie Holiday Theatre, New York, Apr. 1975.

MARTIN, HERBERT WOODWARD

Dialogue. A cop stops a black man on the street in a downpour; through conversation, it appears that the cop is somewhat human—but he isn't. *Cast:* 1 BM, 1 WM. *Length:* 1 Act. *Pubn: The Urban Reader*, ed. by Susan Cahill and Michele Cooper, Englewood Cliffs: Prentice-Hall, 1971. *Lib Source:* SCHOM.

MARTIN, SHARON STOCKARD

Canned Soul. (1974). Protest Absurdist. Over a delicious meal, a couple examines the nuance and nuisance of the black presence, while the subject of the conversation is conspicuously and ominously absent. *Length:* 1 Act. *Perm:* Author.

Deep Heat. Absurdist. Two couples obsessed with departed pets deal with the dissolution of their marriage. *Cast:* 2 M, 2 F. *Length:* 1 Act. *Prod:* Yale Drama School, Yale University, New Haven, Conn., 1975. *Perm:* Author.

Disintegration: A Television Play. (1974). The effects of integration on a middle class family. *Cast:* 1 BM, 1 BF, 1 BB, 1 BG, 8 WM, 1 WF. *Length:* 1 Act. *Perm:* Author.

Edifying Further Elaborations on the Mentality of a Chore. Domestic Ritual. The inevitability of impermanence is examined by a couple who have recently evolved from Negro to Black and who must prepare themselves for the next change. *Cast:* 2 BM, 2 BF, 1 BB. *Length:* 1 Act. *Prod:* FST, New Orleans, La., 1972. *Perm:* Author.

Entertaining Innumerable Reflections on the Sunset at Hand. Domestic Playlet. A couple argues about who's going to take out the garbage. *Cast:* 1 BM, 1 BF. *Prod:* Dashiki Project Theatre, New Orleans, La., 1973. *Perm:* Author.

A Final Exultation Followed by the First Execution of the Obsession of an Imaginary Color from a Temporary Scene. (1974). Fantasy. A man rids the world of the color white. *Cast:* 1 BM, 1 BF. *Length:* 1 Act. *Perm:* Author.

The Interim. (1973). Domestic Drama. The sanctity of late night television viewing is interrupted by a mysterious visitor. *Cast:* 2 BM, 1 BF. *Length:* 1 Act. *Perm:* Author.

Make It Funky Now: The Scentactical Error. (1974). Four college students act to eliminate a foul odor. *Cast:* 4 BM, 2 BF, extras. *Length:* 1 Act. *Perm:* Author.

Moving Violation. Futuristic Protest. Characters are confronted with the double meaning of race in a time when they are not allowed to move. *Cast:* 5 BM, 3 BF, 2 WM, 1 WF. *Length:* 1 Act. *Prod:* Reading, Frank Silvera Writers' Workshop, Harlem Performance Center, New York, Nov. 1976.

The Ole Ball Game: A Song without Words or Music. (1972). Pantomime. Symbolic characters act out the competitive notion of race through a struggle to control the ball in an atypical game. Characters are designated by their costumes, e.g., one man in white-on-white, one man in black-on-black. *Cast:* 9 B M & F. *Perm:* Author.

Proper and Fine. Protest Play. The frustration of a black couple in a department store. *Cast:* 1 BM, 1 BF, 1 WM, 1 WF. *Length:* 1 Act. *Prod:* BLKARTSOUTH, New Orleans, La., 1968. *Pubn: Scholastic Black Literature Program: Search*, New York: Scholastic Books, 1972. *Lib Source:* Typescript, HBA. *Perm:* Author.

Second Story. (1975) Domestic Play. A family of women deals with the conflict between men and women, between races and classes, and with the expression and suppression of the realization of ambition. *Cast:* 5 BM, 5 BF, 1 BB, 2 BG, 3 WM, 1 WF. *Length:* 3 Acts. *Perm:* Author.

To My Eldest and Only Brother. (1969). Playlet. A rural family reacts to the unorthodox marriage of one of its members. *Cast:* 4 BM, 4 BF. *Length:* 1 Act. *Perm:* Author.

The Undoing of the 3-Legged Man. (1972). Morality Play. A man with three legs searches for the meaning of his condition. *Cast:* 7 M, 1 F. *Length:* 1 Act. *Perm:* Author.

MASON, CLIFFORD

Gabriel, the Story of a Slave Rebellion. (1968). Historical Drama. Based on the Gabriel Prosser slave rebellion in Virginia in 1800, with scenes on the plantation, in the bush, and a trial at the end. *Cast:* 8 BM, extras. *Length:* 3 Acts. *Prod:* Staged reading, New Dramatists, Inc., New York, Fall 1968. *Pubn: Black Drama Anthology*, ed. by Woodie King, Jr. and Ron Milner, New York: New Amer. Lib., 1972. *Lib Source:* HBA. *Perm:* Author.

Half-Way Tree Brown. (1972). Drama. This non-realistic play is about a class struggle set in the West Indies; it deals with the conflicts within a ruling class black family (that is jaded and a part of the colonial past) and between them and the workers of the lower class, who are trying to throw off their economic shackles. *Cast:* 10 BM, 5 BF, 2 BC, 1 WM. *Length:* 3 Acts. *Perm:* Author.

Jimmy X. (1969). Domestic Play. Concerns a black youth who is trying to find his revolutionary identity in a world where revolution only leads to disaster. *Cast:* 5 BM, 2 BF, 1 BB. *Length:* 1 Act. *Perm:* Author.

MASON, CLIFFORD (Cont.)

Midnight Special. Set in a bar, this realistic play concerns the black experience. All types are there except children. *Cast:* 9 BM, 2 BF, 2 WM, extras. *Length:* 3 Acts. *Prod:* Staged reading, New Dramatists, Inc., New York, Spring 1972. *Perm:* Author.

Sister Sadie. Domestic Drama. Problem of a black family with classic prototypes: strong-willed mother; a broken father, left only with his dreams; a son trying to survive the black estate of his impoverished inheritance. *Cast:* 4 BM, 3 BF, 3 M teenagers. *Length:* 3 Acts. *Prod:* Staged reading, New Dramatists, Inc., New York, June 1968. *Lib Source:* Typescript, HBA. *Perm:* Author.

The Trial of Denmark Vesey. Historical Drama. The trial of Vesey after his slave rebellion in Charleston, S.C., in 1823. Except for the short first scene, all the action takes place in the courtroom after the first arrests are made. *Cast:* 8 BM, 10 WM. *Length:* 3 Acts. *Prod:* Staged reading, New Dramatists, New York, Spring 1974. *Perm:* Author.

MASON, JUDI ANN

$Living Fat$. Soul Farce. "The story deals with a young black intellectual working as a bank janitor who brings home $15,000 that robbers had stolen and left behind. Should he keep it?"—Townsend Brewster, *Newsletter* of the Harlem Cultural Council, vol. 2, no. 11. *Prod:* NEC, New York, May 1976.

A Star Ain't Nothin' but a Hole in Heaven. A dramatic chronicling of the agonies of a young black girl who is breaking the bonds of the old way of life in the country to take advantage of newly offered opportunities for education and personal development. Winner of Lorraine Hansberry Award for best play on The Black American Experience, 1976. *Prod:* Grambling University, La., 1976.

MAST, ANDREA

In the Bedroom. Comedy. He'd like her to be like he'd like her, but she is as she is. *Cast:* 1 M, 1 F. *Length:* 1 Act.

MATHEUS, JOHN F.

Black Damp. (1929). Drama. Coal miners of mixed ethnic origins are trapped in a mine cave-in. *Cast:* 2 BM, 3 WM. *Length:* 1 Act. *Pubn: Carolina Magazine*, vol. 59, no. 7, Apr. 1929. *Lib Source:* HBA. *Perm:* Author.

'Cruiter. (1926). Folk Drama. Sonny and his wife abandon their farm to travel north for a job in a factory. *Cast:* 1 BM, 2 BF, 1 WM. *Length:* 1 Act. *Pubn: Black Theater USA*, ed. by James V. Hatch and Ted Shine, New York: Free Pr., 1974. *Lib Source:* HBA. *Perm:* Author.

Ouanga. (1929). Opera/Drama. Music by Clarence Cameron White. Haitian opera centered around the life of Jean Jacques Dessalines, former emperor of Haiti. *Cast:* 5 BM, 3 BF, extras. *Length:* 3 Acts. *Prod:* Central High School, South Bend, Ind., 1949. *Lib Source:* Libretto, HBA. *Perm:* Author.

Tambour. (1929). Folk Comedy Incidental music by Clarence Cameron White. Mougalou, a Haitian peasant who has a passion for his drum, wins a victory over the chief of the army and also wins Zabelle, a beautiful woman. Original production directed by Maud Cuny-Hare. *Cast:* 12 BM, 5 BF, extras. *Length:* 1 Act. *Prod:* Allied Arts Players, Boston, Mass., Oct. 1929. *Lib Source:* HBA. *Perm:* Author.

Ti Yette. (1929). Drama. Creole brother hates his sister when she dates a white man during Mardi Gras. *Cast:* 2 BM, 1 BF, 2 WM. *Length:* 1 Act. *Pubn: Plays and Pageants from the Life of the Negro,* ed. by Willis Richardson, Washington, D.C.: Associated Publishers, 1930.

Voice. Pageant. Celebrates the twenty-fifth anniversary of the founding of the NAACP. The stage director and arranger of dances was Mrs. Irving Gravely. *Cast:* 12 BM, 5 BF. *Prod:* Garnet High School Auditorium, Charleston, W.Va., Feb. 1934. *Perm:* Author.

MATHEUS, SALOME BEY. *See* Bey, Salome

MATURA, MUSTAPHA

As Time Goes By.

Black Pieces.

Play Mas.   *Prod:* Urban Arts Corps, New York, 1976.

MAUTI

Cop'n Blow. (1972). A brother out of the "slams" is having job problems. Play has an ironic twist. *Cast:* 3 BM, 6 WM, 1 WF. *Length:* 1 Act. *Pubn: Who Took the Weight (Black Voices from Norfolk Prison),* Boston, Little, 1972. *Lib Source:* HBA.

MAYFIELD, JULIAN

Fount of the Nation. (1963). Drama. Plot concerns the desire of the president of the West African State of Songhay to build a twenty million dollar harbor, which he can only do with American aid; he finally accepts the aid but sacrifices his oldest friend, whom he allows to be framed for treason.

"417." (1971). Domestic Drama. Harlem life in the early 1950s. *Pubn: Black Scenes,* ed. by Alice Childress, New York: Doubleday, 1971.

The Other Foot. (1952). *Length:* 1 Act.

A World Full of Men. (1952). *Length:* 1 Act.

MERCER, WILL, and RICHARD GRANT

The Southerners. (1904).

MEYER, ANNIE NATHAN

Black Souls. *Prod:* 1932. *Pubn:* Bedford, Mass.: Reynolds Pr., 1932.

MILES, CHERRILYN

Eleanora.

To Each His Own.

X Has No Value. (1970).

MILES, WALTER, HAZEL BRYANT, and GERTRUDE GREENIDGE

Makin' It. *Prod:* Afro-American Total Theatre, International House, New York, Jan. 1972.

MILLER, AL

God Is Back, Black, and Singing Gospel. Musical Entertainment. "The audience participates in a camp meeting presided over by a red-gowned revivalist preacher, who gives out sermonettes. . . . There was joyful singing and dancing in the aisles."—Leonard Archer.

MILLER, ALAN E.

The Death of Man. Drama. *Length:* 1 Act. *Pubn:* New York: Amuru Pr., 1974, possibly never published.

I Am My Brother's Soul. Surrealistic Drama. *Length:* 1 Act. *Pubn:* New York: Amuru Pr., 1974, possibly never published.

Kiss Life for Me. Mythic Drama. Concerns Nat Turner's little boy. *Length:* 2 Acts. *Pubn:* New York: Amuru Pr., 1974, possibly never published.

Mama! We Have Rats. Drama. Play of "social life" when a guard pushes dope on black inmates. *Length:* 1 Act. *Pubn:* New York: Amuru Pr., 1974, possibly never published.

MILLER, ALLEN C.

The Opener of Doors. *Prod:* FTP. *Pubn:* Excerpt in *Negro One Act Plays*, 1923.

The Unending War. (1928). Historical Drama. The inhabitants of Haiti take drastic action against the treatment rendered to them by the whites. *Cast:* Large B. *Length:* 3 Acts. *Lib Source:* Typescript, SCHOM.

MILLER, CLIFFORD LEONARD

Wings Over Dark Waters. (1954). Historical Poetic Drama. Some of the elements of this drama set in the early seventeenth century are: Africanus enslavement; slaves land in Jamestown; the War of 1812; Harriet Tubman; the North wins the Civil War. *Cast:* Large B. *Length:* 5 Parts. *Pubn:* New York: Great Concord, 1954. *Lib Source:* HBA; SCHOM.

MILLER, FLOURNOY

Sugar Hill. Comic Opera. Music by James P. Johnson. Rose, who is in love with Harry, is threatened during his absence by a racketeer; when Rose hires Punk to pretend that he is her husband, her real fiancé returns unexpectedly. *Subtitled:* **Meet Miss Jones.** *Cast:* 4 M, 4 F, extras. *Length:* 2 Acts. *Prod:* Las Palmas Theatre, Hollywood, Calif., July 1950. *Lib Source:* HBA.

MILLER, FLOURNOY, EUBIE BLAKE, AUBREY LYLES, and NOBLE SISSLE

Shuffle Along. Musical Comedy. Story possibly based on Miller and Lyles' play *Mayor of Dixie*, 1907. Concerns the efforts of three candidates to win the mayoralty campaign and the complications when one wins. Subtitled: *Mayor of Jim Town.* *Cast:* 15 BM, 4 BF, chorus. *Length:* 2 Acts. *Prod:* Sixty-third Street Music Hall, New York, May 1921. *Pubn: Best Plays of 1920-21,* ed. by Burns Mantle, New York: Dodd, 1921.

MILLER, FLOURNOY, EUBIE BLAKE, and NOBLE SISSLE

Shuffle Along of 1933. Musical Comedy. About the financing of a molasses factory. *Cast:* 13 BM, 7 BF, extras. *Length:* 2 Acts. *Prod:* Mansfield Theatre, New York, Dec. 1932. *Pubn: Best Plays of 1932-33,* ed. by Burns Mantle, New York: Dodd, 1933.

MILLER, FLOURNOY, EUBIE BLAKE, NOBLE SISSLE, and PAUL GERARD SMITH

Shuffle Along of 1952. Musical Comedy. "Woven around a group of GIs and WACs who meet in the army just before the end of World War II and then get together to run a dressmaking establishment in New York."—*New York Times,* May 9, 1952. *Cast:* 15 BM, 7 BF. *Prod:* Broadway Theatre, New York, May 1952.

MILLER, FLOURNOY, and AUBREY LYLES

Keep Shufflin'. (1928). Musical Comedy. Steve and Sam plan to blow up a bank, "thereby releasing a lot of lazy capital loafing in the vaults." *Cast:* 10 BM, 10 BF. *Length:* 2 Acts. *Prod:* Daly's Theatre, New York, Feb. 1928. *Pubn: Best Plays of 1927-28,* ed. by Burns Mantle, New York: Dodd, 1928.

Lazy Rhythm. (c. 1931). Musical.

Rang Tang. Musical Revue. *Cast:* 10 BM, 10 BF. *Length:* 2 Acts. *Prod:* Royale Theatre, New York, July 1927. *Pubn: Best Plays of 1927-28,* ed. by Burns Mantle, New York: Dodd, 1928.

Runnin' Wild. Musical Comedy. The adventures of Sam Peck (Sharpster) and Steve Jenkins (Boob). *Cast:* 15 BM, 7 BF. *Length:* 2 Acts. *Prod:* Colonial Theatre, New York, Oct. 1923. *Pubn: Best Plays of 1923-24,* ed. by Burns Mantle, New York: Dodd, 1924.

MILLER, FLOURNOY, AUBREY LYLES, and HAL REID

The Oyster Man. Musical Revue. Music by Henry Creamer, Ernest Hogan, and William Vodrey. *Prod:* Yorkville Theatre, New York, Dec. 1907.

MILLER, FLOURNOY, AUBREY LYLES, and CHARLES TAZEWELL

Sugar Hill. "A story of the Negro colony in Harlem, having to do with the recent activities of colored racketeers involving Steve Jenkins and Sam Peck, Miller and Lyles."—Miller and Lyles. *Cast:* 8 BM, 6 BF, extras. *Length:* 2 Acts. *Prod:* Forrest Theatre, New York, Dec. 1931. *Pubn: Best Plays of 1931-32,* ed. by Burns Mantle, New York: Dodd, 1932.

MILLER, FLOURNOY, and ANDY RAZAF

Blackbirds of 1930 or *Lew Leslie's Blackbirds.* Musical Revue. Music and lyrics by Eubie Blake and Andy Razaf. Cast included Ethel Waters, Buck and Bubbles, Mantan Moreland, and Flournoy Miller. *Prod:* Royale Theatre, New York, Oct. 1930. *Pubn: Best Plays of 1930–31*, ed. by Burns Mantle, New York: Dodd, 1931.

MILLER, HENRY

Death of a Dunbar Girl.   *Length:* 1 Act. *Prod:* Afro-American Repertory Theatre Company, Masque Theatre, New York, Mar. 1975.

MILLER, IRVIN C.

Brownskin Models of 1954. Musical Revue.

Brownskin Models of 1926. Musical Revue. Special numbers by Arthur Porter, Wally Asher, James Johnson, and Shelton Brooks. *Prod:* Lafayette Theatre, New York, Sept. 1927.

Dinah. Musical Comedy.   *Prod:* Lafayette Theatre, New York, Dec. 1924.

Liza. Musical Comedy. Music by Maceo Pinkard. This play may have introduced the Charleston dance to Broadway.   *Cast:* 13 BM, 4 BF. *Prod:* Daly's Theatre, New York, 1922. *Pubn: Best Plays of 1922–23*, ed. by Burns Mantle, New York: Dodd, 1923.

Put and Take. Musical Revue.   *Length:* 2 Acts. *Prod:* Town Hall, New York, Aug. 1921.

MILLER, JEFFREY

The Last Ditch Junkie.

Who Dreamed of Attica.

MILLER, LAURA ANN

The Cricket Cries. (1967).   *Length:* 1 Act. *Prod:* UCLA Theatre, Los Angeles, Calif., 1967.

The Echo of a Sound. (1968).   *Length:* 1 Act. *Prod:* UCLA Theatre, Los Angeles, Calif., 1968.

Fannin Road, Straight Ahead. (1968).   *Length:* 3 Acts.

Freight Train. Domestic Drama. Two girls residing at a boardinghouse; one becomes pregnant by a downtrodden man while the other falls in love with a handsome rich boy. The former's lover commits suicide because of his state of affairs.   *Cast:* 4 BM, 3 BF. *Length:* 3 Acts. *Lib Source:* Typescript, HBA.

Git Away from Here Irvine, Now Git. (1969).   *Length:* Full Length.

MILLER, MAY

The Bog Guide. Awarded third prize in the *Opportunity Literary Contest* magazine, May 1925. *Length:* 1 Act. *Perm:* Author.

Christophe's Daughters. Historical Melodrama. It is the fatal day of a black king's reign and the two princesses, alone in the deserted throne room, face the suicide of their father and the tragedy of revolution. *Cast:* 2 BF, 2 BG, 3 M. *Length:* 1 Act. *Pubn: Negro History in Thirteen Plays*, ed. by Willis Richardson and May Miller, Washington, D.C.: Associated Publishers, 1935. *Lib Source:* SCHOM. *Perm:* Author.

The Cuss'd Thing. Received honorable mention in the second *Opportunity Literary Contest* magazine, May 1926. *Length:* 1 Act.

Freedom's Children on the March. Dramatic Folk Ballad. *Prod:* Commencement, Frederick Douglass High School, Baltimore, Md., June 1943.

Graven Images. Children's Play. The introduction of prejudice (in biblical times) when Miriam spoke against Moses on account of the Ethiopian woman ho had married and the fancied reaction of their youngest son. *Cast:* 1 BM, 1 BF, 1 BC, 2 WM, 1 WF, extras. *Length:* 1 Act. *Pubn: Black Theater USA*, ed. by James V. Hatch and Ted Shine, New York: Free Pr., 1974. *Lib Source:* HBA. *Perm:* Author.

Harriet Tubman. Historical Drama. About the extraordinary feats of this lone black woman who, on numerous trips, led groups of slaves through the Underground Railway to freedom. *Cast:* 2 BM, 3 BF, 2 WM, extras. *Length:* 1 Act. *Pubn: Negro History in Thirteen Plays*, ed. by Willis Richardson and May Miller, Washington, D.C.: Associated Publishers, 1935. *Lib Source:* SCHOM. *Perm:* Author.

Nails and Thorns. Awarded third prize in Southern University Contest, 1933. *Perm:* Author.

Riding the Goat. Comedy. Problem a young black physician has reconciling his ideas with the mores of the community in which he practices and how the girl he loves solves the problem. *Cast:* 2 DM, 2 DF. *Length:* 1 Act. *Pubn. Plays and Pageants from the Life of the Negro*, ed. by Willis Richardson and May Miller, Washington, D.C.: Associated Publishers, 1930. *Lib Source:* HBA. *Perm:* Author.

Samory. Historical Drama. The story of a fabled leader of the African Sudan and his strategy that outwitted a French scheme to forestall the capture of a native town. *Cast:* 3 BM, 3 WM, extras. *Length:* 1 Act. *Pubn: Negro History in Thirteen Plays*, ed. by Willis Richardson and May Miller, Washington, D.C.: Associated Publishers, 1935. *Lib Source:* SCHOM. *Perm:* Author.

Scratches. A pool game determines the future life plans of two men and one woman—the aim at one thing that hits two. *Cast:* 3 BM, 2 BF. *Length:* 1 Act. *Pubn: Carolina Magazine*, vol. 59, no. 7, N.C.: Apr. 1929. *Lib Source:* HBA. *Perm:* Author.

Sojourner Truth. Historical Play. One of the many occasions on which Sojourner Truth's preaching was effective, changing the minds of a group of white boys bent on destruction. *Cast:* 1 BF, 2 WM, 4 (or more) WB. *Length:* 1 Act. *Pubn: Negro History in Thirteen Plays*, ed. by Willis Richardson and May Miller, Washington, D.C.: Associated Publishers, 1935. *Lib Source:* SCHOM. *Perm:* Author.

Stragglers in the Dust. (c. 1930). *Perm:* Author.

MILLER, MAY (*Cont.*)

Within the Shadow. Awarded first prize, Howard University Drama Award, 1920. *Perm:* Author.

MILLS, BILLY, and LEIGH WHIPPER

Yeah Man. Musical Revue. *Cast:* 9 BM, 5 BF, chorus, extras. *Length:* 2 Acts. *Prod:* Park Lane Theatre, New York, May 1932. *Pubn: Best Plays of 1931-32*, ed. by Burns Mantle, New York: Dodd, 1932.

MILNER, RON

Color Struck. (c. 1970).

The Greatest Gift. Children's Play. *Prod:* Detroit Public Schools, Mich., 1973.

Life Agony. *Length:* 1 Act. *Prod:* Concept East Theatre, Detroit, Mich., 1971.

M(ego) and the Green Ball of Freedom. Ritual. A group of dancers discover they cannot reach the Green Ball of Freedom unless they cooperate and give up their own egos. *Length:* 1 Act. *Prod:* Theatre of Shango, Detroit, Mich., 1971. *Pubn: Black World*, vol. 20, no. 6, Apr. 1971. *Lib Source:* HBA.

The Monster. A Negro dean does not meet the needs of black students and is programmed to commit suicide. *Cast:* 5 BM, 1 BF. *Length:* 1 Act. *Prod:* Louis Theatre, Chicago, Ill., Oct. 1969. *Pubn: Drama Review*, vol. 12, no. 4, Summer 1968. *Lib Source:* HBA.

Season's Reasons: Just a Natural Change. Musical. Music by Charles Mason. Changes black people have gone through from the 1960s to the 1970s. *Length:* Full Length. *Prod:* Langston Hughes Theatre, Detroit, Mich., 1976.

These Three. *Prod:* Concept East Theatre, Detroit, Mich.

The Warning—A Theme for Linda. Domestic Drama. Black girl sees how black men were negative figures in the lives of her mother and grandmother. *Cast:* 3 BM, 6 BF. *Length:* 1 Act. *Prod:* Chelsea Theatre Center, New York, 1969. *Pubn: Black Quartet*, New York: New Amer. Lib., 1970. *Perm:* Agency, NASABA.

What the Wine-Sellers Buy. Drama. A young junkie attempts to recruit his girl friend to dope and prostitution. *Cast:* 12 BM, 6 BF (doubling). *Length:* 3 Acts. *Prod:* NFT, New York, Dec 1973; Vivian Beaumont Theatre, Lincoln Center, New York, Jan. 1974. *Pubn:* SF, 1974. *Perm:* Agency, SF.

Who's Got His Own. (1971). Domestic Drama. Family is forced to examine the powerlessness of the deceased husband and father. *Cast:* 3 BM, 2 BF. *Length:* 3 Acts. *Prod:* APT, New York, Sept. 1966. *Pubn: Black Drama Anthology*, ed. by Woodie King, Jr. and Ron Milner, New York: New Amer. Lib., 1972. *Perm:* Agency, NASABA.

MILTON, NERISSA LONG

The Challenge—a Fantasy. Children's Morality Play. The Spirit of Truth challenges every youth to learn the true history of the black people in America.

Cast: 8, chorus. *Pubn: The Negro History Bulletin,* Oct. 1953. *Lib Source:* HBA.

MITCHELL, LIONEL H.

L'Ouverture. (1972). Historical Ritual. Dramatization of Haitian revolution with emphasis on three historical principles. *Cast:* 30–35. *Length:* 3 Acts. *Perm:* Author.

Uncle Tom's Cabin. Historical Tragi-Comedy. Dramatization of the full American social and racial miasma with new transcendental vision of Tom. Subtitled: *Life among the Lowly.* *Cast:* 50. *Length:* 3 Acts. *Prod:* WPA Theatre, New York, Feb. 1975. *Perm:* Author.

MITCHELL, LOFTEN

The Afro-Philadelphian. (1970).

And the Walls Came Tumbling Down. See Sojourn to the South of the Wall.

Ballad for Bimshire. Musical Play. Music by Irving Burgie. Deals with a girl growing up in Barbados. *Cast:* 5 BM, 6 BF, 1 WM, dancers. *Length:* 2 Acts. *Prod:* Mayfair Theatre, New York, 1963; Recording, London Records. *Perm:* Author.

Ballad of a Blackbird. (1968). Musical Play. Story patterned after the life and death of actress Florence Mills. *Cast:* 14 BM, 7 BF, 2 WM (doubling). *Length:* Full Length. *Perm:* Author.

The Bancroft Dynasty. Domestic Drama. About a Harlem upper middle class family struggling to resist the changes brought about by modern times. The influence of the white standard of beauty is dealt with here. *Cast:* 3 BM, 3 BF, *Length:* 3 Acts. *Prod:* 115th Street People's Theatre, New York, 1948. *Pubn:* Scheduled in playwright's collected works, n.d. *Perm:* Author.

Bubbling Brown Sugar. Musical Revue. Based on a concept by Rosetta LeNoir. About Harlem from 1910 through the 1940s. *Cast:* 5 BM, 5 BF, 2 WM, 2 WF. *Length:* 2 Acts. *Prod:* AMAS Repertory Theatre, Inc., New York, Feb. 1975; ANTA Theater, New York, Mar. 1976. *Perm:* Author.

The Cellar. Drama. About middle-aged black fugitive from southern justice, befriended by a female folksinger in Harlem. *Cast:* 3 BM, 1 BF, 1 WM. *Length:* 2 Acts. *Prod:* 115th Street Theatre, New York, 1952. *Pubn:* Scheduled in playwright's collected works, n.d. *Perm:* Author.

Cocktails. Comedy/Satire. Music by Catherine Richardson. Father Divine is elected president of the U.S. *Length:* 1 Act. *Prod:* Pioneer Drama Group of Harlem, New York, 1938. *Perm:* Author.

Crossroads. Drama. About the Harlem riot of 1935, led by a young hero who is subsequently framed for murder. *Length:* 1 Act. *Prod:* Pioneer Drama Group of Harlem, New York, c. 1938. *Perm:* Author.

The Final Solution to the Black Problem in the United States of America or The Fall of the American Empire. (1973). Play deals with genocide. *Cast:* 3 BM, 2 WM. *Length:* 1 Act. *Perm:* Author.

MITCHELL, LOFTEN *(Cont.)*

Harlem, USA. Tells of the struggles of the Afro-American in Harlem, woven together with traditional black American music and dance. *Cast:* 24. *Prod:* FESTEC, Lagos, Nigeria, Feb. 1977. *Perm:* Author.

A Land beyond the River. (1963). Historical Drama. Amidst white harassment and intimidation, black parents attempt to desegregate the school system in their town under the leadership of Reverend DeLaine. *Cast:* 7 BM, 5 BF, 2 BB, 2 WM. *Length:* 3 Acts. *Prod:* Greenwich Mews Theatre, New York, Mar. 1957. *Pubn: The Black Teacher and the Dramatic Arts*, ed. by William Reardon and Thomas Pawley, Westport: Negro Universities Pr., 1970. *Lib Source:* HBA. *Perm:* Author.

The Phonograph. The struggle of a Harlem family when the winds of change burst into a small, happy home. *Cast:* 4 BM, 2 BF, 3 BB, 1 WM, 2 WF. *Length:* 2 Acts. *Prod:* State University of New York at Binghamton, 1974. *Lib Source:* Typescript, HBA. *Perm:* Author.

Sojourn to the South of the Wall. Play deals with black people in New Amsterdam in the year 1664 and their efforts to rally the Dutch to fight against the British. Subtitled: *And the Walls Came Tumbling Down. Cast:* 5 BM, 2 BF, 1 BB, 6 WM, 1 WF. *Perm:* Author.

Star of the Morning. (1971). Musical Play. Original score by Louis D. Mitchell and Romare Bearden. Deals with the years 1895–1910 in the life of Bert Williams, black theatrical pioneer and vaudevillian; depicts the fall of a black theatre company when big business assumes control of the American theatre. *Cast:* 5 BM, 3 BF, 4 WM, 2 WF. *Length:* 2 Acts. *Prod:* Cleveland, Ohio, 1955. *Pubn: Black Theater USA*, ed. by James V. Hatch and Ted Shine, New York: Free Pr., 1974. *Lib Source:* HBA. *Perm:* Author.

Tell Pharaoh. A concert reading with spirituals depicts the history of the black American from the seventeenth century to the present day. *Cast:* 2 BM, 2 BF, singers. *Prod:* University of California at Santa Barbara, Summer 1968. *Pubn: The Black Teacher and the Dramatic Arts*, ed. by William Reardon and Thomas Pawley, Westport: Negro Universities Pr., 1970. *Lib Source:* HBA. *Perm:* Author.

The Walls Came Tumbling Down. Opera. Music by Willard Roosevelt. Operatic version of play about first blacks on Manhattan Island in 1664. *Length:* 1 Act. *Prod:* Harlem School of the Arts, Alice Tully Hall, Lincoln Center, New York, Mar. 1976.

The World of a Harlem Playwright.

Young Man of Williamsburg.

MITCHELL, LOFTEN, and JOHN O. KILLENS

Ballad of the Winter Soldiers. Historical Drama. Depicts freedom fighters throughout history. *Cast:* 4 BM, 2 BF, 1 BG, 3 WM, 5 WF, dancers, singers. *Length:* 2 Acts. *Prod:* Benefit for CORE, Philharmonic Hall, Lincoln Center, New York, Sept. 28, 1964. *Perm:* Author.

MITCHELL, MELVIN

The American Dream.   *Length:* 1 Act. *Pubn: Black Creation*, Summer 1970.

MOLETTE, BARBARA, and CARLTON MOLETTE

Booji Wooji.   *Prod:* Atlanta University Summer Theatre, Ga., revised into screen-play (unproduced), Fall 1971; stage version rewritten and produced, More-house-Spelman Players, Atlanta, Ga., Dec. 1972.

Noah's Ark.   *Prod:* Morehouse-Spelman Players, Atlanta, Ga., Feb. 1974.

Rosalee Pritchett. (1969). Satirical Drama. A group of upper-class black women have secluded themselves from their fellow black brothers and sisters. In the midst of the "revolution," one of them has an unforgettable experience. *Cast:* 4 BM, 5 BF. *Length:* 1 Act. *Prod:* Morehouse-Spelman Players, Atlanta, Ga., 1970; NEC, New York, Jan. 1971. *Pubn:* DPS. *Lib Source:* HBA. *Perm:* Agency, DPS.

MOLETTE, BARBARA, CHARLES MANN, and CARLTON MOLETTE

Dr. B. S. Black. Musical. Adaptation of Moliere's *Doctor Inspite of Himself.* *Prod:* Atlanta University, Ga., July 1972; Morehouse-Spelman Players, At-lanta, Ga., Apr. 1973.

MONTE, ERIC

Cooley High. (1974). Screenplay. Growing up in the sixties at Cooley High School and the Motown sound that accompanied and complemented life in the ghetto. *Length:* Full Length. *Prod:* Film released in 1975.

Revolution.

MOORE, BILL

Butchman. (1970). Drama. A black man seeks revenge on a group responsible for his only son's drug overdose.   *Cast:* 6-8 BM, 4 BF, 2 WM. *Length:* 1 Act. *Lib Source:* Typescript, SCHOM. *Perm:* Author.

MOORE, ELVIE A.

Angela Is Happening. (1971). Historical Ritual. The trial of Angela Davis is visited by John Brown, Frederick Douglass, Harriet Tubman, and others who have been in the struggle.   *Cast:* 8 BM, 3 BF, 3 WM, 2 WF. *Length:* 1 Act. *Prod:* Watts, Los Angeles, Calif., Mar. 1971. *Pubn: The Disinherited: Plays*, ed. by Abe Ravitz, Encino: Dickenson Pub. Co., 1974. *Lib Source:* HBA.

MOORE, HOWARD

Don't Call Me Man. Drama. "In which jazz singer Betty Carter made her acting debut as a jazz singer reaching out for respect from her man."—*Black World*, vol. 25, no. 6, Apr. 1976.   *Prod:* Billie Holiday Theatre, New York, July 1975.

MOORE, MAL

Where?

MORGAN, ELMO, PHYLLIS HALL, and DELORES McKNIGHT

Two Wings. Performed as a continuing series for Brown University's Afro-American Studies Program and as a complement to a course, "Images and Myths of African People in New World Consciousness." *Length:* 6 Episodes. *Prod:* Brown University, Providence, R.I., Feb.-May 1975.

MORGENSTERN, ARLEEN. *See* Darrelle, Dharvi

MORRELL, PETER, and J. AUGUSTUS SMITH

Turpentine. (1936). Drama. Black turpentine workers protest their destitute conditions with a strike that eventually leads to warfare and victory. *Cast:* 16 M, 4 F. *Length:* 3 Acts. *Lib Source:* FTP, GMU.

MORRIS, GARRETT

A Secret Place. *Prod:* Frederick Douglass Creative Arts Center, New York, Jan. 1975.

MOSES, GILBERT

Roots. Comedy/Parody. An elderly black couple feel they have not led a fulfilled life because of poverty, prejudice, and never having had a family. *Cast:* 1 BM, 1 BF. *Length:* 1 Act. *Prod:* FST, New Orleans, La., Sept. 1966. *Pubn: The Free Southern Theatre*, ed. by Tom Dent, Gilbert Moses, and Richard Schechner, Indianapolis: Bobbs-Merrill, 1969. *Lib Source:* HBA.

MOTOJICHO

Changes. Musical. Music by Valerian Smith. "Here we hear the language styles familiar to Blacks—the 'dozens,' tall tales, street rhymes. Self discovery and belief in and appreciation of oneself were themes sounded again and again."—Jeanne-Marie Miller, *Black World*, vol. 23, no. 6, Apr. 1974. *Prod:* D.C. Black Repertory Company, Washington, D.C. 1973.

The Creeps. (1969). *Length:* 1 Act.

In Sickness and in Health. (1966). *Length:* 1 Act.

Wanted. *Prod:* D.C. Black Repertory Company, Washington, D.C., Oct. 1973.

MULET, PAUL. *See* Rivers, Lou

MUNGU, KIMYA ABUDU

And. *Prod:* University of Massachusetts, Amherst, 1974.

The Black Egg: A Spiritual in Three Movements. Drama with Music. The play speaks of the difficulties black students have getting culturally relevant education in predominantly white educational institutions. Two rival college students reveal the conflicting insights of the serious student and the student who is just trying to pass. Their aspirations are mixed with problems of youth and the expectations of their families. *Cast:* 5 BM, 3 BF, 1 WF, musicians. *Length:* 3 Acts. *Prod:* University of Massachusetts, Amherst, Mar. 1975. *Perm:* Author.

The Contract: A Black Assed Tragedy. Morality Melodrama. The central character falls into the debt of a mysterious underworld figure. The harder he tries to get out of debt, the further in he gets. The daughter of the underworld character drives the man to his demise. *Cast:* 13 BM, 5 BF (doubling). *Length:* 1 Act. *Prod:* California State University, San Jose, Dec. 1972. *Perm:* Author.

A Roast Beef Sandwich. *Prod:* University of Massachusetts, Amherst, c. 1974.

MURRAY, JOHN

The Prince of Mandalore. Comedy. About three Blacks who pose as Indian potentates while visiting the South. *Prod:* Possibly at Karamu House, Cleveland, Ohio.

MURRAY, LUCILLE M.

The Soul Doctor. (1969). Comedy. Adapted from the Moliere play, *Tartuffe.* *Cast:* 3 BM, 3 WM, 7 F. *Length:* 2 Acts.

MUTIMA, NIAMANI

The Revolution Has Been Concealed. Drama. Concerns a young black woman's decision to commit herself to a career in the arts. Subtitled: *Silent Sister.* *Cast:* 2 BM, 3 BF. *Length:* 1 Act. *Prod:* Hansberry Arts Workshop, Princeton, N.J., 1973. *Perm:* Author.

That's All. Drama. Concerns the decision of a young black woman to commit herself to her career or to her social life. *Cast:* 2 BM, 2 BF. *Prod:* Hansberry Arts Workshop, Princeton, N.J., 1972. *Perm:* Author.

MYERS, GAYTHER LEFORDIE

Memphis Aside. (1975) Drama. "Deals with the problems that arise when a white student moves in with his black friend's family and becomes a part of their lives."—*Black World,* vol. 25, no. 6, Apr. 1976.

Teachers, Teaching.

To Be Attacked by the Enemy Is Not a Bad Thing but a Good Thing. (1971). Drama. Capitalism is the enemy here, as two wheelin' and dealin' preachers who share the characteristics of chivalry and criminality are compared to their counterparts on the street. *Cast:* 5 BM, 4 BF. *Length:* 2 Acts.

MYERS, PAULINE

Mama. A woman's tribute to her mother and other black mothers through two centuries of American life. *Cast:* 1 BF. *Prod:* Hollywood, Calif., May 1975. *Perm:* Author.

The World of My America. A one woman presentation from the black author Paul Laurence Dunbar's poems of love, plantation days, and black war heroes. The political satire and humor of Langston Hughes and some riot rhymes of Raymond R. Patterson are included. *Cast:* 1 BF. *Prod:* Hollywood, Calif., Jan. 1963; Greenwich Mews, New York, Oct. 1966. *Perm:* Author.

NAJEE-ULLAH, MANSOOR

And Then There Was Won. *Prod:* Frank Silvera Writers' Workshop, Studio Museum of Harlem, New York, Mar. 1977.

NAYO

Fourth Generation. *Prod:* FST, New Orleans, La., Summer 1969.

NEAL, LARRY

The Glorious Monster in the Bell of the Horn. Lyric Drama. A poetic interpretation of the hopes and aspirations of black artists and the middle class on the eve of the dropping of the A-bomb on Hiroshima. *Prod:* Reading, Frank Silvera Writers' Workshop, Harlem Cultural Council, New York, May 1976.

NEALS, BETTY HARRIS

The Miracle of Sister Love. Drama. Sister Love, after two years of illness, returns to teaching black children and giving them love, even though she has no voice. *Cast:* 2 BM, 2 BF, 3 BG, 3 BB, 2 WM, extras. *Length:* 3 Acts. *Perm:* Author.

NEELY, BENNIE E.

Sue.

NELSON, MARCUS

The Essence of Pathos. A play about the author Richard Wright. *Prod:* New Concept Theatre, Chicago, Ill., 1975.

NELSON, NATALIE

More Things That Happen to Us. Didactic Drama. Presents a story in dialogue and photographs on what elementary school children should do if they know someone on drugs or are approached by a pusher. *Cast:* B & W children. *Length:* 4 Scenes. *Pubn:* New York: New Dimensions, 1970. *Lib Source:* HBA.

Things That Happen to Us. Didactic Drama. Presents a story in dialogue for elementary school children on what to do if approached by a drug pusher. *Cast:* B & W children. *Length:* 4 Scenes. *Pubn:* New York: New Dimensions, 1970. *Lib Source:* HBA.

NEMIROFF, ROBERT,* and CHARLOTTE ZALTZBERG*

Raisin. Domestic Musical. Music by Judd Woldin. Lyrics by Robert Brittan. Based on Lorraine Hansberry's play *A Raisin in the Sun.* Explores essentially the same conflicts and values as the original play, but moves beyond the Younger's apartment into the streets, bars, churches, and work-a-day settings of the people of Chicago's South Side; the score incorporates idioms of gospel, jazz, blues, soul, and the dance, and is based on Afro-American and African traditions; it heightens and underscores the subtleties, humor, and high spirits, the strength and heroism of the Younger family's reaffirmation of their black heritage. *Cast:* 4 BM, 1 BB, 4 BF, 1 WM, extras. *Prod:* Forty-sixth Street Theatre, New York, Oct. 1973. *Pubn:* SF; Recording, original cast, Columbia Records. *Perm:* Agency, SF.

NEW DAY TROUPE

The Lament of the Black Toiler. A revue aimed at whites that tells whites, in their imagery and language, how great the black man is. *Prod:* San Francisco East Bay Area, Calif., 1969.

NEW LAFAYETTE THEATRE

A Black Time for Black Folk. Ritual. A play without words. *Prod:* NLT, New York, Aug. 1970.

The Devil Catchers. (1970). Ritual. *Prod:* NLT, New York, Nov. 1970.

The Psychic Pretenders. Ritual. A black magic show. *Prod:* NLT, New York, Dec. 1971.

Ritual to Bind Together and Strengthen Black People so They Can Survive the Long Struggle That Is to Come. Ritual. *Prod:* NLT, New York, Aug. 1969.

To Raise the Dead and Foretell the Future. (1970). Ritual. *Prod:* NLT, New York, Mar. 1970.

NEWLON, NEIL, and RICHARD WRIGHT

Lawd Today. Drama. Adapted from Wright's novel of the same name. One day in the life of Jake Jackson, a man who is getting beaten from all sides—his wife, his job, "the man"—and his attempt to get a little something for himself. *Cast:* 6 BM, 3 BF, 3 WM, 1 WF. *Length:* 3 Acts. *Lib Source:* HBA. *Perm:* Paul R. Reynolds.

NICHOL, JAMES W.

Home Sweet Home. (1969).

NODELL, ALBERT CHARLES

A River Divided. (1964).

NORFORD, GEORGE

Head of the Family. Comedy. A revision of *Joy Exceeding Glory*, by the same playwright. *Prod:* Westport County Playhouse, Conn., 1950.

Joy Exceeding Glory. (1939). Satire/Comedy. Minerva's the support of a "mad" family. She's got religion (Father Divine) and goes around saying "Joy!" The plot is episodic—Minerva switches to Communism with the same passion. Subtitled: *The Head of the Family.* *Cast:* 12 BM, 7 BF, extras. *Length:* 3 Acts. *Prod:* Rose McClendon Workshop Theatre, New York, 1939.

NSabe, NINA

Moma Don't Know What Love Is. (1971). Drama. Unwed mother-to-be is going through some changes with her mother, who doesn't want her to go through the same changes she has gone through. *Cast:* 2 BM, 1 BB, 4 BF, 1 BG. *Length:* 1 Act. *Pubn: Three Hundred and Sixty Degrees of Blackness Comin' at You*, ed. by Sonia Sanchez, New York: 5X Pub. Co., 1971. *Lib Source:* HBA.

OKPAKU, JOSEPH O.

Born Astride the Grave. (1966).

The Frogs on Capitol Hill. Satire/Comedy. An adaptation of Aristophanes' play *The Frogs.*

The Virtues of Adultery. (1966).

O'NEAL, JOHN

Black Power, Green Power, Red in the Eye. (1972).

Hurricane Season. (1973).

O'NEAL, JOHN, and BEN SPILLMAN

Where Is the Blood of Your Fathers. (1971). *Prod:* Free Southern Theatre, New Orleans, La., Nov. 1975.

O'NEAL, REGINA

And Then the Harvest. Domestic Television Drama. Uses the conflicts and frustrations faced by a black family, at the hands of whites in the rural South, and the urban ghetto to illustrate the forces that spawned the 1967 riots. *Cast:* 5 BM, 2 BF, 4 WM, 1 WF. *Pubn: And Then the Harvest*, Detroit: Broadside Pr., 1975. *Lib Source:* HBA. *Perm:* Author.

Night Watch. Television Drama. Designed to show that the liberalism of whites is frequently abandoned when actually faced with certain experiences involving a Black. *Cast:* 1 BM, 6 WM, 4 WF, 2 W children. *Pubn: And Then the Harvest*, Detroit: Broadside Pr., 1975. *Lib Source:* HBA. *Perm:* Author.

Walk a Tight Rope. Television Drama. Problems and conflicts experienced by a young black teacher as the first Black assigned to an all-white school. *Cast:* 1 BM, 2 BF, 4 WM, 2 WB, 13 WF, 1 WG. *Pubn: And Then the Harvest*, Detroit: Broadside Pr., 1975. *Lib Source:* HBA. *Perm:* Author.

ONYZ, NAKIA

Chance & What Lovers Say. *Length:* 1 Act. *Prod:* Regal Roots for the Performing Arts, St. Joseph Hospital Auditorium, Paterson, N.J., July 1975.

OSBORNE, PEGGY ADAMS

The Meeting. Historical. Based on the black national heritage—Sidney Poitier, Frederick Douglass, Jean Baptiste Pointe Du Sable, etc. *Length:* 1 Act. *Pubn:* Chicago: Afro-American Pub. Co., 1968.

OTTLEY, ROI

Negro Domestic. Radio Play.   *Pubn: Radio Drama in Action,* ed. by Erik Barnouw, New York: Farrar, 1945.

OVERSTREET, JOE, STEVE CANNON, and CORRINE JENNINGS

Snakeshiiit. Pageant Play. Tragic-Comic Farce. Headman at the White House tries to contain the black revolution and is assassinated.   *Cast:* 6 BM, 2 BF, 5 WM, 2 WF, extras. *Length:* 3 Acts. *Prod:* Reading, NFT, New York, 1975. *Lib Source:* Typescript, HBA.

OWA

EGWUWU.   *Cast:* 3 BM, 4 BF. *Length:* 2 Acts. *Prod:* Reading, Frank Silvera Writers' Workshop, Martinique Theatre, New York, Dec. 1974.

Hip Niggas. Tragedy. Two young hip punks mug an old black woman for three dollars for wine.   *Cast:* 3 BM, 1 BF. *Length:* 1 Act.

The Soledad Tetrad. The four plays that compose this group are *A Short Piece for a Naked Tale, Transitions for a Mime Poem, In Between the Coming and the Going,* and *That All Depends on How the Drop Falls.*   *Prod:* Playwrights Workshop of NEC, New York, Spring 1975.

The Soledad Tetrad (Part III) Rejections. (1973). Morality Drama. A white man on a park bench strikes up a conversation with a young black boy, which leads to confrontation and to death.   *Cast:* 1 BM, 1 BF, 1 WF. *Length:* 1 Act.

OWENS, DANIEL W.

Acife and Pendabis. The problem of color prejudice among Blacks, and also the results of what happens when one disregards his or her past. Subtitled: *The Noirhommes.*   *Cast:* 6 BM, 5 BF, dancers, musicians. *Length:* 3 Acts. *Prod:* Afro-American Theatre, New York, Mar. 1975. *Perm:* Author.

Bargainin' Thing. The results of a "bargainin'" made by one to save another's life and what happens when payment comes due—all centering around one black family. Subtitled: *Debts.*   *Cast:* 2 BM, 3 BF. *Length:* 3 Acts. *Prod:* Reading, Frank Silvera Writers' Workshop, New York, Apr. 1975. *Perm:* Author.

The Box. (1969). Allegorical Drama. Young black people trapped in a box gradually recognize their situation and also realize that they must relate to the "old man" (slave) and must understand his attitudes, which differ from their own. *Cast:* 3 BM, 1 BF. *Length:* 1 Act. *Perm:* Author.

Bus Play. This play revolves around five hospital workers vying for the same supervisory position.   *Cast:* 5 BF. *Length:* 1 Act. *Prod:* Summer Thing, Boston, Mass., 1972. *Perm:* Author.

Clean. Young black brother admires a black pimp (Clean) and, through a turn of events, the young brother loses his life.   *Cast:* 5 BM, 2 BF, extras. *Length:* 1 Act. *Prod:* New African Co., Boston, Mass., 1969. *Perm:* Author.

Debts. Deals with what happens when past debts come due.   *Prod:* National Playwrights Conference of the Eugene O'Neill Memorial Theater Center, Waterford, Conn., July 1975.

OWENS, DANIEL W. *(Cont.)*

Emily T. (1973). Deals with a young black woman coming to grips with the world and her vision of herself in it.   *Cast:* 1 BM, 3 BF. *Length:* 1 Act. *Perm:* Author.

Imitatin' Us, Imitatin' Us, Imitatin' Death. (1970). Absurdist. Bizarre look at black revolutionaries and the contradictions within the revolutionary struggle.   *Cast:* 7 BM, 7 BF. *Length:* 1 Act. *Perm:* Author.

Joined. Melodrama. A black assassin is out to exterminate a white liberal. Conflict: Can he go through with one more job?   *Cast:* 2 BM, 2 BF, 2 WM. *Length:* 1 Act. *Prod:* People's Theatre, Cambridge, Mass., 1970. *Perm:* Author.

Misunderstanding. Vignette. The relationship between a black man and his woman and the fact that she does not believe in his dreams.   *Cast:* 1 BM, 1 BF. *Prod:* National Center of Afro-American Artists, Roxbury, Mass., 1972. *Perm:* Author.

Nigger, Nigger, Who's the Bad Nigger. Drama. Two brothers, one light and one dark, and the class conflict.   *Cast:* 2 BM. *Length:* 1 Act. *Prod:* New African Co., Boston, Mass., Summer 1969.   *Perm:* Author.

One Shadow Behind. (1974). Poetic Drama. A woman and two men, all sensitive and talented, struggle with themselves and each other for self-expression until one dies.   *Cast:* 2 M, 1 F, dancer, musicians. *Length:* 2 Acts. *Perm:* Author.

Refusal. Concerns the writer and those for whom he is writing—black people or the white critical world's acclaim and acknowledgment.   *Cast:* 4 BM, 1 BF. *Length:* 1 Act. *Prod:* National Center of Afro-American Artists, Roxbury, Mass., 1973. *Perm:* Author.

What Reason Could I Give. Musical Drama. The story of an obsessed, guilty writer who is incapable of experiencing love or creating.   *Cast:* 3 BM, 3 BF. *Length:* 3 Acts. *Perm:* Author.

Where Are They? Entertains the question of what has happened to the revolutionary brothers of the 1960s.   *Cast:* 7 BM. *Length:* 2 Acts. *Prod:* Black students at Yale Drama School, New Haven, Conn., 1972. *Perm:* Author.

OYAMO

The Advantage of Dope. Drama.   *Cast:* 2 BM, 1 BF, 2 WM. *Length:* 2 Acts; also as a screenplay. *Perm:* Agency, Helen Marie Jones.

The Barbarians. (1972). Ritual. A play on the real barbarians of this society, and their ultimate submission to their source of power as that power is transferred to the hands of others.   *Cast:* 4 BM, 1 BF, 5 WM, 2 WF. *Length:* 2 Acts. *Prod:* Reading, Frank Silvera Writers' Workshop, Martinique Theatre, New York, Dec. 1975. *Perm:* Agency, Helen Marie Jones.

The Breakout. (1969). Protest Morality Comedy. A play full of humor that shows, among other things, that we are all in prison and can "break out" if we simply *move* instead of theorizing and procrastinating.   *Cast:* 13 BM, 1 BF; revised to 8 BM, 1 BF, 2 WM. *Length:* 2 Acts. *Prod:* Manhattan Theatre Club, New York, Apr. 1975. *Pubn: Black Drama Anthology,* ed. by Woodie King, Jr. and

Ron Milner, New York: New Amer. Lib., 1972. *Lib Source:* HBA *Perm:* Agency, Helen Marie Jones.

Called Ur Fear. Comedy/Satire. A play about the black experience. *Cast:* 2 BM, 2 WM. *Length:* 1 Act. *Prod:* Jan. 1974. *Perm:* Agency, Helen Marie Jones.

Chumpanzee. (1970). Street Ritual. *Cast:* 7 BM, 1 BF. *Prod:* July 1973. *Perm:* Agency, Helen Marie Jones.

Chump Changes. (1971). Comedy. *Cast:* 2 BM. *Perm:* Agency, Helen Marie Jones.

Crazy Niggers. A play showing who the real niggers (and other folks) are. *Cast:* 10 BM, 7 BF, 3 WM, 1 WF. *Length:* 3 Acts. *Prod:* May 1975. *Perm:* Agency, Helen Marie Jones.

Fuck Money. (1969). Guerilla Tactics. *Cast:* 3 BM. *Perm:* Agency, Helen Marie Jones.

His First Step. (1970). Satire. Based on contradictions. *Cast:* 4 BM, 1 BF. *Length:* 2 Acts. *Prod:* NEC Workshop, New York, Jan. 1971; Public Theatre, New York, June 1972. *Pubn: The New Lafayette Theatre Presents*, ed. by Ed Bullins, New York: Anchor Books, 1974. *Lib Source:* HBA.

The Juice Problem. An erotic love "chartune" about doing whatever is necessary to survive and "get over" (succeed). *Cast:* 4 BM, 5 BF. *Length:* 3 Acts. *Prod:* Reading, Frank Silvera Writers' Workshop, Martinique Theatre, New York, Jan. 1975. *Perm:* Agency, Helen Marie Jones.

Kindest of the Finest. Quota time and paddy wagon pickup time for New York's "finest" on 119th Street and St. Nicholas Avenue. *Cast:* 14 BM, 3 BF, 4 WM. *Length:* 1 Act. *Perm:* Agency, Helen Marie Jones.

Last Party. (1969). Street Ritual. *Cast:* 5 BM, 1 BF. *Perm:* Agency, Helen Marie Jones.

The Lovers. Street Ritual. *Cast:* 1 BM, 1 BF. *Prod:* Feb. 1970. *Perm:* Agency, Helen Marie Jones.

The Negroes. (1969). Street Ritual. *Cast:* 2 BM. *Perm:* Agency, Helen Marie Jones.

Never Look a Word in the Face. (1970). Surrealistic Mythic. The male psyche encounters the She in a "continuing level of consciousness." *Cast:* 1 M, 1 F, extras. *Length:* 1 Act. *Perm:* Agency, Helen Marie Jones.

Nine as One. (1972). Play/Screenplay. The various levels and universality of oppression and how it is dealt with. *Cast:* 3 BM, 1 WM, 1 WF. *Length:* 3 Acts. *Perm:* Agency, Helen Marie Jones.

Out of Site. (1969). Street Ritual. *Cast:* 2 BM, 2 BF. *Pubn: Black Theatre*, no. 4. *Perm:* Agency, Helen Marie Jones.

The Ravishing Moose. (1972). Written for the National Theatre of the Deaf. *Cast:* 8 M & F. *Perm:* Agency, Helen Marie Jones.

The Revelation. (1970). Ritual. *Cast:* B M & F dancers, drummers, singers. *Perm:* Agency, Helen Marie Jones.

Screamers. (1973). *Length:* 3 Acts. *Perm:* Agency, Helen Marie Jones.

OYAMO (*Cont.*)

A Star Is Born. Children's Play. Adapted from the story *The Star That Could Not Play*, by the same playwright. *Cast:* Children, dancers, drummers, singers. *Pubn:* Privately published, 1974. *Perm:* Agency, Helen Marie Jones.

The Store. (1969). Guerilla tactics. *Cast:* 3 BM. *Perm:* Agency, Helen Marie Jones.

The Surveyors. (1969). Guerilla tactics. *Cast:* 3 BM. *Perm:* Agency, Helen Marie Jones.

The Thieves. Morality. Shows contradictions in Blackness. *Cast:* 6 BM. *Prod:* n.p., Sept. 1970. *Perm:* Agency, Helen Marie Jones.

Unemployment. (1969). Guerilla tactics. *Cast:* 2 BM. *Perm:* Agency, Helen Marie Jones.

Upcrusted. (1969). Guerilla tactics. *Cast:* 3 BM, 4 BF. *Perm:* Agency, Helen Marie Jones.

When Our Spirit Awakens, Then Black Theatre Opens. (1969). A play that asks when black theatre is going to discover what it really is. *Cast:* 21 BM, 4 BF, dancers, drummers, singers. *Length:* 4 Acts. *Perm:* Agency, Helen Marie Jones.

Willie Bignigga. (1969). Street Ritual/Comedy. Shows that no matter what a "nigga" has got or has gotten to, he is still a "nigga." *Cast:* 4 BM, children. *Length:* 1 Act. *Prod:* Henry Street Settlement House, New York, 1970. *Perm:* Agency, Helen Marie Jones.

OYEDELE, OBAMOLA

The Struggle Must Advance to a Higher Level. A cry from the needs of Blacks brings varied responses. *Cast:* 4 BM, 1 BF. *Length:* 1 Act. *Pubn: Black Theatre*, no. 6, 1972. *Lib Source:* HBA.

OYEWOLE, BIODUN

Comments. Poetry/Dance. Advertised as "an answer to *For Colored Girls Who Have Considered Suicide/When the Rainbow Is Enuf*," a play. *See* SHANGE, NTOZAKE. *Prod:* Seventh Avenue Theatre, New York, Spring 1977.

PANNELL, LYNN K.

Conversation.

It's a Shame. Tells the tale of a brother who "runs a game down" on a sister in order to get over. She fails and he cops, and later realizes that he has used her. *Prod:* Theatre Black, New York, 1972.

PARIS-BAILEY, LINDA, and DAVID FULLER

Circus Maxim. Circus/Ritual. "Using the form of a circus freak show . . . the freaks are presented as symbols of black American reality. The play ends with 'We must be freaks no longer.'"—Tom Dent, *First World*, vol. 1, no. 2, Mar.-Apr. 1977. *Prod:* Carpetbag Theater, Festival of the Southern Black Cultural Alliance, New Orleans, La., Nov. 1976.

PARKER, CHARLES

Affirmation. Five mini-plays of impressionism. Included are *The Grave, The Message, The Hour, Benares,* and *Sans.*   *Pubn:* New York: Amuru Pr., 1974, possibly never published.

PARKS, JOHN

You and the Ladies. A series of portraits of black women as mother, sister, girl friend, etc.—that embodies "a considerable amount of anger."   *Prod:* Bijou Theater, New York, Dec. 1976.

PASSMORE, KAREN MADELENE

The Faces of Bron. Tragi-Comedy. Confrontation in a park between two characters, one representing the reality of the black man, the other, his dreams.   *Cast:* 2 BM. *Length:* 2 Acts.

PATTERSON, CHARLES

Circle in the Square.

The Clowns.

Legacy. Domestic. Young black woman leaves her reactionary middle class family for romantic young warrior.   *Cast:* 5 BM, 4 BF. *Length:* 2 Acts. *Pubn: 19 Necromancers from Now,* ed. by Ishmael Reed, Garden City: Doubleday, 1970. *Lib Source:* HDA.

The Liberal.

Longhair.

The Super. (1965).

PAWLEY, THOMAS

Crispus Attucks. (1948). Historical Drama. An ex-slave becomes involved in a protest against the British presence in America and loses his life.   *Cast:* 4 BM, 1 BF, 13 WM, 1 WF, extras. *Length:* 3 Acts. *Lib Source:* University of Iowa Library, Iowa City. *Perm:* Author.

F.F.V. (1963). Domestic Historical Drama. The young son of a color-conscious, near-white Negro family precipitates a crisis by deciding to marry a dark skinned Negro girl.   *Cast:* 2 BM, 5 BF. *Length:* 3 Acts. *Perm:* Author.

Freedom in My Soul. (1939). Protest Play. A group of black hotel employees decides to strike against the white management.   *Cast:* 13 BM, 1 WM, extras. *Length:* 1 Act. *Lib Source:* University of Iowa Library, Iowa City. *Perm:* Author.

Jedgement Day. Comedy. A backsliding churchgoer reforms after a nightmarish dream about the final judgment.   *Cast:* 7 BM, 2 BF. *Length:* 1 Act. *Pubn: Negro*

PAWLEY, THOMAS (*Cont.*)

Caravan, ed. by Sterling Brown et al., New York: Dryden Pr., 1941. *Lib Source:* HBA.

Messiah. (1948). Historical Drama. Nat Turner, a mystic and slave, leads an abortive rebellion against white slave owners in Southampton, Virginia. *Cast:* 8 BM, 2 BF. *Length:* 8 Scenes. *Lib Source:* University of Iowa Library, Iowa City. *Perm:* Author.

Rise Up Shepherd. Domestic Farce. An old alcoholic upsets his relatives in a middle class black family. Subtitled: *Zebedee.* *Cast:* 5 BM, 2 BF, extras. *Length:* 3 Acts. *Perm:* Author.

Smokey. (1939). Protest Melodrama. A black farmhand, who is about to be taken from a jail and lynched, sacrifices himself so his buddy can escape. *Cast:* 2 BM, 4 WM. *Length:* 1 Act. *Lib Source:* University of Iowa Library, Iowa City. *Perm:* Author.

The Tumult and the Shouting. Historical Domestic Drama. A black college professor loses his struggle against the system. *Cast:* 9 BM, 4 BF, 1 WM, 1 WF, extras. *Length:* 2 Acts. *Prod:* Lincoln University, Jefferson City, Mo., 1969. *Pubn: Black Theater USA*, ed. by James V. Hatch and Ted Shine, New York: Free Pr., 1974. *Lib Source:* HBA. *Perm:* Author.

PAYTON, LEW

A Bitter Pill. Historical Drama. A black man asserts himself in a southern town, and it costs him his life. *Cast:* 8 BM, 2 BF, 3 WM, extras. *Length:* 1 Act. *Pubn: Did Adam Sin? Also Stories of Negro Life*, Los Angeles, Calif.: privately published, 1937. *Lib Source:* HBA.

Did Adam Sin? Domestic Melodrama. Emotionally disturbed black youngster kills his sister's boyfriend for threatening his older brother. *Cast:* 6 BM, 3 BF, 2 WM, extras. *Length:* 3 Acts. *Pubn: Did Adam Sin? Also Stories of Negro Life*, Los Angeles, Calif.: privately published, 1937. *Lib Source:* HBA.

A Flyin' Fool. Comedy. A "colored" couple take their first airplane ride. *Cast:* 1 BM, 1 BF. *Length:* 1 Act. *Pubn: Did Adam Sin? Also Stories of Negro Life*, Los Angeles, Calif.: privately published, 1937. *Lib Source:* HBA.

Some Sweet Day. Comedy. The harmonious relations of a black family headed by a blind woman. *Cast:* 4 BM, 2 BF, 2 WM. *Length:* 1 Act. *Pubn: Did Adam Sin? Also Stories of Negro Life*, Los Angeles, Calif.: privately published, 1937. *Lib Source:* HBA.

Two Sons of Ham. Comedy. A series of sketches of two Negro characters—not unlike Bert Williams and George Walker—in the vaudeville era. *Cast:* 3 BM. *Length:* 1 Act. *Pubn: Did Adam Sin? Also Stories of Negro Life*, Los Angeles, Calif.: privately published, 1937. *Lib Source:* HBA.

Who Is de Boss. Satire. The servants of such noted "show biz" personalities as Clark Gable, Bette Davis, etc., act in a movie. *Cast:* 2 BM, 2 BF. *Length:* 1 Act. *Pubn: Did Adam Sin? Also Stories of Negro Life*, Los Angeles, Calif.: privately published, 1937. *Lib Source:* HBA.

PAYTON, LEW, EUBIE BLAKE, and NOBLE SISSLE

In Bamville. Musical Revue. Deals with aspects of horse racing.   *Prod:* Chicago, Ill., 1923-1924; New York, Mar. 1924. *Pubn: Best Plays of 1923-24*, ed. by Burns Mantle, New York: Dodd, 1924.

PAYTON, LEW, and NOBLE SISSLE

The Chocolate Dandies. Musical Revue. Music by Eubie Blake.   *Cast:* 20 BM, 7 BF. *Length:* 2 Acts. *Prod:* Colonial Theatre, New York, Sept. 1924. *Pubn: Best Plays of 1924-25*, ed. by Burns Mantle, New York: Dodd, 1925.

PENNY, ROB.   *See* Kilonfe, Oba

PERKINS, EUGENE

Assassination of a Dream. Morality Drama. An opportunistic black politician finds himself confronted by black justice.   *Cast:* 5 BM, 1 WM. *Length:* 2 Acts. *Prod:* 1967. *Perm:* Author.

Black Fairy. Mythic Children's Musical. A black fairy, who lacks understanding about her culture, feels she has nothing to offer black children.   *Cast:* 3 BM, 2 BF, 5 BB, 4 BG, 1 WM. *Length:* 2 Acts. *Prod:* n.p., 1974. *Pubn:* Chicago: Third World, 1976. *Perm:* Author.

Black Is So Beautiful. Children's Play. Stresses and shows the importance of having pride.   *Cast:* 3 BB, 3 BG, 1 BF, 1 WF. *Length:* 1 Act. *Prod:* n.p., 1970. *Perm:* Author.

Brothers. (1974). Domestic Drama. The story of four brothers who are divided because of their political ideologies.   *Cast:* 7 BM, 3 BF. *Length:* 3 Acts. *Perm:* Author.

Cinque. (1975). Historical Drama. Depicts the events that led to the *Amistad* mutiny and the implications they have for black survival.   *Cast:* 8 BM, 4 BF, 6 WM. *Length:* 3 Acts. *Perm:* Author.

Cry of the Black Ghetto. Domestic Drama. Depicts the problems confronting a black policeman and his family.   *Cast:* 2 BM, 1 BF, 1 BB, 1 WM. *Length:* 1 Act. *Prod:* n.p., 1970.

Fred Hampton. (1970). Historical Drama. Demonstrates the conspiracy behind the police raid that caused the death of Fred Hampton, chairman of the Illinois Black Panther Party.   *Cast:* 3 BM, 4 WM. *Length:* 1 Act. *Prod:* n.p., 1975. *Perm:* Author.

Ghetto Fairy. Children's Play.

God Is Black, but He's Dead. (1968). Morality Drama. A confrontation between black militants and the black Christian church.   *Cast:* 6 BM, 2 BF. *Length:* 1 Act. *Prod:* n.p., 1975. *Perm:* Author.

The Image Makers. Satire/Drama. Concerns the movie industry and black exploitation films.   *Cast:* 6 BM, 4 WM, 1 WF. *Length:* 2 Acts. *Prod:* n.p., 1973. *Perm:* Author.

PERKINS, EUGENE *(Cont.)*

It Can Never Be in Vain. (1973). Drama. A revolutionary leader becomes dis-illusioned with the struggle and takes refuge in the West Indies.   *Cast:* 4 BM, 1 BF. *Length:* 1 Act. *Perm:* Author.

The Legacy of Leadbelly. (1966). Historical Drama. Depicts the circumstances surrounding the death of the blues singer, Huddie Leadbelly.   *Cast:* 1 BM, 1 BF, 4 WM. *Length:* 1 Act. *Perm:* Author.

Maternity Ward.

Nothing but a Nigger. (1969). Drama. A play about a pool hall scene that unites five "street brothers" around a common enemy.   *Cast:* 5 BM, 1 WM. *Length:* 1 Act. *Perm:* Author.

Our Street.   *Prod:* KUUMBA, Chicago, Ill., 1974.

Professor J. B. Domestic Play. A drama about a black middle class family torn between political aspiration and the Afrikan Liberation Movement.   *Cast:* 7 BM, 2 BF. *Length:* 3 Acts. *Prod:* Experimental Black Actors Guild, Chicago, Ill., 1973. *Perm:* Author.

Quinn Chapel. (1975). Historical Play. A play about the development of Quinn Chapel, A.M.E. Church, the first black institution in Chicago (1844).   *Cast:* 10 BM, 4 BF. *Length:* 3 Acts. *Perm:* Author.

Thunder Is Not Yet Rain. (1968). Drama. A group of revolutionaries attempt to wage a battle against the white establishment.   *Cast:* 9 BM, 1 BF, 2 WM, 1 WF. *Length:* 3 Acts. *Perm:* Author.

Turn a Black Cheek. Historical Protest Drama. Based on the lives of the four black students who started the sit-in demonstrations in Greensborough, North Carolina.   *Cast:* 6 BM, 1 BF, 2 WM. *Length:* 3 Acts. *Prod:* n.p., 1965. *Perm:* Author.

PERKINS, JOHN

The Yellow Pillow.   *Prod:* NEC, New York, Feb. 1975.

PERRY, FENTON

Buy the Bi and Bye. The play centers around five actors and actresses who go to the first reading of a play entitled *Killing Flo.* The play-within-the-play is a stereotypical view of black, lower-class life as depicted by a white writer-director.   *Cast:* 5 B M & F. *Prod:* Ralph Waite's Actor's Theatre, Los Angeles, Calif., Spring 1976.

Or.   *Length:* Full Length. *Prod:* Evergreen Stage, Hollywood, Calif., n.d.

PERRY, LESLIE DAVID

The Minstrel Show. (1970).

Rats! Musical Drama. Adaptation of the English poet Robert Browning's poem "The Pied Piper of Hamlin," wherein the rats are human corruption.   *Cast:* 10

M, 3 F (doubling). *Length:* 2 Acts. *Prod:* California State University, Hayward, 1974.

The Side Show.   *Prod:* San Francisco Bay area, Calif., 1971.

Sis' Goose an' de Fox. Folk Fable. A short play on justice, American-style, told in the form of an animal story from black folklore.   *Cast:* 13. *Length:* 1 Act. *Prod:* Afro-American Studies, University of California, Berkeley, n.d. *Pubn: Yardbird Reader*, vol. 4, Berkeley: Yardbird Pub. Co., 1975. *Lib Source:* HBA.

PERRY, MANOKAI

The House That Was a Country.

PERRY, SHAUNEILLE

Mio. (1971).

Presenting the Pettifords. Children's Play. The story of a circus family that decides they will exchange the excitement of their lives for ordinary jobs.   *Prod:* Arts for Living Center, New York, Dec. 1976.

PERRY, SHAUNEILLE, and DONALD JACKSON

Last Night, Night Before. (1971). Morality Melodrama. Good people on the block have a party while "The Cat Man" hooks a sixteen-year-old boy on dope, which kills him.   *Cast:* 11 BM, 10 BF, children. *Length:* 3 Acts. *Prod:* Empoet Productions, New York, n.d.

PERRY, SHAUNEILLE, and NEAL TATE

Music Magic. Musical Odyssey. Book by Shaunoille Porry. Music and lyrics by Neal Tate.   *Prod:* Billie Holiday Theatre, New York, Nov. 1976.

PETERSON, LOUIS

Crazy Horse Have Jenny Now.

Entertain a Ghost. (1962).

Joey. Teleplay.

Take a Giant Step. (1954). Domestic Drama. Spencer Scott; growing into manhood in an integrated neighborhood, meets racism and discovers maturity.   *Cast:* 3 BM, 7 BF, 5 W adolescents, 1 B adolescent. *Length:* 2 Acts. *Prod:* Lyceum Theatre, New York, Sept. 1973. *Pubn: Black Theater USA*, ed. by James V. Hatch and Ted Shine, New York: Free Pr., 1974. *Lib Source:* HBA.

PETERSON, QUENTIN

Another Nigger Dead. Domestic Drama. An urban black family, held together by a strong willed mother, encounters explosive tensions in a world they never made. Despite one son's passiveness and another's unsuccessful attempt at theft, the family fights to hold itself together.   *Cast:* 4 BM, 2 BF. *Prod:* University of Wisconsin, Green Bay, 1976.

PEYTON, BRUCE, and RENEE ROASHE

Street King. Historical. Exploration of the various kinds of slavery endured by black people through the ages, from their royal beginnings in Africa to the present. *Cast:* 2 BM, 2 BF. *Length:* 1 Act. *Prod:* Project of the Work Release Program, Theatre for the Forgotten, Riker's Island Prison, New York, 1973.

PIELMEIER, JOHN

Soledad Brother. (1971). Protest Drama. Adaptation of George Jackson's prison letters. *Cast:* 6 BM, 2 BF, 6 WM (doubling). *Length:* 1 Act.

PIÑERO, MIGUEL

Short Eyes. (1974). Protest Drama. A young white boy sent to prison for child molestation is harassed and killed by the inmates. *Cast:* 4 BM, 5 WM, 3 Latins. *Length:* 2 Acts. *Prod:* Public Theatre, New York Shakespeare Festival, N.Y., Mar. 1974; film: produced by Lewis Harris; entry in New York Film Festival, Sept. 1977.

Sideshow. Protest Play. Portrays a day in the life of ghetto youths on New York's Lower East Side. *Length:* 1 Act. *Prod:* Space Theatre, New York, Jan. 1975.

The Sun Always Shines for the Cool. A High Noon confrontation at the Hustlers and Players bar, where loss of pride is worse than death. *Length:* Full Length. *Prod:* Booth Theatre, New York, Feb. 1976.

PIÑERO, MIGUEL, and NEIL HARRIS

Straight from the Ghetto. Musical Revue. Songs, sketches, poems, and mimes about Harlem street life. *Cast:* 5 BM, 2 BF, musicians. *Length:* Full Length. *Prod:* The Family, a Street Theatre, New York, Summer 1976; Theater for the New City, New York, Jan. 1977.

PITCHER, OLIVER

The Bite. (1970). "Ladies of the evening," and why they do what they do. *Cast:* 2 BM, 3 BF. *Length:* 1 Act. *Pubn: Atlanta University Center Sampler*, ed. by Oliver Pitcher, Atlanta: Atlanta University, c. 1970. *Lib Source:* HBA.

The Daisy. Mythic Drama. A play utilizing avant-garde techniques to convey a symbolic night's journey-dream, the underworld, and the past-of-a-man seeking the source and essence of his existence. *Cast:* 2 BM, 2 BF, 1 WF. *Length:* 2 Acts.

The Meaning of Strings. Drama. The metaphor that all the world's a stage is carried by two female actresses—one black and the other white—both trying to figure out who pulls the strings. *Cast:* 1 BF, 1 WF, 1 M. *Length:* 1 Act.

The One. (1971). Ritual. A single character becomes several characters in transition. *Cast:* 1 BM. *Length:* 1 Act. *Prod:* NEC Workshop, New York, Jan. 1971. *Pubn: Black Drama Anthology*, ed. by Woodie King, Jr. and Ron Milner, New York: New Amer. Lib., 1972. *Lib Source:* HBA.

Snake! Snake! *Prod:* New York Poets Theatre, c. 1961. *Lib Source:* SCHOM.

PITTS, LUCIA MAE

Let Me Dream.

PLANT, PHILIP PAUL

Different Strokes from Different Folks. Domestic Drama. Conflicting values within a black family bring out the problems of sexual and political impotence and its antidote.   *Cast:* 3 BM, 2 BF. *Length:* 1 Act.

Switcharoo. Drama. Fantasy and reality merge as the main character and his alter ego battle it out over a girl; the main question of the play is: what makes a man?   *Cast:* 5 BM, 1 BF. *Length:* 1 Act. *Lib Source:* Typescript, SCHOM.

POINDEXTER, GWENDOLYN

We'll Show Them. (1975). Black folktale for marionettes. An eighty-nine-year-old grandfather spellbinds children with the tale of true love between two slaves who were sold apart, but the conjure woman changes the man and his son into birds so they can remain with the wife/mother.   *Cast:* 4 BM, 2 BF, 1 BB, 1 BG, 1 dog. *Length:* 4 Scenes. *Prod:* Karamu Theatre, Cleveland, Ohio, Nov. 1975. *Perm:* Author.

POLE, CHARLES, JR.

Forty Years—Later. Domestic Play. This is a story about a black family that has constant arguments and disagreements about one another's life-styles, but they nonetheless have coherence and unity.   *Cast:* 4 BM, 3 BF, 1 BB. *Length:* 3 Acts. *Perm:* Author.

POLLARD, AL

Laiser Beam. (1972). Courtroom Drama/Fantasy. This is a peoples' day in court, the court of life, unyielding. The poor and the rejected are all too often the misunderstood.   *Cast:* 2 BM, 1 BF, 4 WM. *Length:* 1 Act. *Lib Source:* Typescript, HBA.

POTTS, JIM

Beautiful Black Cat. Musical Satire. Story of a Black Cat's ordeal as she gives up her freedom for civilization and then returns to her field.   *Cast:* 1 BM, 1 BF, 2 WM, 2 WF, chorus. *Length:* 1 Act. *Perm:* Author.

Deadline for Michael. Domestic Drama. Concerns the death of a black playwright, who dies before he gets to see his first play produced, and the hypocrisy of his fellow playwrights.   *Cast:* 4 BM, 5 BF. *Length:* 1 Act. *Perm:* Author.

A Play for Me. Morality Play. The interaction of a black writer and a black prostitute.   *Cast:* 1 BM, 1 BF, 1 WM. *Length:* 1 Act. *Perm:* Author.

Requiem for Bethany Baptist. Drama. The pressures put on a black youth who integrates a white college in the sixties in Louisiana.   *Cast:* 8 BM, 4 BF. *Length:* 2 Acts. *Perm:* Author.

POTTS, JIM *(Cont.)*

Roots of Evil. Musical Play. The travels of a twenty dollar bill from the bank through the community and back to the mint to be burned.   *Cast:* 6 BM, 2 BF, extras. *Length:* 1 Act. *Perm: Author.*

Unfinished Portrait. Historical Musical. Traces the life of a black woman, from her birth in 1619 to her struggles in today's revolutionary movement.   *Cast:* 3 BM, 3 BF, extras. *Length:* 1 Act. *Prod:* Benjamin Franklin Junior High School, San Francisco, Calif., July 1971.

PRESTON, ROBERT S. *See* Sauti, Insan

PRESTON, TONY

On the Road.   Length: 1 Act. *Prod:* Afro-American Total Theatre, International House, New York, Jan. 1972.

Rags and Old Iron.   Prod: Afro-American Total Theatre, International House, New York, Jan. 1972.

PRICE, DORIS

The Bright Medallion. (1931–1932). Black man, labeled shiftless, finds a medal from World War I and says he won it for bravery. To prove his gallantry, he saves a baby in a burning house, and afterward dies.   *Cast:* 10 BM, 2 BB, 4 BF, 1 BG, 1 WM, extras. *Length:* 1 Act. *Pubn: University of Michigan Plays,* ed. by Kenneth Rowe, Ann Arbor: Univ. of Michigan Pr., 1932. *Lib Source:* SCHOM.

The Eyes of the Old. (1931–1932). Young girl, tired of the mundane life with her grandmother, elopes with her male friend.   *Cast:* 2 BM, 4 BF. *Length:* 1 Act. *Pubn: University of Michigan Plays,* ed. by Kenneth Rowe, Ann Arbor: Univ. of Michigan Pr., 1932. *Lib Source:* SCHOM.

Two Gods: A Minaret.   Length: 1 Act. *Pubn: Opportunity* magazine, Dec. 1932.

PRINGLE, RONALD J.

Dead Flowers on a Great Man's Grave.

Deep Roots of Rotted Wood.

The Fall of the Chandelier.

Feed the Lion.

The Finger Meal. (1968). Drama. The story, set in a timeless, decaying, southern town, explores the slave-master relationship.   *Cast:* 2 BM, 1 WM, 1 WF. *Length:* 1 Act. *Pubn: 19 Necromancers from Now,* ed. by Ishmael Reed, Garden City: Doubleday, 1970. *Lib Source:* HBA.

The Lesser Sleep.

The Price.

PROVIDENCE, WAYNE

Where Are You Black Dream. (1971). Ritual. The Black Dream is the future of all "bloods," but his frozen state imprisons him because of his people's ignorance and immobilization.   *Cast:* 2 BM, 1 BF. *Length:* 1 Act. *Pubn: Three Hundred and Sixty Degrees of Blackness Comin' at You,* ed. by Sonia Sanchez, New York: 5X Pub. Co., 1971. *Lib Source:* HBA.

QUALLES, PARIS H.

A Song for My People. (1977). Drama. Period piece dating from 1937–1942. About a poor black family in Montgomery and Pike Counties, Alabama, focusing on an eighty-six-year-old black man and a thirteen-year-old black boy, who sit out in the woods one day and reflect on their experiences growing up in the South. Their stories are graphically depicted in flashbacks.   *Cast:* 5 BM, 4 BF, 4 WM. *Length:* 2 Acts. *Prod:* Mark Taper Forum, Los Angeles, Calif., June 1977. *Lib Source:* Los Angeles Public Library, Calif. *Perm:* Author.

RADISON, NELSON

Exiles in the Kingdom. Poetic Drama. Flashes into the past life of a Puerto Rican junkie poet.   *Cast:* 4 M, 3 F (doubling). *Length:* 1 Act. *Prod:* Hatch/Billops Studio, New York, May 1972. *Lib Source:* Typescript, HBA.

RAHMAN, AISHAH

In Men's Eyes. (1976). Teleplay/Drama. A black assistant principal of a high school commits suicide during a crisis over the integration of his school.   *Length:* 90 Minutes. *Perm:* Author.

The Jukebox. (1974). Drama. Deals with the integration problem in American high schools.   *Cast:* 6 BM, 2 BF, 5 WM, 4 WF. *Length:* 1 Act. *Perm:* Author.

The Knitte Shop. (1968).   *Length:* 1 Act.

The Lady and the Tramp. (1976). Drama. Shows the alienation between men and women in modern society. Companion piece to *Transcendental Blues,* by the same playwright.   *Cast:* 1 M, 1 F, extras. *Length:* 1 Act. *Perm:* Author.

Lady Day: A Musical Tragedy. Historical. Music by Archie Shepp; lyrics by Aishah Rahman. The tragedy of Billie Holiday.   *Cast:* 30 M, 8 F (doubling). *Length:* 3 Acts. *Prod:* Chelsea Theatre Center, New York, 1972. *Lib Source:* Typescript, HBA. *Perm:* Author.

Linus Song.   *Length:* 1 Act. *Prod:* Howard University, Washington, D.C., 1968.

The Mama, A Folk's Tale. (1974). Ritual/Drama. This play, inspired by the story of George Jackson, explores the relationship between a political prisoner and his mother. Part of trilogy *The Mama.*   *Cast:* 4 BM, 2 BF, 4 WM, extras. *Length:* 1 Act. *Perm:* Author.

Mother to Son. Part of trilogy *The Mama.*   *Prod:* Reading, Frank Silvera Writers' Workshop, Harlem Cultural Council, New York, May 1976.

Portrait of a Blues Lady. (1974). Memory Play. A middle-aged black woman reviews her life and finds the strength to go on. Part of trilogy *The Mama.*   *Cast:* 6 BM, 2 BF, 3 BC. *Length:* 1 Act. *Perm:* Author.

Transcendental Blues. (1976). Drama. A middle-aged woman reviews her life after she is abandoned by her young lover. Companion piece to *The Lady and the*

RAHMAN, AISHAH *(Cont.)*

Tramp, by the same playwright. Audelco Awards Nomination, 1976.   *Cast:* 5 BM, 2 BF. *Length:* 1 Act. *Prod:* Frederick Douglass Creative Center, New York, Aug. 1976. *Perm:* Author.

Unfinished Women Cry in No Man's Land while a Bird Dies in a Gilded Cage. (1976). Drama. Deals with the events in a home for unwed mothers on the last day of jazz musician Charlie Parker's life, March 12, 1955.   *Cast:* 1 BM, 7 BF, 3 WF. *Length:* 3 Acts. *Prod:* New York Shakespeare Festival Mobile Theatre, New York, Aug. 1977. *Perm:* Author.

Voodoo America. Drama.   *Length:* 3 Acts. *Prod:* Howard University, Washington, D.C., 1968.

RAMIREZ, RAMIRO

Mondongo. Historical Musical. Concerns black and Latin coexistence.   *Prod:* New York, Summer 1976.

RANDALL, LEE, and EDDIE HUNTER

On the Border of Mexico. (1920). Vaudeville Sketch/Comedy.

RANDOLPH, FORBES, and ZORA NEALE HURSTON, et al.

Fast and Furious. Musical Revue. Cast included Jackie "Moms" Mabley, Juano Hernandez, Dusty Fletcher, Etta Moten, and Tim Moore.   *Prod:* New Yorker Theatre, Sept. 1931. *Pubn: Best Plays of 1931–32,* ed. by Burns Mantle, New York: Dodd, 1932.

RANDOLPH, JEREMY

Blow Up in "A" Major. Satirical Farce. This play deals with the political wrongdoings of senators, who try to plan a scheme against Blacks.   *Cast:* 5 M & F. *Length:* 2 Acts. *Pubn:* New York: Rannack, 1971.

Cartouche.   *Pubn:* New York: Amuru Pr., 1973, possibly never published.

Negro Mama, Black Son. Domestic. A dream of absurdity. A play about the division of black families in the South.   *Cast:* 3 M & F. *Length:* 1 Act. *Pubn:* New York: Amuru Pr., possibly never published.

To the Slave Mountain Alone. Drama. Depicts reverse loyalty in the ethical and metaphysical problems of a young Black torn between the ways of God and the ways of Man.   *Length:* 3 Acts. *Pubn:* New York: Amuru Pr., possibly never published.

Whiteman's Seal of Approval. Psychological Drama. Publishers confront a female egotist.   *Cast:* 3 M & F. *Length:* 1 Act. *Pubn:* New York: Amuru Pr., possibly never published.

RAPHAEL, LENNOX

Che! (1968). Drama. A symbolic drama of modern ideologies in which nudity, explicit sex, the character of Che Guevara, the president of the U.S., and a nymphomaniac nun are all stirred together in a kind of sociological/political metaphor. *Cast:* 4 M, 2 F. *Length:* 1 Act. *Prod:* Free State Theatre, New York, Mar. 1969. *Pubn:* North Hollywood, Calif.: Contact Books, 1969. *Lib Source:* HBA.

RAVELOMANANTSOA, GLEN ANTHONY. *See* Butler, Glen Anthony

RAYNER, STEPHEN N. *See* Etienne

RAZAF, ANDY

Hot Chocolates. "A Colored Revue." Music by Thomas Waller and Harry Brooks. *Cast:* 8 BM, 10 BF, chorus, extras. *Prod:* Hudson Theatre, New York, June 1929. *Pubn: Best Plays of 1929-30,* ed. by Burns Mantle, New York: Dodd, 1930.

RAZAF, ANDY, and FLOURNOY MILLER

Blackbirds of 1930 or *Lew Leslie's Blackbirds.* Musical Revue. Music and lyrics by Eubie Blake and Andy Razaf. Cast included Ethel Waters, Buck and Bubbles, Mantan Moreland, and Flournoy Miller. *Prod:* Royale Theatre, New York, Oct. 1930. *Pubn: Best Plays of 1930-31*, ed. by Burns Mantle, New York: Dodd, 1931.

REAGON, BERNICE

Upon This Rock. Musical. Features black traditional music. *Length:* 1 Act. *Prod:* D.C. Black Repertory Company, Washington, D.C., 1974.

REDDIE, MILTON, EUBIE BLAKE, and CECIL MACK

Swing It. Revue. "A potpourri of minstrelsy, singing, dancing, mugging, clowning, spirituals, jazz swing, tapping, and the carrying of Harlem's throaty torch." *New York Times*, July 23, 1937. *Cast:* 19 BM, 7 BF. *Prod:* Adelphi Theatre, New York, July 1937.

REDMOND, EUGENE B.

The Face of the Deep. Mythic Choral Drama. Adaptations of works by several black poets: Margaret Walker, Owen Dodson, Henry Dumas—and blues singers. A play-ritual about forces and mystical strengths and powers: a praise-ballet of black endurance including speculation on the origins and habitats of spirits, deities, myths. *Cast:* singers, dancers, musicians. *Prod:* Southern University, Baton Rouge, La., Summer 1971. *Perm:* Author.

Kwanza: A Ritual in 7 Movements. (1971). Choral Ritual. A verse-play that extends from the concept and practice of Kwanza, an African holiday ("First Fruits") observance. The seven movements are choralized poems, one from each of the seven principles of Nguzo Saba; the setting, however, is one of African-American origin. *Cast:* 7 B M & F. *Prod:* California State University, Sacramento, Winter 1971. *Perm:* Author.

The Night John Henry Was Born. (1972-1974). Historical Choral Ritual. Adaptations of many poets' works, with choral interludes. A celebration of the great black cultural folk hero, John Henry, along with a salute to the endurance and struggles of Blacks; a poetic tapestry of black history and thought; the mythic "tablets" of Africans in America. *Cast:* 1 WM, chorus, musicians, drummer,

REDMOND, EUGENE B. (*Cont.*)

dancers. *Prod:* Southern University, Baton Rouge, La., Summer 1972; Cliff Top, W. Va., Summer 1974. *Perm:* Author.

9 Poets with the Blues. (1971). Musical/Verse Ritual. Adaptation from the poetry of Edward Brathwaite. Aims at displaying the oral and gestural rudiments of tradition and current black expression; an act of tapping the reservoir of black musicography and mysticism.   *Cast:* chorus, singer, drummer. *Length:* 1 Act. *Prod:* n.p., May 1971. *Perm:* Author.

River of Bones. Historical Verse Ritual. This adaptation from the works of black poets, but mostly the author's own works, represents a program of black ritualistic rudiments. Centered around the drum as concept, instrument-voice, and repository of ancestral wisdom, the play relies heavily on audience participation and ideas associated with birth, death, puberty, love, age, and initiation.   *Cast:* 1 M dancer-singer, 1 F dancer, 2 drummers, chorus. *Perm:* Author.

Shadows before the Mirror. (1965).

There's a Wiretap in My Soup or *Quit Bugging Me.* Morality Satire. Satirizes the Watergate situation via a mock celebration of Independence Day. Abraham Lincoln, George Washington, Sigmund Freud, Nixon, and Franz Fannon, black psychiatrist and author, are all alluded to or mentioned.   *Cast:* saxophone player, drummer, chorus. *Length:* 1 Act. *Prod:* Miller's Park, Sacramento, Calif., June 1974. *Perm:* Author.

Will I Still Be Here Tomorrow? (1972). Ritual. A eulogistic meditation on the December 3, 1972, shooting of fifteen-year-old Raymond Brewer in Sacramento. The eulogy has been generalized to deal with global expression—the dead youth speaks from the grave about his potentialities and possibilities: "I am tomorrow, but they killed me today."   *Cast:* 4 BM, 4 BF, drummer, chorus. *Length:* 1 Act. *Prod:* n.p., May 1972; Reading, Frank Silvera Writers' Workshop, Martinique Theatre, New York, May 1975. *Perm:* Author.

REDMOND, EUGENE B., and KATHERINE DUNHAM

Ode to Taylor Jones. (1967–1968).

REDWOOD, JOHN

But I Can't Go Alone.

Hope of the Lonely.

REED, EDWENA

A Man Always Keeps His Word. Historical Drama. Based on research into the historical record, this play centers around President Lincoln's decision to write the Emancipation Proclamation.   *Cast:* 7 WM, 1 WB, 1 WF. *Length:* 1 Act. *Pubn:* Negro History Bulletin, vol. 26, no. 4, Jan. 1963. *Lib Source:* NYPL. *Perm:* Author.

REEL, ARTHUR

Gray Cocks Will Crow. (1972). Drama. The war in Vietnam is explored as well as its effects, racially and emotionally, on three men who lose the boundaries of color. *Cast:* 2 BM, 5 WM, 1 Vietnamese M. *Length:* 3 Acts.

REID, HAL, AUBREY LYLES, and FLOURNOY MILLER

The Oyster Man. Musical Revue. Music by Henry Creamer, Ernest Hogan, and William Vodrey. *Prod:* Yorkville Theatre, New York, Dec. 1907.

REID, HAZEL

H.E.W. Down the People.

Midnight Maze.

Ritual for: A New Liberation Covenant. *Prod:* Reading, Frank Silvera Writers' Workshop, Teachers, Inc., New York, Nov. 1976.

REID, IRA De A.

John Henry. (c. 1937).

REILLY, J. TERRENCE

Bogey. The problems of Bogey Price, a black cab driver who nearly wins at the race-tracks. *Cast:* 2 BM, 1 BF, 6 WM. *Pubn: Black!,* Poughkeepsie: Myra House, 1972. *Lib Source:* HBA. *Perm:* Author.

Confrontation. "An anti-abortion tract that ends with a couple considering African names for their child-to-be."—Townsend Brewster, *Newsletter* of the Harlem Cultural Council, vol. 2, no. 6. *Length:* 1 Act. *Prod:* Weusi Kuumba Troupe, New York, 1975.

Enter at Your Own Risk. Three black actors gradually assault and shoot the white audience in a small studio theatre-in-the-round. *Cast:* 3 BM, extras. *Length:* 1 Act. *Pubn: Black!,* Poughkeepsie: Myra House, 1972. *Lib Source:* HBA. *Perm:* Author.

Jejune Ju Ju. Monologue. The theme of this poem-like piece is "black is beautiful." *Cast:* 1 B, M or F. *Length:* 1 Act. *Pubn: Black!,* Poughkeepsie: Myra House, 1972. *Lib Source:* HBA. *Perm:* Author.

Montage: An All Black Play. E. Z. Rapper gets shot by the Shades at the end of his flamboyant pro-Puerto Rican speech. *Cast:* 1 BM, extras. *Length:* 1 Act. *Pubn: Black!,* Poughkeepsie: Myra House, 1972. *Lib Source:* HBA. *Perm:* Author.

Waiting on the Man. Three black men named Yellow, Brown, and Black debate what course of action they should take, while they wait on "The Man." *Cast:* 3 BM. *Length:* 1 Act. *Pubn: Black!,* Poughkeepsie: Myra House, 1972. *Lib Source:* HBA.

RHONE, TREVOR

Smile Orange.

The Web. (c. 1972).

RICHARDS, BEAH

One Is a Crowd. Drama. A black woman's quest for revenge and regeneration. *Cast:* 2 BM, 3 BF, 1 WM. *Prod:* Inner City Cultural Center, Los Angeles, Calif., May 1971. *Perm:* Author.

RICHARDSON, MEL

The Break. A play about marriage. Subtitled: *The Breach.*   *Prod:* Merritt College, Oakland, Calif., Mar., c. 1969.

RICHARDSON, THOMAS

Dead Men Don't Dance and Protest. This playwright's first play uses Lawrence Gellert's Negro Songs of Protest and reveals the harsh injustices in Afro-American existence.

Place: America. Historical. A dramatization of the history of the National Association for the Advancement of Colored People (NAACP). The play was first produced at the thirtieth annual conference of the NAACP.   *Cast:* 17 BM, 6 BF, 16 WM (doubling). *Prod:* NAACP Conference, Negro Community Theatre, Richmond, Va., July 1939. *Lib Source:* Typescript, SCHOM.

RICHARDSON, VIRGIL

After Hours. (1972). Morality Drama. Bama, a bar owner, attempts an extortion scheme that leads to killing and more blackmail.   *Cast:* 7 BM, 2 BF. *Length:* 3 Acts. *Perm:* Author.

RICHARDSON, WILLIS

Alimony Rastus. (c. 1920). Farce. A "darkey farce" on the matrimonial affairs of Rastus and Mandy. (Not the Willis Richardson who wrote *The Chip Woman's Fortune,* etc.)   *Pubn:* Syracuse: Willis N. Bugby Co.

A Ghost of the Past. (c. 1923). Historical Drama. A play about fugitive slaves from South Carolina in the early 1860s. (Not the Willis Richardson who wrote *The Chip Woman's Fortune,* etc.)   *Length:* 1 Act. *Pubn:* Dayton, Ohio: Paine Pub. Co.

RICHARDSON, WILLIS

The Amateur Prostitute. Social Comedy. A scheming woman, with the aid of her daughter, traps the younger son of a prosperous black family, and the boy's father forces his son to marry the girl; when the father learns the truth, he has the marriage annulled.   *Cast:* 3 BM, 3 BF. *Length:* 3 Acts. *Lib Source:* Typescript, HBA. *Perm:* Author.

Antonio Maceo. Historical Tragedy. The Cuban leader Maceo is stabbed by a spy and the general's wife revenges her husband's death. Subtitled: *Flight for Freedom.*   *Cast:* 5 BM, 2 BF, 2 Spanish. *Length:* 1 Act. *Pubn:* Negro History in Thirteen Plays, ed. by Willis Richardson and May Miller, Washington, D.C.: Associated Publishers, 1935. *Lib Source:* SCHOM.; Typescript, HBA. *Perm:* Author.

Attucks, the Martyr. Historical Drama. About Crispus Attucks, the first American patriot to be killed by the British in the Boston Massacre.   *Cast:* 1 BM, 6 WM. *Length:* 1 Act. *Pubn:* Negro History in Thirteen Plays, ed. by Willis Richardson and May Miller, Washington, D.C.: Associated Publishers, 1935. *Lib Source:* SCHOM. *Perm:* Author.

The Black Horseman. (1929). Historical Mythic. Black warrior, Massinissa, threatened by the treachery of a neighboring state, reaffirms his alliance with Rome by rejecting a white woman of Carthage.   *Cast:* 7 BM, 3 BF, 1 WM, extras. *Length:* 1 Act. *Prod:* Playground Athletic League, Baltimore, Md., Oct. 1931. *Pubn: Plays and Pageants from the Life of the Negro,* ed. by Willis Richardson, Washington, D.C.: Associated Publishers, 1930. *Lib Source:* HBA. *Perm:* Author.

Bold Lover. Domestic Play. Black middle class family wherein the mother's choice of spouse for the daughter is not the daughter's choice.   *Cast:* 3 BM, 5 BF. *Length:* 1 Act. *Lib Source:* Typescript, HBA. *Perm:* Author.

The Bootblack Lover. Domestic Comedy. Hoggy Wells, the bootblack, manages to win the daughter and to provide a job for her father—in spite of the fact, nearly everyone looked down on him. First Prize in *Crisis* magazine contest, 1926. *Cast:* 4 BM, 4 BF. *Length:* 3 Acts. *Lib Source:* Typescript, HBA. *Perm:* Author.

The Broken Banjo. (1925). Domestic Protest Drama. Matt, a mean man with a good heart, is trapped by his own anger when it's revealed he committed a murder. *Cast:* 4 BM, 1 BF. *Length:* 1 Act. *Pubn: Plays of Negro Life,* ed. by Alain Locke and Montgomery Gregory, New York: Harper, 1927. *Lib Source:* HBA. *Perm:* Author.

The Broken Banjo. (1965). Tragi-Comedy. A development of the one-act play of the same title.   *Cast:* 6 BM, 3 BF. *Length:* 3 Acts. *Lib Source:* Typescript, HBA. *Perm:* Author.

The Brown Boy.   *Length:* 1 Act. *Lib Source:* Typescript, SCHOM. *Perm:* Author.

The Chip Woman's Fortune. Domestic Folk Drama. The money laid aside by an old chipwoman for her son in jail is given, by the son, to save the job and possessions of the poor black family who cared for his mother. First nonmusical play by a Black on Broadway.   *Cast:* 4 BM, 3 BF. *Length:* 1 Act. *Prod:* Ethiopian Art Players, Frazier Theatre, New York, May 1923. *Pubn: Black Drama in America: An Anthology,* ed. by Darwin T. Turner, Greenwich: Fawcott, 1971. *Lib Source:* HBA. *Perm:* Author.

The Chip Woman's Fortune. (1923). Domestic Folk Drama. A full length development of the one act play of the same title.   *Length:* 3 Acts. *Perm:* Author.

Compromise. (1926). Domestic Drama. Misfortune strikes and tragic compromises are revealed when the daughter of a black rural family confesses she is pregnant by the son of a white neighbor. Her mother seeks further compromise, but her brother strikes back. First black playwright produced by Gilpin Players. *Cast:* 1 BM, 3 BF, 1 WM. *Length:* 1 Act. *Prod:* Gilpin Players, Karamu Theater, Cleveland, Ohio, Feb. 1925. *Pubn: The New Negro,* ed. by Alain Locke, New York: Atheneum, 1969 (reprint). *Lib Source:* HBA. *Perm:* Author.

The Curse of the Shell Road Witch. Folk Drama. Deals with superstition and Christianity among Blacks.   *Cast:* 2 BM, 3 BF. *Length:* 1 Act. *Lib Source:* Typescript, SCHOM. *Perm:* Author.

The Dark Haven. Folk Melodrama. Dan Baker traps his enemy, beats him, and turns him over to the sheriff.   *Cast:* 2 BM, 3 BF. *Length:* 1 Act. *Lib Source:* Typescript, HBA. *Perm:* Author.

The Deacon's Awakening. Domestic Protest Play. The women in the Deacon's family let him know that, contrary to his opinion, they want the right to vote.

RICHARDSON, WILLIS *(Cont.)*

    Cast: 2 BM, 3 BF. *Length:* 1 Act. *Prod:* St. Paul Players, St. Paul, Minn., 1921. *Pubn: Crisis* magazine, Nov. 1920. *Lib Source:* SCHOM. *Perm:* Author.

The Dragon's Tooth. (1956). Children's Fairy Tale. Children contending for leadership award prove bravery by stealing a dragon's tooth on which is written the secret of the future: Love and Brotherhood. *Cast:* 3 B & W B, 2 B & W G, 2 BM, extras. *Length:* 1 Act. *Pubn: The King's Dilemma and Other Plays,* ed. by Willis Richardson, New York: Exposition, 1956. *Lib Source:* HBA. *Perm:* Author.

The Elder Dumas. Historical Play. Alexander Dumas becomes involved in a challenge to a duel over criticism of one of his plays. Subtitled: *Invitation to a Duel.*   *Cast:* 1 BM, 2 WM, 4 WF. *Length:* 1 Act. *Pubn: Negro History in Thirteen Plays,* ed. by Willis Richardson and May Miller, Washington, D.C.: Associated Publishers, 1935. *Lib Source:* SCHOM; Typescript, HBA. *Perm:* Author.

Fall of the Conjurer. Honorable Mention in *Opportunity* magazine Contest Awards, 1925. *Length:* 1 Act. *Perm:* Author.

Family Discord. Domestic Drama. Son brings home a "white" wife and shocks his family, especially Kate, the eldest daughter, who decides "to get" the new wife by making it seem that she has stolen money, but the new wife turns out to be "colored." *Cast:* 3 BM, 4 BF, 1 WM. *Length:* 3 Acts. *Lib Source:* Typescript, HBA. *Perm:* Author.

The Flight of the Natives. (1927). Historical Drama. A group of slaves plots successfully to escape from a plantation. *Cast:* 5 BM, 2 BF, 1 WM. *Length:* 1 Act. *Prod:* Krigwa Players, Washington, D.C., May 1927. *Pubn: Black Theater USA,* ed. by James V. Hatch and Ted Shine, New York: Free Pr., 1974. *Lib Source:* HBA. *Perm:* Author.

The Flight of the Natives. (1963). Historical Drama. A development of the one act play of the same title, adding the character of Sojourner Truth. *Cast:* 5 BM, 4 BF, 2 WM. *Length:* 3 Acts. *Lib Source:* Typescript, HBA. *Perm:* Author.

The Gypsy's Finger Ring. (1956). Children's Fairy Tale. Children encounter a gypsy and see three ages of men: chattel slavery, wage slavery, and age of free men (future). *Cast:* 2 BM, 1 BB, 2 BG. *Length:* 1 Act. *Pubn: The King's Dilemma and Other Plays,* ed. by Willis Richardson, New York: Exposition, 1956. *Lib Source:* HBA. *Perm:* Author.

Hope of the Lowly. Domestic Folk Play. Set in the 1920s in Georgia, the play deals with a sharecropper and his family and their attempt to save enough money to go North. *Cast:* 5 BM, 4 BF, 1 WM. *Length:* 3 Acts. *Lib Source:* Typescript, HBA. *Perm:* Author.

The House of Sham. (1929). Domestic Satire. John Cooper, real estate agent with two daughters engaged to marry, is found to be bankrupt because of his family's middle class tastes. *Cast:* 4 BM, 3 BF. *Length:* 1 Act. *Pubn: Plays and Pageants from the Life of the Negro,* ed. by Willis Richardson, Washington, D.C.: Associated Publishers, 1930. *Lib Source:* HBA. *Perm:* Author.

The Idle Head. (1927). Protest Drama. George Broadus refuses to grin and to "Tom" in order to get a job; instead, he steals a piece of jewelry. *Cast:* 4 BM, 2 BF.

Length: 1 Act. *Pubn: Black Theater USA,* ed. by James V. Hatch and Ted Shine, New York: Free Pr., 1974. *Lib Source:* HBA. *Perm:* Author.

Imp of the Devil. Domestic Melodrama. John Henry, mean and crippled stepson, is discovered to be the thief who stole from Mr. Jim.   *Cast:* 4 BM, 2 BF. *Length:* 1 Act. *Lib Source:* Typescript, HBA. *Perm:* Author.

In Menelik's Court. Historical Drama. Love and intrigue at the court of the King of Abyssinia in 1898.   *Cast:* 5 BM, 1 BF, 2 Italian M, extras. *Length:* 1 Act. *Pubn: Negro History in Thirteen Plays,* ed. by Willis Richardson and May Miller, Washington, D.C.: Associated Publishers, 1935. *Lib Source:* SCHOM. *Perm:* Author.

The Jail Bird.   *Length:* 1 Act. *Lib Source:* Typescript, SCHOM. *Perm:* Author.

Joy Rider. (1969). Domestic Melodrama. The younger son of a "better class" black family falls in love with and marries a girl who has been the mistress of his sister's husband.   *Cast:* 3 BM, 4 BF. *Length:* 3 Acts. *Lib Source:* Typescript, SCHOM. *Perm:* Author.

The King's Dilemma. (1929). Children's Fairy Tale. The white king's son chooses a black friend and refuses to give him up.   *Cast:* 1 BB, 4 WM, 1 WF, 1 WB, extras. *Length:* 1 Act. *Pubn: Plays and Pageants from the Life of the Negro,* ed. by Willis Richardson, Washington, D.C.: Associated Publishers, 1930. *Lib Source:* HBA. *Perm:* Author.

Man of Magic. (1956). Children's Play. Riarmi, man of magic, is of a "new race," neither black nor white. The play deals with his goodness to strangers, friends, and enemies.   *Cast:* 6 BM, 3 BF. *Length:* 1 Act. *Pubn: The King's Dilemma and Other Plays,* ed. by Willis Richardson, New York: Exposition, 1956. *Lib Source:* HBA. *Perm:* Author.

The Man Who Married a Young Wife. Domestic Comedy. A young woman is duped into marrying a young man who professes to be wealthy. His wealth lies in Confederate money.   *Cast:* 3 BM, 2 BF. *Length:* 1 Act. *Lib Source:* Typescript, SCHOM. *Perm:* Author.

Miss or Mrs. Social Comedy. The small town gossips are not certain if Betty is married or not; they find out.   *Cast:* 2 BM, 5 BF. *Length:* 1 Act. *Prod:* Engraving Dramatic Club, Washington, D.C., May 1941. *Lib Source:* Typescript, HBA. *Perm:* Author.

Mortgaged. (1923). Domestic Drama. Quarrel between two brothers (one, an exploitive businessman and the other, a research scientist) involves whether wealth or intellectual achievement will further racial harmony.   *Cast:* 4 BM, 2 BF. *Length:* 1 Act. *Prod:* Howard University Players, Washington, D.C., Mar. 1924. *Pubn: Readings from Negro Authors,* ed by Otelia Cromwell, Eva B. Dykes, and Lorenzo Dow Turner, New York: Harcourt, 1931. *Perm:* Author.

Near Calvary. Biblical Drama. Simon, a black man who carried the cross for Jesus, is pursued by the law.   *Cast:* 3 BM, 1 BF, 1 WM, 2 BB, 1 WB, 3 BG. *Length:* 1 Act. *Pubn: Negro History in Thirteen Plays,* ed. by Willis Richardson and May Miller, Washington, D.C.: Associated Publishers, 1935. *Lib Source:* SCHOM. *Perm:* Author.

RICHARDSON, WILLIS *(Cont.)*

The New Lodgers. (c. 1926).   *Cast:* 3 BM, 4 BF. *Length:* 1 Act. *Perm:* Author.

The New Santa Claus. (1956). Christmas Play / Fairy Tale. A vagabond Santa Claus appears on Christmas Eve, bearing gifts and saying Santa Claus may come in many forms.   *Cast:* 1 BM, 1 BF, 3 BB, 4 BG. *Length:* 1 Act. *Pubn: The King's Dilemma and Other Plays,* ed. by Willis Richardson, New York: Exposition, 1956. *Lib Source:* HBA. *Perm:* Author.

The Nude Siren. Domestic Comedy. A rather prudish father is revealed to be secretly interested in reading the book *The Nude Siren.*   *Cast:* 3 BM, 2 BF. *Length:* 1 Act. *Lib Source:* Typescript, HBA. *Perm:* Author.

The Peacock's Feathers. (1928). Domestic Satire. About middle class people who prefer class over character in selecting friends.   *Cast:* 3 BM, 3 BF. *Length:* 1 Act. *Lib Source:* Typescript, HBA. *Perm:* Author.

A Pillar of the Church. Domestic Play. A father in an extremely religious home refuses to allow his daughter to finish school.   *Cast:* 1 BM, 4 BF. *Length:* 1 Act. *Lib Source:* Typescript, HBA. *Perm:* Author.

Rooms for Rent. Domestic Play. A black female roomer with no apparent husband is the target of vicious gossip.   *Cast:* 2 BM, 2 BF, 1 BG. *Length:* 1 Act. *Lib Source:* Typescript, SCHOM. *Perm:* Author.

A Stranger from Beyond. Folk Drama. Out of the night comes a stranger who saves the family's dying mother for no fee.   *Cast:* 3 BM, 1 BF. *Length:* 1 Act. *Lib Source:* Typescript, HBA. *Perm:* Author.

Victims. Folk Melodrama. Sarah borrows fifty dollars on the strength of her husband's job; when the job fails, tragedy follows. Subtitled: *The Deep Regret.* *Cast:* 3 BM, 3 BF. *Length:* 1 Act. *Lib Source:* Typescript, HBA. *Perm:* Author.

The Visiting Lady. (1967). Social Comedy. A middle-aged gossip goes from house to house in her neighborhood and tells whatever juicy news she has heard. *Cast:* 2 BM, 3 BF, 2 WF. *Length:* 3 Acts. *Lib Source:* Typescript, HBA. *Perm:* Author.

The Wine Seller. (1927). Domestic Comedy. A family of bootleggers have their ups and downs until Sadie, the wife, makes a killing.   *Cast:* 4 BM, 1 BF, 4 WM, extras. *Length:* 3 Acts. *Lib Source:* Typescript, HBA. *Perm:* Author.

RICKMAN, CARL

Brown Buddies. Musical Comedy. Wartime adventures of a group of enlisted black men.   *Cast:* 21 BM, 5 BF. *Prod:* Liberty Theatre, New York, Oct. 1930. *Pubn: Best Plays of 1930–31,* ed. by Burns Mantle, New York: Dodd, 1931.

RIDER, CYPRIAN

Garvey! Historical Drama. The Marcus Garvey story centered around the purchase and disaster of the Black Star Line, a shipping company.   *Cast:* 22 BM, 7 BF, 6 WM. *Length:* 5 Acts.

RIKER'S ISLAND INMATES, and ANN EARLY

I Am. Blues Musical.

RILEY, CLAYTON

Gilbeau. Drama. Gilbeau, an aging pimp who has fallen on evil days, becomes involved in a double game with drug dealers and surburban revolutionaries. *Cast:* 7 BM, 3 BF. *Length:* Full Length. *Prod:* Staged reading, Urban Arts Corps, New York, Apr. 1975; NFT, New York, Jan. 1976.

Over. *Prod:* Reading, Frank Silvera Writers' Workshop, Martinique Theatre, New York, Dec. 1975.

RILEY, NORMAN

Runaway People. Drama. Two idealistic young people trapped in the ghetto plan to leave, but fail. *Cast:* 1 BM, 1 BF, 1 WM. *Length:* 1 Act. *Prod:* Harlem School of the Arts, New York, Mar. 1972.

RILEY, ROBERT

Pretty Black. Dramatic Commentary. *Prod:* Theatre-in-Black Players, Detroit Society for the Advancement of Culture and Education, D-SPACE, Mich., Jan. 1972.

RIVERS, CONRAD KENT

To Make a Poet Black.

Who's Afraid of Malcolm X. (1967). Morality Play. A white playboy assumes that his quiet black servant Walter shares his own attitudes toward class and race, but Walter has his own game. *Cast:* 1 BM, 1 BF, 1 WM, extras. *Length:* 1 Act. *Lib Source:* Incomplete typescript, HBA.

RIVERS, LOU

Black English (1974) Domestic Comedy. The time—1974 in New York City. When the main character, a college student who's having trouble passing an English examination, experiences a temporary setback in his ability to make love to the chairman of the English department, he begins to evaluate his life as a black man and attempts to change it. *Length:* 2 Acts. *Perm:* Author.

Black Pictures. Monologues and dialogues portraying different black characters. No setting, the time is the present, and the monologues are classified as follows: *Cast:* "In the House" 6 M, 9 F; "On the Porch" 2 M, 3 F; "On the Public Bus" 3 M, 2 F; "In the Barber Shop" 3 M, 2 F; "In the Beauty Salon" 2 M, 3 F; "In the Bar" 3 M, 2 F; "On the Street Corner" 3 M, 2 F; "In the Church" 2 M, 3 F. *Perm:* Author.

Bouquet for Lorraine. Morality Play. The time is the present, and the place is a small city in Georgia. The play is concerned with the black struggle between classes in their concepts, values, roles, and sexes. *Cast:* 3 BM, 5 BF. *Length:* 2 Acts. *Perm:* Author.

A Case of Peppermint Gum. Drama. Set in a small city in Georgia. An ego struggle between a black woman and a white man. She is the maid in a five-and-dime store; he is the manager. *Cast:* 1 BM, 1 BF, 4 WM, 1 WF. *Length:* 2 Acts. *Perm:* Author.

Crabs in the Bucket. Domestic Play. Struggles of a black woman in a southern city in 1943, during World War II, to motivate her son and her community to achieve

RIVERS, LOU *(Cont.)*

progress in a political campaign.   *Cast:* 5 BM, 2 BF,.1 WM. *Length:* 1 Act. *Perm:* Author.

Ghosts. Historical Fantasy. The play is the reliving of a struggle between Blacks and whites for ownership of land during Reconstruction.   *Cast:* 4 BM, 4 BF, 1 WM, 1 WF. *Length:* 1 Act. *Lib Source:* Typescript, HBA. *Perm:* Author.

Madam Odum. Domestic Comedy. The interactions take place on the campus of a small southern black college in the late 1960s. It is concerned with the resistance of a female college professor and musical prima donna, Madam Odum, who is being forced to retire.   *Cast:* 4 BM, 5 BF. *Length:* 2 Acts. *Prod:* NHT, New York, Sept. 1973. *Perm:* Author.

Mr. Randolph. Domestic Drama. Problem of a black man who gets caught up in a struggle for power, and it almost destroys him.   *Cast:* 6 BM, 8 BF. *Length:* 2 Acts. *Perm:* Author.

Nights Passage into Purple Passion. Domestic Mythic. The play takes place in 1969 on a southern black college campus and concerns the revolts of students and a faculty committee trying to deal with the situation.   *Cast:* 5 BM, 6 BF, dancer, chorus. *Length:* 1 Act. *Perm:* Author.

Pictures for Jimmy Jr. Domestic Play. Problems of a young, black rural southern couple who recently married and moved to Harlem in the 1930s to improve their lot. They, however, have a baby, Jimmy Jr., before they are ready, and as a result their situation worsens.   *Cast:* 9 BM, 6 BF, 1 WM, 1 WF. *Length:* 1 Act. *Perm:* Author.

The Scabs. Domestic Play. The struggle in Harlem in 1934 between white waiters and a group of unemployed black musicians who agree to scab the jobs of the white waiters, who are out on strike.   *Cast:* 10 BM, 3 BF, 7 WM, musicians. *Length:* 1 Act. *Lib Source:* Published script, HBA. *Perm:* Author.

Seeking. Domestic Tragedy. Problems of a black religious woman struggling to reunite her family, torn apart by politics, war, and alcoholism.   *Cast:* 4 BM, 7 BF, 1 WM. *Length:* 2 Acts. *Perm:* Author.

Spiritual Rock Incident at Christmas Time. Musical Ritual. Music by Benn Carter. The play tests both the faith of those who say they do and don't believe in the divine conception of Jesus. While the play is most meaningful at Christmas time, it is a musical that will have significance at any time.   *Cast:* 5 BM, 8 BF. *Length:* 2 Acts. *Perm:* Author.

The Piece of Land. Domestic. Music by Benn Carter. The play takes place on a small farm in South Carolina during 1934. The heroine, who is terminally ill, is determined to help her husband hold on to a piece of land much longer than the present circumstances might allow.   *Cast:* 5 BM, 3 BF, 1 WM. *Length:* 1 Act. *Prod:* American Theatre Company, New York, Dec. 1974. *Perm:* Author.

The Witnesses. Drama. The time of the play is 1949, and the focus is on the problem of a black college professor who tries to convince other colleagues to remain loyal to a white professor who is being called before a legislative investigating committee to account for his loyalty to his country.   *Cast:* 4 BM, 3 BF, 1 WM. *Length:* 1 Act. *Perm:* Author.

RIVERS, SAM, and ED TAYLOR

Solomon and Sheba. Jazz Opera.   *Cast:* 2 BM, 5 BF. *Length:* 2 Acts. *Prod:* Harlem Opera Society, Harlem Cultural Council, New York, 1973.

ROACH, FREDDIE

Soul Pieces. 1969.

ROASHE, RENEE, and BRUCE PEYTON

Street King. Historical. Exploration of the various kinds of slavery endured by black people through the ages, from their royal beginnings in Africa to the present. *Cast:* 2 BM, 2 BF. *Length:* 1 Act. *Prod:* Project of the Work Release Program, Theatre for the Forgotten, Riker's Island Prison, New York, 1973.

ROBERSON, ARTHUR

Don't Leave Go My Hand. Tragedy. A folk story about a youth and his devastating experience with his fanatical, lecherous grandfather and sweet, loving grandmother who raised him.   *Length:* Full Length. *Prod:* Aldridge Players West, San Francisco, Calif., 1965.

Melanosis. (1969).

Run Sweet Child to Silence. (1968).

Two Years, No Fears. A Musical Collage.   *Prod:* D.C. Black Repertory Theatre, Washington, D.C., 1974.

ROBERSON, WILLIAM. *See* Robinson, William

ROBERTS, VICTORIA

A Time to Laugh.

ROBINSON, DEE

Drawers Down, Bottoms Up. Comedy. Music by Mel Edwards.   *Prod:* New Hope Creative Art Center, New York, Oct. 1974.

ROBINSON, DEE, and ROGER FURMAN

Fat Tuesday or *Drawers Down, Bottoms Up.* Musical Comedy. The action takes place in New Orleans in the "dirty" 1930s, in a run-down brothel, where the girls are a bit too brassy and the house madam, on the wrong side of forty, has a much too young "loverboy."   *Length:* Full Length. *Prod:* NHT, New York, Oct. 1975. *Perm:* Author.

ROBINSON, GARRETT

Golden Autumn. A love story of two senior citizens.   *Perm:* Author.

Hamhocks. Domestic Comedy. A tall story about a husband who lives to eat, a wife who isn't getting much romance, and a visitor who helps himself both to the man's wife and to his supper.   *Cast:* 2 BM, 1 BF. *Length:* 1 Act. *Prod:* NHT, New York, Aug. 1968. *Perm:* Author.

ROBINSON, GARRETT (*Cont.*)

Karma II. About Appalachian whites and religion.   *Perm:* Author.

Land of Lem. The play concerns some of the concepts that whites have used to oppress and to corrupt Blacks.   *Length:* 5 Acts. *Prod:* Afro-Arts Cultural Center, New York, Apr. 1971. *Perm:* Author.

The Magic Drum. Children's Play. Based on a fable by Robinson, the play centers on three teenagers living alone in a Ghanaian village in Africa.   *Cast:* 1 BM, 2 BF, storyteller, dancers. *Prod:* I. S. 201, New York, May 1973. *Perm:* Author.

The Village of Disrespect. Children's Play. The play uses animal dances.   *Length:* 1 Act. *Perm:* Author.

Whiteshop. Metaphorical Fantasy. Play is about a quack who can change black people into white people for a price.   *Cast:* 2 BM, 3 BF. *Length:* 1 Act. *Prod:* NHT, New York, Aug. 1968. *Perm:* Author.

ROBINSON, WILLIAM

The Anger of One Young Man. (1959).

The Passing Grade. (1958).

RODERICK, D. B.

Blues for Kingston Street. Domestic Drama. This play focuses on the problems of a southern family that migrates to New York City and lives in Brooklyn in the late 1940s. It focuses on the problem of assimilation in an urban society, as well as in a Jewish community. Adapted for the screen.   *Cast:* 3 BM, 1 BB, 3 BF, 2 WM, 2 WF. *Length:* 3 Acts. *Prod:* NEC, New York, 1975. *Perm:* Author.

The Gilded Window Box. (1974). Morality Drama. This play deals with the problems of one black man and his struggle to find his identity, on the physical as well as the spiritual plane.   *Cast:* 3 BM, 2 BF, 1 WM, 1 WF. *Length:* 3 Acts. *Perm:* Author.

Man, Woman, Life, Death, Infinity. (1975). Existential Drama. This play deals with man's attempt to define himself and incorporates the use of multimedia to portray levels of consciousness that man exists upon. It is interwoven into everyday situations, and is meant to raise consciousness and spirituality. *Cast:* 1 BM, 1 BF, 1 WM, 1 WF. *Length:* 3 Acts.

Secondhand Rose. (1975). Morality Drama. This play focuses on the problems of a black man, his struggle to escape alcoholism, and his return to his youth. *Cast:* 4 BM, 1 BF, 1 WF. *Length:* 3 Acts. *Perm:* Author.

ROGERS, ALEX

Baby Blues. (1919).

Go-Go. (1923). Musical Comedy. Music by Luckyeth Roberts. Twin sisters, one a nurse, the other a cabaret singer, are confused by "their" boyfriend.   *Cast:* 5 M, 5 F. *Length:* 2 Acts. *Pubn: Best Plays of 1922–23,* ed. by Burns Mantle, New York: Dodd, 1923.

Here and There. (1912). Musical Comedy.

Sharlee. (1923). Musical Comedy   *Cast:* 5 M, 7 F. *Length:* 2 Acts. *Pubn: Best Plays of 1923–24,* ed. by Burns Mantle, New York: Dodd, 1924.

ROGERS, ALEX, and HARRY CORT

Charlie. (1923).

ROGERS, ALEX, and HENRY CREAMER

The Old Man's Boy. Musical Farce.   *Prod:* n.p., 1914.

The Traitor. (1912). Musical.

ROGERS, ALEX, PAUL L. DUNBAR, and JESSE A. SHIPP

In Dahomey. Musical Comedy. The president of the Dahomey Colonization Society hires two detectives (Bert Williams and George Walker) to find a missing treasure. They all end up in Dahomey, where they are nearly executed. They decide there's no place like home.   *Cast:* 15 BM, 3 BF. *Length:* 2 Acts, Prologue. *Prod:* Boston Music Hall, Mass., Sept. 1902.

ROGERS, ALEX, and J. LEUBRIE HILL

Darktown Follies. Musical Revue. According to Fannin Belcher, the 1916 show, *My Friend from Kentucky (Dixie),* was a reworking of this piece.   *Prod:* Lafayette Theatre, New York, 1913.

ROGERS, ALEX, and EDDIE HUNTER

My Magnolia. (1926). Revue.   *Cast:* 9 BM, 5 BF. *Length:* 2 Acts. *Pubn: Best Plays of 1926–27,* ed. by Burns Mantle, New York: Dodd, 1927.

My Friend from Kentucky (Dixie). See Darktown Follies.

ROGERS, ALEX, and JESSE A. SHIPP

Bandanna Land. Musical Comedy. Music by Will Marion Cook. Book with Bert Williams and George Walker. "The story, set on the outskirts of a city in northern Georgia, centered about a group of Negroes who by song and rip-snorting pranks, finally sell their property adjoining the white park to whites."—Fannin Belcher.   *Prod:* Majestic Theatre, New York, Feb. 1908.

(In) Abyssinia. Musical Oddity in Prologue and Four Scenes. Music with Will Marion Cook and Bert Williams. Book with Bert Williams and George Walker. "A young man spends his inheritance in taking a group of friends to visit Abyssinia."—Fannin Belcher.   *Prod:* Majestic Theatre, New York, Feb. 1906.

Mr. Lode of Kole (Koal). Musical Comedy. Music by Rosamund Johnson. Book with Bert Williams. "Musical melange built around a story of an island intrigue in which the kidnapped ruler (Big Smoke), released just in time to prevent the crowning of his successor, appoints the would-be king, chief of the coal department."—Fannin Belcher.   *Prod:* Majestic Theatre, New York, Nov. 1909.

ROGERS, ALEX, and JAMES T. VAUGHN

The Sultan of Zulu. (c. 1900). Musical Comedy.

ROHAN, FRED

Hot Sand. Literary Comedy. Battle between the sexes—female wit versus male ego.   *Cast:* 5 M, 5 F. *Length:* 1 Act. *Perm:* Author.

Why de Donkey So Stubborn. Literary Comedy. Depiction of the present situation between native islanders and down-islanders in St. Thomas, W.I.   *Cast:* 2 M, 3 donkeys, 1 mule, 1 horse. *Length:* 1 Act. *Prod:* St. Thomas, W.I., Sept. 1975. *Perm:* Author.

ROLLINS, BRYANT, and JULIE PORTMAN*

Riot. Drama. A panel of two blacks and two whites is brought together, representing four points of view on America's racial problem, but before the discussion is concluded, a riot breaks out in the theatre. Obie Award as Best Off-Broadway play, 1971.   *Cast:* 10 B, 10 W. *Length:* 1 Act. *Prod:* Om Theatre Workshop, Boston, Mass., Dec. 1967. *Lib Source:* Typescript, HBA.

ROSEMOND, HENRI CHRYSOTOME

Haiti Our Neighbor. Melodrama. A play about Haiti from over a century ago until the present day. One-time slaves, through their struggles and determination, obtain an independent and self-governing Negro republic.   *Length:* 2 Acts. *Pubn:* New York: Haitian Pub. Co., 1944. *Lib Source:* HBA.

ROSIER, MEL

Maddog. (1971). Ritual. A black man struggling with life and trying to enlighten his people has a bitter struggle.   *Cast:* 2 BM, 1 BF, 2 WM, 1 WG. *Length:* 1 Act. *Lib Source:* Typescript, HBA.

ROSS, JOHN M.

Aztec Qzin. Tragedy.   *Length:* 3 Acts. *Prod:* Arkansas A. M. & N. College, Pine Bluff, 1968.

Dog's Place. (1935).

Half Caste Moon.

House or No House. Satiric Comedy.   *Length:* 3 Acts. *Prod:* Arkansas A. M. & N. College, Pine Bluff, 1967.

I Will Repay. Tragedy.   *Length:* 3 Acts. *Prod:* Arkansas A. M. & N. College, Pine Bluff, 1963.

One Clear Call. Tragi-Comedy.   *Pubn:* Nashville: Fisk University, 1935.

The Purple Lily.

Rho Kappa Epsilon. Tragi-Comedy.   *Length:* 3 Acts. *Pubn:* Nashville: Fisk University, 1935.

Strivin'. Satire on Negro middle class.   *Prod:* Nashville: Fisk University, 1937.

The Sword. Tragedy. Set in 1850.   *Length:* 3 Acts. *Prod:* Arkansas A. M. & N. College, Pine Bluff, 1948.

Wanga Doll. Tragedy. Set in 1850.   *Length:* 3 Acts. *Pubn:* New Orleans: Dillard University, 1954.

RUSSELL, CHARLIE

Five on the Black Hand Side. (1969). Domestic Comedy. Various members of a
black family seek black consciousness and awareness in an attempt to unify
their family.   *Cast:* 8 BM, 7 BF, extras. *Length:* 3 Acts. *Prod:* APT, New York,
Dec. 1969; United Artists film, 1973. *Pubn:* SF. *Perm:* Agency, SF.

RUSSELL, CHARLES, and BARBARA ANN TEER

A Revival: Change! Love! Organize! Ritual/Happening. About black culture
and life, teaching unity, health, and problem solving with dance, skits, drums,
and song.   *Cast:* 28 B M & F. *Length:* Full Length. *Prod:* National Black Theatre, New York, July 1972.

SAGGITTARUS

I Am Ishmael, Son of the Blackamoor. Drama. This play deals with the first black
president of the United States and the problems he faces, which are due in
part to his white spouse   *Cast:* 2 BM, 6 BF, 6 WM, 3 WF. *Length:* 4 Acts. *Pubn:*
Washington, D.C.: Nuclassics and Science Pub. Co., 1975. *Lib Source:* HBA.
Perm: Author.

SALAAM, KALAMU YA

Black Liberation Army. Didactic Play. Consciously aware Blacks attempt to
enlighten their siblings to the needs of Blacks.   *Cast:* 6 BM, 1 BF. *Length:* 1
Act. *Prod:* FST, BLKARTSOUTH, New Orleans, La., Spring 1969. *Lib Source:*
Typescript, HBA.

Black Love Song #1. Ritual. The positive and negative images of black life.   *Cast:*
4 BM, 3 BF, extras. *Length:* 1 Act. *Prod:* FST, BLKARTSOUTH, New Orleans,
La., 1969.   *Pubn:* Black Theater USA, ed. by James V. Hatch and Ted Shine,
New York: Free Pr., 1974. *Lib Source:* HBA.

Cop Killer.   *Length:* 1 Act. *Prod:* FST, New Orleans, La., Summer 1968.

The Destruction of the American Stage. Ritual. The White Stranger (Devil) attempts to corrupt black people and succeeds with some whose consciousness of black unity is undeveloped.   *Cast:* 5 BM, 2 BF, chorus, extras.
Length: 1 Act. *Pubn:* Black World, vol. XXI, no. 6, Apr. 1972. *Lib Source:* HBA.

Homecoming. Domestic Drama. After being subjected to the racism of the military, returning black veteran is not the same man he was prior to leaving
home.   *Cast:* 2 BM, 4 BF, 1 WM. *Length:* 1 Act. *Prod:* FST, BLKARTSOUTH,
New Orleans, La., Summer 1969. *Lib Source:* Typescript, HBA.

Mama. Domestic Play. Members of a black family try desperately to keep unified
family group by trying to get each other to examine themselves.   *Cast:* 3
BM, 3 BF. *Length:* 1 Act. *Prod:* FST, BLKARTSOUTH, New Orleans, La., 1968.
Lib Source: Typescript, HBA.

The Picket. Didactic Drama. Black man attempts to show the double standards
a civil rights activist has set up for white and black families.   *Cast:* 2 BM,
2 BF, 1 WF. *Length:* 1 Act. *Prod:* FST, BLKARTSOUTH, New Orleans, La.,
1968. *Lib Source:* Typescript, HBA.

SALAAM, KALAMU YA, and TOM DENT

Song of Survival. *Length:* 1 Act. *Prod:* FST, BLKARTSOUTH, New Orleans, La., Dec. 1969.

SALIMU

Growin' into Blackness. (1969). Domestic Drama. Black girl is determined to be a black woman in all respects, although her mother opposes her actions. *Cast:* 5 BF. *Length:* 1 Act. *Pubn: New Plays from the Black Theatre,* ed. by Ed Bullins, New York: Bantam, 1969. *Lib Source:* HBA. *Perm:* Agency, NASABA.

SAMPSON, JOHN PATTERSON

The Disappointed Bride or *Love at First Sight:* Comedy. *Prod:* Possibly at Hampton Institute, Va., 1883. *Pubn:* Hampton: Hampton School Steam Pr., 1883.

SAMUELS, GEORGE

Tell Pharaoh. *Prod:* Federation Youth Project, New York, Dec. 1974.

SANCHEZ, SONIA

The Bronx Is Next. (1967). Morality Melodrama. A group of revolutionaries decides to destroy slum ghettos. *Cast:* 4 BM, 2 BF, 1 WM. *Length:* 1 Act. *Prod:* Theatre Black, University of the Streets, New York, 1970. *Pubn: Drama Review,* vol. 12, no. 4, Summer 1968. *Lib Source:* HBA. *Perm:* Agency, NASABA.

Dirty Hearts. Ritual. In this play, an incident at a card game with a white man triggers the move of a black man, a co-player in the game, to leave and follow up a dream he had about separation; in so doing, he is reborn. *Cast:* 4 BM, 1 BF. *Length:* 1 Act. *Pubn: Scripts,* vol. 1, no. 1, Nov. 1971. *Lib Source:* HBA. *Perm:* Author.

Malcolm Man Don't Live Here No Mo. (1970). Ritual. Malcolm X's life and ideals; to be performed by children. *Cast:* 1 BM, 1 BF, chorus. *Length:* 1 Act. *Pubn: Black Theatre,* ed. by Ed Bullins, no. 6, 1972. *Lib Source:* HBA. *Perm:* Author.

Sister Son/ji. (1969). Morality Ritual. The transition of a black woman from yesterday to the future and her involvement with her people. *Cast:* 1 BF. *Length:* 1 Act. *Prod:* Concept East Theatre, Detroit, Mich., Dec. 1970; Public Theatre, New York Shakespeare Festival, N.Y., Feb. 1972. *Pubn: New Plays from the Black Theatre,* ed. by Ed Bullins, New York: Bantam, Inc., 1969. *Lib Source:* HBA. *Perm:* Author.

Uh, Uh; But How Do It Free Us. (1970). Didactic Ritual. An examination of the black man/woman relationship in the struggle for liberation. *Cast:* 6 BM, 4 BF, 1 WM, 2 WF. *Length:* 3 Scenes. *Pubn: The New Lafayette Theatre Presents,* ed. by Ed Bullins, New York: Anchor Books, 1974. *Lib Source:* HBA. *Perm:* Agency, NASABA.

SANDERS, JOE, JR.

All Men Are Created. Adaptation of J. A. Roger's book *From Man to Superman.* Prod: Experimental Actors Guild, Chicago, Ill., 1973.

SAUNDERS, RUBY CONSTANCE X.

Goddman July. (1969). *Length:* 1 Act

SAUTI, INSAN

The Installment Plan. Drama. Relationship of black prisoner recidivism to the social and political realities of Amerikkka, and the ordeal of one black man attempting to overcome them. *Cast:* 18 BM, 7 BF, 2 WM. *Length:* 1 Act. *Pubn: Drama and Theater Magazine,* vol. 2, no. 1, 1972. *Perm:* Author.

SAYIF. *See* Geary, Bruce C.

SCHUYLER, GEORGE

The Witch Hunt. Parody Skit. An anti-Communist piece based on the witches' scene in Shakespeare's *Macbeth. Cast:* 2 M, 3 F. *Length:* 5 Pages. *Pubn: Plain Talk* magazine, Jan. 1948; *Black and Conservative,* New Rochelle: Arlington House, 1966. *Lib Source:* HBA.

SCOTT, HAROLD

Dream Deferred. Prod: Chelsea Theatre, New York, 1965-66.

SCOTT, JIMMY

Money. Prod: North Richmond Theatre Workshop, University of California, Berkeley, Summer 1968.

SCOTT, JOHN

The Alligator Man. Musical. Tommie Lee, a black jazz musician, attempts to escape the academic queries of a white Ph.D. and a black girl singer by developing and furnishing an apartment in the sewer system beneath a nightclub. *Cast:* 1 BM, 1 BF, 2 WM. *Length:* 1 Act. *Prod:* Bowling Green State University, Ohio, 1967. *Perm:* Author.

Black Sermon Rock. Sister Rose, a black storefront church "preacheress," attempts to conduct a simple burial ceremony for two black men. Her commercial ceremony is complicated by the spiritual return of the dead men and the ensuing strange effects their presence wields on the sermon, which ends in an orgiastic testimonial to the indestructible beauty of the black essence. Part 3 of a trilogy, which includes *Ride a Black Horse* and *Time Turns Black. Cast:* 4 BM, 1 BF, singers, musicians, extras. *Length:* 1 Act. *Prod:* Bowling Green State University, Ohio, 1972. *Perm:* Author.

The Good Ship Credit. HooDoo Musical. A HooDoo captain manipulates the inhabitants (patients) toward a deeper understanding of the spirit of racial and personal identity. They devise ingenious ways to abuse the credit sys-

SCOTT, JOHN *(Cont.)*

tem to get from the Island of Harloom to the Island of Haitu. The blacks, Ivan-the-Terrific, Grace-the-Great, the Baby-Ru, and Madame Manong, decide to include whites on the voyage, which leads to some comic reversals. *Cast:* 3 BM, 2 BF, 1 WM, 1 WF. *Length:* 2 Acts. *Prod:* Reading, Frank Silvera Writers' Workshop, Martinique Theatre, New York, 1974. *Perm:* Author.

I Talk with the Spirits.

Karma's Kall. Drama. Karma, a black writer/activist, finds herself groping through the conflicting vagaries of pursuing love with her man while also fighting the demands of her junkie ex-husband. This woman's play examines the problems of black women, particularly those who must maintain their femininity while struggling to develop the toughness required to survive. *Cast:* 4 BM, 4 BF. *Length:* 2 Acts. *Prod:* Bowling Green State University, Ohio, 1973. *Perm:* Author.

Play Division.

Ride a Black Horse. A black sociologist is confronted by the bizarre demands of ghetto militants when he attempts to join with them to force commitments from the civic and educational leaders of the city. Failing, he is driven to the brink of irrationality, then pushed toward self-destruction by his wife and former girl friend, who is the mother of his only child. Part 1 of a trilogy, which includes *Time Turns Black* and *Black Sermon Rock.* *Cast:* 7 BM, 3 BF, 2 WM, 1 WF. *Length:* 2 Acts. *Prod:* National Playwright's Conference of the Eugene O'Neill Memorial Center Theater, Waterford, Conn., 1970. *Perm:* Author.

Shades. Drama. The theme of interracial romance is examined through two couples who must look at the economic, career, social, and family pressures that their respective romances cause. *Cast:* 3 BM, 3 BF, 2 WM, 2 WF, chorus (doubling). *Length:* 2 Acts. *Prod:* Reading, Frank Silvera Writers' Workshop, Martinique Theatre, New York, 1974. *Perm:* Author.

Time Turns Black. Drama. Rufus, a black West Indian taxi driver, and Weldon, a black lawyer, abduct the white liberal mayor of a city in an attempt to force civil rights and economic commitments at the national level. This intricate attempt is undermined by unforeseen and uncontrollable revolutionary forces that precipitate a holocaust. Part 2 of a trilogy, which includes *Ride a Black Horse* and *Black Sermon Rock.* *Cast:* 4 BM, 1 BF, 1 BB, 1 WM, 1 WB. *Length:* 2 Acts. *Prod:* Bowling Green State University, Ohio, 1972. *Perm:* Author.

SCOTT, JOSEPH

Hocus-Pocus. Domestic Comedy. Willy, a veteran, returns from war, can't find a job, and hires out as a black maid to a wealthy family in Scarsdale, New York. *Cast:* 2 BM, 2 BF, 2 WF, 2 WM. *Length:* 2 Acts. *Perm:* Author.

SCOTT, SERET

Funnytime. Satire/Comedy. Married man decides to make a full night's commitment to his girl friend. *Cast:* 1 M, 1 F. *Length:* 1 Act. *Perm:* Author.

No You Didn't. (1972).   *Perm:* Author.

Wine and Cheese. (1970).   *Perm:* Author.

SEBREE, CHARLES

The Dry August. (1972). Fantasy/Drama. Adapted from three act version written
in 1949, *My Mother Came Crying Most Pitifully.* Young black girl, Teddy
Hicks, dreams of running away to wealth and fame in Chicago and is offered
help by the devil.   *Cast:* 2 BM, 4 BF, 5 WF. *Length:* 1 Act. *Pubn: Black Theater USA*, ed. by James V. Hatch and Ted Shine, New York: Free Pr., 1974.
Lib Source: HBA.

My Mother Came Crying Most Pitifully. (1949). Fantasy/Drama. *The Dry
August*, by the same playwright, is a subsequent adaptation of this play.
Teddy, a young black girl, dreams of being a rich white lady like Mrs. Pat-
terson, who is corrupt and selfish.   *Cast:* 3 BM, 5 BF, 5 WF. *Length:* 3 Acts.
Lib Source: Typescript, HBA.

SEBREE, CHARLES, and GREER JOHNSON*

Mrs. Patterson. Musical Fantasy. Teddy, a young black girl, is tempted to run
away from her rural shack to become like the rich white lady, Mrs. Patterson.
Cast: 3 BM, 5 BF, 4 WF. *Length:* 3 Acts. *Prod:* National Theatre, New York,
Dec. 1954. *Pubn: Best Plays of 1954-55*, ed. by Louis Kronenberger, New
York: Dodd, 1955.

SEILER, CONRAD

Darker Brother.   *Prod:* Gilpin Players, Karamu Theatre, Cleveland, Ohio, Mar.
1938.

End of the World.

Sweet Land. Drama.   *Prod:* Lafayette Theatre, New York, Jan. 1935. *Pubn:* FTP.

SÉJOUR, VICTOR

André Girard.   *Pubn:* Paris: M. Lévy Frères, 1858. *Lib Source:* NYPL.

L'Argent du Diable.   *Pubn:* Paris: M. Lévy Frères, 1854. *Lib Source:* NYPL.

Les Aventuriers.   *Pubn:* Paris: M. Lévy Frères, 1863. *Lib Source:* NYPL.

The Brown Overcoat. See *Le Paletot Brun*

La Chute de Séjan. Legendary Verse Drama. Depicts the Roman Emperor Ti-
berius and his minister Séjanus and their struggle for power.   *Length:* 5
Acts. *Prod:* Paris, France, 1849.

Compère Guillery. (1860).

Cromwell. Manuscript.

Diégarias. Romantic Verse Drama. Set in fifteenth-century Spain, it depicts a
revenge drama involving a disguised Jew, his daughter, and her husband,
Don Juan.   *Prod:* Paris, France, 1844. *Pubn:* Paris: Imprimèrie de Boule,
1861.

SÉJOUR, VICTOR (*Cont.*)

Les Fils de Charles Quint. *Pubn:* Paris: M. Lévy Frères, 1865. *Lib Source:* NYPL.

Les Fils de la Nuit. *Pubn:* Paris: M. Lévy Frères, 1856. *Lib Source:* NYPL.

Les Grands Vassaux. *Pubn:* Paris: M. Lévy Frères, 1859. *Lib Source:* NYPL.

La Madone des Roses. *Pubn:* Paris: M. Lévy Frères, 1869. *Lib Source:* SCHOM.

Le Marquis Caporal. *Pubn:* Paris: M. Lévy Frères, 1865. *Lib Source:* SCHOM.

Le Martyr du Coeur. *Pubn:* Paris: M. Lévy Frères, 1858. *Lib Source:* NYPL.

Les Massacres de la Syrie. *Pubn:* Paris: J. Barbe, c. 1860.

Les Mystères du Temple. *Pubn:* Paris: Colman Lévy, c. 1860. *Lib Source:* SCHOM.

Les Noces Venitiennes. Legendary. The story of hatred and rivalry between two powerful families in Venice, the Orseoles and the Falieros. *Length:* 5 Acts. *Pubn:* Paris: M. Lévy Frères, 1855. *Lib Source:* NYPL.

The Outlaw of the Adriatic or *The Female Spy and the Chief of the Ten.* *Pubn:* London: T. H. Lacy. *Lib Source:* NYPL.

Le Paletot Brun. Comedy. A woman of fashion discards a lover. *Translation title: The Brown Overcoat.* *Cast:* 1 M, 1 F. *Length:* 1 Act. *Prod:* Circle in the Square, New York, Dec. 1972. *Pubn:* Paris: M. Lévy Frères, 1859; *Black Theater USA*, ed. by James V. Hatch and Ted Shine, New York: Free Pr., 1974. *Lib Source:* HBA.

Richard III. Historical. The rise and fall of the English king. *Length:* 5 Acts. *Pubn:* Paris: D. Giraud et J. Dagneau, 1852.

La Tireuse de Cartes. Melodrama. The story of a mother who demands the return of her kidnapped daughter; when refused, she swears to kill the husband-abductor. *Length:* 5 Acts. *Prod:* Paris, France, 1850. *Pubn:* Paris: M. Lévy Frères, 1860. *Lib Source:* NYPL.

Le Vampire. Manuscript.

Les Volontaires de 1814. *Pubn:* Paris: M. Lévy Frères, 1862. *Lib Source:* SCHOM.

SÉJOUR, VICTOR, and THEODORE BARRIÈRE*

Les Enfants de la Louvre. *Pubn:* Paris: M. Lévy Frères, 1865. *Lib Source:* NYPL.

SELF, CHARLES

The Smokers. *Prod:* Afro-American Festival, Dillard University, New Orleans, La., Feb. 1968.

SEWELL, E. G.

The Voice from Dunberry Hill. Domestic Drama. The play deals with an influential black university leader and his family and the racial problems they face in spite of the status they have achieved. *Cast:* 6 BM, 4 BF, 9 WM, 1 WF. *Length:* 3 Acts.

SHABAKA, KHARI K. *See* Hooks, Barnett Ulyses, II

SHAHAN, HARVEY

Evaline. (1974). Drama with Music. A talented and aspiring young singer confronts conflicting influences in trying to decide the course of her life and her career. *Cast:* 5 BM, 3 BF, 1 WM, 1 WF. *Length:* 3 Acts.

SHANGE, NTOZAKE

For Colored Girls Who Have Considered Suicide/When the Rainbow Is Enuf. Choreopoem. A series of poems about life and love from the viewpoint of a black woman. *Cast:* 7 BF. *Length:* Full Length. *Prod:* NFT, Booth Theatre, New York, Sept. 1976. *Pubn:* New York: Macmillan, 1977.

A Photograph: A Still Life with Shadows/A Photograph: A Study of Cruelty. (In Progress).

SHANNON, JAMES EDWARD

The Menials. (1976). "The younger of two blood sisters, one a domestic, the other a nursing home attendant, has, with the encouragement of the son of their employers, become sufficiently interested in Malcolm X to wish to put his picture on the wall along with those of Christ and Martin Luther King."—Townsend Brewster, *Newsletter* of the Harlem Cultural Council, vol. 2, no. 11. *Length:* 1 Act. *Prod:* New York, 1976.

Truth Tabernacle. Comedy. "Bishop Ozol W. Johnson, a figure reminiscent of Reverend Ike, awards a clock radio to the sister who has made the largest contribution toward his trip to the Holy Land."—Townsend Brewster, *Newsletter* of the Harlem Cultural Council, vol. 2, no. 11. *Length:* 1 Act. *Prod:* New York, 1976.

SHARP, SAUNDRA

Sistuhs. Play with Music. About black women in America (not historical). *Cast:* 3 BM, 7 BF, musicians. *Length:* 2 Acts. *Prod:* Reading, Frank Silvera Writers' Workshop, Martinique Theatre, New York, Jan. 1975. *Perm:* Author.

SHAW, G. TITO

Guerra. (1967). Protest Drama. A portrait of a proud black musician, once successful, now having lost his talent, and his wife, loses his only son in Vietnam. *Cast:* 1 BM, 1 WM. *Length:* 1 Act. *Prod:* Paperback Theatre, New York, June 1970. *Perm:* Agency, Esther Sherman, William Morris.

He's Got a Jones. (1969). Historical Domestic Drama. During the depression, a pair of black brothers in the South struggle for a better life amidst the rampant racial bigotry and oppression of that day. *Cast:* 2 BM, 1 BF, 1 WF. *Length:* 3 Acts. *Prod:* Greenwich Mews Theatre, New York, Jan. 1973. *Perm:* Agency, Esther Sherman, William Morris.

Jingle in a Broken Tongue. (1973). Historical Domestic Drama. The day-to-day struggle for survival and dignity of a family of black sharecroppers in

SHAW, G. TITO (*Cont.*)

the South in the 1920s. *Cast:* 3 BM, 1 BF. *Length:* 1 Act. *Perm:* Agency, Esther Sherman, William Morris.

An Orchid for Romy. (1968). Morality. The moral conflicts and emotional struggles of a young, inexperienced, homosexual soldier who goes AWOL to stop his white friend's marriage, only to discover he doesn't have the "soul" of his people. *Cast:* 4 BM, 2 BF, 2 WM, 1 WF. *Length:* 1 Act. *Prod:* Paperback Theatre, New York, Nov. 1970. *Perm:* Agency, Esther Sherman, William Morris.

SHELTON, IRVING

Soul Iconoclast. Union management contract negotiations compounded with racial discrimination; struggle of a black man in a hamlet of racial prejudice. Subtitled: *Union.* *Cast:* 4 BM, 1 BF, 8 WM, 1 WF, extras. *Length:* 1 Act. *Lib Source:* Typescript, SCHOM. *Perm:* Author.

SHEPP, ARCHIE

The Communist. *Prod:* Chelsea Theatre Center, New York, 1965–66 season.

Junebug Graduates Tonight. (1971). Ritual. A musical model in structure, complete with band, chorus, and scenic transitions that focus the message of a black youth's disillusionment in the blues changes of sharps or flats, the entire matrix giving expression to the kind of harsh lyricism of an oppressed reality of a young black man in America. *Cast:* 2 BM, 4 BF, 2 WM, 1 WF. *Length:* 2 Acts. *Prod:* Chelsea Theatre Center, New York, Feb. 1967. *Pubn:* Black Drama Anthology, ed. by Woodie King, Jr. and Ron Milner, New York: New Amer. Lib., 1972. *Lib Source:* HBA.

Revolution. Ritual. A black man and woman through all metamorphoses of roles still find themselves up against an inhuman racist system. *Cast:* 2 BM, 1 BF. *Length:* 1 Act. *Prod:* Brooklyn College, New York, 1969. *Lib Source:* Typescript, HBA.

Skulls. (1969). Ritual/Farce with Music. In "De Vali" of the jungle of central Harlem, the white father missionary is slain by his former black mistress and the junkie slaves are thereby set free. *Cast:* 5 BM, 3 BF, 1 WM. *Length:* 1 Act. *Lib Source:* Typescript, HBA.

SHEARS, CARL L. *See* Saggittarus

SHERMAN, JIMMIE

A Ballad for Watts.

SHINE, TED

The Bats out of Hell. (1955). Comedy. Orphan children seeking their mother disrupt what was once a peaceful neighborhood in their efforts to find her. *Cast:* 6 BM, 9 BF, extras. *Length:* 1 Act. *Perm:* Agency, Flora Roberts.

Coca-Cola Boys. (1969). *Length:* 1 Act.

Cold Day in August. (1950). Domestic Play. Problems between young married couple living in the cramped quarters of the wife's domineering mother. *Cast:* 3 M, 3 F. *Length:* 1 Act. *Prod:* Howard University, Washington, D.C., 1950. *Perm:* Agency, Flora Roberts.

Come Back after the Fire. (1967). Drama. A female evangelist's struggle to find a place for herself following a nervous breakdown. *Cast:* 6 M, 4 F, extras. *Prod:* Lincoln University, Jefferson City, Mo., 1969. *Perm:* Agency, Flora Roberts.

Contribution. (1968). Comedy/Drama. A grandmother, not able to march the streets for freedom, shows her grandson that she does her share in her own way. *Cast:* 1 BM, 2 BF. *Length:* 1 Act. *Prod:* NEC, New York, Spring 1969; Tambellini's Gate Theatre, New York, Mar. 1970. *Pubn: Black Drama: An Anthology,* ed. by William Brasmer and Dominick Consolo, Columbus, Ohio: Merrill Pub. Co., 1970. *Lib Source:* HBA. *Perm:* DPS.

Dry August. (1952). Comedy/Drama. The story of a young black male caught in the bitter trap of racial injustice in the deep South. *Cast:* Large. *Perm:* Agency, Flora Roberts.

Entourage Royale. (1958). Musical. Gypsy family invades a southern community with the intention of ridding the inhabitants of all their possessions, only to discover love and respectability. *Cast:* 7 M, 6 F, extras. *Perm:* Agency, Flora Roberts.

Epitaph for a Bluebird. (1958). Comedy/Fantasy. Young girl in mourning finds love in a small military town, only to be deserted by her soldier-lover. *Cast:* 6 BM, 4 BF. *Length:* 3 Acts. *Prod:* University of Iowa, Iowa City, 1958. *Perm:* Agency, Flora Roberts.

Flora's Kisses. (1965). Comedy. A welfare mother meets a stranger and desperately tries to find love. *Cast:* 2 BM, 1 BF. *Length:* 1 Act. *Prod:* Theatre U., Baltimore, Md., 1969. *Perm:* Agency, Flora Roberts.

Hamburgers at Hamburger Heaven Are Impersonal. (1969). Comedy/Drama. Lonely school teacher falls for a sensual manic in a crude Dallas tavern. *Cast:* 2 BM, 4 BF. *Length:* 1 Act. *Perm:* Agency, Flora Roberts.

Herbert III. Domestic Play. The channels of communication between husband and wife have deteriorated to near nothing, as shown by their early morning quarrel over their absent son. *Cast:* 1 BM, 1 BF. *Length:* 1 Act. *Pubn: Black Theater USA,* ed. by James V. Hatch and Ted Shine, New York: Free Pr., 1974. *Perm:* Agency, Flora Roberts. *Lib Source:* HBA.

Idabel's Fortune. (1969). Protest Satire/Melodrama. Black domestic outwits her white employer for her own financial benefits. *Cast:* 1 BF, 1 WM, 2 WF, extras. *Length:* 1 Act. *Prod:* Howard University, Washington, D.C., Oct. 1969. *Lib Source:* Typescript, HBA. *Perm:* Agency, Flora Roberts.

Jeanne West. (1968). Musical. *Perm:* Agency, Flora Roberts.

Miss Victoria. (1965). *Length:* 1 Act.

Morning, Noon, and Night. (1964). Drama. Old woman eliminates people that she feels have mistreated her and those that have developed relationships

SHINE, TED (*Cont.*)

    with her grandson and son. *Cast:* 1 BM, 3 BF. *Length:* 3 Acts. *Prod:* Howard University, Washington, D.C., 1964. *Pubn: The Black Teacher and the Dramatic Arts*, ed. by William Reardon and Thomas Pawley, Westport: Negro Universities Pr., 1970. *Lib Source:* HBA. *Perm:* Agency, Flora Roberts.

The Night of Baker's End. Drama. A black father's struggle to hold his family together results in tragedy. *Cast:* 4 BM, 5 BF, extras. *Length:* 3 Acts. *Prod:* Lincoln University, Jefferson City, Mo., Dec. 1974. *Perm:* Agency, Flora Roberts.

Packard. (1971). Comedy. Southern white lady is faced with the problem of removing the dead body of her black chauffeur from her bed. *Cast:* 2 M, 1 F, extras. *Length:* 1 Act. *Perm:* Agency, Flora Roberts.

Plantation. (1970). Protest Drama. White plantation head discovers he is a mulatto and refuses to accept his black-skinned offspring. *Cast:* 1 BM, 1 BF, 2 WM, 1 WF. *Length:* 1 Act. *Prod:* Tambellini's Gate Theatre, New York, Mar. 1970. *Pubn:* DPS. *Lib Source:* HBA. *Perm:* Agency, DPS.

Pontiac. (1967). *Length:* 1 Act.

A Rat's Revolt. (1959).

Revolution. (1968).

Shoes. (1970). Domestic Play. A young man's priority of a pair of alligator shoes is questioned by his peers. *Cast:* 5 BM. *Length:* 1 Act. *Prod:* Howard University, Washington, D.C., Oct. 1969; Tambellini's Gate Theatre, New York, Mar. 1970. *Pubn:* DPS. *Lib Source:* HBA. *Perm:* Agency, DPS.

Sho Is Hot in the Cotton Patch. (1951). Comedy. Conflict between the older and younger generations of Blacks working in the YWCA kitchen in Dallas. Subtitled: *Miss Weaver.* *Cast:* 5 BM, 5 BF. *Length:* 1 Act. *Prod:* Howard University, Washington, D.C., 1951; NEC, New York (as *Miss Weaver*), 1968. *Pubn: Encore* magazine, vol. 11, Tallahassee, Fla., Florida A & M University, 1967.

Waiting Room. (1969). *Length:* 1 Act.

SHIPP, JESSE A.

Seeing Chinatown. Musical Comedy. An oriental and Afro-American fantasy. *Prod:* Lafayette Players, New York, 1919.

Senegamian Carnival. Musical Revue. *Prod:* 1898.

This and That. (1919).

SHIPP, JESSE A., and WILL MARION COOK

The Policy Players. Musical Revue. Subtitled: *4-11-44.* *Prod:* 1900.

SHIPP, JESSE A., PAUL L. DUNBAR, and ALEX ROGERS

In Dahomey. Musical Comedy. The president of the Dahomey Colonization Society hires two detectives (Bert Williams and George Walker) to find a

missing treasure. They all end up in Dahomey, where they are nearly executed. They decide there's no place like home. *Cast:* 15 BM, 3 BF. *Length:*
2 Acts, Prologue. *Prod:* Boston Music Hall, Mass., Sept. 1902.

SHIPP, JESSE A., and ALEX ROGERS

Bandanna Land. Musical Comedy. Music by Will Marion Cook. Book with Bert
Williams and George Walker. "The story, set on the outskirts of a city in
northern Georgia, centered about a group of Negroes who by song and rip-
snorting pranks, finally sell their property adjoining the white park to whites."—
Fannin Belcher. *Prod:* Majestic Theatre, New York, Feb. 1908.

(In) Abyssinia. Musical Oddity in Prologue and Four Scenes. Music with Will
Marion Cook and Bert Williams. Book with Bert Williams and George Walker.
"A young man spends his inheritance in taking a group of friends to visit
Abyssinia."—Fannin Belcher. *Prod:* Majestic Theatre, New York, Feb. 1906.

Mr. Lode of Kole (Koal). Musical Comedy. Music by Rosamund Johnson. Book
with Bert Williams. "Musical melange built around a story of an island intrigue
in which the kidnapped ruler (Big Smoke), released in time to prevent the
crowning of his successor, appoints the would-be king, chief of the coal
department."—Fannin Belcher. *Prod:* Majestic Theatre, New York, Nov.
1909.

SHIPMAN, WILLIE B.

Pepper. (1972).

SHORT, QUINCY.

Delon. Drama. A rent strike in a hotel apartment building turns into a fight for
power and money. *Cast:* 7 BM, 3 BF, 2 WM. *Length:* 3 Acts.

SHULL, LEO

What's Your Epitaph. In a community of "policy writers, prostitutes, gamblers,
and crooked politicians," a harassed social worker and an embittered organizer take steps to salvage the community. *Cast:* 4 BM, 5 BF, 4 WM, 1
WF, extras *Length:* 3 Acts. *Lib Source:* Typescript, SCHOM.

SILVERA, FRANK

Unto the Least. (c.1938). Domestic. Adapted from Maxim Gorky's play *The Lower
Depths.* A drama of Negro life, their hopes, fears, and aspirations. *Cast:*
7 BM, 5 BF. *Length:* 3 Acts. *Lib Source:* SCHOM.

SILVERA, JOHN D., and ABRAM HILL

Liberty Deferred. (1936). Drama. Chronicle of the Negro, Federal Theatre epic
style. *Cast:* Large B & W M. *Length:* Full Length. *Lib Source:* Typescript, PAL,
GMU, & FTP.

SINGLETON, PAT

Seven till Two in the Morning. *Prod:* Bed-Stuy Street Academy, New York.

SISSLE, NOBLE, EUBIE BLAKE, AUBREY LYLES, and FLOURNOY MILLER

Shuffle Along. Musical Comedy. Story possibly based on Miller and Lyles' *Mayor of Dixie*, 1907. Concerns the efforts of three candidates to win the mayoralty campaign and the complications when one wins. Subtitled: *Mayor of Jim Town.*   *Cast:* 15 BM, 4 BF, chorus. *Length:* 2 Acts. *Prod:* Sixty-third Street Music Hall, New York, May 1921. *Pubn: Best Plays of 1920-21*, ed. by Burns Mantle, New York: Dodd, 1921.

SISSLE, NOBLE, EUBIE BLAKE, and FLOURNOY MILLER

Shuffle Along of 1933. Musical Comedy. Having to do with the financing of a molasses factory.   *Cast:* 13 BM, 7 BF, extras. *Length:* 2 Acts. *Prod:* Mansfield Theatre, New York, Dec. 1932. *Pubn: Best Plays of 1932-33*, ed. by Burns Mantle, New York: Dodd, 1933.

SISSLE, NOBLE, EUBIE BLAKE, FLOURNOY MILLER, and PAUL GERARD SMITH

Shuffle Along of 1952. Musical Comedy. "Woven around a group of GIs and WACs who meet in the army just before the end of World War II and then get together to run a dressmaking establishment in New York."—*New York Times*, May 9, 1952.   *Cast:* 15 BM, 7 BF. *Prod:* Broadway Theatre, New York, May 1952.

SISSLE, NOBLE, EUBIE BLAKE, and LEW PAYTON

In Bamville. Musical Revue. Deals with aspects of horse racing.   *Prod:* Chicago, Ill., 1923-1924; New York, Mar. 1924. *Pubn: Best Plays of 1923-24*, ed. by Burns Mantle, New York: Dodd, 1924.

SISSLE, NOBLE, and LEW PAYTON

The Chocolate Dandies. Musical Revue. Music by Eubie Blake.   *Cast:* 20 BM, 7 BF. *Length:* 2 Acts. *Prod:* Colonial Theatre, New York, Sept. 1924. *Pubn: Best Plays of 1924-25*, ed. by Burns Mantle, New York: Dodd, 1925

SISSLE, NOBLE, and ED SULLIVAN*

Harlem Cavalcade. Musical Revue.   *Prod:* Ritz Theatre, New York, May 1942.

SMITH, DEMON. *See* Abubakari, Damani

SMITH, DJENIBA

Please Reply Soon. (1971).

SMITH, EDWARD G.

Games. Ritual. From games that children play to the games that adults play, like the burning of the Sunday school in Birmingham, Alabama, to the assassination of Martin and Malcolm.   *Cast:* 10-12 M & F. *Length:* 1 Act. *Prod:* Buffalo, N.Y., Aug. 1972. *Perm:* Author.

It's Easier to Get Dope than It Is to Get a Job. Didactic. The problems of drug
traffic in the black communities, given from the viewpoint of the child, teenager,
junkie, pusher, and a law enforcement agency.   *Cast:* 14 M, 9 F, 1 BB, 1 BG.
Length: 1 Act. *Prod:* Buffalo, N.Y., Aug. 1971. *Perm:* Author.

Now Time. Radio Drama. A revolutionary drama that consists of one man's obli-
gation to the order.   *Cast:* 5 M, 3 F. *Length:* 30 Minutes. *Prod:* Buffalo, N.Y.,
Apr. 1970. *Perm:* Author.

SMITH, J. AUGUSTUS

Louisiana. Drama. In the bayou region of Louisiana, a Christian and a voodoo
group vie for control of Pastor Amos Berry and his niece.   *Cast:* 10 BM, 7 BF,
extras. *Prod:* Forty-eighth Street Theatre, New York, Feb. 1933. *Pubn: Best
Plays of 1932-33*, ed. by Burns Mantle, New York: Dodd, 1933.

SMITH, J. AUGUSTUS, and PETER MORRELL

Turpentine. (1936). Drama. Black turpentine workers protest their destitute conditions with a strike, which finally leads to warfare and victory.   *Cast:* 16 M,
4 F. *Length:* 3 Acts. *Lib Source:* FTP, GMU.

SMITH, JEAN

O.C.'s Heart. Drama. This psychological drama about racial revenge concerns
the brother of a dead black youth who gets back his heart, which has been
transplanted into the body of a white man. Excerpts from a three act play of
the same name.   *Pubn: Negro Digest*, Apr. 1970. *Lib Source:* SCHOM.

SMITH, LOIS A.

A Reversible Oreo. Domestic Comedy. Play depicts present-day life in the homes
of two southern families—one black, the other white—and how everyday life
pressures affect them; with an out-of-the-ordinary ending that was created
primarily to arouse concern and help direct thought and action toward estab-
lishing better human relations among all the people in a given community.
Cast: 2 BM, 3 BF, 1 BB, 1 WM, 2 WF, 1 WB. *Length:* 3 Acts. *Prod:* n.p., Apr. 1974.
Perm: Author.

What's Wrong. Domestic Comedy. Play is a contemporary Christmas holiday
happening that demonstrates the present pace and condition of most individuals—always in a hurry and thinking selfishly.   *Cast:* 2 BM, 2 BF, 3 BB, 1
BG, children's choir, extras. *Length:* 1 Act. *Prod:* n.p., Dec. 1974. *Perm:* Author.

SMITH, OTIS, RICHARD DEDEAUX, and KILLU ANTHONY HAMILTON

The Rising Sons—Wisdom and Knowledge.   *Pubn:* Los Angeles: The Watts
Prophets, 1973.

SMITH, PAUL GERARD, EUBIE BLAKE, FLOURNOY MILLER, and NOBLE SISSLE

Shuffle Along of 1952. Musical Comedy. "Woven around a group of GIs and WACs
who meet in the army just before the end of World War II and then get together

SMITH, PAUL GERARD, EUBIE BLAKE, FLOURNOY MILLER, and NOBLE SISSLE *(Cont.)*

to run a dressmaking establishment in New York."—*New York Times*, May 9, 1952.   *Cast:* 15 BM, 7 BF. *Prod:* Broadway Theatre, New York City, May 1952.

SMITH, VANCE

S.T.R.E.S.S. This play describes for black communities the Detroit police department's stratagem in using police decoys to apprehend street robbers. S.T.R.E.S.S., an acronym for "Stop The Robbers—Enjoy Safe Streets," shows how all the police unit's victims, nineteen blacks, fell to their fatal shooting. *Prod:* Mwongi Arts, Detroit, Mich., 1973.

SMYRL, DAVID LANGSTON

On the Lock-in. Musical. A collage of scenes, soliloquies, and songs that give a picture of prison life where men have lost their "plans."   *Cast:* 11 M. *Length:* Full Length. *Prod:* Public Theatre, New York Shakespeare Festival, N.Y., Apr. 1977.

On the Goddam Lock-in or Lights Out. (1972). Drama. Deals with the relationship that develops among men sharing the experience of being imprisoned together.   *Cast:* 10 BM, 2 WM. *Length:* 1 Act. *Prod:* Reading, Frank Silvera Writers' Workshop, Martinique Theatre, New York, Mar. 1975; Hotel Alden Theatre, New York, July 1975.

SNAVE, ELMAS

Little Dodo.

The Park on 14th Street.

Skin Deep.

SNIPES, MARGARET F. TAYLOR

Folklore Black American Style.

Hotel Happiness.   *Prod:* Karamu Theatre, Cleveland, Ohio, 1971.

I Want to Fly.   *Prod:* Karamu Theatre, Cleveland, Ohio, 1971.

Sing a Song of Watergate. Musical. Spoof based on Watergate shenanigans. *Prod:* Humanists Theatre, Cleveland, Ohio, Feb. 1975.

Will Somebody Please Die.   *Prod:* One World Theatre Project, Cleveland, Ohio, July 1973.

SNIPES, MARGARET F. TAYLOR, and AL FANN

The Hymie Finkelstein Used Lumber Company. Musical. *Prod:* Karamu Theatre, Cleveland, Ohio, 1973-74 Season.

SPENCE, EULALIE

Brothers and Sisters of the Church Council. (c. 1920).

Fool's Errand. (1927). Comedy. Busybody neighbors assume that the unmarried daughter of a church member is pregnant, and they attempt to force a marriage. Second prize at the National Little Theatre Tournament at the Frolic Theatre, New York, 1927.   *Cast:* 4 BM, 4 BF, extras. *Length:* 1 Act. *Prod:* Krigwa Players, Little Negro Theatre of Harlem, New York, 1927. *Pubn:* SF.

Foreign Mail. Second prize in 1926 *Crisis* magazine contest.   *Prod:* 1927. *Pubn:* SF. *Perm:* Agency, SF.

Help Wanted.   *Pubn:* Boston: *Saturday Evening Quill,* Apr. 1929.

Her. (1927).   *Length:* 1 Act.

The Hunch. Comedy. About Harlem life. Second prize in *Opportunity* magazine contest, 1927.   *Length:* 1 Act.

The Starter. (1927). Comedy. A young man loves women but not marriage.   *Cast:* 1 BM, 3 BF. *Length:* 1 Act. *Pubn: Plays of Negro Life,* ed. by Alain Locke and Montgomery Gregory, New York: Harper, 1927. *Lib Source:* HBA.

Undertow. (1929). Domestic Melodrama. Hattie refuses to let her man find happiness with another woman.   *Cast:* 2 BM, 3 BF. *Length:* 1 Act. *Pubn: Black Theater USA,* ed. by James V. Hatch and Ted Shine, New York: Free Pr., 1974. *Lib Source:* HBA.

The Whipping. (1932). Screenplay.   *Length:* Full Length. *Prod:* Optioned by Paramount Pictures but never produced.

SPENSLEY, PHILIP

The Nitty Gritty of Mr. Charlie. (1969).

SPILLMAN, BEN, and JOHN O'NEAL

Where Is the Blood of Your Fathers. (1971).   *Prod:* Free Southern Theatre, New Orleans, La., Nov. 1975.

ST. CLAIR, WESLEY

The Station. (1969).

STANBACK, THURMAN W.

Tomorrow Has Been Here and Gone. Domestic Drama. Family facing eviction because of riots; militant son's wife causes conflict with Vietnam veteran brother; violent death of militant brother brings family together. Subtitled: *A Change Has Got to Come.*   *Cast:* 6 BM, 6 BF. *Length:* 3 Acts. *Prod:* Fla., Feb. 1970. *Perm:* Author.

STEED, RUTH

A Raindrop of Thunder. Social Drama. The conflicting values of black brothers and sisters.   *Pubn:* New York: Amuru Pr., 1974, possibly never published.

STEEL, JOHN

Vigil of Candles.   *Cast:* 1 BM, 2 BF, 1 WF. *Length:* 1 Act. *Prod:* Reading, Frank Silvera Writers' Workshop, Martinique Theatre, New York, Oct. 1974.

STEELE, RICHARD

The Matter of Yo Mind.

STEVENSON, WILLIAM ADELL, III

Bugles.

Bulldogs.

Love, Love.

One the Two of Us. Black man tries to relate to his woman what is expected of the two of them in the revolution. *Cast:* 4 BM, 2 BF, extras. *Length:* 1 Act. *Pubn: Scripts*, vol. 1, no. 7, May 1972. *Perm:* Agency, Diana Hunt.

STEWARD, ARTIE

Voyages. Subtitled: *Trek.*   *Prod:* Theatre Black at School of Continuing Education, New York University, Apr. 1969.

STEWARD, SAM

Involuntary Slavery.   *Prod:* La Mont Zeno Community Theatre, Chicago, Ill., 1973.

STEWARD, RON, and LOUIS JOHNSON

Sambo or *A Black Opera with White Spots.* Jazz Musical. Based on nursery rhymes. Sambo grows up in a white world that evidences its sickness.   *Cast:* 2 BM, 2 BF, 3 WM, 2 WF. *Length:* 2 Acts. *Prod:* Public Theatre, New York Shakespeare Festival, New York, Dec. 1969.

STEWART, DELANO

Rerun.   *Prod:* Bed-Stuy Theatre, New York, May 1973.

Uncle Tom. Historical. A purposeful examination of the past.   *Prod:* Bed-Stuy Theatre, New York, Sept. 1973.

Welcome Home Joe.   *Prod:* Bed-Stuy Theatre, New York, Nov. 1973.

STEWART, JAMES

Agbanli and the Hunter. A secret entrusted to a woman is told, thus causing strife in a home where polygamy is practiced. Subtitled: *Why One Never Tells the Truth to Women.*   *Cast:* 2 M, 4 F. *Length:* 1 Act. *Pubn: Black Lines*, vol. 2, no. 1, ed. by Larry Coleman and Clarence Turner, Fall 1971. *Lib Source:* HBA.

The Gourd Cup. Children's Play. The play, using song and dance, deals with trickery and ends in a paroxysm of contorted and exaggerated agony. *Cast:* 4 M, 3 F. *Length:* 1 Act. *Pubn: Black Lines*, vol. 2, no. 1, ed. by Larry Coleman and Clarence Turner, Fall 1971. *Lib Source:* HBA.

How Men Came into the World. Children's Play. Mother tries to rid herself of her eleven children. The attempt is futile. Subtitled: *How the Lesser Gods Came into the World.*   *Cast:* 6 M & F, 21 children. *Length:* 1 Act. *Pubn: Black Lines*, vol. 2, no. 1, ed. by Larry Coleman and Clarence Turner, Fall 1971. *Lib Source:* HBA.

The Messenger of God. Ritual. The messenger of God perplexes the villagers by his behavior. Subtitled: *Mamu's Ways Are Just.* *Cast:* 7 M, 1 F. *Length:* 1 Act. *Pubn: Black Lines*, vol. 2, no. 1, ed. by Larry Coleman and Clarence Turner, Fall 1971. *Lib Source:* HBA.

The Storytellers. Children's Play. Two short morality skits: one involves two brothers, the other a wayward father. *Cast:* 5 M, 2 F, extras. *Length:* 1 Act. *Pubn: Black Lines*, vol. 2, no. 1, ed. by Larry Coleman and Clarence Turner, Fall 1971. *Lib Source:* HBA.

STILES, THELMA JACKSON

No One Man Show. Domestic Comedy. Afraid to live her own life, a single woman in her late thirties usurps the responsibilities of those around her. She encourages her dependent twenty-year-old underemployed brother and eighteen-year-old sister to support themselves, yet frustrates their efforts to become mature, independent adults. A cousin who lives rent free with the family, and the younger sister's married boyfriend, as well as two outspoken members of a black nationalist organization also clash with the female head of the house. *Cast:* 5 M, 2 F. *Length:* 1 Act. *Prod:* n.p., 1971. *Perm:* Author.

STOKES, HERBERT

The Man Who Trusted the Devil Twice. Drama. Negro principal makes a deal with white authorities that backfires, thus causing him to lose his life. *Cast:* 5 BM, 2 WM. *Length:* 1 Act. *Pubn: New Plays from the Black Theatre*, ed. by Ed Bullins, New York: Bantam, 1969. *Lib Source:* HBA.

The Uncle Toms. The conversion of distorted minds to black consciousness. *Cast:* 5 BB. *Length:* 1 Act. *Pubn: Drama Review*, vol. 12, no. 4, Summer 1968. *Lib Source:* HBA.

STOKES, TONY

Movements. (1974). A play of ghetto life—with its bravery and its horror. *Length:* 1 Act.

STOREY, CHARLES

The Oneness of It All. (1973). The play deals with black power and solidarity. *Cast:* 8 BM, 2 BF, 1 WM, 2 WF, chorus. *Length:* 3 Acts.

STOREY, RALPH

Doww.

STREATOR, GEORGE

New Courage. A woman listens to "white America" on a bus ride, takes the bus driver's number, and panics him. *Cast:* 1 BF, 5 WM, extras. *Pubn: Crisis* magazine, Jan. 1934. *Lib Source:* SCHOM.

STREATOR, GEORGE (*Cont.*)

A Sign. A parson and his wife exploit California Governor Ralph's remark that lynching of kidnappers was an object lesson to America and the world. *Pubn: Crisis* magazine, Feb. 1934. *Lib Source:* SCHOM.

STRICKLAND, WILBUR, and RANDOLPH EDMONDS

G.I. Rhapsody. G.I. Musical Revue. Features skits, solos, music and dance numbers. *Cast:* 18 M, 5 F, extras. *Prod:* The Special Service Division, Fort Huachuca, Ariz., 1943.

STRONG, ROMANER JACK

A Date with the Intermediary. (1968). Drama. *Length:* Full Length. *Prod:* Theatre of UCLA, Los Angeles, Calif., 1968.

A Direct Confrontation in Black. (1968). Drama. *Length:* 1 Act. *Prod:* Theatre of UCLA, Los Angeles, Calif., 1968.

Mesmerism of a Maniac. (1967). Tragedy. *Length:* Full Length. *Prod:* Theatre of UCLA, Los Angeles, Calif., 1967.

Metamorphisms. (1966). Drama. *Length:* 1 Act. *Prod:* Theatre of UCLA, Los Angeles, Calif., 1966.

The Psychedelic Play or a Happening. (1967). Tragedy. *Length:* 1 Act. *Prod:* Theatre of UCLA, Los Angeles, Calif., 1967.

STUART, HAROLD

Calais and the Last Poets. (1972). Ritualistic Play. A group of teenagers in a drug rehabilitation program decide to act out the poetry of the "Last Poets," for their therapy. *Cast:* 5-20 B M & F. *Length:* 2 Acts. *Perm:* Author.

Hunter. (1974). Comedy. A middle-aged woman brings a middle-aged man to her home to take care of her and her son . . . and he seems willing . . . until he finds out the son can't hear, see, or talk. *Cast:* 2 BM, 1 BF. *Length:* 1 Act. *Perm:* Author.

There's a Struggle Going On. (1973). Musical. A young Vietnam veteran in search of a new life finds truth, love, reality, and the struggle. *Cast:* 7 BM, 3 BF, 1 BB, 1 BG, dancers, singers. *Length:* 2 Acts. *Perm:* Author.

The Truth about the Truth. (1974). Drama. A wise human being talks about economics and its effects on the black and third world peoples. *Cast:* 1 B, M or F. *Length:* 1 Act. *Perm:* Author.

SUBLETTE, WALTER

Natural Murder. (1973).

SULLIVAN, MAY MILLER. *See* Miller, May

SWAIN, ROCKO. *See* Ali, Lateef

SWANN, DARIUS LEANDER

The Circle beyond Fear. Choral Drama.   *Pubn:* New York: Friendship Pr., 1960.

The Crier Calls. Drama. For a verse choir.   *Pubn:* New York: Friendship Pr., 1956.

A Desert, a Highway.   *Length:* 1 Act. *Pubn:* New York: Friendship Pr., 1957.

A House for Marvin. About discrimination in housing.   *Cast:* 5 WM, 3 WF. *Length:* 1 Act. *Pubn:* New York: Friendship Pr., 1957.

I Have Spoken to My Children. Verse Chorus.   *Length:* 1 Act. *Pubn:* New York: Friendship Pr., 1957.

SWEETING, EARLE, and EDDIE HUNTER

The Lady. (1944). Comedy. A black maid and her boss, Lady Chesterfield.   *Cast:* 1 BF, 1 WF. *Length:* 1 Act. *Lib Source:* Typescript, SCHOM.

TANNER, WILLIAM H.

The Birth of Freedom and the Present Age.   *Pubn:* Dayton: 1919.

TAPIA, JOSE

Ego. Musical Comedy.   *Prod:* Amsterdam, Holland, 1970.

Kenya. Musical Mystery Play.   *Prod:* Public School 29, New York, 1969.

Outrage. Musical.

Satin Man. Musical.

Welcome to the Space Ship O.R.G.Y. (1971)

TARBELL, SHIRLEY, and ED BULLINS

The Game of Adam and Eve. (1966).   *Length:* 1 Act.

TATE, NEAL

No More Dragons to Kill.

Searchin'. Musical.

Surprise. Musical.

You Gotta Deal with It. Musical.

TATE, NEAL, and SHAUNEILLE PERRY

Music Magic. Musical Odyssey. Book by Shauneille Perry. Music and lyrics by Neal Tate.   *Prod:* Billie Holiday Theatre, New York, Nov. 1976.

TAYLOR, CECIL, and ADRIENNE KENNEDY

A Rat's Mass/Procession in Shout. Improvizational Jazz Opera. Staged and adapted by Cecil Taylor from Ms. Kennedy's play, *A Rat's Mass.*   *Cast:* 17 M & F, 5 musicians. *Length:* 1 Act (2 hours). *Prod:* La Mama E.T.C., New York, Mar. 1976.

TAYLOR, ED, and SAM RIVERS

Solomon and Sheba. Jazz Opera.   *Cast:* 2 BM, 5 BF. *Length:* 2 Acts. *Prod:* Harlem Opera Society, Harlem Cultural Council, New York, 1973.

TAYLOR, EMORY

Black Cowboys. "An adult Western and Jass [sic] Form." Music by Sam Rivers. *Prod:* Afro-American Singing Theatre, New York, May 1970.

TAYLOR, JACKIE

The Other Cinderella.   *Prod:* Chicago's Black Ensemble, Ill., 1975.

TAYLOR, JEANNE

A House Divided.   *Prod:* Possibly by Douglass House Foundation, Washington, D.C., 1968.

TAYLOR, MARGARET F. *See* Snipes, Margaret F. Taylor

TAYLOR, PATRICIA

If We Grow Up. A television adaptation of Audience Association's Off-Broadway production.   *Prod:* WCBS-TV, New York, 1963. *Perm:* Author.

The People Watchers. A television series for children.   *Prod: Camera Three,* CBS-TV, Philadelphia, Pa., 1965. *Perm:* Author.

The Play People. Traditional Afro-American games, rhymes, chants, songs, for children aged 5–9.   *Prod:* Voices, Inc., Town Hall, New York, Dec. 1971. *Perm:* Author.

Unfinished Business. A television adaptation of Audience Associate's Off-Broadway production.   *Prod:* Repertoire Workshop, WCAV-TV, 1964. *Perm:* Author.

Walk Down Mah Street. Music by Norman Curtis. A television adaptation of Audience Associate's Off-Broadway production.   *Cast:* 2 BM, 2 BF, 1 WM, 1 WF. *Prod: Camera Three,* CBS-TV, New York, 1967; The Players Theatre, New York, June 1968. *Perm:* Author.

A Whole Lotta World. An adventure series created and developed for children. *Prod:* NET-TV series, "The Electric Company," 1971. *Perm:* Author.

TAYLOR, ROD, and CECIL ALONZO

Strike One Blow. The plot involves a black prisoner's determination not to succumb to the pressures of being imprisoned, which causes him both physical and psychological anguish. *Length:* 1 Act. *Prod:* Tompkins Square Park Players, New York, June 1975.

TAZEWELL, CHARLES, AUBREY LYLES, and FLOURNOY MILLER

Sugar Hill. "A story of the Negro colony in Harlem having to do with the recent activities of colored racketeers involving Steve Jenkins and Sam Peck."—

Millor and Lyles.   *Cast:* 8 BM, 6 BF, extras. *Length:* 2 Acts. *Prod:* Forrest Theatre, New York, Dec. 1931. *Pubn: Best Plays of 1931–32*, ed. by Burns Mantle, New York: Dodd, 1932.

TEAGUE, BOB, and LANGSTON HUGHES

Soul Yesterday and Today. (1969).

TEER, BARBARA ANN

Soljourney into Truth. The theme is love, and the real purpose is to teach self-appreciation, how to love yourself, and how to expand your ability to feel good about who you are.   *Length:* Full Length. *Prod:* National Black Theatre, New York, 1975.

TEER, BARBARA ANN, and CHARLES RUSSELL

A Revival: Change! Love! Organize! Ritual/Happening. About black culture and life, teaching unity, health, and problem solving with dance, skits, drums, and song.   *Cast:* 28 B M & F. *Length:* Full Length. *Prod:* National Black Theatre, New York, July 1972.

TERRELL, VINCENT

Another Man Called William. Concerns the dedicated determination of William Monroe Trotter and members of the Boston Equal Rights League in their attempts to voice nine important questions about the questionable leadership of Booker T. Washington while he spoke at the Roxbury church meeting. That meeting subsequently turned into a riot that led to the arrest of Trotter and others.   *Cast:* 2 BM, narrator. *Length:* 1 Act. *Pubn:* Boston: Solar Pr., 1975. *Perm:* Agency, The Society of Creative Concern.

Apollo #19. Interplanetary space drama that depicts the interactions of two astronauts during a special space flight.   *Cast:* 1 BM, 1 BF, 2 WM, 1 WF, 2 WG. *Length:* 1 Act. *Pubn:* Boston: Solar Pr., 1970. *Perm:* Agency, The Society of Creative Concern.

The Caskets. (1969). Mythic Ritual/Drama. Concerns three slain civil rights activists, Medgar Evers, Malcolm X, and Reverend Dr. Martin Luther King, Jr.   *Cast:* 4 BM, 1 BF, 1 WM, 1 WF. *Length:* 1 Act. *Pubn:* Boston: Solar Pr., 1969. *Perm:* Agency, The Society of Creative Concern.

An Evening with William Wells Brown. Historical Drama. A play about William Wells Brown's escape from the evils of slavery, and his travels and wit as a free man and race spokesman.   *Cast:* 1 BM. *Length:* 1 Act. *Pubn:* Boston: Solar Pr., 1974. *Perm:* Agency, The Society of Creative Concern.

From These Shores or *Good Olde Crispus.* Historical Drama. A play about the martyr Crispus Attucks, black freedom fighter of the Boston Massacre, the first to give his life for freedom.   *Cast:* 1 BM, 1 BF. *Length:* 2 Acts. *Pubn:* Boston: Solar Pr., 1974. *Perm:* Agency, The Society of Creative Concern.

A Genuine Minstrel Show. Historical Musical Comedy.   *Cast:* 15 BM, 5 BF, 5 WM, 2 WF. *Length:* 3 Acts. *Pubn:* Boston: Solar Pr., 1969. *Perm:* Agency, The Society of Creative Concern.

TERRELL, VINCENT (Cont.)

God's a Faggot (A Biblical Confession). Morality Ritual/Drama. Designed to show contradictions of the Holy Bible, this play concerns the damnation of man's soul as determined by conflicting cultural and spiritual values. *Cast:* 2 BM, 4 WF. *Length:* 1 Act. *Pubn:* Boston: Solar Pr., 1970. *Perm:* Agency, The Society of Creative Concern.

Miss Phillis. Historical Drama. A play that shows black American poet Phillis Wheatley's (1753?–1784) youthful literary development during Boston's colonial times. *Cast:* 1 BM, 1 BF, 2 WM, 3 WF. *Length:* 1 Act. *Pubn:* Boston: Solar Pr., 1974. *Perm:* Agency, The Society of Creative Concern.

Right, Reverend Nat Turner. Historical Drama. The life and times of black freedom fighter Reverend Nat Turner, great minister and leader of the Virginia Slave Rebellion. *Cast:* 1 BM. *Length:* 1 Act. *Pubn:* Boston: Solar Pr., 1974. *Perm:* Agency, The Society of Creative Concern.

Sarge. Drama. The tribulations of a young black combat soldier who defects to the Vietnamese forces and who is later captured and sentenced to life in prison. *Cast:* 2 BM, 1 BB, 2 BF, 1 WM. *Length:* 1 Act. *Pubn:* Boston: Solar Pr., 1970. *Perm:* Agency, The Society of Creative Concern.

Several Barrels of Trash. (1970). Domestic Morality Drama. Play depicts a contemporary life situation of trash and garbage collectors faced with a questionable dilemma after finding a large sum of money. *Cast:* 4 BM. *Length:* 1 Act. *Perm:* Agency, The Society of Creative Concern.

Shoot-out at St. Rafael County Courthouse. Protest Political Drama. About fearless commitment of a younger brother to plan and implement the escape of his incarcerated brother. *Cast:* 5 BM, 4 WM, 1 WF. *Length:* 1 Act. *Pubn:* Boston: Solar Pr., 1974. *Perm:* Agency, The Society of Creative Concern.

Shuttle U.S.A. Political Drama. Revolutionary-mission oriented play that espouses radical solutions for problems facing America. *Cast:* 1 BM, 1 BF, 1 WF, dancer. *Length:* 1 Act. *Pubn:* Boston: Solar Pr., 1970. *Perm:* Agency, The Society of Creative Concern.

The Sunday the Preacher Did Not Show Up. Morality Drama. Depicts a human situation of what happened when mysteriously, throughout the land, the black preachers failed to show up at their Sunday services. *Cast:* 3 BF, 1 WF. *Length:* 1 Act. *Pubn:* Boston: Solar Pr., 1975. *Perm:* Agency, The Society of Creative Concern.

13th Day after Christmas. Protest Political Drama. Details the daily routine of an urban sniper and the mission he undertakes. *Length:* 1 Act. *Perm:* Agency, The Society of Creative Concern.

Trotter. Relates the tragic last days and hours of William Monroe Trotter's life. *Cast:* 3 BM, 1 B, narrator. *Length:* 1 Act. *Pubn:* Boston: Solar Pr., 1972. *Perm:* Agency, The Society of Creative Concern.

Trotter Debates. Depicts William Monroe Trotter's famous White House encounter with President Woodrow Wilson on race issues. *Cast:* 6 BM, 6 BF, 2 WM, 2 WF, narrator. *Length:* 1 Act. *Pubn:* Boston: Solar Pr., 1973. *Perm:* Agency, The Society of Creative Concern.

Trotter Woman. Depicts William Monroe Trotter (journalist, human rights activist, and editor) in the early years of his marriage to his beloved and completely dedicated wife, Geraldine Louise Pindell Trotter. *Cast:* 2 BM, 1 BF, narrator. *Length:* 1 Act. *Pubn:* Boston: Solar Pr., 1974. *Perm:* Agency, The Society of Creative Concern.

Us. Political Drama. Play espouses radical solutions for the problems of black and white Americans. *Cast:* 1 BM, 1 BF, 1 WM. *Length:* 1 Act. *Pubn:* Boston: Solar Pr., 1971. *Perm:* Agency, The Society of Creative Concern.

We Fought Too! Historical Drama. About the early black revolutionary heroes Peter Salem and Salem Poor and the role they played in the Battle of Bunker and Creed's Hill. *Cast:* 10 BM, 4 WM. *Length:* 1 Act. *Pubn:* Boston: Solar Pr., 1975. *Perm:* Agency, The Society of Creative Concern.

Will It Be Like This Tomorrow. Drama. A play about the physical transformation of the president of the U.S. and the effect it has on his presidency. *Cast:* 1 BM, 1 WM, 2 WF *Length:* 1 Act. *Pubn:* Boston: Solar Pr., 1972. *Perm:* Agency, The Society of Creative Concern.

Yours for the Cause. Historical Drama. Written and dedicated to the late, great William Monroe Trotter, 1872-1934, journalist, human rights activist, and editor of the now defunct *Boston Guardian* newspaper. *Perm:* Agency, The Society of Creative Concern.

THEATRE BLACK COMPANY

Destination Ashes. *Prod:* University of the Streets, New York, June 1970.

THIRD WORLD REVELATIONISTS

The Blanket Play. Historical. This play deals with how colonization took place. *Prod:* Third World Revelationists, New York, 1969.

The Screaming Play. Skit. Opens with a sister on her knees, hands tied, screaming. In front of her are two brothers and two sisters, potential revolutionaries. Two armed troops enter with a solution to the black restlessness problem— devise TV programs for Blacks. *Prod:* Third World Revelationists, New York, 1969.

THOMAS, CARL

Once Upon a Time in Buffalo. *Prod:* Reading, Frank Silvera Writers' Workshop, Martinique Theatre, New York, Mar. 1974.

THOMAS, FATISHA

Choice of Worlds Unfilled.

It's Been a Long Time Comin'.

Twenty Year Nigger.

THOMAS, JOYCE CAROL

Black Mystique. *Prod:* Berkeley Community Little Theatre, Calif., 1974.

How I Got Over. *Prod:* Los Medanos College, Calif., 1976.

THOMAS, JOYCE CAROL (*Cont.*)

Look! What a Wonder! Musical. The purpose of this piece is not only to hold up a mirror for Afro-Americans to focus more sharply on their collective consciousness, but to share with the total community in America the meaning and impact of the contributions of black Americans. *Prod:* Berkeley Community Theatre, Calif., Oct. 1976.

A Song in the Sky. Musical. *Prod:* Montgomery Playhouse, San Francisco, Calif., 1976.

THOMAS, STAN

In the City of Angels.

THOMAS, VALERIE M.

The Blacklist. (1971). Morality Drama. Focuses on the dilemma of middle class Blacks as a series of unexplainable firings of high salaried Blacks begins. The principal character, himself a victim of the assimilation of the "professional Black," is faced with the conflict of recognizing the crisis and choosing a course of action. *Cast:* 3 BM, 2 BF. *Length:* 1 Act. *Prod:* n.p., 1971. *Perm:* Author.

THOMPSON, CAROLE

I'd Go to Heaven if I Was Good. Drama. Matriarchal black family living in Brooklyn. The story centers on the struggle between a mother and her teenaged daughter. *Prod:* Manhattan Theatre Club, New York, July 1973.

THOMPSON, CHEZIA B.

The Concubines. (1973). Ritual/Drama. Based on traditional Yoruba religious figures and the phenomenon of Haley's Comet in 1910, this is a story about the appearance of three orishas during the Mardi Gras festival in New Orleans and their relationship with the entity of Time. *Cast:* 7 BM, 11 BF, extras. *Prod:* Mallincrodt Performing Arts Center, St. Louis, Mo., 1973. *Perm:* Author.

Death Walk. (1974). Ritual/Drama. Based on Haitian legends of two women who were carried off by "loas" (Haitian voodoo cult deities) to the "land beneath the water" and how each was transformed by the experience. *Cast:* 9 BM, 9 BF. *Perm:* Author.

Once Upon a Time in a Garden. (1972). Ritual/Drama. Delineates the invasion of Africa by Europeans; also proposes a theory about Earth's invasion by hostile intergalactic forces. *Cast:* 8 BM, 9 BF, 8 WM, 8 WF. *Prod:* The Learning Center, St. Louis, Mo.; Graham Chapel, Washington University, St. Louis, Mo. *Perm:* Author.

THOMPSON, ELOISE A.

Africannus. *Prod:* Los Angeles, Calif., c. 1922.

Caught. *Prod:* The Ethiopian Players, Chicago, Ill., 1925. *Pubn: Best Plays of 1925-26*, ed. by Burns Mantle, New York: Dodd, 1926. *Lib Source:* PAL.

Cooped Up. *Prod:* Lafayette Players, New York, 1924.

THOMPSON, GARLAND LEE

Incantations or the Incarnation of Reverend Goode Black Dresse. A work in progress. Astro study of intergalactic war as seen through the eyes of a former Egyptian tomb chiseler.

Papa Bee on the D Train. Surrealistic Spoof with Music. A play-within-a-play look at the New York, late 1960s, black rhetoric play. The writer stops the play. Is it the death of a play or the playwright? *Length:* Full Length. *Prod:* Reading, Second Annual Black Theatre Alliance Festival, Howard University, Washington, D.C., 1972; Howard University, Washington, D.C., 1974. *Perm:* Author, c/o Frank Silvera Writers' Workshop.

Sisyphus and the Blue-Eyed Cyclops. A black astral plane play dealing with one of the seven levels of consciousness. Sisyphus, a black man, explores the areas between madness and sanity, this world and others. *Cast:* 3 BM, 2 BF. *Length:* 2 Scenes, Prologue. *Prod:* Actor's Studio West, Los Angeles, Calif., Summer 1970; Frank Silvera Writers' Workshop, Afro-American Total Theatre, New York, July 1975. *Perm:* Author, c/o Frank Silvera Writers' Workshop.

THOMPSON, LARRY

A Time to Die. Skit.

THOMPSON, SISTER MARY FRANCESCA

Black Vignettes. Black poetry, music, and dance. *Prod:* Marion College, Indianapolis, Ind., 1974.

THORNE, ANNA V.

Black Power Every Hour. (1970).

THURMAN, LEO L.

Hooray for the Crazy People. (1974). Comedy. A couple living in New York's Greenwich Village (the man is an artist) face problems when confronted with two white millionaires who want to help further their careers. *Cast:* 1 BM, 1 BF, 1 WM, 1 WF, voice. *Length:* 3 Acts.

THURMAN, WALLACE

Jeremiah the Magnificent. (c. 1930). Melodrama/Satire. Drawing on material from Marcus Garvey and the back-to-Africa theme. Jeremiah is sincere but hoodwinked by schemers out to make money. A post office fraud is included. *Cast:* Large. *Length:* 3 Acts. *Lib Source:* Typescript, SCHOM, FTP.

THURMAN, WALLACE, and WILLIAM JOURDAN RAPP*

Harlem. Drama. The Williams family, who has recently arrived from South Carolina, struggle for existence in Harlem and are gradually destroyed. *Cast:* 10 BM, 7 BF, extras. *Length:* 3 Acts. *Prod:* Apollo Theatre, New York, Feb. 1929. *Pubn: Best Plays of 1928-29,* ed. by Burns Mantle, New York: Dodd, 1929. *Lib Source:* Typescript, YL.

TILLMAN, KATHERINE DAVIS

Aunt Betsy's Thanksgiving. Domestic. Mother quarrels with husband—leaving her infant daughter for dead—and returns years later to heap riches on daughter and her mother, who has taken care of her. *Cast:* 1 BM, 3 BF, 1 WM. *Length:* 1 Act. *Pubn:* Philadelphia, Pa.: AME Book Concern, 191? *Lib Source:* SCHOM.

Fifty Years of Freedom or *From Cabin to Congress.* Historical. Based on the life of Benjamin Banneker. Runaway servant is given a chance to go to school in the North. He returns to his southern abode a proud and much praised man. *Cast:* 6 BM, 5 BF, 12 WM, 3 WF. *Length:* 5 Acts. *Pubn:* Philadelphia, Pa.: AME·Book Concern, 191? *Lib Source:* SCHOM.

TODD, B., and HAZEL BRYANT

Origins. *Prod:* Afro-American Total Theatre, Riverside Church Theatre, New York, Oct. 1969.

TOLSON, MELVIN B.

Black Boy. (1963).

Black No More. (1952). Adaptation of George Schuyler's novel of the same name.

The Fire in the Flint. Adaptation of Walter White's book of the same name.

The Moses of Beale Street.

Southern Front.

TOOMER, JEAN

Balo. (1924). Poetic Drama. Balo, a young man on a Georgia farm, has a mystic vision during a prayer meeting in his home. *Cast:* 5 BM, 2 BF, 1 WM, children, extras. *Length:* 1 Act. *Pubn: Black Theater USA,* ed. by James V. Hatch and Ted Shine, New York: Free Pr., 1974. *Lib Source:* HBA.

The Colombo-Madras Mail. (1940). A family on a train discussing the likes and dislikes of their own people and the people surrounding them. *Cast:* 1 WM, 2 WF, extras. *Length:* 1 Act. *Lib Source:* Original script (incomplete), Fisk University Special Collections.

The Gallowerps or Diked. Satirical Farce. This play shows how the power of suggestion can be used. *Cast:* 2 WM, 1 WF. *Length:* 3 Acts. *Lib Source:* Fisk University Special Collections.

Kabnis. (1951). Historical Ritual. Memories of oppression in a southern Georgia town, *Kabnis* is taken from the last part of this author's novel *Cane.* *Cast:* 7 BM, 3 BF. *Length:* 6 Scenes. *Pubn: Kuntu Drama,* ed. by Paul Carter Harrison, New York: Grove, 1974. *Lib Source:* HBA.

Man's Home Companion. A man makes new inventions to keep him company while his family is away. *Cast:* 1 WM, 3 WF. *Length:* 1 Scene. *Lib Source:* Fisk University Special Collections.

Natalie Mann. (1922). About the plight of the middle class black woman. *Cast:* Large B. *Lib Source:* Fisk University Special Collections.

The Sacred Factory. (1927). Religious Drama. A conversation between a husband and his wife in which he tells her the moral and ethical things that are wrong with her and she in turn tells him about his faults.   *Cast:* 1 M, 2 F, 1 child. *Lib Source:* Fisk University Special Collections.

Tourists in Spite of Themselves. Sketch. About Americans in India. Normal conversation of a family while on a train in India.   *Cast:* 1 WM, 1 WF, 1 WC, extras. *Length:* 1 Act. *Lib Source:* Fisk University Special Collections.

TOUSSAINT, RICHARD

If You Get Stepped On . . . Tough! Domestic. Black youth fights to get out of his ghetto environment and is opposed by his family and some of his defeated friends.   *Cast:* 11 BM, 6 BF, 1 WM. *Length:* 3 Acts. *Prod:* Under the title of *These Black Ghettos*, n.p., 1969. *Perm:* Agency, Damani Productions.

A Visitor with a Mission. Mythic Drama. A black prostitute is propositioned by a strange character, who reveals himself as the "Angel of Death."   *Cast:* 1 M, B or W, 1 BF. *Length:* 1 Act. *Prod:* n.p., Oct. 1970. *Perm:* Agency, Damani Productions.

TOWNSEND, WILLA A.

Because He Lives.   *Pubn:* Nashville: Sunday School Publications, Board of the National Baptist Convention, 1924.

TRASS, VEL

From Kings and Queens to Who Knows What.   *Prod:* The Paul Robeson Players, Los Angeles, Calif., 1975.

TRELLING, URSALA. *See* Andrews, Regina

TRENIER, DIANE

Rich Black Heritage. (1970). Satire. Two black men attempt to revenge the wrongs done to black people by abusing a white child.   *Cast:* 2 BM, 1 WB. *Length:* 1 Act. *Lib Source:* Typescript, HBA.

TROY, HENRY, and S. H. DUDLEY

Dr. Beans from Boston. (1911).

TROY, HENRY, and LESTER A. WALTON

Black Bohemia. Musical Revue. Music by Alex Rogers and Will Marion Cook. Lyrics by Lester A. Walton.   *Prod:* n.p., Oct. 1911.

Darkeydom. Musical Revue. Music by Will Marion Cook.   *Prod:* n.p., 1914.

TOWNS, GEORGE A.

The Sharecroppers.

TURNER, BETH

Come Liberty. *Prod:* Reading, Frank Silvera Writers' Workshop, Teachers, Inc., New York, December, 1976.

Ode to Mariah—(A Miracle of Sunshine). *Prod:* Reading, Frank Silvera Writers' Workshop, Martinique Theatre, New York, Apr. 1975.

Sing On, Ms. Griot. Children's Musical. "Mansa Musa, the African ruler summoned up from the fourteenth century to judge a contest arising from an argument over whether Afro-Americans have maintained their heritage fully as much as native Africans."—Townsend Brewster, *Newsletter* of the Harlem Cultural Council, vol. 2, no. 11. *Prod:* Afro-American Total Theatre, Richard Allen Center for Culture and Art, New York, July 1976.

TURNER, DENNIS

Charlie Was Here and Now He's Gone.

TURNER, JOSEPH

The Scheme. (1968). Drama. Black officers in the National Guard are faced with corruption and moral choice during a time of riots. *Cast:* 5 BM, 1 WM. *Length:* 1 Act. *Perm:* Author.

TURPIN, WALTER

Let the Day Perish. Domestic Drama. Play explores the bleak prospects of a family living in poverty in Harlem that cannot stay within the bounds of the law and survive. *Cast:* 4 BM, 6 BF, extras. *Length:* 3 Acts.

TUTT, J. HOMER

Up and Down.

TUTT, J. HOMER, DONALD HEYWOOD, and SALEM WHITNEY

Jim Crow. Musical Drama.

TUTT, J. HOMER, and SALEM WHITNEY

Children of the Sun. (1919-1920). Musical Revue.

Darkest Americans.

De Gospel Train. Dramatic Musical Comedy. Rewritten from the unproduced musical drama, *Jim Crow*, by J. Homer Tutt, Donald Heywood, and Salem Whitney. A southern "Jim Crow" car headed for the North (Washington, D.C.) and its passengers, with their peculiarities, have a morbid end. *Cast:* 6-8 BM, 6 BF, 2 WM, extras. *Length:* 3 Acts. *Lib Source:* Typescript, SCHOM.

Deep Harlem. Musical Comedy. *Cast:* 14 M, 13 F. *Length:* 2 Acts. *Prod:* Biltmore Theatre, New York, Jan. 1929. *Pubn: Best Plays of 1928-29*, ed. by Burns Mantle, New York: Dodd, 1929.

Expresident of Liberia.

George Washington Bullion Abroad.

His Excellency the President.

Mayor of Newton.

My People.

Oh Joy.

TYREE, E. WAYNE

"Yesterday . . . Continued." Drama. The play examines the effects of integration in the rural South and the subsequent death of a school as experienced by a rural family, an old school teacher, and a son who returns home from the North. *Prod:* East River Players, New York, 1974.

ULLMAN, MARVIN

And I Am Black. (1969).

URBAN THEATRE (Houston, Texas)

Stay Strong for the Harvest. Historical Pageant. Begins in Africa, tracing saga through Middle Passage and slavery, then bringing us to the black Southwest and alliances with native Americans. *Prod:* Festival of Southern Black Cultural Alliance, New Orleans, La., Nov. 1976.

VANE, THADDEUS

The Alligators Are Coming. Comedy. *Prod:* Inner City Cultural Center, Los Angeles, Calif., Summer 1970.

VAN PEEBLES, MELVIN

Ain't Supposed to Die a Natural Death. Tunes from Blackness. All music, song, and pantomime—no dialogue. A picture of prostitution, drugs, rats, gambling, police corruption, and despair as forced on the residents of the ghetto. *Cast:* 12 BM, 7 BF. *Length:* 2 Acts. *Prod:* Premiere at Sacramento State College, Calif., Nov. 1970; Ambassador Theatre, New York, Oct. 1971 *Pubn:* New York: Bantam, 1973. *Lib Source:* HBA.

Don't Play Us Cheap. (1967). Musical Comedy. Play is about two of the devil's imps who attempt to break up a Saturday night party Miss Maybelle is giving for her niece. Their efforts are doomed; the devil's scheming is too weak to go up against the love, laughter, and genuine warmth of the folks. *Length:* Full Length. *Prod:* Ethel Barrymore Theatre, New York, May 1972. *Pubn:* as *La Fête à Harlem*, Paris: Jérome Martineau, 1967; New York: Bantam, 1973. *Lib Source:* HBA.

VAN SCOTT, GLORY

Miss Truth. (1971). Poetic Musical. The life of Sojourner Truth, a black slave who took her freedom and went out to preach about the ills of slavery; she became the first female Freedom Rider and a champion of women's rights. *Cast:* 4 BM, 5 BF. *Length:* 1 Act. *Prod:* NEC, New York, Jan. 1972. *Perm:* Agency, Jonathan Pearlman, William Morris.

VAN SCOTT, GLORY (*Cont.*)

Poetic Suite on Arabs and Israelis. (1969). Poetic Musical. A nonpartisan view of the conflict and dramatic pathos of Arabs and Israelis who are locked in an emotional, spiritual, and physical battle with each other. *Cast:* 4 M, 4 F. *Length:* 1 Act. *Prod:* Lincoln Center Auditorium, New York, May 1969. *Lib Source:* Typescript, HBA. *Perm:* Agency, Jonathan Pearlman, William Morris.

Syvilla Fort. Dance/Poem. A poetic documentary tribute to dancer and teacher Syvilla Fort. *Cast:* 4 BF, musicians. *Length:* 1 Act. *Prod:* Lincoln Center Auditorium, New York, May 1977.

VAUGHN, JAMES T., and ALEX ROGERS

The Sultan of Zulu. (c. 1900). Musical Comedy.

VOICES, INC.

The Beauty of Blackness. Musical/Dramatic Statement. Traces the black man from his homeland in Africa to slavery in America.

WADUD, ALI

Kingdom. Drama. "A young black man who has killed a policeman for brutalizing a black woman during a St. Louis race riot in 1968, and who has been shot himself, seeks help at the house of two sisters."—Townsend Brewster, *Newsletter* of the Harlem Cultural Council, vol. 2, no. 10. *Length:* Full Length. *Prod:* NEC Season-within-a-Season, New York, Spring 1976.

WAKEFIELD, JACQUES

Brotherly Love. (1972). Drama. A story about Joe, who's strung out on dope. His buddy cares enough for him to beat him up behind it. *Cast:* 5 BM, 1 BF. *Length:* 1 Act. *Pubn:* Mimeograph, New York, 1972. *Lib Source:* HBA.

WALCOTT, BRENDA

The Black Puppet Show.

Fantastical Fanny.

Look Not Upon Me.

Temporary Lives.

WALCOTT, DEREK

The Charlatan. Music by Gail McDermot. *Prod:* New Theatre for Now, Mark Taper Forum, Los Angeles, Calif., 1974. *Perm:* Agency, Bridget Aschenberg, ICM.

Dream on Monkey Mountain. Mythic Drama. A ritualized play set in the West Indies, combining fantasy, voodoo, and poetry to explore the deeper, unconscious sources of identity, the nature of freedom. *Cast:* 7 BM, 1 WF, dancer, singer, M chorus, drummers, extras. *Length:* 2 Acts. *Prod:* Central Library

Theatre, Toronto, Can., Aug. 1967; NEC, New York, Apr. 1971. *Pubn:* Dream
on Monkey Mountain and Other Plays, New York: Farrar, 1970. *Lib Source:*
HBA. *Perm:* Agency, Bridget Aschenberg, ICM.

In a Fine Castle.   *Prod:* New Theater for Now, Mark Taper Forum, Los Angeles,
Calif., 1972. *Perm:* Agency, Bridget Aschenberg, ICM.

Malcochon or the Six in the Rain. Mythic Drama. A metaphorical drama set
on a timeless and isolated island (West Indies) during the rainy season.
Relates the reappearance of the mythic hero Chantal, "the Tiger who un-
ravels lies and makes me account for their sins and dreams." *Cast:* 5 BM,
1 BF, singers, musicians, chorus. *Length:* 1 Act. *Prod:* St. Lucia Arts Guild,
W.I. 1959. *Pubn:* Dream on Monkey Mountain and Other Plays, New York:
Farrar, 1970. *Lib Source.* HBA. *Perm:* Agency, Bridget Aschenberg, ICM.

The Sea at Dauphin. Mythic Drama. The sea is a metaphor in this play as two
fishermen confront their lives and regeneration on a West Indian island.
Cast: 5 BM, 1 BB, 1 BF, *Prod:* Errol Hill, Whitehall Players, 1954. *Pubn:* Dream
on Monkey Mountain and Other Plays, New York: Farrar, 1970. *Lib Source:*
HBA. *Perm:* Agency, Bridget Aschenberg, ICM.

Ti-Jean and His Brothers. Mythic Drama. A parable of three sons and how each
fares with the devil, especially Ti-Jean, "a fool like all heroes," who "passed
through the tangled opinions of this life, loosening the rotting faggots of
knowledge from old men to bear them safely on his shoulder. . . ." *Cast:*
7 M, 1 F, extras. *Length:* Full Length. *Prod:* Little Carib Theatre, Port of Spain,
Trinidad, W.I., 1958. *Pubn:* Dream on Monkey Mountain and Other Plays, New
York: Farrar, 1970. *Lib Source:* HBA. *Perm:* Agency, Bridget Aschenberg, ICM.

WALKER, EVAN

Coda. Morality Drama. Discovery within a black family of its corruption by the
larger white society.   *Cast:* 5 BM, 2 BF. *Prod:* D.C. Black Repertory Theatre, Washington, D.C., Dec. 1972. *Perm:* Author.

Dark Light In May. (1960).   *Length:* 1 Act.

East of Jordan. Morality Drama. Problems of black man trying to obtain a house
for his wife.   *Cast:* 10 BM, 6 BF, 2 WM. *Length:* 2 Acts. *Prod:* FST, New Orleans, La., Apr. 1969. *Perm:* Author.

The Message. Morality Comedy. About a middle class black couple about to be
assimilated by American society.   *Cast:* 2 BM, 1 BF, 1 WM. *Length:* 1 Act.
Prod: D.C. Black Repertory Theatre, Washington, D.C., June 1973. *Perm:*
Author.

A War for Brutus. Drama. A young black paratrooper learns the facts of life in
an all black, airborne infantry regiment a few months before the outbreak of
the Korean War.   *Cast:* 14 BM, 2 WM. *Length:* 3 Acts. *Perm:* Author.

WALKER, FAI

The Everlasting Arm. Domestic Drama. Siblings are faced with the problem of
what is to happen to their aging, widowed mother.   *Cast:* 2 BM, 2 BF. *Prod:*
Reading, Frank Silvera Writers' Workshop, New York, Dec. 1975. *Perm:* Author.

WALKER, GEORGE, and BERT WILLIAMS

The Sons of Ham. Musical Comedy. "Williams and Walker, mistaken for long absent twin brothers, are royally feted until the real brothers appear."— Fannin Belcher. The vaudevillians Williams and Walker collaborated on several works. *See* Paul L. Dunbar, Alex Rogers, and Jesse A. Shipp for collaborations. *Prod:* Grand Opera House, New York, Mar. 1902.

WALKER, JOSEPH A.

Harangue. Drama. Action takes place on Avenue B on New York's Lower East Side. The last of four plays in a production called *The Harangues. Cast:* 4 BM, 1 BF. *Length:* 1 Act. *Prod:* NEC, New York, Jan. 1970. *Perm:* Author.

The Lion Is a Soul Brother. Jazz-Rock Musical. Music by Dorothy Dinroe. Set in an African village, a medicine man tells the story of a lion who talked and was a friend to man. *Length:* Full Length. *Prod:* Demi-Gods, New York, May 1976.

Ododo. (1968). Historical Ritual. A conjurer conjures up the spirits of the original black people and traces the black man's history from his beginnings in Africa to the present. *Cast:* 11 B M & F. *Length:* 2 Acts. *Prod:* NEC, New York, Dec. 1970. *Pubn: Black Drama Anthology*, ed. by Woodie King, Jr. and Ron Milner, New York: New Amer. Lib., 1972. *Perm:* Author.

Out of the Ashes. (1974). Satire. In two parts (the Legacy and the Vow). An ensemble piece that mixes old minstrel and modern scenes with actors that metamorphose from role to role until central character, Joe, can save his pop from death and alcohol. Subtitled: *A Minstrel Show. Perm:* Author.

The River Niger. (1973). Domestic Melodrama. A son returns home to his father, not quite the hero the father anticipated nor the staunch militant his former buddies once knew. The father becomes the hero. *Cast:* 9 BM, 4 BF. *Length:* 3 Acts. *Prod:* NEC, New York, Dec. 1972; Brooks Atkinson Theatre, Mar. 1973. *Pubn:* New York: Mermaid, 1973. *Perm:* Agency, SF.

Theme of the Black Struggle. Prod: NEC, New York, Fall 1970. *Perm:* Author.

Tribal Harangue One. Historical Mythic. The action takes place in an African dungeon on the coast of West Africa in the fourteenth and fifteenth centuries. One of four plays in a production called *The Harangues. Cast:* 1 BM, 1 BF. *Length:* 1 Act. *Prod:* NEC, New York, Jan. 1970. *Perm:* Author.

Tribal Harangue Two. (1969). Drama. A black revolutionary's plot to kill the rich white stepfather of his lover is foiled by the white man's control of money. One of four plays in a production called *The Harangues. Cast:* 5 BM, 1 WM, 1 WF. *Length:* 1 Act. *Pubn: The Best Short Plays, 1971*, ed. by Stanley Richards, New York: Chilton, 1971. *Lib Source:* HBA. *Perm:* Author.

Tribal Harangue Three. Mythic. Action takes place in the future. One of four plays in a production called *The Harangues. Cast:* 1 BM, 1 BF. *Length:* 1 Act. *Prod:* NEC, New York, Jan. 1970. *Perm:* Author.

Yin Yang. Ritual. Music by Dorothy D. Walker. A potpourri of black thought forms, projected through poetry, drama, dance, and music. *Cast:* 3 BM, 6 BF. *Prod:* Afro-American Studio, New York, June 1972. *Perm:* Author.

WALKER, JOSEPH A., and JOSEPHINE JACKSON

The Believers. Musical. Action takes place in the "Gone Years" and the "Then and Now Years." Subtitled: *The Black Experience in Song.* *Cast:* 7 BM, 6 BF. *Length:* 2 Acts. *Prod:* Garrick Theatre, New York, May 1968. *Pubn: Best Plays of 1967–68*, ed. by Otis L. Guernsey, Jr., New York: Dodd, 1968. *Perm:* Author.

WALKER, MARGARET, and DONALD DORR

Jubilee. Opera. Music by Ulysses Kay. Libretto by Donald Dorr. Adapted from Margaret Walker's novel, *Jubilee.* The story of Vyry, a plantation slave who survives to make a place for herself as a free woman, mother, and wife. *Length:* Full Length. *Prod:* Opera/South, Jackson State University, Miss., Nov. 1976.

WALKER, MARK

A Near Fatality. A two scene statement: "for niggers only." *Pubn: Black Expressions*, Fall 1968.

WALKER, SULLIVAN

8 O'Clock Time. Montage Play. It presents aspects of Caribbean life in Trinidad and in the U.S. through sketches, ritualistic poems, and dance. *Prod:* The New World Theatre, Lincoln Square Community Centre, New York, July 1977.

A Tribute to the Black Woman. *Prod:* Church of St. Matthew and St. Thomas, New York, July 1974.

WALLACE, G. L.

Them Next Door (1974) Black and white couples cannot adjust to being neighbors due to conditioned stereotypes they both possess. *Cast:* 2 BM, 1 BF, 1 WM, 2 WF. *Length:* 1 Act. *Pubn:* SF. *Lib Source:* HBA. *Perm:* Agency, SF.

WALLACE, RUDY

Brothers of Blood and Thunder. Tragi-Comedy. Ideological conflict between the five pledges of a black fraternity and the three Big Brothers. *Cast:* 8 BM, 3 BF. *Length:* 2 Acts. *Prod:* Annenburg Center, Philadelphia, Pa., 1974. *Perm:* Author.

The Dark Tower. Psycho-Symbolic Drama. Old street-fighter artist matches thoughts and emotions against young, conservative academic poet. *Cast:* 2 BM. *Length:* 1 Act. *Prod:* NEC, New York, May 1975. *Perm:* Author.

The Friends of Leland Stone. Domestic Tragedy. After the father shoots the accused rapist of his youngest daughter, his wife and their three sons are forced to deal with some deep agonizing truths. *Cast:* 1 BM, 3 BF. *Length:* 1 Act. *Prod:* Theatre Advocate, Philadelphia, Pa., Dec. 1974. *Perm:* Author.

The Moonlight Arms. Domestic Tragedy. Young married couple destroys two-month-old marriage over sex, violence, and immaturity. *Cast:* 1 BM, 1 BF.

WALLACE, RUDY (*Cont.*)

Length: 1 Act. *Prod:* Theatre Advocate, Philadelphia, Pa., Dec. 1974; NEC, New York, May 1975. *Perm:* Author.

The People Play. (1975). Psycho-Symbolic Drama. Four avant-garde intellectuals get together in a cold apartment to fight over the possibilities of human perfectibility.   *Cast:* 2 BM, 2 BF. *Length:* 2 Acts. *Perm:* Author.

The Phillis Wheatley Story. (1975). Ritual/Drama. During the delirium of childbirth, Phillis Wheatley (1753?–1784), the first black woman poet in America, recalls scenes from her bittersweet existence from a free little girl in Africa to the frail, impoverished wife of a proud John Peters.   *Cast:* 5 BM, 5 BF. *Length:* 2 Acts. *Perm:* Author.

The Philosopher Limer. (1974). Caribbean Comedy. Mandy deserts his wife and six children to live on a beach; while on the beach, he helps and is helped by a beautiful young island girl.   *Cast:* 1 BM, 2 BF, 6 children. *Length:* 1 Act. *Perm:* Author.

WALLER, G. HOBSON

The Ladies.   *Prod:* Reading, Frank Silvera Writers' Workshop, Harlem Cultural Council, New York, May 1976.

WALMSLEY, DEWDROP

Genius in Slavery. Historical Drama. A slave plots a way to educate slaves. *Cast:* 12 M & F. *Length:* 1 Act. *Pubn:* New York: Amuru Pr., 1976, possibly never published.

WALTON, LESTER A., and HENRY TROY

Black Bohemia. Musical Revue. Music by Alex Rogers and Will Marion Cook. Lyrics by Lester A. Walton.   *Prod:* n.p., Oct. 1911.

Darkeydom. Musical Revue. Music by Will Marion Cook.   *Prod:* n.p., 1914.

WALTOWER, EARL

The Landlord. Domestic Drama. Portrays the deterioration of a struggling southern black family—on the brink of being dispossessed by an unscrupulous southern white landlord.   *Length:* 1 Act. *Prod:* Tompkins Square Park Players, New York, June 1975.

WARD, DOUGLAS TURNER

Brotherhood. (1970). Satire/Comedy. Two couples—one black, one white—attempt to hide the enmity they have for each other.   *Cast:* 1 BM, 1 BF, 1 WM, 1 WF. *Length:* 1 Act. *Prod:* NEC, New York, Mar. 1970. *Pubn: Black Drama Anthology*, ed. by Woodie King, Jr. and Ron Milner, New York: New Amer. Lib., 1972. *Lib Source:* NYPL. *Perm:* Agency, DPS.

Day of Absence. (1966). Satire. The chaos of a southern town when the entire black population takes a holiday and the whites realize the varied jobs that

Blacks did. Winner, Obie Award, and Vernon Drama Desk Award. *Cast:* 14 BM, 7 BF. *Length:* 1 Act. *Prod:* St. Marks Playhouse, New York, Nov. 1965; NEC, New York, Mar. 1970. *Pubn: Black Drama: An Anthology*, ed. by William Brasmer and Dominick Consolo, Columbus, Ohio: Merrill Pub. Co., 1970. *Lib Source:* NYPL. *Perm:* Agency, DPS.

Happy Ending. (1966). Satire/Comedy. Two black domestics lament over possible unemployment with white family, thus ending their household pilfering. Winner, Obie Award, and Vernon Drama Desk Award. *Cast:* 2 BM, 2 BF. *Length:* 1 Act. *Prod:* St. Marks Playhouse, New York, Nov. 1965. *Pubn: Black Drama: An Anthology*, ed. by William Brasmer and Dominick Consolo, Columbus, Ohio: Merrill Pub. Co., 1970. *Lib Source:* NYPL. *Perm:* Agency, DPS.

The Reckoning. (1970). Satire. Black radical traps white governor and subjects him to blackmail. Subtitled: **A Surreal Southern Fable.** *Cast:* 2 BM, 2 BF, 3 WM. *Length:* 2 Movements. *Prod:* NEC, New York, Sept. 1969. *Pubn:* DPS. *Lib Source:* HBA. *Perm:* Agency, DPS.

WARD, FRANCIS, and VAL GRAY WARD

The Life of Harriet Tubman. A dramatic reenactment of the life of the great black heroine. *Prod:* Kuumba Workshop, Chicago, Ill., 1971.

WARD, RICHARD

Penitence. *Cast:* 13 M & F. *Prod:* Open Space, New York, May 1975.

WARD, THEODORE

The Bell and the Light. (1962). Historical Musical. Slaves, including the colonel's own mulatto daughter, depend upon the colonel for their "good" treatment, but when the chips are down, they discover that they must be free and save themselves. *Cast:* 9 BM, 11 BF, 4 WM, 2 WF, extras. *Length:* 2 Acts. *Lib Source:* Typescript, HBA. *Perm:* Agency, James V. Hatch.

Big Money. (1961). Musical Comedy. Thunderbird suddenly gets $85,000 and all his friends want to help him spend it, but the police interfere. *Cast:* 15 BM, 5 BF, 8 WM, 1 WF, extras. *Length:* 2 Acts. *Lib Source:* Typescript, HBA. *Perm:* Agency, James V. Hatch.

Big White Fog. (1938). Domestic Drama. Victor Mason, husband, father, and Garveyite (follower of Marcus Garvey) fights to keep his dream alive while his family and the world fall down around him. *Cast:* 6 BM, 6 BF, 4 BC, 2 WM, extras. *Length:* 3 Acts. *Prod:* FTP, Great Northern Theatre, Chicago, Ill., Apr. 1938. *Pubn: Black Theater USA*, ed. by James V. Hatch and Ted Shine, New York: Free Pr., 1974. *Lib Source:* HBA. *Perm:* Agency, James V. Hatch.

Candle in the Wind. (1966). Historical Protest. Charles Caldwell, black senator from the state of Mississippi, 1875, fights to keep a black and white coalition in power and is killed for it. *Cast:* 10 BM, 3 BF, 18 WM (doubling). *Length:* 4 Acts. *Lib Source:* Typescript, HBA. *Perm:* Agency, James V. Hatch.

WARD, THEODORE (*Cont.*)

Charity. (1960). Historical Musical. This is the true story of the Negro musician, Blind Tom, and how he was exploited. *Cast:* 4 BM, 5 BF, 10 WM, 3 WF, extras. *Length:* 3 Acts. *Lib Source:* Typescript, HBA. *Perm:* Agency, James V. Hatch.

The Daubers. (1953). Drama. A middle class black family, in its efforts to achieve political power and property, loses its daughter to drug addiction. *Cast:* 3 BM, 6 BF, 1 WM, 1 WF. *Length:* 3 Acts. *Prod:* Experimental Black Actors Guild, Chicago, Ill., 1973. *Lib Source:* Typescript, HBA. *Perm:* Agency, James V. Hatch.

Deliver the Goods. (1941). Historical Drama. First National Defense Play for World War II defense effort. It shows the struggle of longshoremen against fascists and corrupt bosses while trying to support the army overseas. *Cast:* 2 BM, 18 WM, 6 WF (doubling). *Length:* 3 Acts. *Prod:* Greenwich House, New York, 1942. *Lib Source:* Typescript, HBA. *Perm:* Agency, James V. Hatch

Even the Dead Arise. (1938). Historical Mythic Drama. The black revolutionaries of the past refuse to lie quietly in their graves until justice is done. *Cast:* 8 BM, 4 BF, 2 WM, extras. *Length:* 1 Act. *Prod:* Chicago, Ill., 1938. *Lib Source:* Typescript, HBA. *Perm:* Agency, James V. Hatch

Falcon of Adowa. (1938). Drama. Set during the Italian invasion of Ethiopia; Gugsa, a collaborator, is executed by the Italians when he defects and calls for Abyssinian unity and loyalty to Haile Selassie. *Lib Source:* Manuscript, HBA. *Perm:* Author.

John Brown. Historical Political Drama. *See also Of Human Grandeur. Prod:* People's Drama, New York, Apr. 1950. *Pubn:* (Act I, scene II) *Masses and Mainstream,* Oct. 1949.

John de Conqueror. (1953). Folk Opera. Warrior and leader, John de Conqueror, leads his people into the sea rather than submit to white slavery. *Cast:* 9 BM, 4 BF, 3 WM, extras. *Length:* 2 Acts. *Lib Source:* Typescript, HBA. *Perm:* Agency, James V. Hatch.

Madison. (1956). Historical Musical. Adapted from Frederick Douglass' short story, "The Heroic Slave" (1853). Slaves being taken from Richmond to New Orleans on the S.S. *Creole* seize control through leadership of Madison and sail to Nassau and freedom. Subtitled: *Creole. Cast:* 7 BM, 5 BF, 4 WM, extras. *Length:* 2 Acts. *Lib Source:* Typescript, HBA. *Perm:* Agency, James V. Hatch.

Of Human Grandeur. (1949). Historical Political Drama. The story of John Brown from 1835 until his execution. *Cast:* 7 BM, 1 BF, 20 WM, 2 WF (doubling). *Length:* 4 Acts. *Prod:* As *John Brown,* People's Drama, New York, Apr. 1950. *Lib Source:* Typescript, HBA. *Perm:* Agency, James V. Hatch.

Our Lan'. (1941–1946). Historical Drama. A band of freed slaves receives a Georgia island from General William Tecumseh Sherman to raise crops, build a school and community; they are later told by the federal government to leave; they refuse. *Cast:* 13 BM, 7 BF, 6 WM, 1 WF, BC. *Length:* 2 Acts. *Prod:* Henry Street

Playhouse, New York, 1946; Royale Theatre, New York, Sept. 1947. *Pubn: Black Drama in America*, ed. by Darwin T. Turner, Greenwich: Fawcett, 1971. *Lib Source:* PAL. *Perm:* Agency, James V. Hatch.

Shout Hallelujah. (1941). Tragedy. Young Sammy, talented musician, stands a chance to escape West Virginia mines, but discovers that his mother is a prostitute and kills himself. *Cast:* 11 BM, 5 BF, 2 WM. *Length:* 3 Acts. *Lib Source:* Typescript, HBA. *Perm:* Agency, James V. Hatch.

Sick and Tired (Sick and Tiahd). Historical Drama. A black man goes to a commissary where a white man tries to cheat him and a scuffle follows; the white man falls on a plow and is killed. The black man refuses to run because he is sick and "tiahd" of white folks. Received second prize in city-wide contest sponsored by the New Theatre League, Chicago, Ill. *Cast:* 2 BM, 1 BF, 3 BC, 1 WB. *Length:* 1 Act. *Prod:* n.p., 1938; revised version, 1964. *Lib Source:* HBA. *Perm:* Agency, James V. Hatch.

Throwback. (1952). Folk Protest. A black man kills a white mill owner for messing with his wife. *Cast:* 1 BM, 2 BF, 1 WM, child. *Length:* 1 Act. *Prod:* n.p., 1952. *Lib Source:* Typescript, HBA. *Perm:* Agency, James V. Hatch.

Whole Hog or Nothing. (1952). Drama. A group of black American servicemen fighting in World War II fight white racism in New Guinea as well and win. *Cast:* 5 BM, 11 WM. *Length:* 1 Act. *Prod:* n.p., 1952. *Lib Source:* Typescript, HBA. *Perm:* Agency, James V. Hatch.

WARD, VAL GRAY, and FRANCIS WARD

The Life of Harriet Tubman. A dramatic reenactment of the life of the great black heroine. *Prod:* Kuumba Workshop, Chicago, Ill., 1971.

WARING, DOROTHY, and ZORA NEALE HURSTON

Polk County. (1944). Comedy. Based partially on Ms. Hurston's experiences collecting folk materials in Florida. A play of black life in a sawmill camp, with authentic music. *Cast:* 10 BM, 6 BF, 1 WM, extras, musicians. *Length:* 3 Acts. *Lib Source:* Typescript, PAL.

WARNER, MARION

The Bag. Drama. The struggle of a family in Harlem to keep on keeping on against dope, poverty, and family conflict; they succeed. *Cast:* 4 BM, 2 BF, 3 WM. *Perm:* Author.

WASHINGTON, CAESAR G.

The Gold Front Stores, Inc. Farce/Satire. *Length:* Full Length. *Prod:* National Ethiopian Art Theatre, New York, Mar.-Apr. 1924.

WASHINGTON, CHARLES L. B.

To Hell with It. (1974). Screenplay. Personal struggle for morals, equilibrium, justice, salvation, and love. *Cast:* 12 BM (2 boys), 5 BF (2 teenagers), 7 WM (1 teenager), 3 WF, extras. *Length:* Full Length. *Perm:* Author.

WASHINGTON, ERWIN

Oh Oh Freedom. Terrance Stone, a forty-five-year-old Black, is king of his house and boss of his family because the white world won't let him be king or boss of anything else. Second place in Lorraine Hansberry Award for best play on the Black-American experience, 1976. *Cast:* 11 M, 2 F. *Prod:* University of California at Los Angeles, Calif., 1976.

WASHINGTON, SAM

A Member of the Fateful Gray. (1969).

WATI, JASO

Lazarus. *Prod:* Reading, Frank Silvera Writers' Workshop, City College of New York, Mar. 1977.

Trouble Don't Last Always. *Prod:* Frank Silvera Writers' Workshop, The Teachers, Inc., New York, Jan. 1977.

WATKINS, GORDON

Caught in the Middle. *Perm:* Agency, Breakthrough Press.

A Lion Roams the Streets. (1971). Choral Verse Drama. The implications of racism for Blacks and whites are presented in shifting scenes with choral response. *Cast:* 1 BM, 1 BF, 1 WM, 1 WF, extras. *Length:* 1 Act. *Pubn:* New York: Breakthrough Pr., 1971. *Lib Source:* HBA. *Perm:* Agency, Breakthrough Press.

Sojourner Truth. Poetic Drama.

Too Late. *Prod:* The Toussaint Group, Cliffside Park, N.J., July 1975.

WATSON, HARMON

Clown in Three Rings.

The Golden Gates Fall Down. *Pubn: Black Insights*, ed. by Nick A. Ford, New York: Wiley, 1971.

The Middle Man. (1972). Drama. Joe, a black man married to a white woman, pays a high price for having a foot in both camps. *Cast:* 6 BM, 2 BF, 1 WM, 1 WF, extras. *Length:* 3 Acts. *Perm:* Author.

Toy of the Gods. (1964).

WATT, BILLIE LOU

Phillis. Historical Drama. The life of black American poet Phillis Wheatley (1753?–1784). *Pubn:* New York: Friendship Pr., 1969.

WEAVER, ABIOLA ROSELLE

The Matriarchs. *Prod:* Reading, Frank Silvera Writers' Workshop, Teachers, Inc., New York, Nov. 1976.

WEBB, LORRAINE

Why Do You Think They Call It Dope. *Prod:* Billie Holiday Theatre, New York, May 1974.

WEBER, ADAM

Spirit of the Living Dead.   *Prod:* FST, New Orleans, La., Fall 1969.

To Kill or Die.   *Prod:* FST, New Orleans, La., Summer 1969.

WEBSTER, PAUL

Under the Duppy Parasol. Domestic Comedy. The plot is a satire on Barbadians who return from Brooklyn to Barbados with arrogant airs and accents.   *Length:* Full Length. *Prod:* Barbados Theatre Workshop, Billie Holiday Theatre, New York, Spring 1975.

WESLEY, RICHARD

Ace Boon Coon. (1971). Drama. Explores the conflict that arises when one's political and social beliefs conflict with one's moral obligations.   *Cast:* 8 BM, 1 BF. *Length:* 1 Act. *Prod:* Black Arts/West, San Francisco, Calif., Feb. 1972. *Perm:* Agency, NASABA.

The Black Terror. (1970). Political Melodrama. Explores the conflict between moderation and non-African oriented political ideologies in pursuit of the black man's freedom, justice, and equality.   *Cast:* 8 BM, 2 BF. *Length:* 1 Act. *Prod:* WASTSA, Ira Aldridge Theatre, Washington, D.C., Feb. 1971; Public Theatre, New York Shakespeare Festival, N.Y., Nov. 1971. *Pubn: Scripts,* vol. I, no. 2, Dec. 1971. *Lib Source:* HBA. *Perm:* Agency, NASABA.

Gettin' It Together. (1970). Domestic Drama. Centers around the conflicts between a man and a woman who have dreams of love and a better life for themselves and the attempts of each to realize that goal.   *Cast:* 1 BM, 1 BF. *Length:* 1 Act. *Prod:* Theatre Black, New York, 1970; Public Theatre, New York Shakespeare Festival, N.Y., Feb. 1972. *Lib Source:* Typescript, HBA. *Perm:* Agency, NASABA.

Goin' thru Changes. Drama. Explores the social pressures that affect healthy relationships between men and women in black America.   *Cast:* 2 BM, 3 BF. *Length:* 1 Act. *Prod:* Billie Holiday Theatre, New York, Dec. 1973.

Headline News.   *Perm:* Agency, NASABA.

Knock Knock Who Dat? (1970). Political Comedy. A bickering black family unites with gunfire when the police break down the door.   *Length:* 1 Act. *Prod:* Theatre Black, University of the Streets, New York, Oct. 1970. *Perm:* Agency, NASABA.

The Last Street Play. Drama. Revision of *The Mighty Gents,* by the same playwright. Ten years have passed since the Gents ruled the Central Ward in Newark, and over the years the gang has stagnated. At thirty, the members have become a "surplus" people.   *Cast:* 6 BM, 1 BF. *Length:* Full Length. *Prod:* Frank Silvera Writers' Workshop, Urban Art Corps, New York, Jan. 1977; Manhattan Theater Club, New York, May 1977.

Let's Do It Again. Screenplay/Comedy/Satire. Sequel to *Uptown Saturday Night,* by the same playwright.   *Prod:* Film, 1975.

The Mighty Gents. (1973). Revised as *The Last Street Play,* by the same playwright. Explores the refusal of men to deal with the reality that they can no longer live in the past.   *Cast:* 6 BM. *Length:* 1 Act. *Prod:* National Playwright Conference of the Eugene O'Neill Memorial Theater Center, Waterford, Conn. *Perm:* Agency, NASABA.

WESLEY, RICHARD (*Cont.*)

The Past Is the Past. (1973). Drama. Explores the relationship between father and son and their need to understand one another and thereby change the direction of their lives.   *Cast:* 2 BM. *Length:* 1 Act. *Prod:* Billie Holiday Theatre, New York, Dec. 1973. *Perm:* Agency, NASABA.

Put My Dignity on 307. Drama/Satire. A black factory worker strives for middle class status and plays the numbers for the means to obtain it. Citation of Award, Samuel French National Playwriting Contest, 1965.   *Length:* 1 Act. *Prod:* Howard University, Washington, D.C., WRC-TV, 1967.

The Sirens. (1973). Drama. Explores male/female conflicts that sometimes result in lifelong damage.   *Cast:* 3 BM, 3 BF. *Length:* 1 Act. *Prod:* Manhattan Theatre Club, New York, May 1974. *Pubn:* DPS. *Lib Source:* HBA. *Perm:* Agency, NASABA.

Springtime High. (1968).   *Length:* 1 Act. *Perm:* Agency, NASABA.

The Street Corner. (1969).

Strike Heaven in the Face. (1972). Drama. Deals with the destructive effects of war on a black veteran returning to the negative effects of racism in America.   *Cast:* 2 BM, 2 BF, 2 WM. *Length:* Full Length. *Prod:* Phoenix Theatre Showcase, New York, 1973. *Perm:* Agency, NASABA.

Uptown Saturday Night. Screenplay/Comedy/Satire. *Let's Do It Again* is a sequel to this title.   *Prod:* Warner Bros., 1974.

WEST, VERN

Circles.   Prod: Afro-American Total Theatre, International House, New York, Feb. 1970.

WESTBROOK, EMANUEL

In a Safe Place. (1975). Comedy. An evil tempered comic miser is conned out of some of his money by his own children.   *Cast:* 6 BM, 3 BF. *Length:* 7 Scenes. *Prod:* Reading, Frank Silvera Writers' Workshop, Teachers, Inc., New York, Nov. 1976.

WHIPPER, LEIGH, and PORTER GRAINGER

De Board Meetin'. (1925). Comedy. Black pastor is removed from office for flirting with women, bootlegging, and misappropriating church funds.   *Cast:* 6 BM, 1 BF, extras. *Length:* 1 Act. *Lib Source:* Typescript, SCHOM.

We's Risin'. (1927). Musical Comedy. The story of the rivalry of two "colored" fraternal organizations in a small town in Mississippi.   *Cast:* 15-20 B M & F. *Length:* 2 Acts. *Lib Source:* Typescript, SCHOM.

WHIPPER, LEIGH, and J. C. JOHNSON

Runnin' de Town. (1930). The story is based on the rivalry of two fraternal organizations in a small town in Mississippi.

WHIPPER, LEIGH, and BILLY MILLS

Yeah Man. Musical Revue.   *Cast:* 9 BM, 5 BF, chorus, extras. *Length:* 2 Acts. *Prod:* Park Lane Theatre, New York, May 1932. *Pubn: Best Plays of 1931-32,* ed. by Burns Mantle, New York: Dodd, 1932.

WHITE, EDGAR

The Burghers of Calais. (1970). Historical. The story of the Scottsboro boys from 1931 to 1950. Uses whiteface.   *Cast:* 25 BM, 3 BF. *Length:* 7 Scenes. *Prod:* Billie Holiday Theatre, New York, 1972. *Pubn: Underground (Four Plays),* New York: Morrow, 1970. *Lib Source:* HBA. *Perm:* Agency, Wender & Associates.

The Cathedral of Chartres.   *Prod:* 1969. *Pubn: Liberator,* vol. 8, July 1968.

The Crucificado. Morality Drama. Morose, a junkie existing in a haunting world of beggar prophets and trapped women, frees himself from the slavery imposed upon him by the white man by killing his white father. Uses whiteface.   *Cast:* 6 BM, 5 BF. *Length:* 24 Scenes. *Prod:* Vinnette Carroll's Urban Arts Corps, New York, 1972. *Pubn:* New York: Morrow, 1972. *Lib Source:* HBA. *Perm:* Agency, Wender & Associates.

The Defense. Mythic Drama. Dread, a guard in a Lower East Side (New York) housing project, has had a dream of death. The play is a summoning of a defense, images from his past, events in his present—to justify his life.   *Cast:* 7 BM, 10 BF. *Length:* 23 Scenes. *Prod:* NFT, New York, Nov. 1976.

Dija. Children's Play/Fantasy. This is the inside of a black child's dream, a child who is searching for her birthday.   *Cast:* 3 BM, 2 BF, 1 BB, 1 BG, extras. *Length:* 1 Act. *Pubn: Scripts,* vol. 1, no. 10, Oct. 1972. *Lib Source:* HBA. *Perm:* Agency, Wender & Associates.

Les Femmes Noires. Slices from the lives of a variety of black women. Subtitled: *The Black Ladies.*   *Cast:* 9 BM, 15 BF. *Prod:* Public Theatre, New York Shakespeare Festival, N.Y., Mar. 1974. *Perm:* Agency, Wender & Associates.

Fun in Lethe. (1970). Tragic-Comedy. The play involves the journey of a young Negro poet through Great Britain; it makes use of Chinese classical drama, as well as Greek comedy. Subtitled: *Or the Feast of Misrule.* Uses whiteface. *Cast:* 18 BM, 5 BF. *Length:* 4 Acts. *Pubn: Underground (Four Plays),* New York: Morrow, 1970. *Lib Source:* HBA. *Perm:* Agency, Wender & Associates.

La Gente. Spanish/Black Domestic Drama.   *Cast:* 24 BM, 16 BF. *Prod:* Public Theatre, New York Shakespeare Festival, N.Y., July 1973.

Lament for Rastafari. West Indian Ritual.   *Cast:* 7 BM, 5 BF. *Prod:* Billie Holiday Theatre, New York, 1971. *Perm:* Agency, Wender & Associates.

The Life and Times of J. Walter Smintheus. Morality Play. Smintheus, a black bourgeois intellectual, while working on a massive sociological study entitled "The Contributions of the Negro Intellectual to American Society and His Resultant Impotence," avoids dealing with the more concrete problems of his life—his failing marriage, his black identity, his values, etc.—until his only friend, Robert, dies in jail and Smintheus finally confronts reality and goes mad. Uses whiteface.   *Cast:* 10 BM, 3 BF. *Prod:* Theatre DeLys, ANTA Matinee Series,

WHITE, EDGAR *(Cont.)*

New York, Feb. 1971. *Pubn: The Crucificado,* New York: Morrow, 1972. *Lib Source:* HBA. *Perm:* Agency, Wender & Associates.

The Mummer's Play. (1970). Morality Comedy. Bellysong and Pariah, whose age difference could make them father and son, are actually two black artists at different stages of development—experiencing, loving, and chiding the world and its maker for not giving them a break. Uses whiteface.   *Cast:* 9 BM, 4 BF. *Length:* 15 Scenes. *Prod:* Public Theatre, New York Shakespeare Festival, N.Y., 1971. *Pubn: Underground (Four Plays),* New York: Morrow, 1970. *Lib Source:* HBA. *Perm:* Agency, Wender & Associates.

Ode to Charlie Parker. Subtitled: *Study for Sunlight in Park.*   *Cast:* 10 BM, 7 BF. *Prod:* Studio Rivbea, New York, Sept. 1973. *Perm:* Agency, Wender & Associates.

Offering for Nightworld. Domestic Morality Play.·   *Cast:* 9 BM, 9 BF. *Prod:* Brooklyn Academy of Music, Black Theatre Alliance Festival, New York, 1973. *Perm:* Agency, Wender & Associates.

The Pygmies and the Pyramid. "An Africanized version of a story familiar to us from the Bible. Act I (The Creation) presents Adam; Act II is an allegory of events surrounding an updated Crucifixion."—Townsend Brewster, *Newsletter* of the Harlem Cultural Council, no. 11, vol. 2.   *Length:* 2 Acts. *Prod:* Yardbird Theatre Co., New York, Spring 1976.

The Rastafarian. Children's Play/Fantasy. A boy child's acceptance of death and life.   *Cast:* 2 BM, 1 BB, 1 BG, dancer, singer, extras. *Length:* 1 Act. *Pubn: Scripts,* vol. I, no. 10, Oct. 1972. *Lib Source:* HBA. *Perm:* Agency, Wender & Associates.

Seigismundo's Tricycle. (1971). Poetic Fantasy. An old white man on a silver tricycle and a Negro who walks with crutches examine their state of affairs. Subtitled: *A Dialogue of Self and Soul.*   *Cast:* 1 BM, 1 WM. *Length:* 1 Act. *Prod:* Public Theatre, New York Shakespeare Festival, N.Y., Apr. 1971. *Pubn: Black Review,* no. 1, ed. by Mel Watkins, New York: Morrow, 1971. *Lib Source:* HBA. *Perm:* Agency, Wender & Associates.

The Wonderfull Yeare. (1970). Domestic. The allusion in this Spanish/black play is London's deliverance from a plague, among other impending disasters. But even while plagues rage, the living have a way of ignoring them. This deeply ironic play is about the gift of life in the midst of death. Uses whiteface.   *Cast:* 18 BM, 7 BF. *Length:* 23 Scenes. *Prod:* Public Theatre, New York Shakespeare Festival, 1971. *Pubn: Underground (Four Plays),* New York: Morrow, 1970. *Lib Source:* HBA. *Perm:* Agency, Wender & Associates.

WHITE, JAMES E., III

African Adventure. (1975). Historical Ritual/Musical. Normalcy of an African tribe is disrupted by the advent of the white man. Tribe weighs merits of the white man's materialism and its gains against retention of cultural values and customs.   *Cast:* 4 BM, 3 BF, 1 WM. *Length:* 1 Act. *Perm:* Author.

The Candy Store Is Still Closed. (1973). Domestic Drama. Problem of a black family in the South during the early 1950s, where the older brother takes care of family by being subservient to whites and the younger brother rebels against this; includes a white middle class family, a poor white trash family, a rape, a murder, and a lynching.   *Cast:* 3 BM, 2 BF, 4 WM, 2 WF. *Length:* 2 Acts. *Perm:* Author.

Don't Go to Strangers. (1974). Domestic Musical/Drama. About widowed grandmother who comes to live with her son and his family, and how she is rejected and sent to a nursing home, and how she rebels against such treatment by her strength.   *Cast:* 6 BM, 7 BF. *Length:* 2 Acts. *Perm:* Author.

WHITE, JOSEPH

The Blue Boy in Black.   *Prod:* Masque Theatre, New York, Apr. 1963. *Pubn:* Best Plays of 1962-63, ed. by Henry Hewes, New York: Dodd, 1963.

The Hustle.   *Prod:* Kuumba House, Newark, N.J., 1970.

The Leader. Head of organization designed to help Blacks is found to be only interested in his own prestige.   *Cast:* 3 BM, 2 BF, 2 WM, 1 WF. *Length:* 1 Act. *Pubn:* Black Fire, ed. by LeRoi Jones and Larry Neal, New York: Morrow, 1968. *Lib Source:* HBA. *Perm:* Agency, William Morrow.

Old Judge Mose Is Dead. Comedy. The shenanigans of two black janitors in a funeral home where the body of "a mean ole white man" lies—and how they treat him!   *Cast:* 2 BM, 1 WM, 1 WF. *Length:* 1 Act. *Pubn:* Drama Review, vol. 12, no. 4, Summer 1968.

WHITE, KATHLEEN YVONNE

The Greatest Show on Earth.   *Prod:* St. Marks-on-the-Bowery, New York, Oct. 1972.

WHITEHEAD, JAMES X.

Justice or Just Us (Part II). (1972). Protest Play. This play deals with the reasons a prisoner gives for stating that the parole board is not the way to determine whether a man is ready for society.   *Cast:* 3 BM, 5 WM. *Length:* 1 Act. *Pubn:* Who Took the Weight (Black Voices from Norfolk Prison), Boston: Little, 1972. *Lib Source:* HBA.

WHITFIELD, GRADY D.

All about Money. Morality Drama. A man reads about a leak from a tank of silicon tetrafluoride on Chicago's South Side. A woman, age 69, was found dead from inhaling the fumes. Thinking that it is his mother, the man tries to borrow enough money to go home, but is unable to. In order to raise the money, he lets a prostitute use his place.   *Cast:* 2 BM, 2 BF, 1 WM, 1 WF, 1 Cuban M. *Length:* 1 Act. *Prod:* Reading, Frank Silvera Writers' Workshop, The Teachers, Inc., New York, Jan. 1976. *Perm:* Author.

Spiritually Trapped.   *Prod:* Reading, Frank Silvera Writers' Workshop, Harlem Performance Center, New York, Nov. 1976.

WHITFIELD, GRADY D. (*Cont.*)

Trapped in Cobweb. (1974). Political Drama. A minister's daughter, forced to leave home in her third year of high school, returns ten years later to avenge the death (caused by a white politician) of her baby sister and father. Subtitled: *A Woman's World.*   *Cast:* 3 BM, 5 BF, 3 WM, 2 WF. *Length:* 3 Acts. *Perm:* Author.

WHITFIELD, VANTILE. *See* Motojicho

WHITNEY, ELVIE

Center of Darkness. (1968).

The Hostages.

Pornoff.   *Prod:* Possibly by Douglass House Foundation, Washington, D. C., 1968.

Up a Little Higher. (1969).

WHITNEY, SALEM, DONALD HEYWOOD, and J. HOMER TUTT

Jim Crow. Musical Drama.

WHITNEY, SALEM, and J. HOMER TUTT

Children of the Sun. (1919-1920). Musical Revue.

Darkest Americans.

Deep Harlem. Musical Comedy.   *Cast:* 14 M, 13 F. *Length:* 2 Acts. *Prod:* Biltmore Theatre, New York, Jan. 1929. *Pubn: Best Plays of 1928-29*, ed. by Burns Mantle, New York: Dodd, 1929.

De Gospel Train. Dramatic Musical Comedy. Rewritten from the unproduced musical drama *Jim Crow* by Salem Tutt Whitney, Donald Heywood, and J. Homer Tutt. A southern "Jim Crow" car headed for the North (Washington, D.C.) and its passengers, with the peculiarities, have a morbid end.   *Cast:* 6-8 BM, 6 BF, 2 WM, extras. *Length:* 3 Acts. *Lib Source:* Typescript, SCHOM.

George Washington Bullion Abroad.

His Excellency the President.

Mayor of Newton.

My People.

Oh Joy.

WHITTEN, JAMES

Traps. A play about men in prison and their families who come to visit. The major concern is the inability of these people to reach out to each other.   *Prod:* Afro-American Studio, New York, 1974.

WIGGINS, ERNEST

Song Way Mom Way Dewey. (1976). Comedy/Drama. Explores the conflict between black men and women.   *Cast:* 2 BM, 2 BF. *Length:* 1 Act. *Perm:* Author.

WILKERSON, MARGARET

The Funeral. Drama. "The play focuses on the effects of death and how a black family views death and how death is celebrated."—*Black World*, vol. 25, no. 6, Apr. 1976.   *Prod:* Kumoja Players, Richmond, Calif., 1975.

WILKINS, PATRICIA ANN

In Search of Unity. (1972). Morality Play. Three black couples deal, each with his partner, in different ways with varying degrees of success and failure.   *Cast:* 3 BM, 3 BF. *Length:* 2 Acts. *Prod:* Reading, Frank Silvera Writers' Workshop, New York.

WILKS, PETER YOUNG, III. *See* Alamaji, Jiwe

WILLIAMS, BERT, and GEORGE WALKER

The Sons of Ham. Musical. "Williams and Walker, mistaken for long absent twin brothers, are royally feted until the real brothers appear."—Fannin Belcher. *See* Paul L. Dunbar, Alex Rogers, and Jesse A. Shipp for collaborations. *Prod:* Grand Opera House, New York, Mar. 1902.

WILLIAMS, CLARENCE

Bottomland. Musical Revue.   *Cast:* 15 BM, 4 BF. *Prod:* Savoy Theater, Atlantic City, N.J., June 1927; Princess Theater, New York, June 1927. *Pubn: Best Plays of 1927-28*, ed. by Burns Mantle, New York: Dodd, 1928.

WILLIAMS, CURTIS L.

The Auction. (1970). Domestic Play. A mother tries to decide between burying her son's body or selling it to a foundation so that she can buy things for her other children.   *Cast:* 2 BM, 2 BB, 3 BF. *Length:* 1 Act. *Prod:* Off-Broadway, N.Y., n.d. *Perm:* Author.

Crispus. (1975). Historical Morality. Problems of Crispus Attucks, on the last day of his life, decision to join white pro-slavery Bostonians as they rebel against British occupation.   *Cast:* 3 BM, 2 BF, 10 WM. *Length:* 2 Acts. *Perm:* Author.

Fairy Tales.

Maiden Voyage. Drama. Deals with three days in the life of Lorenzo, who returns home to preach to people who remember him as a petty criminal. He becomes involved in a killing that threatens to destroy his already shaky career as a preacher.   *Cast:* 6 M, 6 F. *Length:* Full Length. *Prod:* Albany State College, Ga., Nov. 1976. *Perm:* Author.

M-ssing in Act-on. (1974). Domestic. A husband and wife try to adjust to his having lost his procreative extremity in Vietnam.   *Cast:* 2 BM, 2 BF. *Length:* 2 Acts. *Perm:* Author.

Single Indemnity. (1972). Domestic Drama. Problems of a fatally ill young Black trying to leave some sort of legacy for his wife and his young brother.   *Cast:* 4 BM, 2 BF, 2 WM, 1 WF. *Length:* 2 Acts. *Perm:* Author.

WILLIAMS, CURTIS L., and T. MARSHALL JONES

Ghetto Vampire. (1973). Comedy. Blacks try to gain apprenticeship in the Vampire
Union to escape the ghetto.   *Cast:* 6 BM, 3 BF. *Length:* 2 Acts. *Perm:* Author.

Swap Face. (1974). Children's Play/Musical. The problem explored is one of
identity. A black youth tries to obtain a face, for which he has swapped his own
oft-criticized face.   *Cast:* 7 BM, 6 BF. *Perm:* Author.

WILLIAMS, EDWARD G.

Great Day for a Funeral. (1974). Domestic. Concerns family conflicts that arise
over the death of the main character's husband.   *Cast:* 2 BM, 6 BF, extras.
Length: 2 Acts.   *Prod:* Reading, Frank Silvera Writers' Workshop, New York,
Oct. 1975. *Perm:* Author.

Remembrance of a Lost Dream.   *Prod:* Reading, Frank Silvera Writers' Workshop,
Harlem Cultural Council, New York, May 1976.

WILLIAMS, ELLWOODSON

Mine Eyes Have Seen the Glory. (1970). Historical. The life of Booker T. Washington (1856–1915).   *Length:* 3 Acts.

Only Her Barber Knows for Sure.   *Prod:* Reading, Frank Silvera Writers' Workshop, Studio Museum of Harlem, New York, Mar. 1977.

Voice of the Gene. Drama. A black, light-skinned father has two sons by a black-
skinned woman. One has extremely light skin, the other has dark skin like the
mother. Out of old-fashioned ignorance, the father rejects the black-skinned
son and drives the mother and child away.   *Cast:* 3 BM, 2 BF, 1 WM, extras.
Length: 3 Acts. *Prod:* Bed-Stuy Theatre, New York, Aug. 1969. *Lib Source:*
Typescript, SCHOM.

WILLIAMS, HAROLD

With the Right Seed My Plant Will Grow Green.

WILLIAMS, JOHN AJALA

Essence of Time.   *Length:* 1 Act. *Prod:* Taft Community Players, New York, Nov.
1976.

WILLIAMS, JOHN AJALA, and CECIL ALONZO

1999 or Ghetto 1999. (1974).   *Length:* 1 Act. *Prod:* Alonzo Players, Harlem Cultural
Council, New York, Jan. 1975.

WILLIAMS, JOHN ALFRED

Reprieve for All God's Children.

WILLIAMS, JOHN VANLEER

The Face of Job. Domestic Drama. The death of a matriarch in a powerful black
family is the catalyst that exposes the true nature of those that remain behind

and how their lives are changed as a result of the will bequeathed. *Cast:* 5 BM, 5 BF, 1 WF. *Length:* 3 Acts. *Prod:* Reading, Frank Silvera Writers' Workshop, New York, Oct. 1975.

WILLIAMS, LEWIS

Give Yourself to Jesus.   *Length:* 1 Act. *Prod:* Kuumba Workshop, Eugene Perkins Theatre, Chicago, Ill., Oct. 1976.

WILLIAMS, MANCE

What's the Use of Hanging On? Two soul brothers discuss the possibilities and aims of rebellion and conclude they have to hang on. *Pubn: Roots*, Texas Southern University, Houston, 1970.

WILLIAMS, MARSHALL

The Diary of a Black Revolutionary. (1974). Satirical Drama. A revolutionary delivers a monologue from his cell. *Cast:* 1 BM. *Length:* 1 Act.

WILLIAMS, SAMM

The Coming. (1974). Morality Drama. Concerns a bum on New York's skid row that meets and talks with God, who appears before him as a prostitute, a field slave, and a junkie. *Cast:* 4 BM, 2 BF. *Length:* 1 Act. *Perm:* Author.

Do Unto Others. (1974). Domestic Drama. The life of a Chicago numbers banker who for ten years thought that he had killed his wife in a fire, but she returns to seek revenge. *Cast:* 4 BM, 2 BF. *Length:* 1 Act. *Perm:* Author.

Kamilia. (1975). Morality Drama. The life and trials of a young, upper-class woman who discovers, as a result of a recurring dream—after she is married—that she is a lesbian. *Cast:* 3 BM, 3 BF, 1 WF. *Length:* 2 Acts. *Perm:* Author.

A Love Play. Drama. "The four female characters size up their situation and decide that lesbianism is their best bet, and, given the men in their lives, it is difficult to say nay."—Townsend Brewster, *Newsletter* of the Harlem Cultural Council, vol. 2, no. 10. *Cast:* 2 BM, 4 BF. *Length:* Full Length. *Prod:* NEC Season-within-a-Season, New York, Spring 1976. *Perm:* Author.

Welcome to Black River. (1974). Ritual/Drama. Life and problems of a southern sharecropper and the impact that a hurricane has on his life, coupled with the voodoo religious beliefs of his neighbors. *Cast:* 4 BM, 3 BF, 1 WM. *Length:* 2 Acts. *Prod:* NEC, New York, May 1975. *Perm:* Author.

WILLIAMS, SANDRA BETH

The Family.

Hey Nigger Can You Dig Her.

Jest One Mo. This play led to the playwright's award of a New York State Council on the Arts grant.

Sunshine Loving.   *Prod:* Billie Holiday Theatre, New York, Feb. 1975.

Zodiac Zenith.

WILSON, ALICE T.

How a Poet Made Money and Forget-Me-Nots. Screenplay. Includes poems. *Pubn:* New York: Pageant, 1968.

WILSON, ANDI A. D.

Blacksheep. Drama. Story of a young man who makes the painful decision of what his new role is in an independent country (Bahamas). *Prod:* Horace Mann Theater, New York, May 1976.

Eleuthera My Wife, Eleuthera My Home.

The Youths.

WILSON, CAL

The Pet Shop.   *Prod:* Possibly by Douglass House Foundation, Washington, D.C., 1968.

WILSON, FRANCIS H.

Confidence. Sketch. Deals with Negro life.   *Prod:* Quality Amusement Corporation, New York, 1920, as noted from *The New York Age*, Sister Francesca Thompson.

WILSON, FRANK

Back Home Again.

Brother Mose. Comedy/Drama with Music. Rewrite of Wilson's *Meek Mose* (1928). Mose, under white pressures, leads his community to settle in the swamplands, but they are saved from disaster when oil is discovered there.   *Length:* Full Length. *Prod:* FTP, New York, Aug. 1934. *Lib Source:* Typescript, GMU.

The Good Sister Jones.   *Length:* 1 Act.

Meek Mose. (1928). Comedy/Drama. Rewritten by Wilson as *Brother Mose.* Mose leads his community to settle in the swamplands, but they are saved from disaster when oil is discovered there.   *Cast:* 12, 5 F. *Length:* 3 Acts. *Prod:* New York, Feb. 1928. *Pubn: Best Plays of 1927-28*, ed. by Burns Mantle, New York: Dodd, 1928.

The Prison Life.

Sugar Cane. (1920). Folk Melodrama. Sugar, the daughter, is pregnant by a neighboring white man, who raped her. Her father thinks a northern Negro named Howard is responsible. Howard returns and kills the white man and the father nearly kills Howard, but the truth is learned.   *Cast:* 3 BM, 3 BF. *Length:* 1 Act. *Pubn: Plays of Negro Life*, ed. by Alain Locke and Montgomery Gregory, New York: Harper, 1927. *Lib Source:* HBA.

Walk Together Chillun. Drama. A hundred Blacks are imported from the South to work for little money in the North, where they meet prejudice from Blacks and whites.   *Cast:* 13M, 7 F, extras. *Length:* 2 Acts. *Prod:* Lafayette Theatre, New York, Feb. 1936. *Pubn: Best Plays of 1935-36*, ed. by Burns Mantle, New York: Dodd, 1936. *Lib Source:* Typescript, FTP; PAL.

WILSON, LESTER

$600 and a Mule. Musical Experience. The history of black people in America is told in music, dance, and song.   *Prod:* Los Angeles, Calif., 1973.

WILSON, MATTIE MOULTRIE

Charity Suffereth Long. (1975). Dramatic Gospel Musical. Deals with the struggle of a good Christian woman to save her husband from the devil.

WINKLER, MEL

The Reachers. Astrological Drama. It is November of 1975. The jet stream has shifted, the polar caps are melting, the ionosphere is thinning out, new vibrations are getting through, and the earth's axis is beginning to tilt the other way. *Length:* 1 Act. *Prod:* The New Genesis Theatre Company, New York, Jan. 1976.

WINTER, ELLA, and LANGSTON HUGHES

Blood on the Fields. (1935). Proletarian Drama. Play deals with conditions among migrant cotton workers and their attempts to organize a union.   *Length:* 1 Act. *Lib Source:* Manuscript, possibly incomplete, YL.

WISE, EDWARD, and RANDY CURRIE

Zelda and Lucas Plotz.   *Length:* 1 Act. *Prod:* Regal Roots for the Performing Arts, St. Joseph Hospital Auditorium, Paterson, N.J., July 1975.

WISE, ROBERT

Tho Game. Melodrama. A black hymn-singing mother kills the detective who killed her son.   *Length:* 1 Act. *Prod:* Weusi Kuumba Troupe, New York, 1975.

Portsmouth. A handsome, talented young writer exploits his charm until the hard-working sister puts him out.   *Length:* 1 Act. *Prod:* Weusi Kuumba Troupe, New York, 1975.

WOLFE, ELTON C.

The After Party. Comedy. Two black men discuss "Negro" vs. "black" attitudes and they end in a fight with audience participation invited.   *Cast:* 2 BM, 2 BF. *Length:* 1 Act. *Prod:* n.p., 1970. *Perm:* Author.

All Men Wear Mustaches. Domestic Drama. Mary returns to her old home to discover the husband she left is still there; she decides she made a mistake but it's too late.   *Cast:* 5 BM, 7 BF. *Length:* 1 Act. *Perm:* Author.

The Big Shot. (1969). Situation Comedy. After a seven-year absence, a son returns to his mother's home in the South in an expensive Rolls Royce that he has "borrowed" from his wealthy employer, for whom he works as a chauffeur, and discovers that his mother has spread the misinformation that he is rich.   *Cast:* 3 BM, 4 BF. *Perm:* Author.

WOLFE, GEORGE C.

Block Play. Story Theatre. A troupe of "niggas" and whores sing and tell of what happens to people who sell "fantasies" out on the block.   *Cast:* 4-6 BM, 4-6 BF, 1 WM. *Length:* 2 Acts. *Prod:* Pomona College Theatre, Claremont, Calif., Dec. 1976. *Perm:* Author.

Up for Grabs. Epic Comedy/Satire. As Joe Thomas discovers the secret to being black and the reasons for his existence, he receives a lesson in American exploitation and power, all the while being an unknown contestant on the ultimate TV game show.   *Cast:* 5 BM, 3 BF, 1 WM, 3 WF. *Length:* 4 1-Act Episodes. *Prod:* Pomona College Theatre, Claremont, Calif., Nov. 1975. *Perm:* Author.

WOOD, DEBBIE

Four Niggers. Sketch. Four drug addicts scratch themselves to death.   *Cast:* 3 BM, 1 BF. *Length:* 1 Act. *Prod:* Ira Aldridge Theatre, Washington, D.C., 1971. *Perm:* Author.

Indiana Avenue.   *Prod:* NEC, New York, Jan. 1973.

WRIGHT, CHARLES STEVENSON

Something Black.

WRIGHT, JAY

Balloons. (1968). Morality Comedy. Benjamin, the balloon man, sees his dream of good people destroyed by racism—black and white.   *Cast:* 2 BM, 1 BF, 1 WM, 1 WF, 1 child. *Length:* 1 Act. *Pubn:* Boston: Baker, 1968. *Lib Source:* HBA.

The Doors.   *Length:* 1 Act. *Prod:* Exodus Coffee House, San Pedro, Calif., n.d.

Prophets and Fools. Morality Play. The play deals with the problems of black people trying to get their community (Watts) together, with emphasis on black pride. *Cast:* 13 BM, 5 BF, extras.

Welcome, Black Boy.   *Length:* 1 Act. *Prod:* Playwright's Workshop, Berkeley, Calif., n.d.

WRIGHT, RICHARD

The Farmer in the Dell. (c. 1949). Children prepare to celebrate Thanksgiving. *Length:* 2 Scenes. *Lib Source:* Manuscript, Paris, France.

Gott ist anders (Man, God Ain't Like That). Radio Play. Translated by Kurt Heinrich Hansen. Published as a short story in Wright's book *Eight Men.* A famous police inspector cannot solve a murder committed by Babu, an African, because he does not understand "racism." *Length:* 45 Minutes. *Prod:* Probably broadcast over North German Radio, Hamburg, 1959. *Lib Source:* Typescripts in German and English, HBA.

Mädchen für Alles (Man of All Work). Radio Play. Translation by Erich Fried; second translation by Erwin Wickert. Published as a short story in Wright's book

Eight Men. A black man, unable to find work to support his family, disguises himself as a woman and takes a job as a maid.   *Length:* 45 Minutes. *Prod:* Broadcast over North German Radio, Hamburg, Jan. 1960. *Lib Source:* Typescripts in German and English, HBA.

The Problem of the Hero. An attempt to reconstruct a sense of the cultural problem found in dramatizing Wright's novel, *Native Son.*   *Lib Source:* Typescript, Paris, France.

WRIGHT, RICHARD, and KITTY FRINGS*

The Long Dream. Protest Drama. Based on Wright's novel of the same name, set in Clintonville, Miss.   *Cast:* 13 M, 4 F, extras. *Length:* 3 Acts. *Prod:* Ambassador Theatre, New York, Feb. 1960.

WRIGHT, RICHARD, and PAUL GREEN*

Native Son. (1941). Protest Drama. The dramatization of Wright's novel of the same name. About the life and death of Bigger Thomas, the central character in *Native Son.*   *Cast:* 4 BM, 3 BF, 7 WM, 1 B, extras. *Length:* 10 Scenes. *Prod:* Mercury Theatre, New York, Mar. 1941. *Pubn: Black Theater USA,* ed. by James V. Hatch and Ted Shine, New York: Free Pr., 1974. *Lib Source:* HBA.

WRIGHT, RICHARD, and NEIL NEWLON

Lawd Today. Drama. Adapted from Wright's novel of the same name. One day in the life of Jake Jackson, a man who is getting beaten from all sides—his wife, his job, "the man"—and his attempt to get a little something for himself. *Cast:* 6 BM, 3 BF, 3 WM, 1 WF. *Length:* 3 Acts. *Lib Source:* HBA.

WRIGHT, RICHARD, and LOUIS SAPIN*

Daddy Goodness. (1956). Comedy. Translated and adapted for the American stage by Richard Wright from a play by Louis Sapin, *Papa Bon Dieu.* The Messiah returns to face all the human contradictions of the black people. *Cast:* 12 BM, 4 BF (doubling). *Length:* 3 Acts. *Prod:* NEC, New York, 1968.

WYATTE, FARICITA

You Gotta Pay Your Dues. Prod: Black Repertory Group, Berkeley, Calif., 1973.

X, MARVIN

The Black Bird. (1969). Didactic Play. A fundamental lesson in the correlation of blackness and the nation of Islam. Subtitled: *Al Tair Aswad.*   *Cast:* 1 BM, 2 BF, dancers. *Length:* 1 Act. *Pubn: New Plays from the Black Theater,* ed. by Ed Bullins, New York: Bantam, 1969. *Lib Source:* NYPL. *Perm:* Agency, NASABA.

A Black Ritual. (1970).

Come Next Summer.   Prod: Blackarts/West Theatre, San Francisco, Calif., 1969.

X, MARVIN (*Cont.*)

Flowers for the Trashman or *Take Care of Business.* Morality Domestic. A jailed black man's wish for a better relationship with his father comes a little too late. *Cast:* 3 BM, 2 WM. *Length:* 1 Act. *Prod:* Blackarts/West Theatre, San Francisco, Calif., Spring 1966. *Pubn: Black Fire*, ed. by LeRoi Jones and Larry Neal, New York: Morrow, 1966. *Lib Source:* NYPL. *Perm:* NASABA.

The Resurrection of the Dead. *Length:* 4 Movements. *Prod:* NLT, New York, 1969. *Pubn: Black Theatre*, ed. by Ed Bullins, no. 3, 1969.

The Trial. *Perm:* NASABA.

YARBROUGH, CAMILLE

And Then There's Negroland. Ritual. A positive statement that black people have survived and will survive. Subtitled: *Ain't No One Monkey.* *Cast:* 13 BM, 8 BF (doubling). *Length:* Full Length. *Perm:* Author.

YOUNG, CLARENCE, III

Black Love. Musical. "The theme is love, which is achievable once the barriers to it are removed."—*Black World.* *Prod:* Theater West, Washington, D.C., 1975.

The Perry's Mission. (1971). Drama. Two white people in a bar manipulate a cross-section of black people to the point of their deaths. *Cast:* 8 BM, 1 WM, 1 WF. *Prod:* NEC, New York, Jan. 1971.

The System. Musical Psycho-Drama. About America. *Prod:* Cleveland State University, Ohio, 1973.

YOUNG, OTIS

Right On Brother. (1969).

YOUNG, WHITNEY

The Coming of the Pink Cheeks. Historical Children's Play. The coming of the white man to Africa. *Cast:* 5 BB, 4 BG, 4 WB, chorus. *Length:* 3 Acts. *Pubn: We Are Black*, Chicago: Science Research Assn., 1969. *Lib Source:* HBA.

ZALTZBERG, CHARLOTTE,* and ROBERT NEMIROFF*

Raisin. Domestic Musical. Music by Judd Woldin. Lyrics by Robert Brittan. Based on Lorraine Hansberry's play, *A Raisin in the Sun.* Explores essentially the same conflicts and values as the original play, but moves beyond the Younger's apartment into the streets, bars, churches, and work-a-day settings of the people of Chicago's South Side; the score incorporates idioms of jazz, gospel, blues, soul, and the dance, and is based on Afro-American and African traditions; it heightens and underscores the subtleties, humor, and high spirits, the strength and heroism of the Younger family's reaffirmation of their black heritage. *Cast:* 5 BM, 1 BB, 4 BF, 1 WM, extras. *Prod:* Forty-sixth Street Theatre, New York, Oct. 1973. *Pubn:* SF; Recording, original cast, Columbia Records. *Perm:* Agency, SF.

ZELLARS, JOHN

Tribute to Otis Redding.   *Prod:* Theatre of The Living Soul, Philadelphia, Pa., 1971.

ZUBER, RON

Three X Love. Ritual. In this work, the black mother, sister, and lover are exalted and praised.   *Cast:* 2 BM, 3 BF, singers. *Length:* 1 Act. *Pubn: Black Drama Anthology*, ed. by Woodie King, Jr. and Ron Milner, New York: New Amer. Lib., 1966. *Lib Source:* NYPL.

BIBLIOGRAPHIES

Selected Bibliography of Books and Sources on Black Drama and Its Theatre Artists

Abdul, Raoul, ed. *Famous Black Entertainers of Today.* New York: Dodd, 1974.

Abramson, Doris E. *Negro Playwrights in the American Theater.* New York: Columbia Univ. Pr., 1969.

Anderson, Doris Garland. *Nigger Lover.* London: L. N. Fowler & Co., n.d.

Angelou, Maya. *Singin' and Swingin' and Gettin' Merry Like Christmas.* New York: Random, 1976.

Arata, Esther Spring, and Rotoli, Nicholas John. *Black American Playwrights, 1800 to the Present.* Metuchen: Scarecrow, 1976.

Archer, Leonard C. *Black Images in the American Theater.* Brooklyn: Pageant, 1973.

Bailey, Pearl. *The Raw Pearl.* New York: Harcourt, 1968.

———. *Talking to Myself.* New York: Harcourt, 1971.

Benston, Kimberly W. *Baraka.* New Haven and London: Yale Univ. Pr., 1976.

Bigsby, C. W., ed. *The Black American Writer, Volume II: Poetry and Drama.* Baltimore: Penguin, 1971.

Birdoff, Harry. *The World's Greatest Hit, Uncle Tom's Cabin.* New York: S. F. Vanni, 1947.

Black Theatre magazine. New Lafayette Theatre Production, nos. 1-6, 1968-1972.

Bolcom, William and Kimball, Robert, eds. *Reminiscing with Sissle and Blake.* New York: Viking, 1973.

Bond, Frederick W. *The Negro and the Drama.* Washington, D.C.: Associated Publishers, 1940.

Bontemps, Arna, ed. *The Harlem Renaissance Remembered.* New York: Dodd, 1972.

Brown, Sterling. *Negro Poetry and Drama and the Negro in American Fiction.* Washington, D.C.: 1937. Reprint. New York: Atheneum, 1969.

Butcher, Margaret Just. *The Negro in American Culture,* 2nd ed. New York: Knopf, 1972.

Calloway, Cab, and Rollins, Bryant. *Of Minnie the Moocher and Me.* New York: Crowell, 1976.

Charters, Ann. *Nobody: The Story of Bert Williams.* New York: Macmillan, 1970.

Cohen, Tom. *Three Who Dared.* New York: Doubleday, 1969.

Cruse, Harold. *The Crisis of the Negro Intellectual.* New York: Morrow, 1967.

Dace, Letitia. *LeRoi Jones (Imamu Amiri Baraka): A Checklist of Works by and about Him.* London: Nether Pr., 1971.

Dandridge, Dorothy, and Conrad, Earl. *Everything and Nothing.* New York: Abelard-Schuman, 1970.

Dent, Tom; Moses, Gilbert; and Schechner, Richard. *The Free Southern Theater.* Indianapolis: Bobbs-Merrill, 1969.

Drama Review: Black Theatre Issue. Vol. 16, no. 4, December 1972.

Dunham, Katherine. *A Touch of Innocence.* New York: Harcourt, 1959.

Emanuel, James. *Langston Hughes.* New York: Twayne, 1967.

Emery, Lynne Fauley. *Black Dance in the United States from 1619 to 1970.* Palo Alto: Mayfield Pub. Co., 1972.

Ewers, Carolyn H. *Sidney Poitier: The Long Journey.* New York: New Amer. Lib., 1969.

Fabre, Geneviève; Fabre, Michel; French, William; and Singh, Amritjit, eds. *Afro-American Poetry and Drama.* Detroit: Gale, forthcoming.

Farrison, William Edward. *William Wells Brown.* Chicago: Univ. of Chicago Pr., 1969.

Fletcher, Tom. *100 Years of the Negro in Show Business.* New York: Burdge & Co., 1954.

Funke, Lewis. *The Curtain Rises: The Story of Ossie Davis.* New York: Grosset, 1971.

Gayle, Addison, Jr., ed. *The Black Aesthetic.* New York: Doubleday, 1971.

Gilliam, Dorothy Butler. *Paul Robeson, All American.* Washington, D.C.: New Republic Book Co., Inc., 1976.

Graham, Shirley. *Paul Robeson.* New York: Messner, 1946.

Hamilton, Virginia. *Paul Robeson.* New York: Harper, 1974.

Harnan, Terry. *African Rhythm American Dance: A Biography of Katherine Dunham.* New York: Knopf, 1974.

Harrison, Paul Carter. *The Drama of Nommo.* New York: Grove, 1972.

Hatch, James V. *Black Image on the American Stage: A Bibliography of Plays and Musicals, 1770-1970.* New York: Drama Book Specialists, 1970.

Horne, Lena, and Schickel, Richard. *Lena.* New York: Doubleday, 1965.

Hoyt, Edwin. *Paul Robeson, the American Othello.* Cleveland: World, 1967.

Hudson, James A. *Flip Wilson, Close-Up.* New York: Avon, 1972.

Hudson, Theodore R. *From LeRoi Jones to Amiri Baraka: The Literary Works.* Durham: Duke Univ. Pr., 1973.

Huggins, Nathan Irvin. *Harlem Renaissance.* New York: Oxford Univ. Pr., 1971.

Hughes, Langston. *The Big Sea.* New York: Hill & Wang, 1940.

————. *I Wonder as I Wander.* New York: Hill & Wang, 1956

————, and Meltzer, Milton. *Black Magic.* Englewood Cliffs: Prentice-Hall, 1967.

Isaacs, Edith J. *The Negro in the American Theater.* New York: Theater Arts, 1947.

Johnson, James Weldon. *Along This Way.* New York: Viking, 1933.

————. *Black Manhattan.* New York: Knopf, 1930.

Jones, LeRoi. *Home: Social Essays.* New York: Morrow, 1966.

Kitt, Eartha. *Alone with Me.* Chicago: Regnery, 1976.

————. *Thursday's Child.* New York: Duell, Sloan, & Pearce, 1956.

Locke, Alain, ed. *The New Negro.* New York: Atheneum, 1925.

Macebuh, Stanley. *James Baldwin.* New York: Third Pr., 1973.

McGill, Raymond D., ed. *Notable Names in the American Theatre.* Clifton: James T. White & Co., 1976.

Marshall, Herbert, and Stock, Mildred. *Ira Aldridge, the Negro Tragedian.* Carbondale: Southern Illinois Univ. Pr., 1968.

Meltzer, Milton. *Langston Hughes.* New York: Crowell, 1968.

Mitchell, Loften. *Black Drama: The Story of the American Negro in the Theatre.* New York: Hawthorn, 1967.

_____. *Voices of the Black Theatre.* Clifton: James T. White & Co., 1976.

Muse, Clarence, and Arlen, David. *Way Down South.* Hollywood, Calif.: David Graham Fischer, 1932.

O'Daniel, Therman B., ed. *Langston Hughes: Black Genius.* New York: Morrow, 1971.

Papich, Stephen. *Remembering Josephine: A Biography of Josephine Baker.* Indianapolis: Bobbs-Merrill, 1976.

Patterson, Lindsay, ed. *Anthology of the American Negro in the Theatre.* New York: Publishers Co., 1967.

Ploski, Harry A., and Marr, Warren, II, eds. "The Black Entertainer in the Performing Arts." *The Afro American.* New York: Bellwether, 1976.

Reardon, William, and Pawley, Thomas. *The Black Teacher and the Dramatic Arts: A Dialogue, Bibliography and Anthology.* Westport: Negro Universities Pr., 1970.

Rollins, Charlemae H. *Black Troubadour: Langston Hughes.* Chicago: Rand McNally, 1970.

_____. *Famous Negro Entertainers of Stage, Screen, and TV.* New York: Dodd, 1967.

Rush, Theressa Gunnels; Myers, Carol Fairbanks; and Arata, Esther Spring. *Black American Writers, Past and Present: A Biographical and Bibliographical Dictionary.* Metuchen: Scarecrow, 1975.

Schiffman, Jack. *Uptown, the Story of Harlem's Apollo Theatre.* New York: Cowles Book Co., 1971.

Schwartz, Charles. *Gershwin, His Life and Music.* Indianapolis: Bobbs-Merrill, 1973.

Shaw, Arnold. *Belafonte.* Philadelphia: Chilton, 1960.

Shockley, Ann Allen, and Chandler, Sue P., eds. *Living Black American Authors: A Biographical Directory.* New York: Bowker, 1973.

Sterns, Marshall, and Sterns, Jean. *Jazz Dance, the Story of American Dance.* New York: Macmillan, 1968.

Toll, Robert C. *Blacking Up.* New York: Oxford Univ. Pr., 1974.

Waters, Ethel. *His Eye Is on the Sparrow.* New York: Doubleday, 1951.

_____. *To Me It's Wonderful.* New York: Harper, 1972.

Wittke, Carl. *Tambo and Bones.* Durham: Duke Univ. Pr., 1930.

Yale/Theatre, African Theatre Issue. Vol. 8, no. 1, Fall 1976.

Selected Bibliography of Anthologies
Containing Scripts by Black Playwrights

Adams, William; Conn, Peter; and Slepian, Barry, eds. *Afro-American Literature: Drama.* Boston: Houghton, 1970.

Amis, Lola Jones. *Three Plays.* New York: Exposition, 1965.

Baraka, Amiri [LeRoi Jones]. *Four Black Revolutionary Plays.* Indianapolis: Bobbs-Merrill, 1969.

Brasmer, William, and Consolo, Dominick, eds. *Black Drama: An Anthology.* Columbus, Ohio: Merrill Pub. Co., 1970.

Brown, Sterling; Davis, Arthur; and Lee, Ulysses, eds. *Negro Caravan.* New York: Dryden Pr., Inc., 1941.

Bullins, Ed. *Five Plays by Ed Bullins.* Indianapolis: Bobbs-Merrill, 1968.

_____, et al. *A Black Quartet.* New York: New Amer. Lib., 1970.

_____. *Four Dynamite Plays.* New York: Morrow, 1972.

_____. *The Theme Is Blackness.* New York: Morrow, 1973.

_____, ed. *New Lafayette Theatre Presents.* New York: Doubleday, 1974.

_____, ed. *New Plays from the Black Theatre.* New York: Bantam, 1969.

The Carolina Magazine. [play issue] Vol. 59, no. 7, April 1929.

Childress, Alice, ed. *Black Scenes.* New York: Doubleday, 1971.

Clark, China. *Neffie and In Sorrow's Room.* New York: ERA Pub. Co., 1976.

Couch, William, Jr., ed. *New Black Playwrights.* Baton Rouge: Louisiana State Univ. Pr., 1968.

Dean, Philip Hayes. *The Sty of the Blind Pig and Other Plays.* Indianapolis: Bobbs-Merrill, 1973.

The Drama Review. [play issue] Vol. 12, no. 4, Summer 1968.

Edmonds, Randolph. *The Land of Cotton and Other Plays.* Washington, D.C.: Associated Publishers, 1942.

_____. *Shades and Shadows.* Boston: Meador Pub. Co., 1930.

_____. *Six Plays for a Negro Theater.* Boston: Baker, 1934.

Goss, Clay. *Homecookin': Five Plays.* Washington, D.C.: Howard Univ. Pr., 1974.

Hansberry, Lorraine. *A Raisin in the Sun/ The Sign in Sidney Brustein's Window.* New York: New Amer. Lib., 1966.

Harrison, Paul Carter. *Kuntu Drama.* New York: Grove, 1974.

Hatch, James V., and Shine, Ted, eds. *Black Theater USA.* New York: Free Pr., 1974.

King, Woodie, Jr., and Milner, Ron, eds. *Black Drama Anthology,* New York: New Amer. Lib., 1972.

Locke, Alain, and Gregory, Montgomery, eds. *Plays of Negro Life.* New York: Harper Bros., 1927.

Nemiroff, Robert, ed. *Les Blancs: The Last Collected Plays of Lorraine Hansberry.* New York: Random, 1972.

Norfolk Prison Brothers. *Who Took the Weight? Black Voices from Norfolk Prison.* Boston: Little, 1972.

Oliver, Clinton, and Sills, Stephanie, eds. *Contemporary Black Drama.* New York: Scribner, 1971.

O'Neal, Regina. *And Then the Harvest, Three Television Plays.* Detroit: Broadside Pr., 1974.

Patterson, Lindsay, ed. *Black Theater.* New York: Dodd, 1971.

Payton, Lew. *Did Adam Sin? Also Other Stories of Negro Life in Comedy-Drama and Sketches.* Los Angeles: Privately published, 1937.

Reardon, William, and Pawley, Thomas, eds. *The Black Teacher and the Dramatic Arts: A Dialogue, Bibliography and Anthology.* Westport: Negro Universities Pr., 1970.

Reed, Ishmael, ed. *19 Necromancers from Now.* New York: Doubleday, 1970.

Richardson, Willis. *The King's Dilemma and Other Plays for Children.* New York: Exposition, 1956.

————, ed. *Plays and Pageants from the Life of the Negro.* Washington, D.C.: Associated Publishers, 1930.

————, and Miller, May, eds. *Negro History in Thirteen Plays.* Washington, D.C.: Associated Publishers, 1935.

Sanchez, Sonia, ed. *Three Hundred and Sixty Degrees of Blackness Comin' at You.* New York: 5X Pub. Co., 1971.

Smalley, Webster, ed. *Five Plays by Langston Hughes.* Bloomington: Indiana Univ. Pr., 1963.

Turner, Darwin T., ed. *Black Drama in America: An Anthology.* Greenwich: Fawcett, 1971.

Walcott, Derek. *Dream on Monkey Mountain and Other Plays.* New York: Farrar, 1970.

White, Edgar. *The Crucificado, Two Plays.* New York: Morrow, 1973.

————. *Underground, Four Plays.* New York: Morrow, 1970.

Bibliography of Dissertations and Theses on the American Theatre

This bibliography contains scholarly works in two categories. One category includes dissertations and theses by black scholars about black and white drama, theatre, and theatre artists. The other includes dissertations and theses by white scholars about black drama, black theatre, and black theatre artists. Those scholars known to be Black are designated by the use of an asterisk (*). The list derives from four sources: *The Black Teacher and the Dramatic Arts: A Dialogue, Bibliography and Anthology*, by Professors William Reardon and Thomas Pawley; "Blacks with Earned Doctorates in Theatre/Drama, 1973," a list compiled by Professor Winona Fletcher; *Educational Theatre Journal*, the annual listing of dissertations in progress; and a list supplied by Professor Errol Hill of Dartmouth College. The bibliography identifies which works are Ph.D dissertations and which works are M.A. theses when the sources, mentioned above, so indicated.

Abramson, Doris E. "From *Harlem to A Raisin in the Sun:* A Study of Plays by Negro Playwrights, 1929-1959." Ph.D. dissertation, Columbia University Teachers College, 1965.

Adubato, Robert. "A History of the Negro Units of Federal Theatre (WPA) in New York City and New Jersey, from 1935 to 1939." Ph.D. dissertation, New York University, 1977.

*Archer, Leonard C. "The National Association for the Advancement of Colored People and the American Theatre, a Study of Relationships and Influences." Ph.D. dissertation, Ohio State University, 1959.

*Austin, Gerlyn Erna. "Moral Attitudes in America as Viewed through Drama, 1865 to 1920." M.A. thesis, Howard University, Department of English, 1964.

*Bailey, Leon Edwin. "The Acting of Walter Huston." Ph.D. dissertation, University of Illinois, 1973.

Baines, J. D. "Samuel S. Sandford and Negro Minstrelry." Ph.D. dissertation, Tulane University, 1967.

Beardsley, Grace H. "The Negro in Greek and Roman Civilization." Ph.D. dissertation, The Johns Hopkins University, 1939.

*Belcher, Fannin S. "The Place of the Negro in the Evolution of the American Theatre, 1767-1940." Ph.D. dissertation, Yale University, 1945.

*Bettis, Charles. "The Spirit of Langston Hughes as Expressed in His Dramas." Ph. D. dissertation in progress, University of California at Santa Barbara.

Blitzgen, Sister Mary John Carol. "Voices of Protest: An Analysis of the Negro Protest Plays of the 1963-64 Broadway and Off-Broadway Season." M.A. thesis, University of Kansas, 1966.

*Bond, Frederick W. "The Direct and Indirect Contribution Which the American Negro Has Made to the Drama and the Legitimate Stage, with Underlying Conditions Responsible." Ph.D. dissertation, New York University, 1938.

Bowles, Warren C. "Black Americans in the Professional Theatre: A Study of Factors Motivating Blacks to Choose Careers in Theatre, from the Emancipation to the Negro Renaissance." Ph.D. dissertation in progress, University of Minnesota.

Bradley, Gerald S. "The Negro in the American Drama." M.F.A. thesis, Carnegie Institute of Technology, 1963.

*Brooks, Gwendolyn. "Attacks on the American Stage for Reasons of Morals." M.A. thesis, Howard University, Department of English, n.d.

*Buchanan, Singer. "A Study of the Attitudes of the Writers of the Negro Press toward the Depiction of the Negro in Plays and Films: 1930-1968." Ph.D. dissertation, University of Michigan, 1968.

Burke, William Lee. "The Presentation of the American Negro in Hollywood Films, 1946-1961: Analysis of a Selected Sample of Feature Films." Ph.D. dissertation, Northwestern University, 1965.

*Cochran, James P. "The Producer-Director on the New York Stage, 1890-1915." Ph.D. dissertation, State University of Iowa, 1958.

*Coleman, Edwin L., Jr. "Langston Hughes: An American Dramatist." University of Oregon, 1971.

Colle, Royal. "Negro Image and the Mass Media." Ph.D. dissertation, Cornell University, 1967.

Collins, John D. "American Drama in Anti-Slavery Agitation." Iowa State University, 1963.

Collins, Leslie M. "A Song, a Dance, and a Play—An Interpretative Study of Three American Artists" [Black performers]. Ph.D. dissertation, Western Reserve University, 1945.

*Cook, Ann. "An Analysis of the Acting Styles of Garrick, Siddons, and Edmund Kean in Relation to the Dominant Trends in Art and Literature of the Eighteenth Century." Ph.D. dissertation, Yale, 1944.

*Cowan, Mary Frances. "The Negro in the American Drama, 1877-1900." M.A. thesis, Howard University, 1950.

Cox, Ken. "The Rhetorical Devices Employed in the Plays of LeRoi Jones." Ph.D. dissertation, University of Nebraska, 1974.

Crumpler, Gloria Thomas. "The Negro in the American Theatre and Drama from 1950-1956." Ph.D. dissertation, New York University, 1952.

Davidson, Frank C. "The Rise, Development, Decline and Influence of the American Minstrel Show." Ph.D. dissertation, New York University, 1952.

Davis, Br. Joseph Morgan. "A Compilation and Analysis of Views Concerning the Contributions of the Negro in the American Theatre in 1950-1960." M.A. thesis, Catholic University, 1962.

Distler, P. A. "The Rise and Fall of Racial Comics in American Vaudeville." Ph.D. dissertation, Tulane University, 1963.

*Dixon, Bessie L. "The Negro Character in American Drama." M.A. thesis, Howard University, 1936.

Eaton, Gregory S. "Black Theatre and Drama in America to Baldwin." Ph.D. dissertation in progress, Washington University.

*Edwards, Flora Mancuso. "The Theatre of the Black Diaspora: Black Drama in Brazil, Cuba, and the United States." Ph.D. dissertation, New York University, 1975.

Eikleberry, Burton. "The Negro Actor's Participation and the Negro Image on the New York Stage, 1954-1964." M.A. thesis, University of Kansas, 1965.

Ellington, Mary David. "Plays by Negro Authors with Special Emphasis upon the Period from 1916-1934." Fisk University, 1934.

*Fisher, Edward. "Imamu Baraka (LeRoi Jones) and Radical Black Thought." Ph.D. dissertation in progress, University of California at Santa Barbara.

*Fletcher, Winona L. "Andrew Jackson Allen: 'Internal and External' Costumer to the Early Nineteenth Century American Theatre." Ph.D. dissertation, Indiana University, 1968.

*Gaffney, Floyd. "Interracial Theatre in the United States." Ph.D. dissertation, Carnegie-Mellon University, 1964.

Garton, Christiana. "The Portrayal of Negro Character in the American Drama and Novel." M.A. thesis, University of Colorado, 1942.

Gary, J. Vaughn, Jr. "The Integration of the Negro on the New York Stage Since 1940." M.A. thesis, Columbia University, 1958.

*Gilliam, T. E. "The Negro Image in Representative American Dramas." Ph.D. dissertation, Tulane Univeristy, 1967.

*Grace, John. [OMANii Abdullah]. "An Annotated Bibliography of Black Drama, 1959-1974." M.A. thesis, University of Tennessee, 1974.

Haley, Elsie Galbreath. "The Black Revolutionary Theatre: LeRoi Jones, Ed Bullins, and Minor Playwrights." University of Denver, 1971.

*Hall, Fred. "The Black Theatre in New York from 1960-1970." Ph.D. dissertation, Columbia University Teachers College, 1972.

Hardwick, Mary R. "The Nature of the Negro Hero in Serious American Drama, 1919-1964." Michigan State University, 1968.
*Hay, Samuel. "The Image of the Black Man as Projected by Representative White American Dramatists, 1900–1963." Ph.D. dissertation, Cornell University, 1971.
*Hill, Errol. "The Trinidad Carnival: Basis for a National Theatre." Ph.D. dissertation, Yale University, 1966.
*Hinklin, Fannie Ella. "The American Negro Playwright 1920-1964." Ph.D. dissertation, University of Wisconsin, 1965.
Holt, Frances E. "The Negro Character in the American Drama from 1914–1934." Fisk University, 1934.
*Hudson, Theodore R. "From LeRoi Jones to Amiri Baraka." Ph.D. dissertation, Howard University, 1971.
*Jackson, Esther M. "The Emergence of a Characteristic Contemporary Form in the American Drama of Tennessee Williams." Ph.D. dissertation, Ohio State University, 1958.
*Jeyifous, Biodun. "Theatre and Drama and the Black Physical and Cultural Presence in America: Essay in Interpretation." Ph.D. dissertation, New York University, 1975.
Kesler, William Jackson. "The Early Productions of the Aiken-Howard Versions of Uncle Tom's Cabin." University of Texas, 1968.
Knowles, Mary Tyler. "Drama and Nationalism: Their Interrelationship as Reflected in the Drama of the Irish Renaissance and Civil War and of Black Amerca." (In progress.) University of Wisconsin.
Kuhlke, William. "They Too Sing America (1918-1930)." M.A. thesis, Adams State College of Colorado, 1952.
Lawson, Hilda H. "The Negro in American Drama." Ph.D. dissertation, University of Illinois, 1939.
Linnehan, E. G. "We Wear the Mask: The Use of Negro Life and Character in American Drama." Ph.D. dissertation, University of Pennsylvania, n.d.
Luck, James William. "The Contribution of the Negro to the Legitimate Theatre in America." M.A. thesis, Emerson College, 1953.
*McGhee, Esther Jordan. "The Secret Lives of the Women in Eugene O'Neill's Plays: A Study in Dramatic Technique." M.A. thesis, Howard University, Department of English, 1954.
*Miller, Althea Ann. "The Negro in American Drama." M.A. thesis, University of Oklahoma, 1958.
*Molette, Carlton. "Concepts about Theatre: A Survey of Some College Students in the Florida Counties of Broward, Dade, and Palm Beach, Comparing Those Who Have Had a Theatre and Drama Appreciation Course against Those Who Have Not." Ph.D. dissertation, Florida State University, 1969.
*Monroe, John G. "Charles Sidney Gilpin: The Emperor Jones." M.A. thesis, Hunter College, 1974.
*Nash, Rosa Lee. "Characterization of Blacks in the Theatre of the Sixties." Ph.D. dissertation, Yeshiva University, 1971.
*Ogunbiyi, Yemi. "The New Black Playwrights in America: Essays in Theatrical Interpretation." Ph.D. dissertation, New York University, 1976.
*Owens, William. "The Dramaturgical Treatment of Character Types by Playwrights of Heroic Drama." Ph.D. dissertation, University of Denver, 1959.

*Pawley, Thomas D., Jr. "Experimental Productions of a Group of Original Plays."
    Ph.D. dissertation, University of Iowa, 1949.
Pembrook, Carrie D. "Negro Drama through the Ages." Ph.D. dissertation, New York
    University, 1946.
Pettit, Paul B. "The Important American Dramatic Types to 1900. A Study of the
    Yankee, Negro, Indian, and Frontiersman." Ph.D. dissertation, Cornell Univer-
    sity, 1943.
*Pinkett, L. Louise. "Folk Elements in American Drama, 1870-1936." M.A. thesis,
    Howard University, 1936.
*Pitts, Ethel M. "A Descriptive Study of the American Negro Theatre in New York City
    in the 1940s." Ph.D. dissertation, University of Missouri, 1975.
*Poag, Thomas C. "The Negro in Drama and the Theatre." Ph.D. dissertation, Cornell
    University, 1943.
Quarnstrom, Isaac Blaine. "Harmount's Uncle Tom's Cabin Company, A Study of a
    Twentieth Century 'Tom' Show." Ohio State University, 1967.
Reed, Laverne M. "Plays of Paul Green—A Study of Technique." Fisk University,
    1934.
Reed, P. I. "Realistic Presentation of American Characters in Native American Plays
    Prior to 1870." Ph.D. dissertation, University of Ohio, 1918.
*Reeves, Elizabeth. "A Program in Speech for the College of Liberal Arts at Howard
    University." Ph.D. dissertation, Columbia University Teachers College, 1956.
Richards, Sandra. "Bert Williams: His Stage Career and Influence on American
    Theatre." Ph.D. dissertation, Stanford University, 1973.
Sandle, Floyd L. "A History of the Development of the Educational Theatre in the
    Negro College and Universities, 1911-1959." Ph.D. dissertation, Louisiana
    State University, 1959.
*Scott, John S. "The Black Spirit: A Trilogy of Original Plays and a Treatise on the
    Dramatic Theory of Contemporary Black Drama." Ph.D. dissertation, Bowling
    Green State University, 1972.
*Senanu, Kojo. "The Theatre of John Arden." Carnegie-Mellon University, 1963.
Sherman, Alfonso. "The Diversity of Treatment of the Negro Character in American
    Drama Prior to 1860." Ph.D. dissertation, Indiana University, 1964.
*Shine, Ted. "Black Characters in American Drama Prior to 1800." Ph.D. disser-
    tation, University of California at Santa Barbara, 1974.
Silver, Reuben. "A History of the Karamu Theatre of Karamu House, 1915-1960."
    Ph.D. dissertation, Ohio State University, 1961.
Smith, Allington E. "The Negro Actor in Legitimate Plays, with Special Emphasis on
    the Period from 1900-1934." M.A. thesis, Fisk University, 1934.
*Stevenson, John M. "An Analysis of Administrators' Attitudes toward Speech in
    Arkansas Public High Schools." Ph.D. dissertation, University of Arkansas,
    1965.
Stevenson, Robert L. "The Image of the White Man as Seen in Plays by Represen-
    tative Black American Dramatists, 1847-1973." Ph.D. dissertation in progress,
    University of Iowa.
Sumpter, Clyde Gene. "Militating for Change: The Black Revolutionary Theatre
    Movement in the United States." University of Kansas, 1970.
Tedesco, John. "The White Image in Black Drama, 1955-1970: A Survey of White
    Characters—Their Dramatic and Rhetorical Functions." Ph.D. dissertation in
    progress, University of Iowa.

*Thompson, Sister Francesca. "The Lafayette Players: 1915-1932." Ph.D. dissertation, University of Michigan, 1972.

Troesch, Helen D. "The Negro in English Dramatic Literature on the Stage and a Bibliography of Plays with Negro Characters." Ph.D. dissertation, Western Reserve University, 1940.

Westmoreland, Beatrice Fultz. "The Negro in American Drama." M.A. thesis, University of Kansas, 1937.

*Wilkerson, Margaret Buford. "Black Theatres in the San Francisco Bay Area and in the Los Angeles Area: A Report and Analysis." Ph.D. dissertation, University of California, 1974.

*Williams, Allen. "Sheppard Randolph Edmonds: His Contributions to Black Educational Theatre." Ph.D. dissertation, Indiana University, 1973.

*Williams, Curtis L. "Two Plays on the Black Experience." Ph.D. dissertation, University of Texas, 1977.

*Williams, Eddie Ray. "The Rise of the Negro Actor in the American Theatre from 1900-1950." M.A. thesis, University of Tennessee, 1951.

Williams, Mance Raymond. "The Aesthetics of the Black Theatre Movement in America, 1960-1970." Ph.D. dissertation, University of Missouri, 1977.

*Wilson, Robert. "The Black Theatre Alliance, a History of Its Founding Members." Ph.D. dissertation, New York University, 1974.

*Yerby, Frank G. "The Little Theatre in the Negro College." M.A. thesis, Fisk University, 1938.

Zietlon, Edward Robert. "Wright to Hansberry: The Evolution of Outlook in Four Negro Writers." Ph.D. dissertation, University of Washington, 1967.

APPENDIX 1: TAPED INTERVIEWS IN THE THEATRE: THE ORAL HISTORY LIBRARY OF THE HATCH-BILLOPS ARCHIVES

This list of tapes pertains to the black American theatre and its artists and is derived from the Oral History Library of the Hatch-Billops Archives (HBA). The HBA collection contains over 400 taped interviews, panel discussions, and lectures about black artists in the areas of dance, music, theatre, visual arts, literature, history, and education. There are also a number of tapes with other ethnic artists and theatre groups associated with black artists.

The Hatch-Billops Library has an ongoing process of abstracting the interviews to aid the researcher in finding material. These abstracts do not represent actual transcriptions of the interviews but summaries of them. At this writing, 173 tape abstracts have been completed. These are available at duplication cost. A published catalog of the Hatch-Billops Archives collection is available for $5 per copy and a list of tapes may be obtained upon request. While most of the interviews are available to scholars, artists, and other interested individuals for listening in the Library by appointment, some have special restrictions that require permission from the interviewee. Any publication of material from the tapes, either by direct or indirect quotation, must credit the Library. No tapes may be duplicated.

The Hatch-Billops Archives is a not-for-profit organization, which is supported in part by the New York State Council on the Arts. Ninety percent of the interviews in its collection are original and were conducted by Hatch-Billops staff members under a grant from the National Endowment for the Humanities and from the Faculty Research Foundation of City University of New York. The remaining interviews are copies of ones conducted on radio and television or are copies of interviews given to the Library by the following individuals and organizations: Ms. Vivian Perlis of Yale University Music Library; Professor Eileen Southern of Harvard University; Professors Lorraine Brown and John O'Connor of the Research Center for the Federal Theatre Project (FTP), George Mason University; Reuben and Dorothy Silver of Karamu Theatre; Loften Mitchell, author; James T. White, publisher; and Robert Wilson, professor.

Further information may be obtained by contacting: Hatch-Billops Archives, 491 Broadway, New York, N.Y. 10012. Telephone: (212) 966-3231.

An asterisk (*) indicates availability of an abstract. Numbers indicate the number of tapes.

Allison, Hughes—radio
Allison, Mrs. Hughes
Andrews, Regina
Archer, Osceola*
Attles, Joseph*
Audelco Awards 1975 and 1976
Baker, Josephine—TV
Bates, Add
Belgrave, Cynthia
Bethel, Pepsi
Black Comedians at the Apollo—TV
Black Film, 1972—panel—TV
Black Film, 1974—panel—TV
Black Playwriting, 1973—panel
Black Theatre, 1972—TV
Black Theatre, 1973—TV
Black Theatre/White Critic, 1973—
    panel
Black Women in the Theatre, 1976—
    panel
Blake, Eubie*3
Branch, William*2
Brewer, Sherri
Brewster, Townsend
Bricktop—TV
Browne, Theodore*
Browning, Ivan*
Bryant, Hazel
Bubbles, John*2
Bubbling Brown Sugar—TV—producers
Bullins, Ed*
Burroughs, Baldwin
Burroughs, Charles 2
Burrows, Vinie*
Bush, Anita*
Butcher, James
Campbell, Dick*2
Carroll, Vinnette*
Childress, Alice*
Coleman, Ralf*
Colon, Miriam*
Couloumbis, Akila
Cullen, Ida*2
Davidson, N. R.*2
Davis, Ossie
de Lavallade, Carmen*
Dendy, Brooks III 2
Dent, Tom

de Paur, Leonard*
Dixon, Ivan and Mary Bohanan
Dodson, Owen*5
Dotson, Josie*
DuBois, Shirley Graham*2
Dunham, Katherine*
Edmonds, Randolph*
Elder, Lonne III
Faulkner, Jeanne
Foster, Frances*
Foxx, Redd—TV
Frank, Benno
Frazier, Levi, Jr.
Freeman, Valdo*3
Furman, Roger
Gilbert, Lou
Gilliam, Ted*
Glanville, Maxwell*
Grant, Micki
Griffin, Charles
Griffinn, Charles
Guillaume, Robert 2
Hairston, Jester*
Harris, Neal
Haynes, Hilda*
Heath, Gordon
Hill, Abram*
Hill, Errol
Hubbard, Ida Forsyne
Hughes, Langston
Hunter, Eddie*
Hyman, Earle
Jeannette, Gertrude*2
Jelliffe, Rowena and Russell Jelliffe*6
Jones, Gary
Jones, Robert Earl*
Jordan, Jack
Karr, Krishna
Kashaska and Sati Jamal
Keiser, Kris
King, Woodie, Jr.*2
Lateef, Sister Lubaba
LeBlanc, Whitney 2
LeNoire, Rosetta
Lewis, Elma*2
Leyba, Claire*
Loft-Lynn, William Jay*
Long, Avon*

McClintock, Ernie*
McQueen, Butterfly*
Mapp, Jim
Markham, Pigmeat
Marshall, William
Matheus, John*2
Mayo, Whitman
Media Meet—Harlem 1975
Mitchell, Arthur
Mitchell, Loften*2
Molette, Barbara and Carlton Molette
Moore, Melba
Moses, Gilbert*
Moten, Etta
Muse, Clarence*2
Myers, Pauline*2
Neal, Larry*2
Nelson, Novella
Nemiroff, Robert
New York Shakespeare Festival, Public
    Theatre
Norman, Maidie*
O'Neal, Fred*
O'Neal, John 3
Oubre, Juanita
Papp, Joseph
Pawley, Thomas
Polndexter, Gwendolyn
Richards, Beah*
Richards, Lloyd
Richardson, Willis*2
Riley, Clayton 2
Rivers, Louis
Roberts, Davis
Robeson, Paul—panel about
Russell, Charlie L.
Salaam, Kalamu Ya
Sanchez, Sonia

Schiffman, Bob and Frank Schiffman
Sebree, Charles*
Shange, Ntozake—TV
Shepp, Archie*
Silver, Dorothy and Reuben Silver
Sissle, Noble*
Spence, Eulalie*
Staton, Joseph*2
Stewart, Delano*
Taylor, Art
Taylor, Clarice*
Teer, Barbara Ann*
Thompson, Sister Francesca*
Thompson, Garland Lee 2
Toole, Letitia
Turner, Tom
Van Scott, Glory*2
Vincent, Irving*
Voices of the Black Theatre (Regina
    M. Andrews, Dick Campbell, Vin-
    nette Carroll, Ruby Dee, Abram
    Hill, Eddie Hunter, and Frederick
    O'Neal)
Walker, Bill
Walker, Evan
Walker, Joseph*2
Ward, Douglas Turner—TV
Ward, Frances and Val Ward
Ward, Ted*5
Webb, Elida
Wesley, Richard*2
Whipper, Leigh*
Whitaker, Mical
White, Edgar
Whitfield, Vantile
Whiting, Napoleon*
Williams, Frances*2
Wood, Maxine

APPENDIX 2: AWARDS
TO BLACK THEATRE ARTISTS

Over approximately the last twenty-five years, black Americans in the theatre
have received increasing recognition in the fields of playwriting, performance,
directing, and the technical aspects of theatre. This list includes awards and fel-
lowships given to black Americans in the theatre and related arts.

AUDELCO (First Annual Award—1973). The names of plays and the categories were not cited for the first year

Ernest Baxter
Hazel Bryant
Vinie Burrows
Al Fann
Woodie King, Jr.
Kirk Kirksey
Ernie McClintock
Joan Sandler
Barbara Ann Teer
Joseph A. Walker
Gary Wheeler

Board of Directors Award: Vinnette Carroll and Roger Furman

AUDELCO (Second Annual Award—1974). The names of plays were not cited
for the second year

Aduke Aremu, producer
Josephy Gandy, scenic design
Helaine Head, production
Barbara Montgomery, performance
Judy Dearing Parks, costume
Shauneille Perry, director
Shirley Prendergast, lighting
Howard Roberts, musical director
Milo Timmons, choreographer
Richard Wesley, playwright
Dick A. Williams, performance

AUDELCO (*Cont.*)

> Board of Directors Award: Herbert Scott-Gibson, Billie Holiday Theatre for the Little Folks (children's theatre) and Douglas Turner Ward, Negro Ensemble Company

> Pioneer Award: Dr. Anne Cooke Reid

AUDELCO (Third Annual Award—1975)

> Zaida Coles, performance, *Cotillion*
> Joseph Gandy, scenic design, *Cotillion*
> Bill Gunn, playwright, *Black Picture Show*
> Woodie King, Jr., producer, *The Taking of Miss Janie*
> Kirk Kirksey, performance, *The Taking of Miss Janie*
> Robbie McCauley, performance, *The Taking of Miss Janie*
> Gil Moses, director, *The Taking of Miss Janie*
> Judy Dearing Parks, costume, general excellence
> Rod Rogers, choreographer, *My Sister, My Sister*
> Saundra Ross, lighting, *Waiting for Mongo*
> Dick A. Williams, performance, *Black Picture Show*

> Board of Directors Award: Woodie King, Jr., Karamu Playhouse, Cleveland, Ohio

> Pioneer Award: Owen Dodson and Theodore Ward

> Play of the Year: *Black Picture Show*

AUDELCO (Fourth Annual Award—1976). An asterisk (*) indicates white producer

> Deborah Allen, choreographer, *Mondongo*
> Trazana Beverley, performance, *For Colored Girls Who Have Considered Suicide/When the Rainbow Is Enuf*
> Bolani, costume, *Soljourney into Truth*
> Graham Brown, performance, *Eden*
> Joseph Gandy, scenic design, *Fat Tuesday*
> Woodie King, Jr., producer, *For Colored Girls Who Have Considered Suicide/When the Rainbow is Enuf*
> Larry Le Gaspi, costume, *Soljourney into Truth*
> Reggie Life, director, *Hail, Hail the Gangs!*
> Lou Meyers, performance, *Fat Tuesday*
> Barbara Montgomery, performance, *Eden*
> Joseph Papp,* producer, *For Colored Girls Who Have Considered Suicide/When the Rainbow Is Enuf*
> Saundra Ross, lighting, *Eden*
> Ntozake Shange, playwright, *For Colored Girls Who Have Considered Suicide/When the Rainbow Is Enuf*

> Board of Directors Award: Ernie McClintock and Garland Lee Thompson

> Pioneer Award: Frederick O'Neal

> Play of the Year: *Eden*

CLARENCE DERWENT AWARD

1969, Ron O'Neal, performance, *No Place to Be Somebody*
1975, Reyno, performance, *The First Breeze of Summer*

CUE   (Entertainer of the Year)

1961   Diahann Carroll
1964   Sammy Davis, Jr.
1967   Pearl Bailey
1972   Diana Ross

DONALDSON AWARD (*Billboard* magazine). This award was discontinued after 1955

1943-1944   Paul Robeson, performance, *Othello*
1945-1946   Pearl Bailey, performance, *St. Louis Woman*
1948-1949   Juanita Hall, performance, *South Pacific*
1949-1950   Todd Duncan, performance, *Lost in the Stars*
1950-1951   Janet Collins, performance, *Out of This World*
1953-1954   Harry Belafonte, performance, *Almanac*

DRAMA DESK AWARD

1964-1965   James Earl Jones, performance, *Othello*
1964-1965   Barbara Ann Teer, performance, *Home Movies*
1965-1966   Douglas Turner Ward, playwright, *Happy Ending* and *Day of Absence*
1967-1968   Ed Bullins, playwright, three plays
1968-1969   Lonne Elder III, playwright, *Ceremonies in Dark Old Men*
1968-1969   Charles Gordone, playwright, *No Place to Be Somebody*
1968-1969   James Earl Jones, performance, *The Great White Hope*
1969-1970   Cleavon Little, performance, *Purlie*
1969-1970   Melba Moore, performance, *Purlie*
1970-1971   Ruby Dee, performance, *Boesman and Lena*
1970-1971   James Earl Jones, performance, *Les Blancs*
1971-1972   Jonelle Allen, performance, *Two Gentlemen of Verona*
1971-1972   Phillip Hayes Dean, playwright, *The Sty of the Blind Pig*
1971-1972   J. E. Franklin, playwright, *Black Girl*
1971-1972   J. E. Gaines, playwright, *Don't Let It Go to Your Head*
1971-1972   Micki Grant, playwright, *Don't Bother Me, I Can't Cope*
1971-1972   Linda Hopkins, performance, *Inner City*
1971-1972   Kain, performance, *The Black Terror*
1971-1972   Gil Moses, director, *Ain't Supposed to Die a Natural Death*
1971-1972   Brock Peters, performance, *Lost in the Stars*
1971-1972   Melvin Van Peebles, playwright, *Ain't Supposed to Die a Natural Death*
1971-1972   Richard Wesley, playwright, *The Black Terror*
1972-1973   Bill Cobbs, performance, *Freeman* and *What the Wine-Sellers Buy*

DRAMA DESK AWARD (*Cont.*)

1972-1973   Ruby Dee, performance, *Wedding Band*
1972-1973   James Earl Jones, performance, *Hamlet* and *The Cherry Orchard*
1972-1973   Ben Vereen, performance, *Pippin*
1972-1973   Joseph A. Walker, playwright, *The River Niger*
1973-1974   Ray Aranha, playwright, *My Sister, My Sister*
1973-1974   Seret Scott, performance, *My Sister, My Sister*
1973-1974   Dick A. Williams, performance, *What the Wine-Sellers Buy*
1974-1975   Charlie Smalls, music and lyrics, *The Wiz*
1975-1976   Vivian Reed, performance, *Bubbling Brown Sugar*

DRAMATISTS GUILD (Elizabeth Hull/Kate Warriner Award)

1971-1972   Phillip Dean Hayes, playwright, *The Sty of the Blind Pig*
1972-1973   Joseph A. Walker, playwright, *The River Niger*

GUGGENHEIM FELLOWSHIP (John Simon Guggenheim Memorial Foundation)

1948   Theodore Ward, playwright
1958   Loften Mitchell, playwright
1959   William Branch, playwright
1965   LeRoi Jones (Imamu Amiri Baraka), playwright
1966   Errol John, playwright
1967   Adrienne Kennedy, playwright
1971   Ed Bullins, playwright
1971   Lonne Elder III, playwright
1973   Charles F. Gordon (Oyamo), playwright
1973   Joseph A. Walker, playwright

MARGO JONES AWARD

1969   Ellen Stewart, Cafe La Mama
1974   Douglas Turner Ward, Negro Ensemble Company

NEW YORK DRAMA CRITICS CIRCLE AWARD

1958-1959   Lorraine Hansberry, play, *A Raisin in the Sun*
1968-1969   James Earl Jones, performance, *The Great White Hope*
1970-1971   Cleavon Little, performance, *Purlie*
1973-1974   Miguel Piñero, play, *Short Eyes*
1974-1975   Ed Bullins, play, *The Taking of Miss Janie*

OBIE (The *Village Voice* Off-Broadway Award)

1958-1959   Harold Scott, performance, *Deathwatch*
1960-1961   Godfrey Cambridge, performance, *The Blacks*
1961-1962   Vinnette Carroll, performance, *Moon on a Rainbow Shawl*
1961-1962   C. Bernard Jackson, playwright, *Fly Blackbird*

1961–1962	James Earl Jones, performance, *Clandestine on the Morning Line*, *The Apple*, *Moon on a Rainbow Shawl* (N.Y. Shakespeare Festival)
1963–1964	Gloria Foster, performance, *In White America*
1963–1964	LeRoi Jones (Amiri Baraka), playwright, *Dutchman*
1963–1964	Adrienne Kennedy, playwright, *Funnyhouse of a Negro*
1963–1964	Diana Sands, performance, *The Living Premise*
1964–1965	Roscoe Lee Browne, performance, *The Old Glory*
1964–1965	James Earl Jones, performance, *Baal*
1965–1966	Gloria Foster, performance, *Medea*
1965–1966	Douglas Turner Ward, performance, *Day of Absence*
1965–1966	Jane White, performance, *Coriolanus*
1967–1968	Moses Gunn, performance, general excellence (Negro Ensemble Company)
1967–1968	Michael A. Schultz, director, *Song of the Lusitanian Bogey*
1968–1969	Boston Om Theatre Workshop, Inc., performance, *Riot*
1968–1969	Nathan George, performance, *No Place to Be Somebody*
1968–1969	Ron O'Neal, performance, *No Place to Be Somebody*
1969–1970	Gil Moses, director, *Slave Ship*
1970–1971	Susan Batson, performance, *AC/DC*
1970–1971	Ed Bullins, playwright, *The Fabulous Miss Marie* and *In New England Winter*
1970–1971	Ruby Dee, performance, *Boesman and Lena*
1970–1971	Sonny Jim, performance, *The Fabulous Miss Marie*
1970–1971	Kirk Kirksey, performance, general excellence
1970–1971	Derek Walcott, playwright, *Dream on Monkey Mountain*
1971–1972	Alex Bradford, performance, *Don't Bother Me, I Can't Cope*
1971–1972	Micki Grant, playwright, *Don't Bother Me, I Can't Cope*
1972–1973	J. E. Gaines, playwright, *What If It Had Turned Up Heads*
1972–1973	William E. Lathan, director, *What If It Had Turned Up Heads*
1972–1973	Roxie Roker, performance, *The River Niger*
1972–1973	Joseph A. Walker, playwright, *The River Niger*
1972–1973	Douglas Turner Ward, performance, *The River Niger*
1973–1974	Marvin Felix Camillo, director, *Short Eyes*
1973–1974	Loretta Greene, performance, *The Sirens*
1973–1974	Paul Carter Harrison, playwright, *The Great MacDaddy*
1973–1974	Barbara Montgomery, performance, *My Sister, My Sister*
1973–1974	Miguel Piñero, playwright, *Short Eyes*
1974–1975	Ed Bullins, playwright, *The Taking of Miss Janie*
1974–1975	Moses Gunn, performance, *The First Breeze of Summer*
1974–1975	Leslie Lee, playwright, *The First Breeze of Summer*
1974–1975	Gil Moses, director, *The Taking of Miss Janie*
1974–1975	Reyno, performance, *The First Breeze of Summer*
1974–1975	Ellen Stewart, 20-year Obie, general excellence
1975–1976	Robert Christian, performance, *Blood Knot*
1976–1977	Oz Scott, director, *For Colored Girls Who Have Considered Suicide/When the Rainbow is Enuf*
1976–1977	Ntozake Shange, playwright, *For Colored Girls Who Have Considered Suicide/When the Rainbow Is Enuf*

PULITZER PRIZE

1969-1970   Charles Gordone, playwright, *No Place to Be Somebody*

SPINGARN MEDAL (Fine Arts Winners)

1917   Harry T. Burleigh, music
1918   William Stanley Braithwaite, literature
1921   Charles S. Gilpin, performance
1924   Roland Hayes, music
1925   James Weldon Johnson, literature
1928   Charles W. Chesnutt, literature
1931   Richard Berry Harrison, performance
1939   Marian Anderson, music
1941   Richard Wright, literature
1945   Paul Robeson, performance
1959   Edward Kennedy (Duke) Ellington, music
1960   Langston Hughes, literature
1965   Leontyne Price, music
1968   Sammy Davis, Jr., performance

THEATRE WORLD AWARD

1961-1962   James Earl Jones, performance, *Moon on a Rainbow Shawl*
1963-1964   Kitty Lester, performance, *Cabin in the Sky*
1963-1964   Gilbert Price, performance, *Jericho-Jim Crow*
1964-1965   Beah Richards, performance, *Amen Corner*
1964-1965   Clarence Williams III, performance, *Slow Dance on the Killing Ground*
1965-1966   Gloria Foster, performance, *Medea*
1965-1966   Robert Hooks, performance, *Where's Daddy?* and *Day of Absence*
1967-1968   Jack Crowder, performance, *Hello Dolly*
1968-1969   Lauren Jones, performance, *Does a Tiger Wear a Necktie?*
1968-1969   Ron O'Neal, performance, *No Place to Be Somebody*
1968-1969   Marlene Warfield, performance, *The Great White Hope*
1969-1970   Donny Burks, performance, *Billy Noname*
1969-1970   Melba Moore, performance, *Purlie*
1970-1971   Clifton Davis, performance, *Do It Again*
1971-1972   Jonelle Allen, performance, *Two Gentlemen of Verona*
1971-1972   Ben Vereen, performance, *Jesus Christ Superstar*
1971-1972   Beatrice Winde, performance, *Ain't Supposed to Die a Natural Death*
1973-1974   Ralph Carter, performance, *Raisin*
1973-1974   Ernestine Jackson, performance, *Raisin*
1973-1974   Joe Morton, performance, *Raisin*
1974-1975   Lola Falana, performance, *Dr. Jazz*
1974-1975   Dorian Harewood, performance, *Don't Call Back*
1975-1976   Chip Garnett, performance, *Bubbling Brown Sugar*
1975-1976   Vivian Reed, performance, *Bubbling Brown Sugar*

TONY (Antoinette Perry Award, American Theatre Wing)

1961–1962	Diahann Carroll, performance, *No Strings*
1967–1968	Pearl Bailey, special award
1967–1968	Leslie Uggams, performance, *Hallelujah Baby!*
1968–1969	James Earl Jones, performance, *The Great White Hope*
1968–1969	Negro Ensemble Company, special award
1969–1970	Cleavon Little, performance, *Purlie*
1969–1970	Melba Moore, performance, *Purlie*
1971–1972	Linda Hopkins, performance, *Inner City*
1972–1973	Ben Vereen, performance, *Pippin*
1973–1974	Virginia Capers, performance, *Raisin*
1973–1974	—, musical, *Raisin*
1973–1974	—, play, *The River Niger*
1974–1975	Dee Dee Bridgewater, performance, *The Wiz*
1974–1975	George Faison, choreography, *The Wiz*
1974–1975	Geoffrey Holder, director/costume designer, *The Wiz*
1974–1975	Ted Ross, performance, *The Wiz*
1974–1975	Charles Smalls, composer, *The Wiz*
1974–1975	—, musical, *The Wiz*
1974–1975	John Kani, performance, *Sizwe Banzi Is Dead* and *The Island*
1974–1975	Winston Ntshona, performance, *Sizwe Banzi Is Dead* and *The Island*
1976–1977	Trazana Beverley, performance, *For Colored Girls Who Have Considered Suicide/When the Rainbow Is Enuf*
1976–1977	Delores Hall, performance, *Your Arms Too Short to Box with God*

VARIETY's Annual New York Drama Critics' Poll

1958	Lena Horne, performance, *Jamaica*
1959	Lorraine Hansberry, playwright, *A Raisin in the Sun*
1962	Diahann Carroll, performance, *No Strings*
1965	Beah Richards, performance, *Amen Corner*
1967	Leslie Uggams, performance, *Hallelujah Baby!*
1969	James Earl Jones, performance, *The Great White Hope*
1970	Cleavon Little, performance, *Purlie*
1970	Melba Moore, performance, *Purlie*
1972	Jonelle Allen, performance, *Two Gentlemen of Verona*

WHITNEY OPPORTUNITY FELLOWSHIP (John Hay Whitney Foundation)

1950–1951	Mattiwilda Dobbs, voice
1951–1952	Rawn Spearman, voice
1953–1954	Betty L. Allen, voice
1956–1957	Esther M. Jackson, drama
1957–1958	Louis Rivers, Jr., theatre
1957–1958	Shirley Verrett, voice
1958–1959	Armenta E. Adams, music
1958–1959	Grace A. Bumbry, voice
1959–1960	Anna Laura Archer, dance

WHITNEY OPPORTUNITY FELLOWSHIP *(Cont.)*

1959–1960	Luther James, drama
1959–1960	James F. Truitte, dance
1960–1961	Robert Wilson, voice
1961–1962	Amiri Baraka (LeRoi Jones), writing
1961–1962	Eleo Pomare, dance
1962–1963	Ronald S. Milner, writing
1962–1963	Veronica Tyler, voice
1963–1964	Lonne Elder III, playwriting
1963–1964	Clarence B. Jackson, music
1964–1965	Pearl A. Reynold, dance
1965–1966	Nathan Barrett, playwriting
1965–1966	Susan A. Batson, acting
1965–1966	E. D. Burbridge, Jr., scenic design
1965–1966	Wayne G. Grice, acting
1965–1966	Gwendolyn Killebrew, voice
1965–1966	Woodie King, Jr., theatre
1965–1966	Rod Rodgers, dance

WORLD THEATRE AWARD (American Theatre Association/International Theatre Institute)

1973	Paul Robeson (awarded posthumously)
1975	Ellen Stewart

APPENDIX 3: ADDRESSES OF PLAYWRIGHTS, AGENTS, AND AGENCIES

This list contains the addresses of playwrights or agents who responded to the editors' inquiries or whose addresses could be verified.

Robert Abney, Jr.
514 Missouri Avenue N.W.
Washington, D.C. 20011

AFRACA, Inc.
Box 656
Morningside Station
New York, N.Y. 10026

Donald Alexander
1414 Harmon Street
Berkeley, Calif. 94702

Diane T. Anderson
222 West 23 Street
New York, N.Y. 10011

Richard Ashley
327 Central Park West
New York, N.Y. 10025

Russell Atkins
6005 Grand Avenue
Cleveland, Ohio 44104

Nathan Barrett
35 East First Street
New York, N.Y. 10003

Damali Bashira
47 Briarcliff Drive
Greenville, S.C. 29607

George Houston Bass
Brown University
Providence, R.I. 02918

Black Theatre Alliance
162 West 56 Street
New York, N.Y. 10019

Norma Blacke-Bragg
19 Knowles Avenue
Middletown, Conn. 06457

Edward Boatner
76 West 69 Street
New York, N.Y. 10023

Gene Boland
c/o Brandt & Brandt
101 Park Avenue
New York, N.Y. 10017

Sylvia Woingust Branchcomb
18 Dearborne Street
Yonkers, N.Y. 10710

Brandt & Brandt
101 Park Avenue
New York, N.Y. 10017

Breakthrough Press
27 Washington Square North
New York, N.Y. 10011

Alexis Brewer
9145 Sunset Boulevard
Los Angeles, Calif. 90069

Roger Brewer
Route 1, Box 123
Roopville, Ga. 30170

Townsend Brewster
171-29 103 Road
Jamaica, N.Y. 11433

Brown-Tiwoni
227 West 149 Street, Apt. 2B
New York, N.Y. 10039

Theodore Browne
286 Seaver Street
Roxbury, Mass. 02121

Vinnette Carroll
Urban Arts Corps
26 West 20 Street
New York, N.Y. 10011

Steve Carter
c/o Negro Ensemble Company
133 Second Avenue
New York, N.Y. 10003

China Clark
101 West 12 Street, Apt. 4L
New York, N.Y. 10011

Sebastian Clarke
c/o Hattie Gossett
775 Riverside Drive
New York, N.Y. 10032

Buriel Clay II
San Francisco Black Writers Workshop
Box 1165
San Francisco, Calif. 94101

Robert Coles
909 South Terrance Road
Box 6101
Tempe, Ariz. 85281

Kelsey E. Collie
7519 12 Street N.W.
Washington, D.C. 20012

Kathleen Collins
796 Piermont Avenue
Piermont, N.Y. 10968

J. Douglas Comer
660 Wilson Avenue
Columbus, Ohio 43205

Jimmie Davis Compton, Jr.
18660 Waxford
Detroit, Mich. 48234

Michael Connor
98-07 204 Street
Hollis, N.Y. 11423

Mel Conway
1127 West McNichols, Apt. B3
Detroit, Mich. 48203

T. G. Cooper
Drama Department
Howard University
Washington, D.C. 20059

Tony Cox
1837 Marvin Avenue
Los Angeles, Calif. 90053

Scott Cunningham
230 West 105 Street
New York, N.Y. 10025

Lorraine Currelley
216 West 140 Street, Apt. 2
New York, N.Y. 10030

Damani Productions
Box 614
Lincolnton Station
New York, N.Y. 10037

Helen Daniel
Box 1733
Fort Valley State College
Fort Valley, Ga. 31030

Dharvi Darrelle
147 West 85 Street
New York, N.Y. 10024

N. R. Davidson
2608 Robert Street
New Orleans, La. 70115

A. I. Davis
60 East 177 Street, Apt. 5F
Bronx, N.Y. 10453

Milburn Davis
Box 248
FDR Station
New York, N.Y. 10022

Philip Hayes Dean
639 West End Avenue
New York, N.Y. 10023

James de Jough
523 West 121 Street
New York, N.Y. 10027

J. Brooks Dendy III
Issac Hathaway Fine Arts Center
University of Arkansas
Pine Bluff, Ark. 71601

Melvin Dixon
245 Fairfield Avenue
Stamford, Conn. 06904

Owen Dodson
350 West 51 Street
New York, N.Y. 10019

Dramatists Play Service, Inc.
440 Park Avenue South
New York, N.Y. 10016

Daisy I. Dumas
148 Clinton Street
Brooklyn, N.Y. 11238

Ann Early
Writers in Residence
1 St. Paul Place
Great Neck, N.Y. 11021

Randolph Edmonds
Box 765
Lawrenceville, Va. 23868

Don Farber
350 Park Avenue
New York, N.Y. 10017

Richard Farley
332 East 53 Street
New York, N.Y. 10022

Maurice Fields
4723 Walnut, Apt. C8
Philadelphia, Pa. 19104

Bil Forde
372 Central Park West, Apt. 19J
New York, N.Y. 10025

Hank Frazier
Box 1188
Manhattanville Station
New York, N.Y. 10027

Levi Frazier, Jr.
1917 Netherwood Avenue
Memphis, Tenn. 38114

Free Southern Theatre
1240 Dryades Street
New Orleans, La. 70113

Harold Freedman
Brandt & Brandt
101 Park Avenue
New York, N.Y. 10017

Samuel French, Inc.
25 West 45 Street
New York, N.Y. 10036

Roger Furman
Box 146
Manhattanville Station
New York, N.Y. 10027

George Mason University (GMU)
Library of Congress Collection of
    Federal Theatre Plays
4400 University Drive
Fairfax, Va. 22030

Clive Goodwin Associates
79 Cromwell Road
London S.W. 7, Eng.

Clay Goss
c/o Dorothea Oppenheimer
866 United Nations Plaza
New York, N.Y. 10017

Hattie Gossett
755 Riverside Drive
New York, N.Y. 10032

Arthur J. Graham
3440 National Avenue
San Diego, Calif. 92113

Rudy Gray
615 Fort Washington Avenue, Apt. 1H
New York, N.Y. 10040

Gertrude Greenridge
715 St. Marks Avenue
Brooklyn, N.Y. 11216

Bill Gunn
c/o Reed, Cannon & Johnson Co.
2140 Shattuck Avenue, Rm. 311
Berkeley, Calif. 94704

Bill Harris
1438 Glynn
Detroit, Mich. 48206

James V. Hatch
Hatch-Billops Archives (HBA)
491 Broadway
New York, N.Y. 10012

Hatch-Billops Archives (HBA)
491 Broadway
New York, N.Y. 10012

Victoria Hershey
Writers in Residence
1 St. Paul Place
Great Neck, N.Y. 11021

Ralph Hicks
3807 Bellefontaine
Kansas City, Mo. 64142

Mars Hill
5 Homestead Avenue
Albany, N.Y. 12203

Ronald Hobbs Literary Agency
211 East 43 Street
New York, N.Y. 10017

Laurence Holder
33-52 Crescent Street
Long Island City, N.Y. 11106

Ulyses Barnet Hooks II
Route 1, Box 260
Lexington, Okla. 73051

Diana Hunt
Literary Agency
246 West 44 Street
New York, N.Y. 10036

Madeline Huntley
2181 Madison Avenue
New York, N.Y. 10037

Grace Cooper Ihunanya
3200 Park Place N.W.
Washington, D.C. 20010

International Creative Management
   (ICM)
40 West 57 Street
New York, N.Y. 10019

C. Bernard Jackson
c/o Reverse Music
Inner City Cultural Center
1308 S. New Hampshire Avenue
Los Angeles, Calif. 90006

Bill Jamison
4640 Folson Street
Philadelphia, Pa. 19139

Gertrude Jeannette
42 West 139 Street
New York, N.Y. 10037

Reginald Vel Johnson
107-26 165 Street
Jamaica, N.Y. 11433

Gene-Olivar Jones
304 West 119 Street, Apt. 2A
New York, N.Y. 10026

Helen Marie Jones
Box 251
Morningside Station
New York, N.Y. 10026

Barry Amyer Kaleem
250 West 16 Street
New York, N.Y. 10014

Ninon Tallon Karlweis
250 East 65 Street
New York, N.Y. 10021

Scott Kennedy
114-91 179 Street
St. Albans, N.Y. 11412

John O. Killens
c/o Phyllis Jackson
International Creative Management
40 West 57 Street
New York, N.Y. 10019

Paul Kohner Inc.
9169 Sunset Boulevard
Hollywood, Calif. 90028

Erma L. Kyser
7728 Reenel Way
Sacramento, Calif. 95823

A. Clifton Lamb
800 East 43 Street
Baltimore, Md. 21212

Ed Lawrence
350 Masten Avenue
Buffalo, N.Y. 14207

Lerb Enterprises
2520 Talbot Road
Baltimore, Md. 21216

David Lewis
655 Burke Avenue
Bronx, N.Y. 10467

Erma D. Lewis
Sojourner Truth Players, Inc.
1060 East Terrell Avenue
Fort Worth, Tex. 76104

Frederick Lights
200 West 90 Street
New York, N.Y. 10024

Liveright Publishers
386 Park Avenue South
New York, N.Y. 10016

Darryle Lloyd
168-10 127th Avenue
Jamaica, N.Y. 11434

W. F. Lucas
Carpetbag Theatre
1930 Prospect Place
Knoxville, Tenn. 37915

Shedrick Lyons
Box 113
Talladega College
Talladega, Ala. 35160

Pat McCaughan
2288 Lothrop
Detroit, Mich. 48206

Melodie Maria McDowell
9406 S. Street
Chicago, Ill. 60619

Jerry Eugene McGlown
Box 521
Oxford, Miss. 38655

Jo-Anne McKnight
184-20 Galway Avenue
Hollis, N.Y. 11412

Sister Malika
393 Dumont Avenue, Suite 14B
Brooklyn, N.Y. 11212

Sharon Stockard Martin
4533 Chantilly Drive
New Orleans, La. 70126

Clifford Mason
800 West End Avenue
New York, N.Y. 10025

John F. Matheus
1743 South Boulevard
Tallahassee, Fla. 32301

May Miller
1632 S. Street S.W.
Washington, D.C. 20009

Lionel H. Mitchell
254 East 11 Street
New York, N.Y. 10003

Loften Mitchell
Drama Department
State University of New York
Binghamton, N.Y. 13901

Bill Moore
477 West 57 Street, Apt. 3F
New York, N.Y. 10019

William Morris Agency
1350 Avenue of the Americas
New York, N.Y. 10019

William Morrow
Subsidiary Rights Department
425 Park Avenue South
New York, N.Y. 10016

Mungu Kimya Abudu
c/o Carl F. Morrison, Jr.
127-I Brittany Manor
Amherst, Mass. 01002

Pauline Myers
8206 Delongpre, Apt. 10
Los Angeles, Calif. 90046

NASABA
1860 Broadway, Suite 910
New York, N.Y. 10023

Betty Harris Neals
134 Roosevelt Avenue
East Orange, N.J. 07017

Ellen Neuwald
905 West End Avenue
New York, N.Y. 10025

Regina O'Neal
Broadside Press
12651 Old Mill Place
Detroit, Mich. 48238

Dorothea Oppenheimer
866 United Nations Plaza
New York, N.Y. 10017

Daniel W. Owens
195 Sullivan Place
Brooklyn, N.Y. 11225

Thomas Pawley
Department of Humanities
Lincoln University
Jefferson City, Mo. 65101

Eugene Perkins
LaMonte Zeno Community Theatre
1512 South Pulaski
Chicago, Ill. 60623

Gwendolyn Poindexter
3706 Rolliston Road
Shaker Heights, Ohio 44120

Charles Pole, Jr.
1171 Sherman Avenue, Apt. 4C
Bronx, N.Y. 10456

Jim Potts
2688 Bush Street
San Francisco, Calif. 94115

Aishah Rahman
c/o Frank Silvera Writers' Workshop
Greenroom Registry, Lobby J
330 West 45 Street
New York, N.Y. 10036

Eugene B. Redmond
3700 Kings Way, Apt. 2
Sacramento, Calif. 95821

Edwena Reed
Route 8, Box 162-A
Birmingham, Ala. 35201

Reverse Music
Inner City Cultural Center
1308 S. New Hampshire Ave.
Los Angeles, Calif. 90006

Paul R. Reynolds
12 East 41 Street
New York, N.Y. 10017

Jack Rich
349 East 149 Street
Bronx, N.Y. 19451

Beah Richards
3690 Fifth Avenue
Los Angeles, Calif. 90018

Robert E. Richardson Productions
200 East 17 Street
New York, N.Y. 10003

Virgil Richardson
Balsos 32-19
Mexico, D.F.

Willis Richardson
2023 13 Street N.W.
Washington, D.C. 20009

Lou Rivers
300 Jay Street
Brooklyn, N.Y. 11201

Flora Roberts Agency
116 East 59 Street
New York, N.Y. 10022

Garrett Robinson
313 East 10 Street
New York, N.Y. 10009

D. B. Roderick
340 East 22 Street
New York, N.Y. 10010

Fred Rohan
Box 3763
St. Thomas, V.I. 00801

Saggittarus
Box 3345
Washington, D.C. 20010

Sonia Sanchez
c/o Driver
10 West 135 Street
New York, N.Y. 10037

Insan Sauti
Box 43
MCI Norfolk
Norfolk, Mass. 02056

Joseph Scott
81 Bedford Street, Apt. 3E
New York, N.Y. 10014

John Scott
Theatre Department
Bowling Green University
Bowling Green, Ohio 43402

Seret Scott
340 West 87 Street
New York, N.Y. 10024

Saundra Sharp
333 West End Avenue
New York, N.Y. 10025

Irving Shelton
391 Grand Avenue
Brooklyn, N.Y. 11238

Frank Silvera Writers' Workshop
c/o Green Room Registry
Lobby J
330 West 45 Street
New York, N.Y. 10036

Ed Smith
Department of Theatre
State University of New York
28 North Harriman
Buffalo, N.Y. 14214

Lois A. Smith
2405 12 Avenue, Apt. B
Chattanooga, Tenn. 37407

The Society of Creative Concern
591 Massachusetts Avenue
Boston, Mass. 02118

T. W. Stanback
Theatre Department
Florida Atlantic University
Boca Raton, Fla. 33432

Thelma Stiles
814 Mandana Boulevard
Oakland, Calif. 94610

Harold Stuart
Box 763, Kenmore Square
Boston, Mass. 02115

Patricia Taylor
215 West 98 Street, Apt. 7C
New York, N.Y. 10025

Valerie M. Thomas
392 Central Park West
New York, N.Y. 10025

Chezia B. Thompson
Roots & Branches
4217 Castleman
St. Louis, Mo. 63110

Richard Toussaint
c/o Damani Productions
Box 614
Lincolnton Station
New York, N.Y. 10037

Joseph Turner
5028 South Woodlawn
Chicago, Ill. 60615

Evan K. Walker
807 Riverside Drive
New York, N.Y. 10032

Fai Walker
143 West 85 Street, Apt. 4
New York, N.Y. 10024

Joseph Walker
605 Maitland Avenue
Teaneck, N.J. 07666

Rudy Wallace
4300 Spruce Street, Apt. C203
Philadelphia, Pa. 19104

Charles L. B. Washington
7033 Jay Street
Houston, Tex. 77028

Harmon C. Watson
910 St. Paul Street
Baltimore, Md. 21201

Wender & Associates
30 East 60 Street
New York, N.Y. 10022

James E. White III
2407 15 Street
Washington, D.C. 20009

Grady D. Whitfield
716 Third Avenue
Valdosta, Ga. 31601

Ernest Wiggins
1075 Grand Concourse, Apt. 2G
Bronx, N.Y. 10452

Tyrone E. Wilkerson
c/o Black Liberated Arts Center
McFarland YWCA
1700 N. Eastern
Oklahoma City, Okla. 73111

Curtis L. Williams
211 Tremont Avenue
Albany, Ga. 31705

Edward G. Williams
801 West End Avenue, Apt. 5B
New York, N.Y. 10025

Samm Williams
244 West 64 Street, Apt. 20
New York, N.Y. 10023

Elton C. Wolfe
390 Page Street
San Francisco, Calif. 94102

George C. Wolfe
c/o Pomona College Theatre
Claremont, Calif. 91711

Debbie Wood
1725 17 Street N.W.
Washington, D.C. 20006

Camille Yarbrough
66 West 82 Street
New York, N.Y. 10024

TITLE INDEX

Bought with Cookies. McBrown, Gertrude Parthenia, 151
Bouquet for Lorraine. Rivers, Lou, 195
Bow Boly. Ayers, Vivian, 11
Box. Owens, Daniel W., 173
Box Office. Bullins, Ed, 33
Boys Like Us. Lights, Frederick L., 147
Brass Medallion. Crawford, Robert, 56
Break. Richardson, Mel, 190
Breakfast Is Served. Alonzo, Cecil, 6
Breakout. Oyamo, 174–175
Breast of Heaven. Hezekiah, Lloyd, 110–111
Breasts Oppressed. Currelley, Lorraine, 58
Broeders. Edmonds, Randolph, 77
Breeders. Lamb, A. Clifton, 142
Brer Soul. Harrison, Paul Carter, 100
Bricks. Groenidge, Gertrude, 102
Bright Medallion. Price, Doris, 184
Broken Banjo (1925). Richardson, Willis, 191
Broken Banjo. Richardson, Willis, 191
Bronx Is Next. Sanchez, Sonia, 202
Brother Marcus. Fuller, Charles H., 90
Brother Mose. Wilson, Frank, 248
Brotherhood. Ward, Douglas Turner, 234
Brotherly Love. Wakefield, Jacques, 230
Brothers. Burr, Anne, 39
Brothers. Perkins, Eugene, 179
Brothers and Sisters of the Church Council. Spence, Eulalie, 214
Brothers of Blood and Thunder. Wallace, Rudy, 233
Brown Boy. Richardson, Willis, 191
Brown Buddies. Rickman, Carl, 194
Brown Overcoat. See Le Paletot Brun
Brownskin Models of 1954. Miller, Irvin C., 162
Brownskin Models of 1926. Miller, Irvin C., 162
Brownsville Raid. Fuller, Charles H., 90–91
Bubba, Connie and Hindy. Lewis, David, 146
Bubbling Brown Sugar. Mitchell, Loften, 165
Buddies. Alladice, Darryl E., 5
Bugles. Stevenson, William Adell, III, 216
Bulldogs. Stevenson, William Adell, III, 216
Burghers of Calais. White, Edgar, 241
Burn, Baby, Burn. Greenwood, Frank, 103
Bus Play. Owens, Daniel W., 173
Businessman. Frazier, Hank, 88
But I Can't Go Alone. Redwood, John, 188
But Never Jam Today. Carroll, Vinnette, 43
But There's Gotta Be Music. McCray, Ivy, 152
Butchman. Moore, Bill, 167
Buy a Little Tenderness. Clay, Buriel, II, 48

Buy the Bi and Bye. Perry, Fenton, 180
Buzzards. Hill, Mars, 113
Byword for Evil. Cullen, Countee, 57

Cabaret Girl. Johnson, Fenton, 130
Cable. Brewster, Townsend, 26
Cadillac Alley. Geary, Bruce C., 94
Cadillac Dreams. Jordan, Norman, 135
Caesar Driftwood. Cotter, Joseph S., Sr., 55
Cage. Hill, Mars, 113
Cain. Fuller, Charles H., 91
Calais and the Last Poets. Stuart, Harold, 218
Caleb, the Degenerate: A Study in Types, Customs, and Needs of the American Negro. Cotter, Joseph S., 31, 55
Call of Jubeh. Edmonds, Randolph, 77
Call to Arms. Jones, Willa Saunders, 135
Called Ur Fear. Oyamo, 175
Campaign. Boyd, Vinetta, 23
Candidate. Fuller, Charles H., 91
Candle in the Wind. Ward, Theodore, 235
Candy Store Is Still Closed. White, James E., III, 243
Candyman's Dance. Cotton, Walter, 56
Canned Soul. Martin, Sharon Stockard, 156
Capricious Crump. Anonymous, 8
Captive. Archer, Dudley, 9
Captive. Brown, Lennox, 29
Car Pool. McDowell, Melodie M., 152
Career or College. Edmonds, Randolph, 77
Carmelita and the Cockatoo. Hughes, Langston, 117
Cartouche. Randolph, Jeremy, 186
Case of Peppermint Gum. Rivers, Lou, 195
Casino Girl. Cook, Will Marion, 54
Caskets. Terrell, Vincent, 221
Castles in the Air. Bahati, Amirh T., 12
Castration. Decoy, Robert H., 64
Cat Called Jesus. Davis, Geri Turner, 61
Catch Me! Catch Me! If You Can! Bell, Robert, Jr., 19
Cathedral of Chartres. White, Edgar, 241
Caught. Thompson, Eloise A., 224
Caught in the Middle. Watkins, Gordon, 238
Calvacade of the Negro Theatre. Bontemps, Arna, and Hughes, Langston, 23, 121
Celebration. Collie, Kelsey E., 51
Cellar. Mitchell, Loften, 165
Center of Darkness. Whitney, Elvie, 244
Ceremonies in Dark Old Men. Elder, Lonne, III, 83